Sightlines

THEATER: Theory/Text/Performance

Enoch Brater, Series Editor

Around the Absurd: Essays on Modern and Postmodern Drama edited by Enoch Brater and Ruby Cohn

Tom Stoppard and the Craft of Comedy: Medium and Genre at Play by Katherine E. Kelly

Performing Drama/Dramatizing Performance: Alternative Theater and the Dramatic Text by Michael Vanden Heuvel

The Plot of the Future: Utopia and Dystopia in Modern Drama by Dragan Klaić

Shaw's Daughters: Dramatic and Narrative Constructions of Gender by J. Ellen Gainor

How Dramas End: Essays on the German Sturm und Drang, *Büchner, Hauptmann, and Fleisser* by Henry J. Schmidt

Critical Theory and Performance edited by Janelle Reinelt and Joseph R. Roach

The Actor's Instrument: Body, Theory, Stage by Hollis Huston

Presence and Resistance: Postmodernism and Cultural Politics in Contemporary American Performance by Philip Auslander

Ionesco's Imperatives: The Politics of Culture by Rosette C. Lamont

The Theater of Michael Vinaver by David Bradby

Rereading Molière: Mise en Scène from Antoine to Vitez by Jim Carmody

O'Neill's Shakespeare by Normand Berlin

Postmodern Theatric(k)s: Monologue in Contemporary American Drama by Deborah R. Geis

The Player's Passion: Studies in the Science of Acting by Joseph R. Roach

To Act, To Do, To Perform: Drama and the Phenomenology of Action by Alice Rayner

Tom Stoppard in Conversation edited by Paul Delaney

After Brecht: British Epic Theater by Janelle Reinelt

Directing Beckett by Lois Oppenheim

Susan Glaspell: Essays on Her Theater and Fiction edited by Linda Ben-Zvi

The Theatrical Gamut: Notes for a Post-Beckettian Stage edited by Enoch Brater

Staging Place: The Geography of Modern Drama by Una Chaudhuri

The Aesthetics of Disturbance: Anti-Art in Avant-Garde Drama by David Graver

Toward a Theater of the Oppressed: The Dramaturgy of John Arden by Javed Malick

Theater in Israel edited by Linda Ben-Zvi

Crucibles of Crisis: Performing Social Change edited by Janelle Reinelt

Fornes: Theater in the Present Tense by Diane Lynn Moroff

Taking It to the Streets: The Social Protest Theater of Luis Valdez and Amiri Baraka by Harry J. Elam Jr.

Hearing Voices: Modern Drama and the Problem of Subjectivity by John H. Lutterbie

Mimesis, Masochism, & Mime: The Politics of Theatricality in Contemporary French Thought edited by Timothy Murray

Approaching the Millennium: Essays on Angels in America edited by Deborah R. Geis and Steven F. Kruger

Rooms with a View: The Stages of Community in the Modern Theater by Richard L. Barr

Staging Resistance: Essays on Political Theater edited by Jeanne Colleran and Jenny S. Spencer

Sightlines: Race, Gender, and Nation in Contemporary Australian Theatre by Helen Gilbert

Edges of Loss: From Modern Drama to Postmodern Theory by Mark Pizzato

Postmodern/Drama: Reading the Contemporary Stage by Stephen Watt

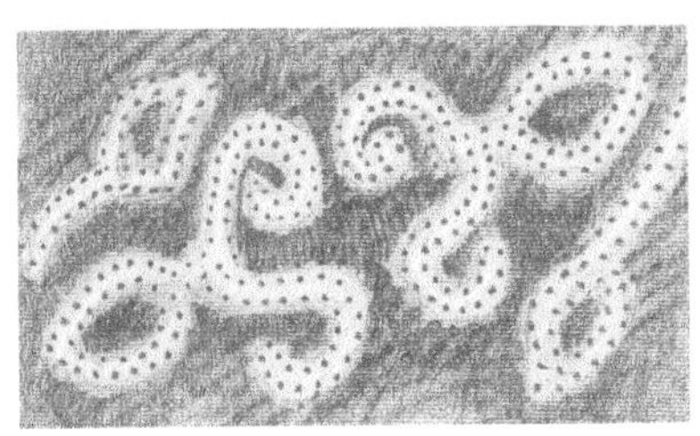

Sightlines

Race, Gender, and Nation in Contemporary Australian Theatre

Helen Gilbert

Ann Arbor

THE UNIVERSITY OF MICHIGAN PRESS

Published in the United States of America by
The University of Michigan Press
Manufactured in the United States of America
⊗ Printed on acid-free paper

2001 2000 1999 1998 4 3 2 1

A CIP catalog record for this book is available from the British Library.

Library of Congress Cataloging-in-Publication Data

Gilbert, Helen, 1956–
Sightlines : race, gender, and nation in contemporary Australian theatre / Helen Gilbert.
p. cm. — (Theater—theory/text/performance)
Includes bibliographical references (p.) and index.
ISBN 0-472-09677-X (cloth : acid-free paper)
ISBN 0-472-06677-3 (pbk. : acid-free paper)
1. Australian drama—20th century—History and criticism. 2. Literature and society—Australia—History—20th century. 3. National characteristics, Australian, in literature. 4. Gender identity in literature. 5. Nationalism in literature. 6. Sex role in literature. 7. Race in literature. I. Title. II. Series.
PR9611.5 .G55 1998
822—ddc21 98-8956
CIP

In memory of my father,
who would have considered it more
of an achievement if I'd gone out
and caught a very big fish.

Preface

Attempts to reconstruct postcolonial subjectivities, to reassert local knowledges and practices into a history marked by gaps and ruptures, are crucial to the artistic endeavors of colonized societies. Although this recuperative project in postcolonial writing has attracted substantial critical debate, less attention has been paid to the role of theatre as a site of negotiation and struggle against imperialist hegemonic structures and their associated models of individual, social, and national identity. The dual aims of this book are to demonstrate how postcolonial criticism offers enabling models for interpreting dramatic images of a nation's past and present, and, concurrently, to show how performance theory *and* practice extend the usual scope of postcolonial inquiry.

My focus is on Australian plays of the last twenty years, a period marked by a historical consciousness that has revitalized the nation's theatrical themes, forms, and styles. This engagement with history in an attempt to unsettle dominant myths of nationhood and to express a range of dissenting knowledges and identities—including those articulated in/through embodied forms of art—lends itself very well to a politicized mode of analysis. In carrying out such analysis, I draw attention to performative aspects of theatre and discuss their potential to expand postcolonial notions of counterdiscursive resistance, a strategy too often located exclusively in language/writing.

In Australia, as in other countries that were colonized by European powers, a wide range of theatre can be usefully examined in relation to current theories about colonial and postcolonial texts and discourses. While Aboriginal theatre is an obvious locus of interest for my inquiry, this book is equally concerned to analyze various kinds of settler theatre, especially that which examines the contradictions of its own positioning within the dominant culture. The application of a broad-based postcolonial model of interpretation is not intended to suggest a homogenized response to the contingencies of imperialism, but rather to highlight difference as well as similarity. Many of the key concepts of postcolonial theory, such as ambivalence, mimicry, hybridity, split subjectivity, and masquerade, are discussed not only in their theatre-specific articulations but also in reference to race, gender, and other particular categories of difference that influence power relations at all levels of society.

The critical models forwarded by this book should not be conceived as specific to Australian theatre but rather applicable (with modifications) to a range of contexts, especially in cultures that are implicated in, or affected by, imperialism. Applied to performance, postcolonial theory urges politicized readings not just of theatrical deployments of voice, body, space, and costume, but of the whole semiotic network of the mise en scène. This kind of analysis presumes that the theatre does not mirror the so-called real but rather opens up new sightlines for reviewing national histories and identities.

Note: In this book, dates given for plays after their first mention refer to the first production. However, quoted references, unless otherwise noted, are to the published text as listed in the bibliography. Where the analysis refers to particular performances, these are specified in footnotes or in the analysis itself.

Acknowledgments

First, I wish to acknowledge a number of intellectual debts to colleagues whose input and support have ensured the completion of this project. Above all, I am deeply grateful to Jacqueline Lo, who has been my critical sounding-board and a constant source of help and encouragement. Her generosity, particularly in the final lap of this project, leaves me ever in her debt. Veronica Kelly's excellent research on contemporary Australian theatre and Helen Tiffin's exemplary work on postcolonial theory have been the critical touchstones informing the development of this book. I thank them for mapping out possible directions and for their input at various stages. I also owe a significant debt to Leigh Dale, whose contribution to my discussion of Orientalism's application in Australian contexts has been invaluable.

Special thanks to Cameron Browne for meticulous proofreading and editing, for running errands at inconvenient times, and for help with numerous other tasks. His unfailing patience over a very long time is a precious gift that I have sometimes taken for granted. Thanks also to Margaret Henderson for help with proofing and indexing; to Judy Smith for helping so cheerfully with references, computer problems, and proofing (not to mention the cooking); to Melinda Mawson for research assistance and witty emails; and to Simone Murray for the judicious edit that made revisions a much easier task. All omissions and errors are mine, not theirs. I'm also grateful to the readers who assessed this book in manuscript form; their comments and criticisms were most valuable in helping me to produce a better piece of work.

A number of other friends and colleagues deserve my gratitude for their assistance and support. Thanks to Joan Ward for encouragement, good cheer, and for listening to my gripes; Chris Worth for his belief in this book's value and for helping me to find the right publisher; Ruth Barcan for moral support, health tips, and much wise advice; Chris Tiffin for jokes and other bits of wisdom; Dick and Roget for always coming up with alternatives; Helen Thomson for the loan of her beach house; Peter Fitzpatrick for collegial support; Gareth Griffiths and Elizabeth Webby for their comments on earlier versions of this book; Terry Threadgold and Charlie Stevens for helping to arrange teaching release so I could work on the project in its earlier stages and the Cathie Fund of Monash University for funding that release; and, not least, my current department's secretarial staff for the many ways in which they have made my work easier.

I wish to thank the University of Michigan Press, and LeAnn Fields in particular, for making a place for this book in the series Theater: Theory/Text/Performance. In a climate when most academic publishing involves some risk, this support for my work demonstrates a particular vision that enriches the field of theatre studies. I'm also grateful to the press's staff for their editorial and production work and their prompt responses to my queries.

Some of the material published in this book has appeared in earlier versions in the following journals: *Australasian Drama Studies, SPAN, New Literatures Review, World Literature Written in English, Australian and New Zealand Studies in Canada, Kunapipi, Southern Review, Southerly, ARIEL*, and *Yearbook of Comparative and General Literature.* I thank all the editors and editorial staff concerned. I would also like to acknowledge Routledge for permission to use material from essays I contributed to *Imperialism and Theatre* (edited by J. Ellen Gainor) and *De-scribing Empire: Colonialism and Textuality* (edited by Chris Tiffin and Alan Lawson).

Particular debts are owed to photographers Di Barrett, Geoff Busby, Christopher Ellis, Melanie Gray, Peter Holderness, David Parker, Fiora Sacco, David Simmonds, Penny Wilkinson, and David Wilson. Their work adds life and color to this book and I am grateful for their generous contributions. Every effort has been made to trace ownership of all copyrighted material in this book and to obtain permission for its use.

Finally, thanks to Margaret Leask of Currency Press for her generous assistance with locating and lending photographs, and to the staff of the following institutions for help with finding production records and visual material: Melbourne Theatre Company, Queensland Theatre Company, La Boite, Playbox, Festival Arts Centre of South Australia, and Black Swan Theatre Company.

Contents

Introduction *1*
History/Theatre/Postcolonialism
Performance and Counterdiscourse

Chapter 1.
Canonical Counterdiscourse:
A Case Study *27*

Chapter 2.
Contemporary Aboriginal Theatre *51*
Spatial Histories
Body Politics: Dance and Costume
De-scribing Orality

Chapter 3.
Settler/Invader Plays *97*
Monumental Moments: The Bicentennial Plays
Cartographies: Stagescape/Landscape
Postcolonial Grotesques: Re-membering the Body

Chapter 4.
Feminist Postcolonial Drama *145*
Convict Women and Gender Power
Travel, Exile, and the (Post)Colonial Woman
Reframing the Gaze: Metatheatre/Feminist Performance

Chapter 5.
Neoimperialism: Gender and Nation *185*
American Neoimperialism
Australian/Asian Relationships

Conclusion *231*
Notes *235*
Bibliography *249*
Index *267*

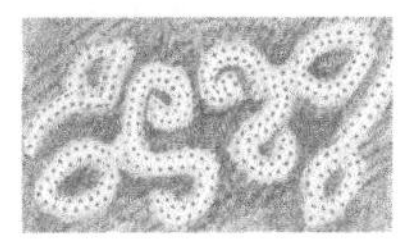

Introduction

History is natural selection. Mutant versions of the past struggle for dominance; new species of fact arise, and old saurian truths go to the wall, blindfolded and smoking last cigarettes.

—*Salman Rushdie,* ***Shame***

History/Theatre/Postcolonialism

In his introduction to *The Road to Botany Bay,* the revisionist historian Paul Carter postulates that "the illusion of the theatre and, more exactly, the unquestioned convention of the all seeing spectator" is the "primary logic" that informs and structures orthodox accounts of white settlement in Australia (1987, xv).[1] Such accounts, he argues, ignore the intentionality of historical narrative, constructing a drama that unfolds as the historian merely *repeats* what happened:

> Australia was always simply a stage where history occurred, history a theatrical performance. It is not the historian who stages events, weaving them together to form a plot, but History itself. History is the playwright, coordinating facts into a coherent sequence: the historian narrating what happened is merely a copyist or amanuensis. He is a spectator like everybody else and, whatever he may think of the performance, he does not question the stage conventions. (xiv)

Constructing an alternative history, Carter maintains, involves firstly exposing the imperial venture implicit in writing history as a theatrical process that occurs on a neutral stage, and then tracing the "spatial forms and fantasies through which a culture declares its presence" (xxii) so that the resultant historical account metaphorically approximates a map that opens up the possibility of going back: "the kind of history where traveling is a process of *continually* becoming" (xxiv). While Carter's preoccupation with the categories of space rather than time exemplifies the postmodern crisis of historicity, the importance of his analysis for my study lies in its postcolonial endeavor to dismantle the self-reinforcing illusions of imperial history and its concomitant notions of linear time and neutral space. Carter claims that such an endeavor "begins and ends in language" (xxiii), but I would argue that any history constructed as a theatrical performance lends itself particularly well to interrogation from the inside, from the specifically dramatic aspects of such narrative construction. This approach reckons with the weight of the theatrical metaphor so that the "stage conventions" of Western historiography *can* be called into question. An examination of the elements that make up the theatre—the dialectic between space and time, the actor, and the spectator—suggests that drama/performance offers significant sites from which to explore the lacunae left by imperialist representations of the past. If, as Carter asserts, the colonization of Australia was a spatial process, a mode of knowing subject to the intentional gaze, an act that was perceived as a theatrical event on the stage of history, then the ongoing process of decolonization can be effected through a series of theatrical counterevents, or rather counterprocesses, that allow the remapping of space, the reframing of time, the relocation of sightlines, and the repositioning of the colonial subject/body in representation.

Even a cursory look at the corpus of contemporary Australian drama reveals numerous plays that take on precisely this challenge. Focusing on the theatre of the last twenty years, this study explores the ways in which diverse playwrights have articulated responses to imperialism as the major historical force still shaping Australian society. The period of drama under examination has been marked by what Peter Fitzpatrick and Helen Thomson call "a series of quiet but significant little revolutions" (1993, 489) that have led to an increasing diversity in the theatrical repertoire and, in some instances, a productive dialogue between very different cultures, with a concomitant extension of theatrical styles and techniques. In contrast to the stridently neonationalist (Anglo-Celtic and male) movement—the so-called new wave—of the late 1960s and early 1970s, these "quiet revolutions" have demanded that narratives of cultural definition be opened up to include the perspectives of marginalized groups, and that dominant representations of these Others[2] be examined critically.

While the 1980s saw David Williamson settle comfortably into the mainstream as most of the other new-wave playwrights faded into obscurity, dramatists such as Louis Nowra and Stephen Sewell rose to prominence with plays that insistently challenged the tastes and conventions of the bourgeois audience, or, as in Michael Gow's case, with works that initially appeared to reinforce its prejudices. These playwrights in turn became part of an established (if more open) order that now constitutes the theatrical mainstream, although all three could be seen as ambivalently positioned within that mainstream.[3] At the same time, the emergence or consolidation of a number of other theatrical "voices" has increasingly fragmented any (false) sense of a monovocal Australian drama. Among the most significant of recent "revolutions" has been the development of an Aboriginal theatre that questions not only the centrality of Anglo-European perspectives but also the forms of their representation. Along with an increasing consciousness of Australia's Asian context, this movement has provoked changes in how racial difference is treated, and how relationships between European and non-European peoples are dramatized. Similarly, the feminist agenda has been an important energizing force in Australian contemporary theatre, and one that has impacted on both its subject matter and its performance styles, though not necessarily in any uniform way. Some women writers/performers have followed the lead of individualist figures such as Dorothy Hewett, while other, often more avowedly political groups, have shaped their art within collective frameworks. In this respect, community theatre has become a prominent arena for the work of feminist collectives, as well as continuing to play a major role in the development of drama by other historically marginalized groups such as migrants from non-English-speaking backgrounds. As an appropriate forum for the expression of "fringe" identities, community theatre also provides a site/model for gay and lesbian performances; this is an increasingly visible aspect of Australian theatrical culture, as the annual Mardi Gras in Sydney now demonstrates.[4]

A review of the critical literature on Australian theatre over the last few decades shows that there have been concerted efforts to examine the works of individual dramatists and often to place them within particular traditions.[5] But, excepting Peta Tait's detailed study of feminism in Australian theatre, *Converging Realities* (1994), there has been no sustained, critically coherent inquiry into a broad cross-section of plays, particularly since the new wave has receded to a postwave swell—or rather, series of swells. Few critics seem to disagree on the characteristics of the new-wave drama even if, as Fitzpatrick has pointed out, they attribute to it a uniform identity that is somewhat misleading (1987a, 166). An aggressive use of Australian vernacular language, a paradoxical celebration/critique of nationalism, and a foregrounding of the offensively masculinist humor associated with Ockerism are by now well recognized as the standard features of the new-wave movement.[6] The work of the postwave writers, despite being tagged as "internationalist," has been much more difficult to define, and this is reflected in the general lack of comparative criticism on the drama of the period,[7] except in the study of easily identified (and usually marginalized) fields such as community, Aboriginal, or multicultural theatre.[8] It is increasingly evident, however, that the internationalist label belies an ongoing interest in cultural self-definition, since most of the plays thus categorized are ultimately "less concerned with looking out from the island than with finding new ways of looking within" (Fitzpatrick 1987a, 172). What is "seen" in the contemporary moment, however, is no more or less definitive than any other assertions of identity. To paraphrase John Romeril, how Australians currently pose the question of "who and what they are," and how they answer it differently in different times, is perhaps the real issue to be addressed in any periodic assessment of Australian theatre (1979–80, 149).

That most critics have not identified a characteristic way of looking at this question in the eighties and nineties points, in many ways, to a welcome recognition of diversity as against the totalizing constructions of the new-wave period; however, as John McCallum argues in his survey of academic discourses on twentieth-century Australian drama, more systematic approaches could lead to some very useful discussion that might address major gaps in critical understanding of the field (1988, 153–54), even as it is recognized that this "field" is discursively constituted rather than simply given. It seems, then, that the time is ripe for a broad-based inquiry that attempts to make connections between disparate texts by examining them within theoretical frameworks designed to elicit comparisons while still respecting differences.

In the culturally diverse theatre I have outlined as characteristic of the period under discussion, history is a recurring thematic, but one that has not attracted a great deal of substantial analytical response. The major exceptions are McCallum's survey of postsixties "history" plays (1987a), along with various articles by Veronica Kelly (1987a, 1987c, 1992b), whose work is, in many respects, the starting point for my overall study. McCallum examines the increasing prevalence of a "sense of history" in Australian drama and identifies three general categories that constitute a more-or-less sequential development of historical consciousness: "Celebrations of the Past, Reassessments of the Past, and the Past as Present" (1987a, 149). In outlining the stylistic and thematic concerns typical to each category, his article is useful in opening up the possibilities of what history itself entails and how it might be dramatized; however, McCallum's taxonomy of "history" plays is somewhat misleading because it suggests that the various modes of representing the past are mutually exclusive, and because it underplays the role of the present in *all* historical reconstruction. As the influential work of Hayden White reminds us, "every representation of the past has specifiable ideological implications" that reveal more about current social conditions than about any putative history (1978, 69). Kelly's assessment of the "historical visions" of such playwrights as Nowra, Sewell, and Gow stresses that history is neither "self-evidently [nor] unproblematically accessible" in their plays, and that their allusive dramatizations of a fragmentary past constitute "potent interventions in ideological struggle" (1987c, 69). Working from the premise that "the 'past' is what we now decide to remember of it for present purposes" (1990a, 140), Kelly argues that history is a particularly powerful site of anxiety for an Australian society still coming to terms with a legacy of convictism, colonial rule, and dispossession of indigenous peoples. This indissoluble link between a society's representations of history and its experiences as a colonized and colonizing culture provides one of the key issues to be explored in more detail throughout this book.

My analysis of the problematic centrality of history, in its many protean forms, in Australian contemporary drama proceeds by isolating ways of (re)viewing texts from a postcolonial perspective, a critical approach that is always concerned with the operations of power articulated in and by representation. In keeping with the concept of history as "culturally motivated and ideologically conditioned" in the present (Slemon 1988a, 159), my choice of texts often extends beyond those obviously about history to include plays that articulate their postcoloniality in other ways. Although largely focused on British imperialism as the major historical force shaping Australian society, this study also examines neoimperial influences in/on Australian culture. Overall, I am much less interested in identifying the particular characteristics of these intersecting hegemonies than in demonstrating how responses to them represent a complex endeavor to express the multiple and ambivalent subjectivities that circulate under the sign *Australian*. In short, the central concern of this book is not with constructions *of* history per se but with constructing the self *in* history. This process is both crucial and problematic for the postcolonial subject whose "historical" role, according to the stage conventions that Carter outlines in the opening quotation of this section, has generally been that of history's Other.

Postcolonialism is only one of the many theoretical discourses that might fruitfully be brought to bear on the subject of contemporary Australian drama,[9] but it is a particularly apposite one in the wake (used in both senses of the term) of the 1988 Bicentenary of European settlement, and in a decade when debates about republicanism, Aboriginal land rights, and race resurface regularly. I would also argue that a postcolonial analysis of Australian drama is long overdue, given the very useful critical insights that have emerged from applications of this approach to other genres of

Australian literature, especially fiction.[10] It is important to note, however, that examining drama through the conceptual frameworks developed in postcolonial studies involves more than a simple and unproblematic transposition of reading strategies because some of the signifying systems through which plays "mean" are vastly different from those of texts not designed for performance. Hence, although this study seeks to demonstrate how its subject area might be illuminated by the chosen theoretical approach, it also aims to extend the current limits of that approach. In this respect, theories of drama and performance have much to add to debates about how imperial power is articulated and/or contested through discourses centered on the body, space, language, and representation, to name just a few of the key topoi of postcolonial studies.

In the light of continuing debate in Australia, and abroad, about what comes under the rubric of *postcolonialism,* it is necessary at this point to clarify my usage of the term. I do not wish to enter into arguments about the suitability of the term itself as a descriptor of the practices operating under its capacious umbrella, but rather to outline the particular brand of postcolonial theory relevant to this study. To adequately assess various opinions on the epistemological scope of postcolonialism would require much more space than this study allows, and that particular territory is already well covered in Peter Childs and Patrick Williams's recent reassessment of postcolonial theory (1997, 1–25). Of the numerous critics who have scrutinized the term *postcolonial,* Tejumola Olaniyan provides perhaps the most cogent argument for its continuing, if provisional, usage when he points out that, regardless of the conceptual blur that often surrounds the term, "a lot of relevant work is being done in its name" (1993, 745). Moreover, he argues, the crisis in naming the practices to which postcolonialism generally refers is merely the latest in a series of identity crises occasioned by Europe's attempt to categorize the discourses of its Others. In response to charges that the term is naively teleological, imperially biased, and geopolitically inexact, Olaniyan suggests that "perhaps we should start to wonder whether, epistemologically speaking, a condition of radical disjunction/incommensurability between (nomenclatural) 'form' and 'substance' is necessarily unhealthy for a subordinate(d) discourse whose strategies of survival or resistance do not exclude, *a priori,* wile and guile" (1993, 745).

Following the authors of *The Empire Writes Back,* I use "postcolonial" literatures as a geopolitical term designating not only those "affected by the imperial process from the moment of colonization to the present day" but also, and at the same time, those that assert a "tension with the imperial power" (Ashcroft, Griffiths, and Tiffin 1989, 2). This does not imply a naive teleological sequence in which *post*colonialism merely supersedes colonialism but rather indicates an engagement with and contestation of its discourses. In Alan Lawson's words, postcolonialism is "a politically motivated historical-analytical movement [that] engages with, resists, and seeks to dismantle the effects of colonialism in the material, historical, cultural-political, pedagogical, discursive, and textual domains" (1992, 156). As a critical discourse, then, postcolonialism is both a textual effect and a reading strategy. Its theoretical practice often operates on two levels, attempting at once to elucidate the postcoloniality that inheres in certain texts, and to unveil and deconstruct any remnant colonialist power.

Contrary to the view of Bob Hodge and Vijay Mishra, this working definition of postcolonialism as inherently oppositional does not suggest that "subversion reigns equally everywhere in all 'postcolonial' societies" (1991, xii). What Hodge and Mishra fail to note is the distinction between postcolonialism as a critical approach specifically designed to counter imperialism's political power, and postcoloniality as the probabilistic effect of that power, however mediated. Obviously, there are many texts produced in colonized cultures that exhibit some degree of complicity with the epistemological biases of imperialism, but this does not rule out the concurrent existence of ambivalent or even oppositional counterdiscourses in such texts, nor should it preclude their analysis from a postcolonial point of view. As Brian Edwards argues, and as the influential work of critics such as Homi Bhabha and Gayatri Spivak has demonstrated, the "possibilities for post-colonialist revisions and rereadings are implicit in the colonizing discourse" (Edwards 1992, 144). The study of colonialist texts therefore has heuristic value as part of the larger project of dismantling imperialism's discursive structures, particularly in the so-called settler colonies such as Australia where the nonindigenous culture is both colonized and colonizing.

The implication of Hodge and Mishra's argument in the Australian context is that only Aboriginal texts may be regarded as postcolonial; non-Aboriginal literature, they contend, remains marked by a "neo-colonial mentality that is still obsessed by the exploited Other" (1991, xiv). While the latter statement holds some truth, to discount the forms of resistance to imperialism embedded in many non-Aboriginal texts is to assert a false essentialism. As Gareth Griffiths maintains, although it is crucial to recognize differences between various groups' experiences of and responses to colonialism, a refusal to consider postcoloniality as a condition of nonindigenous literatures leads to "the recuperation and reinscription of a mystified 'authentic'" that denies the complex, hybridized nature of Australian society (1992b, 329). In an attempt to understand the wide range of textual effects that might be elucidated by a postcolonial approach, the scope of my inquiry extends beyond Aboriginal theatre—itself an important focus—to cover a great number of plays written by, and dealing primarily with, the white settler/invader society. Many of the plays in this category show explicit cognizance (albeit often through metaphor) of the ways in which the colonizing of Australia disempowered indigenous peoples and effectively erased their presence from the discursive con/texts of the nation's official history. Furthermore, by deconstructing the dominant discourse from within its self-privileging framework, some of these plays are deliberately designed to clear a space from which the marginalized might speak.

That references to the indigenous subject as history's Other seem to surface with almost Freudian insistence in much recent mainstream drama confirms, on one level, Hodge and Mishra's claim that Aboriginality is the "Dark side of the [Australian] dream," as the title of their book suggests. To "write" this repressed Other back into history when that history—however revisionist—remains under the control of the settler/invader society is a perilous process that risks reconstructing Aborigines as the inert objects of yet another form of power/knowledge. Following Edward Said's model of Orientalism as a set of discourses that author/ize representations of the Other, Hodge and Mishra have termed this approach "Aboriginalism" (1991, 27). Their appropriation of Said's work undoubtedly yields some perceptive insights, and gestures toward a comparative analysis that might also prove instructive, but, as I will argue in my discussion of Australia's relationships with Asia, the implicit binarism of Said's model, and its insufficient recognition of the ambivalence of colonial power, limit its applicability to this study. Similarly, Aboriginalism does not appear to be the characteristic epistemological mode of the many nonindigenous plays I examine. Rather, they operate within what Bain Attwood has outlined as post-Aboriginalism, a discourse/practice that recognizes that any knowledge of the Other is partial, limited, and discursively constructed. As a reading and/or writing strategy, post-Aboriginalism involves "historicising the processes that have constructed Aborigines" to reveal how their identity has been "contingent on colonial power relations." This inevitably leads to a "new object of knowledge—Ourselves, European Australians, rather than Them, the Aborigines" (Attwood 1992, xv). Such self-knowledge is not only the primary goal of many of the plays I will examine but also, on a metadiscursive level, of my study itself. In this respect, I reserve the right to speak *about* both Aboriginal and non-Aboriginal texts while acknowledging that my reading of them is always an act of interpretation from a specific cultural and critical perspective. As

Attwood points out, the "problematic of our representations lies not in the fact that we speak but in the particular nature of how and what we speak" (1992, xiii).

The comparison of texts across cultural groups has long been one of the hallmarks of postcolonial theory and criticism. As Lawson warns, however, the comparative approach must be driven by "the twin recognitions of similarity and difference." By continuing to ask what is similar, we avoid producing "a false uniqueness and a bogus empiricism," while the question of what is different guards against reproducing "a monolithic *in*difference [and] a bogus generalization" (1992, 153). It is through this insistence on the recognition of difference that postcolonialism distinguishes itself most clearly from other currently fashionable comparative practices and/or frameworks, notably postmodernism and its related but largely theatre-specific movement, interculturalism.[11] As the debates about postmodernism's intersections with postcolonialism have already received much press,[12] I do not intend to rehash them here; suffice it to say that I cannot agree with Arun Mukherjee's suggestion that race is the pivotal factor in distinguishing the two—that white members of colonized cultures typically produce postmodern texts while only nonwhites exhibit a genuinely postcolonial consciousness (1990, 2–3). Nor does the brand of postcolonialism espoused by the more scrupulous "white" critics necessarily produce a "unitary post-colonial subject" as Mukherjee contends (1990, 7). Helen Tiffin, for example, argues for (and practices) "cross-cultural 'humility' and 'homework'" as the necessary conditions for maintaining that "delicate balance of difference and similarity which is inevitably a part of comparative critical practice" (1984a, 30).

In general, this kind of vigilance is precisely what has been lacking in both the theory and the practice of such proponents of interculturalism as Peter Brook, Richard Schechner, and Eugenio Barba.[13] Through a laboratory approach, intercultural criticism typically examines theatre/ritual within anthropological frameworks that seldom acknowledge the operations of power exercised by the documentary team or individual—usually Euro-American—over the subjects studied. An elegant paradox underlies the intercultural method of analysis since it aims to calculate the similarities between all cultures primarily by studying those exoticized Others whose chief interest to the critic is their difference. Perhaps even more insidious is the brand of interculturalism enacted through performance itself, where, in search of the "therapeutic" (Marranca 1991, 15), Western directors appropriate the theatrical raw materials of non-Western cultures in order to enliven their own texts. As Daryl Chin argues, "The idea of interculturalism as simply a way of joining disparate cultural artefacts together has a hidden agenda of imperialism" (1991, 87). This is demonstrated quite clearly by the local example of the Mudrooroo/Müller project, which was initiated by Gerhard Fischer with the stated aim of mobilizing the "innovative and dynamic force" of Aboriginal performance aesthetics to rescue a "moribund if not dead" mainstream Australian theatre (Fischer 1993, 15). In this case, the Aborigines seem to have reappropriated the performance text in the rehearsal/workshopping process, which, according to Mudrooroo, was the arena of the project's "real" political action (1993, 143); but the more common outcome of the intercultural event is an unequal exchange, or a kind of "cultural tourism" that seems to celebrate heterogeneity while merely affirming the theatrical connoisseurship of the more powerful partner. Recently, in his introduction to *The Intercultural Performance Reader* (1996), Patrice Pavis attempts a more systematic appraisal of the effects of this kind of theatre, but many of the essays included in his book nonetheless avoid a critical assessment of their own intercultural theories and/or practices. Rustom Bharucha's earlier point that it is imperative to contextualize the cultures and exchanges at issue in each intercultural event cautions against such approaches: "No theory or critique of interculturalism can begin, to my mind, without confronting the politics of its location. And this, unfortunately, is what continues to elude most seekers of interculturalism who, in their pursuit of 'pre-cultural,' 'transcultural' or 'universal' values and sources, imagine that interculturalism can transcend the particularities of history altogether" (1993, 240).

In the terms of current performance theory, no entirely suitable model for theatrical *practice* has been forwarded to counter the egregious imperialism of the intercultural approach, although *Post-colonial Drama: Theory, Practice, Politics* (Gilbert and Tompkins, 1996) analyzes the theatre of colonized countries with reference to the many performative contexts that impact upon the field. Christopher Balme's writing on the syncretic theatre of colonized peoples in Australia and the Caribbean provides a perspective on the kind of cross-cultural exchange that occurs in the other direction—when marginalized groups "marry" European performance aesthetics with indigenous myths and rituals—but tends to see this process as inherently adaptive rather than potentially subversive (1990, 402–3). His reluctance to examine fully the politics of theatrical syncretism appears to stem from a belief that "the decolonisation process in the Fourth World can be seen as a mutual deepening of trust and respect between the politically dominant and the subjugated, indigenous cultures" (1990, 402). Although Balme's focus on the theatre of the colonized displaces the Eurocentric orientation of interculturalism and therefore makes an important start in developing alternatives, his approach sometimes risks duplicating interculturalism's interest in heterogeneity as mere effect. Postcolonialism, on the other hand, employs such critical concepts as hybridity and cultural contamination to describe not only the effects of imperialism but, more importantly, the deliberately political strategies by which imperial power might be dismantled. As Homi Bhabha argues,

> If the effect of colonial power is seen to be the *production* of hybridisation rather than the hegemonic command of colonialist authority or the silent repression of native traditions, then an important change of perspective occurs. It reveals the ambivalence at the source of traditional discourses on authority and enables a form of subversion, founded on that uncertainty, that turns the discursive conditions of dominance into the grounds of intervention. (1985a, 97)

Robert Young extends Bhabha's model to include two levels of cultural interaction: "organic hybridity, which will tend toward fusion, in conflict with intentional hybridity, which enables a contestatory activity, a politicized setting of cultural differences against each other dialogically" (1995, 22). It is through the latter, genuinely radical, concept of societies as *intentionally* hybrid and multidiscursive that postcolonialism posits a speaking space for the Other. Hence, in their discussion of models of hybridity and syncreticity in postcolonial literatures, Ashcroft, Griffiths, and Tiffin argue that hybridity subverts the establishment of any one way of being as axiomatic (1989, 100), creating a framework of difference in which the perspectives of the marginalized can be heard. Literary contamination, a related strategy, explores the creative potential of cross-cultural contact by seeking to "define differences that do not depend on myths of cultural purity or authenticity but that thrive on interaction" (Brydon 1990, 196). Neither term means to suggest a resolution of tensions between/within cultures; rather, hybridity and contamination operate both at the discursive level and the level of cultural practice within an "antithetical movement of coalescence and antagonism" (R. Young 1995, 22).

The notion of a multidiscursive and dialogic society is central not only to the study of indigenous peoples' resistance to colonization but also to an understanding of the discourses of settler groups positioned more ambivalently in relation to imperial power. This book's treatment of the non-Aboriginal texts that have inspired the bulk of the analysis is therefore designed to demonstrate some paradigmatic patterns of response to colonialism, rather than to insist upon a homogenized category of "settler" drama. Although a case might be forwarded for examining so-called multicultural plays separately from settler works, I have not always made that distinction since the two fields of practice, while certainly distinct and even contestatory at times, nonetheless share common interests in discourses of migration/exile and a similar ambivalence toward Aboriginal cultures.[14] Alan Filewod's point that "post-imperial governments [in Australia and Canada] promoted multiculturalism as an ideology of nationalism to satisfy the post-colonial need for a defining national principle" (1992, 11) also suggests the loose alignment of non-Aboriginal multicultural groups with the values of the dominant society. Individual plays by writers of varied ethnic/cultural origins are included in my study when they stage issues germane to the focus on postcolonialism, but a significant body of Greek and Italian theatre specifically tagged as multicultural is not examined because it speaks to experiences of marginality that are not particularly inflected by a history of colonization. My final chapter's analysis of Asian stereotypes signals the need for an in-depth study of the ways in which imperialism and neoimperialism impact upon various Asian-Australian groups, but, as yet, the body of theatre by this particular section of the multicultural community is relatively small.[15]

The case for a focus on the specificity of women's experiences in the colonial and postcolonial moment is much stronger; hence I devote considerable space to this subject. All too often, postcolonial analyses tend to overlook the ways in which constructions of sexual difference both reproduce and unsettle the hierarchies of empire. That gender critiques are crucial to the dismantling of imperialism's master narrative will be illustrated not only in my discussion of plays by and about women, but also in reference to many other texts. As feminist scholarship has demonstrated, patriarchal hegemony proceeds, by and large, through the privileging of the masculine pole of a series of binary oppositions constructed on gender difference. In imperial contexts, this leads to the implicit gendering of the dominant culture's colonizable Other as feminine, whether that Other is internal—usually figured by the land and/or its indigenous inhabitants in narratives about settlement/invasion—or external, as is often the case in accounts of neocolonialism. The problematic of representation is a key issue here, and one that frequently intersects with current debates about the gendering of performance as a feminized (and feminizing) practice. Hence, my application of feminist theory extends to an analysis of theatrical paradigms of representation and spectatorship in an attempt to dismantle those scopic regimes that Carter's argument forwards as the constitutive basis of imperial history. This is but one of the many areas of postcolonial inquiry that can be significantly informed by recent developments in performance theory.

Performance and Counterdiscourse

This book aims to articulate analytical frameworks that extend both the political reference and the conceptual praxis of conventional drama criticism. Although my examination of specific plays frequently relies on a text that is not the performance but a written transcription of what it might be (or even an approximation of what it was on the opening night), I am concerned that the performative dimension of the theatre under discussion not be overlooked. To this end, I wish to open up the notion of counterdiscourse that is central to postcolonial theory, and to explore its application to readings of performance. Counterdiscourse, according to Tiffin, "involve[s] a mapping of the dominant discourse, a reading and exposing of its underlying assumptions, and the dis/mantling of these assumptions from the cross-cultural standpoint of the imperially subjectified 'local'" (1987a, 23). Most postcolonial criticism has concentrated on the counterdiscursivity effected through written (and occasionally spoken) language, but Tiffin's definition invites broader interpretation to include visual signification and enactment, or perhaps more importantly, *re*enactment. If we accept the notion of discourses to mean "sets of statements—verbal, visual or otherwise—that give expression to the meanings and values of an institution, to the power relations that operate within and define that institution" (Cranny-Francis 1988, 160–61), then the operation of counterdiscourse has, at its disposal, more than simply language-oriented tools. In fact the notion of "mapping the dominant discourse" strongly suggests a spatial as well as rhetorical activity, while the words "exposing" and "dis/mantling" have a close affinity with the concept of costume as employed in theatre's masquerade. Clearly, the challenge to imperial discourses can, and frequently does, take nonlinguistic forms, especially in performance. Here, the subversive power of the "word" will also be significantly affected by the actor/s who utter it, by the audience as culturally positioned "readers," and by other aural and visual signifiers existing in the same theatrical space. As well as identifying the more overt counterdiscourses of the chosen texts, this study aims, therefore, to displace a different kind of logocentrism, to scrutinize those postcolonial critical practices that privilege the very language-based discursive strategies that they claim lie at the heart of imperialism. Such criticism, which has largely ignored the role of drama in the process of decolonization, risks becoming another hegemonic system.

In attempting to consider the theatrical contexts of the plays examined, I draw not only on performance theory but also on an eclectic range of discourses that have foregrounded the impact of ideology on representation. My overall study proceeds through an in-depth analysis of selected texts that lend themselves to a postcolonial reading and that best illustrate the concerns of the category of drama they are discussed under. After beginning with an example of how canonical counterdiscourse can refigure the specific tropes of the imperial text, and, beyond that, of received traditions of "national" theatre, this book treats the following four broad categories: Aboriginal theatre, settler/invader plays, feminist postcolonial drama, and plays about neoimperialism. These categories are designed to facilitate comparison across texts that share some political imperatives and performance features, rather than to suggest a number of mutually exclusive subfields of inquiry. In general, I make no attempt to give a comprehensive survey of relevant plays, choosing instead to explicate certain features of paradigmatic texts through critical frameworks that demonstrate both the diversity and the agency of postcolonial approaches to contemporary Australian theatre. When the prospective field of drama is relatively small or where few exemplary texts are available, my discussion is more extensive than intensive, although its aim remains constant.

Along with an emphasis on the range of postcolonial readings that might fruitfully be applied to its subject, this study is also concerned with issues and performative motifs that surface across all areas of inquiry. A political investment in replaying Australian history and/or the experience of imperialism is not the only common thread connecting apparently diverse plays. Perhaps one of the most prominent features of the theatre discussed here is a widespread tendency to experiment with nonnaturalistic techniques, whether that means inserting epic structures, incorporating expressionist styles and themes, positioning elements of Aboriginal or Asian performance cultures in creative tension with European ones, or including metatheatrical frameworks that foreground the role of the spectator vis-à-vis representation. In many instances, this movement away from a wholly illusionistic theatre can be seen as part of a larger agenda to unsettle both the power relationships and the race and gender hierarchies naturalized by history's narratives. If a postcolonial analysis is intent upon denaturalizing representation, it must then bring into focus such aspects of theatre as space, the body, movement, and costume as elements of an ideologically coded sign system.

In performative genres, unlike in literary modes of representation, narratives unfold in space as well as through time. Whereas words on a page must be interpreted sequentially, theatre offers the possibility of a simultaneous reading, through the senses, of all the visual and aural signifiers embedded in the text as performance. Theatre thus lends itself particularly well to the interrogation of spatial and temporal (teleological) aspects of imperialism and facilitates the telling/showing of oppositional versions of the past that propose not only different constitutive events but also different ways of constructing that past in the present. Theatre's potential to intervene in the epistemological and ontological systems through which the pageant of imperial history is seen simply to "unfold" (in Carter's terms) paves the way for more enabling conceptualizations of historical representation. As Albert Einstein argues, "Time and space are modes by which we think and not conditions in which we live" (qtd. in Forsee 1963, 81).

In keeping with the idea of a spatial history as one of the alternatives that a postcolonial replay of the past might explore, this study regards space as an important field of analysis. Darko Suvin, along with other performance theorists, postulates that space is "analytically distinguishable from but in fact consubstantial with the dramaturgic agents"; because it is neither neutral nor homogeneous, space always "colours all relationships within its limits" (1987, 322, 312). Michel Foucault's work on heterotopian space is instructive here, for he maintains that while "we live inside a set of relations that delineates sites which are irreducible to one another and absolutely not superimposable on one another," certain heterogeneous sites nonetheless relate to all others in a way that destabilizes the set of relations they designate (1986, 23–24). Not surprisingly, theatre features among Foucault's listed heterotopias—sites that are "capable of juxtaposing in a single real place several [incompatible] spaces" (1986, 25). If these spaces are never isolated but dynamic and interactive, where they meet and clash is of crucial significance for a postcolonial reading of a nation's drama because it is in the nexus of debated (and debatable) space that pluralism and difference emerge. And in the larger context of cultural production, the public spaces of the theatre become important venues where the marginalized can claim access to the privilege of self-representation.

Space is often the central feature of dramatized images of the landscape, which is a key site of struggle and anxiety in postcolonial narratives in Australia and in other settler nations such as Canada, New Zealand, and the United States. Although the ideological functions of nature in dominant (nationalist) constructions and marginalized (feminist and/or Aboriginal) contestations of Australian identity have been widely discussed in reference to fiction, poetry, and, more latterly, film,[16] analyses of Australian drama/theatre have tended to subordinate landscape to other thematic and generic concerns, or to read it merely as a scenic device that at best heightens narrative emplotment and at worst recedes as a naturalized backdrop for signal events.[17] While partly excusable due to the *perceived* limitations of the theatre's capacity to conjure nature's expansive dimensions, critical neglect of the landscape as a central feature of contemporary versions of the past demonstrates a false complacency about the preeminence of interpersonal relationships in both history and in theatre. Such approaches can become complicit with imperialism's project not only because they fail to show adequate cognizance of spatial aspects of the European *landnama*—the land taking and land naming—of Australia, but also because they assume that nature can be subsumed by culture.[18] Furthermore, a lack of engagement with nature as expressed through the stagescape suggests an undervaluation of space as a fundamental component of dramatic representation. As Michael Issacharoff demonstrates by reference to Beckett's works, while movement or dialogue can be banished from performance, space is a constant and necessary requirement (1981, 211).

How the landscape/stagescape figures as an important relational space in postcolonial drama is a topic explored in my study not only via an analysis of the "territorial disputes" staged by Aboriginal theatre but also in relation to settler/invader responses to alien space/place, and feminist concerns with dislocation and exile. Mapping, a spatial activity designed to "make sense" of the landscape, and, concomitantly, a discourse with specific ideological implications, recurs in a number of plays across these categories, and is thus a focus motif. Two related cartographic strategies are evident: deconstructing imperial and/or patriarchal maps by exposing how they construct (rather than simply record) space in the nexus of power and culture, and remapping the land/space/stage according to the political imperatives of the colonized group. The rhizomatic[19] properties of the performance text as a spatial discourse that is unbounded and open—and therefore resistant to the closures of imperial cartography—establish theatre as a particularly effective site for decolonizing the map. In addition, when the process of mapping is undertaken within the framework of nonnaturalistic theatre, the disjunctive gap between the map and its referent brings into visibility the "mimetic fallacy" through which subjective and contingent models of "reality" are passed off as objective and universal representations (Huggan 1989b, 117–18).

Like time and space, the body in colonized societies is subject to multifarious inscriptions that tend to produce a dialogic, ambivalent, and unstable signifier rather than a single, independent, and discrete entity. As Tiffin maintains, there is not ever a single colonized "body," but rather "an interplay between colonial and post-colonial *texts* and bodies" (1993a, 47). The metaphorizing of the body as a habit of imperialist representation and part of its larger military, medical, and pedagogical administration of actual subjects/bodies has been both insidious and persuasive throughout the history of Australia's colonization. Such hegemonic systems of codification sometimes appear unassailable, but they always risk recursive dismantlement if those differences that facilitate imperial reductions of the body are also seen to convey an Otherness that exceeds textual containment. The current movement toward cultural decolonization, then, involves not just a verbal/textual counterdiscourse but a counterdiscourse of the body and its signifying practices. Pamela Banting makes the important point that "if the postcolonial begins at the very moment when colonial power inscribes itself onto the body and space of its Others, then we are compelled not only to analyze languages and discourses as sites of resistance but also to consider the inscribed bodies of postcolonial subjects" (1993, 8). This is particularly true of theatre, where the body, brought into focus through performance, becomes an especially charged site of convergence for contesting discourses and, at times, even the vehicle for an incipient expressive language that resists appropriation into dominant linguistic codes.

In examining the subversive possibilities and problematics of the body in a culturally delimited context, I aim to foreground the exercise of imperial power and the ways in which that power may be subverted or compromised through performance. Philip Auslander reminds us that "questions of who or what is speaking through the body and in what language, of what discourses are inscribed on/in the body, are clearly questions of power relations" (1988, 9). The body's potential to articulate disruptive counterdiscourses is closely related to its problematic construction within disciplinary regimes and systems of surveillance:

> If the body is the strategic target of systems of codification, supervision and constraint, it is also because the body and its energies and capacities exert an uncontrollable, unpredictable threat to a regular, systematic mode of social organisation. As well as being the site of

> knowledge-power, the body is thus also a site of *resistance,* for it exerts a recalcitrance, and always entails the possibility of a counterstrategic reinscription, for it is capable of being self-marked, self-represented in alternative ways. (Grosz 1990, 64)

How the reinscription and self-representation of bodies that are colonized or "intextuated"—to use Elizabeth Grosz's term for bodies marked with inscriptions of power/knowledge—translate into performative strategies is a key issue for this study and, again, one that surfaces across a wide variety of plays. Accordingly, my discussion of the body looks at the settler/invader subject as well as more conventionally marginalized figures such as Aborigines, Asians, and women.

As categories constructed through an act of *visual* recognition, race and gender have particular significance in theatrical contexts; however, it is crucial to remember that these categories are historically conditioned rather than simply biologically determined. They are, moreover, unstable and complex markers of difference even if highly significant politically. One of the problems of performing/interpreting such difference is how to avoid essentialist constructions of race and gender while still accounting for the irreducible specificity of their identifications (as opposed to identities). A possible solution, following Ien Ang's work on ethnicity and migration, is to conceptualize race and gender as not based upon a single origin but "experienced as a provisional and partial 'identity,' which must be constantly (re)invented and (re)negotiated" (1993, 42). What performance offers to this process of identity formation is the opportunity to manipulate such codes as costume, gesture, movement, and makeup—all factors in the "recognition" of Otherness outside the art/ificial world of theatre—in ways that destabilize imperial and patriarchal power. This can be effected through the foregrounding of "pure" difference, a form of what Spivak calls "strategic essentialism" (1988, 205), or, alternatively, by using theatre's signifying devices to illustrate the constructedness of race and gender categories. This is where mimicry, masquerade, hybridity, cross-dressing, and other carnivalesque subversions activated through the postcolonial body come into play. If, as Peter Stallybrass and Allon White argue, the carnivalesque is a form of transgression that "mediates between the classical/classificatory body and its negations, its Others, what it excludes to create its identity as such" (1986, 26), then it is particularly relevant to this study. My investigation of the carnivalesque as a resistance strategy, though principally developed in relation to Louis Nowra's work, extends to other plays and to verbal languages as well as somatic states and discourses.

Reading the body as a text denaturalizes constructions of a self grounded primarily in verbal signifiers and avoids reproducing epistemologies that emphasize the Renaissance mind/body dichotomy, a feature of colonialist discourse that can be problematized through performance. Whereas markers of race and gender are generally inscribed on the body, movement and gesture "mean" via the body's own articulation in space. This process is most noticeable when highly coded sequences such as dance—an important motif in this study—bring into focus the body's "languages." Most analyses of drama tend not to look at dance as a signifying practice in itself but to subsume its discourses in the verbal/symbolic codes of the dialogue proper by discussing how dance contributes to the plot, character, and imagery of the particular play in which it is staged.[20] These approaches fix meaning within the hermeneutic world of the play text, deny the historical, geographical, and sociocultural specificity of dance, and effectively ignore issues of representation. Critical analyses of dance in Australian drama are virtually nonexistent even though almost all Aboriginal theatre features it, as do many other plays examined in this study. In general, theatre reviewers either fail to notice dance or else classify it as spectacle, therein eliding its signifying practices with aesthetic (read normative) standards of judgment. In an attempt to foreground dance as a site of negotiation of cultural power and identity, instead of trying to determine what dance means, I will attempt to discuss "how" it means and what it "does."

Dramaturgically speaking, enactment of some kind of dance during a play does a number of things to the text. As a focalizing agent, it draws attention to the rhetoric of embodiment in all performance, something that is less apparent in the dramatization of dialogue, especially within the conventions of realism. Even while bringing the body into focus, dance also spatializes its field of representation, which is to say that it foregrounds the proxemic relationships between characters, spectators, and features of the set. This ever-shifting relational axis of space breaks down binary structures that seek to situate dance as either image or identity, and the spectator as observer rather than coproducer of meaning. Furthermore, situated within a dramatic text, dance often denaturalizes theatre's signifying practices by disrupting narrative sequence and/or genre. What dance "does," then, is draw attention to the various frames of dramatic representation, which suggests that it can function as a historicizing device that locates the action in particular temporal and cultural contexts. This calls for analysis of dance's ideological encoding, an especially important project in criticism of postcolonial texts.

General theories of movement illuminate an examination of "how" dance means and can be applied to theatrical practice that uses highly coded movement as basic to representation. Ann Daly posits that meaning is constructed in the fluid relationships between patterned movement and its many layers of context: "The significance of any given behavior can only be determined in its individual, interactional, institutional, and cultural contexts and in relation to behavioral expectations, for what is *not* done may be as significant as what is done" (1988, 44). Daly's argument that meaning in movement is located in a nexus of intersecting systems demands that we pay attention to the performer and his/her relationship with other actors and spectators, to the conventions of drama and its enactment in theatrical space and time, and to the culture in which it is produced.

Similarly, the reading of costume is both a complicated process and a political act. Like movement, clothing gives the body presence, particularly on stage, where even nakedness becomes a costume of sorts. Theatre practitioners have of course long recognized that the theatrical subject is indelibly marked by costume, but critics and audiences seem less willing to scrutinize the textuality of clothes and fabrics, especially in naturalistic theatre, where they are barely noted unless something does not quite fit, literally or figuratively. What is judged inappropriate or incongruous then becomes significant in terms of Roland Barthes's concept of the "aberrant message which '*surprises*' the code" (1986, 94), but, in general, dress operates to naturalize particular representations—or rather fabrications. Jane Gaines's critique of film as a medium in which costume, paradoxically, is designed to "recede" at the same time as it "registers" (1990, 183) can be aptly applied to much contemporary theatre practice wherein costume delivers as self-evident particular gender, racial, social, and national identities and then recedes into the background as mere clothing, a mood-setting device for the verbal text. From a political standpoint, then, any garment is a problematic signifier because the paradox of its transparency conceals a rhetorical power that is nonetheless expressed through the materiality of clothing as part of the mise en scène, and in its relationship to the body as the most localized site of ideological struggle. My discussions of costume in various sections of this study are designed to show how such power is exercised in the interests of imperialism, and to illustrate the role of particular kinds of dress in constructing, consolidating, and/or contesting cultural and sexual identities on Australian stages. In this way, I hope to suggest some provisional beginnings for an "epistemology of the wardrobe"[21] that emphasizes how the marginalized might de-sign costume for strategic purposes.

Because its power is literal as well as symbolic, clothing has a number of important functions in the processes of imperialism. A brief look at Shakespeare's much discussed colonial paradigm, *The Tempest,* indicates that Prospero maintains his position of authority not only through language but also by sartorial fiat, a strategy designed to achieve full effects in performance. Predictably, he discards his magic robe only when he can don another powerful costume: his rightful attire as duke of Milan. Caliban, in contrast, is clothed in a coarse gaberdine cloak that confers low social status, signifies alterity, and functions as a comic device when he is mistaken for a monster of the isle. His "linguistic capture," so often remarked upon by postcolonial critics,[22] is thus paralleled by corporeal containment. In a text that deploys costume in the interests of the colonizer, Prospero's garments become an object of desire for the oppressed, as suggested by Stephano's and Trinculo's fascination with the glistening apparel that Ariel sets as a trap. Although Caliban himself is not fooled by this "trumpery"—he at least can distinguish between mere adornment and the vestments of power—it nonetheless prevents the trio from overthrowing colonial rule; and because he has merely exchanged one master for another, Caliban is forced to carry the clothes, a strong visual image for "wearing the blame." His failed insurrection can be related directly to his inability to appropriate his master's clothes as successfully as he appropriates his language by learning "how to curse" (1.2.363). Historically, most performances of *The Tempest* have certainly depended on costume to subordinate Caliban as the "missing link" in the evolutionary chain,[23] a predictable tactic given that his language is often far too eloquent to do the trick. The theatrical clout of this kind of characterization is incidentally illustrated by Trevor Griffiths's observation that one early-twentieth-century production that attempted to represent Caliban more sympathetically seemed to flounder because of the difficulty of playing against costume (1983, 175).

The larger historical picture shows that clothing was used throughout the British Empire to instigate similar hierarchies of power. A particularly resonant example in the Australian context is the convict uniform, which, as costume historians point out, was designed not only to signal that a person had committed a crime (or at least had been found guilty of doing so), but also to function as part of the punishment and reformation of criminals insofar as it caused humiliation and even discomfort.[24] Military or police uniforms, on the other hand, not only signal authority but in many instances actually confer it, a point amply—if ironically—illustrated in colonial times by the recruitment of Black[25] trackers as policemen who were then empowered to discipline Aborigines. Western-style civilian clothing also remains a highly charged costume code that patrols certain important borders: it delineates "civilized" from "savage," self from Other, and Christian from heathen. Wearing indigenous dress thus becomes a gesture of recalcitrance on behalf of the colonized but tantamount to barbarism in the case of the European settler/invader because it threatens to dissolve boundaries; hence the implied criticism when someone "goes native." The conative aspects of clothing—that it encourages people to act in prescribed ways—are clearly at work here. The idea that "clothes make the man" (*sic*) underlies discourses that marginalize traditional clothing as a risible sign of difference and explains efforts by imperial powers—the administrators of Aboriginal missions are a good example—to mobilize dress as a means of acculturation of the racial Other.

Outlining how clothing functions to establish and maintain a powerful identity for the imperial self while securing the textual capture and containment of the colonizable Other is one line of inquiry pursued in my examination of costume. The parallel project is to identify ways of resisting this capture, a task at least partly addressed by rewriting, or in this case remodeling, the epistemological frameworks that shape representation. Tiffin's contention that postcolonial literatures are "constituted in counter-discursive rather than homologous practices" (1987a, 18) begs us to consider the ways in which costuming on Australian stages has not simply involved transplanting European codes and fashions, but formulating a complex, sometimes ambivalent, response to their underlying assumptions. The hybrid forms that result from such repatterning provide a key for unlocking imperialism's master wardrobe and dismantling the vestiges of its power. This strategy, particularly evident in contemporary Aboriginal texts, suggests that mixed dress codes operate as a form of cultural negotiation, often through comedy and parody, even while they indicate detribalization and acculturation.

Any discussion of costume inevitably raises questions of gender, in part because dress is one of the main signifiers by which we (mis)identify gender, and also because "dressing up" to perform has been cast as a feminized activity in Western culture despite strong traditions of male transvestite theatres on the Greek and Elizabethan stages. Thus costume also operates as a code through which intersections of gender, nation, and sexuality might be *re*cognized, a subject I explore primarily, but not exclusively, in reference to Australia's relationships with Asia. In particular, transvestism—here taken to include cross-cultural as well as cross-gender dressing—can function as a marker of "gender undecidability and an indication of category crisis" (Garber 1992, 238). Jonathan Dollimore's reminder that "to cross is not only to traverse, but to mix (as in to cross-breed) and to contradict (as in to cross someone)" (1991, 288) suggests some of the subversive possibilities of transvestism as a way of both inverting and displacing the gender and racial binaries that have facilitated imperialist constructions of nationhood (see Brydon 1994, 23–25). The inherently theatrical nature of transvestism is a key issue since how something is worn can signify as much as what is worn. It follows that the wearing of certain clothing as a political act is by no means always collusive with the normative codes of the costume chosen. I am interested here in the iconoclastic potential of performance and the sometimes disjunctive relationships between the actor and his/her clothing as mediated by the role. Nonnaturalistic techniques such as Brecht's alienation effect offer ways to prevent the seamless application of clothing to the performer and/or character, suggesting that costume's race and gender connotations are highly arbitrary. Focus on how costume is worn also explains the effectiveness of parody and masquerade as ways of subverting imperial and patriarchal hierarchies.

The flexible (and sometimes playful) gap between script and performance becomes an important site of intervention in a postcolonial theory of drama. Hence language, like the other signifying codes I have discussed, needs to be examined within the context of its performance. If theatrical dialogue can be understood as the staging of the relationship between what is said and how it is said, then the performance text offers an ideal arena for what Ashcroft, Griffiths, and Tiffin forward as a fundamental strategy of postcolonialism: the abrogation and appropriation of the colonizer's linguistic codes (1989, 37–38 and passim). That this involves "*seizing* the language of the center and re-placing it with a language fully adapted to the colonised *place*" (1989, 38; emphasis added) reminds us to pay attention to both the embodiment of language and its site of enunciation, aspects that are often foregrounded in performance. Stephen Slemon's observation that "European language comes to colonial space through a process of deracination and disruption" (1989, 103) also suggests the corporeal and spatial aspects of verbal expression. My approach to language thus focuses on those spaces from which the colonized speak and on those enactments of voice that precipitate a crisis of authority that deprivileges standard English as the normative code of language. This subject is developed primarily in my analysis of orality in Aboriginal theatre, although it is crucial to remember that all of the plays under discussion mobilize performative aspects of speech (and even silence) as a part of the political text of their dialogue.

The polyphonic nature of theatrical discourse, which generally avoids a single narrative voice, amplifies the possibilities for hearing the Other speak. Accordingly, a postcolonial critique of theatrical language moves away from a search for a "genuine" Australian vernacular toward the acceptance of Other voices and Other languages as viable, and indeed vital, modes of expression. The concept of an Australian voice (white, male, and generally Eurocentric) as identified by drama critics in the 1970s is no longer relevant, if it ever was. I am not suggesting, however, that we simply broaden the category of what might be called "Australian" or develop subcategories that allow for difference to be expressed within an overarching framework of nationalism. Identifying an "authentic" native, migrant, feminist, or any other voice in Australian theatre is much *less* important than examining how the many languages of the larger culture overlap and intersect with each other, how they are hybridized and contaminated in the counterdiscursive process. Here again, the rhizomatic model suggests the importance of multiple and connective structures.

> A rhizome ceaselessly establishes connections between semiotic chains, organizations of power, and circumstances relative to the arts, sciences, and social struggles. A semiotic chain is like a tuber agglomerating very diverse acts, not only linguistic, but also perceptive, mimetic, gestural, and cognitive; there is no language in itself, nor are there any linguistic universals, only a throng of dialects, patois, slangs, and specialized languages. There is no ideal speaker-listener, any more than there is a homogeneous linguistic community. Language is, in Weinreich's words, "an essential heterogeneous reality." There is no mother tongue, only a power takeover by a dominant language within a political multiplicity. (Deleuze and Guattari 1987, 7)

The hierarchies of power enacted through language usage, and how these are established, reinforced, negotiated, challenged, or undermined, are what concern me here.

My final area of recurrent focus vis-à-vis performance is the framing of the stage action and its specular consumption by the audience. This is a potentially problematic subject for a postcolonial inquiry since it is through the intentional gaze of the colonizer, as much as through the linguistic interpellation of the colonized subject, that imperial regimes often become self-legitimizing. The imperial gaze marks out the colonizable subject "as a fixed reality which is at once an 'other' and yet entirely knowable and visible" (Bhabha 1983, 23) and, through networks of representation and surveillance, reproduces this Other as an object of knowledge/power. It is also implicated in the scopic regimes of exploration and settlement that seek to delimit, inhabit and therefore own, alien territory—to penetrate the "inert yet resistant female land" (Ryan 1994, 36). The imperial/patriarchal gaze, therefore, becomes a site/sightline for postcolonial resistance, and if theatrical representation means to undermine its authority, then performance must somehow engage with the looking relations it establishes. Like his language, the colonizer's gaze must be actively seized for subversive purposes, its privileges abrogated, its uses (re)appropriated. The movement away from naturalism is an important step in breaking down the illusory "fourth wall" that facilitates scopic pleasure. Nonnaturalistic theatre allows for the incorporation of techniques designed to challenge paradigms of spectatorship and to foreground the audience's function in narrative construction. In the plays under discussion, these techniques range from direct dialogues with the audience to complex refractory moments in which multiple and intersecting gazes and frames hold up to question the entire theatrical framework. Particularly relevant here is the work done by feminist performance theorists on deconstructing "male gaze" models of representation, a project that meshes very well with postcolonialism's interest in disrupting imperial "looking" relations. This issue is examined at various points in my analysis, notably in chapter 5's discussion of metatheatrical frames in feminist postcolonial drama.

If, as Tiffin maintains, decolonization "invokes an ongoing dialectic between hegemonic centrist systems and peripheral subversions of them" (1987a, 17), then a postcolonial theory/practice of performance must also examine its own biases as an art form still heavily influenced by European conventions. The prominence of metatheatre in the body of drama that has inspired this study calls attention to the ways in which any performance stages the necessary provisionality of all representation. By developing multiple self-reflexive discourses through role playing, role doubling/splitting, plays within plays, interventionary frameworks, and other metatheatrical devices, these works interrogate received models of theatre at the same time as they show, quite self-consciously, that they are "acting out" their histories/identities in a complex replay that can never be finished or final. Co-opting Wilson Harris's creative strategy of "infinite rehearsal" as a particularly apt model for a performative revisioning of imperial history,[26] I see this emphasis on metatheatre as a critical part of the agenda for change. Hena Maes-Jelinek explains "infinite rehearsal" as the process "whereby the artist, convinced of the impossibility of ever reaching final truth," constantly revises versions of it and thus "breaks the rigid mould of history" by rehearsing and rerehearsing its implications (1989, 232–33). This model might well apply to criticism itself, and in that respect, I wish to acknowledge that the approaches I attempt to outline in this study can only ever be partial, provisional, and subject to change.

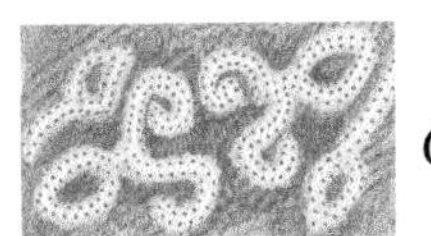

Chapter 1

Canonical Counterdiscourse

A Case Study

But whose idea was it to do Shakespeare? Very silly choice if you ask me.

—Gwen, from Michael Gow's ***Away***

The circulation of "Shakespeare's Books" within educational and cultural spheres has been a powerful hegemonic force throughout the history of the British Empire,[1] and one that continues to operate almost unabated in a number of postcolonial countries including Australia. Not surprisingly, the ideological weight of the Bard's legacy is felt nowhere more strongly than in the theatre, where his work is still widely seen as the measure of all dramatic art, the ultimate test for the would-be actor or director, the mark of audience sophistication, and the uncontested sign of Culture itself. This tendency to deem Shakespeare's worth self-evident and his application universal not only naturalizes a particular Eurocentric (and patriarchal) worldview but also paralyzes the development of local theatrical traditions. In her analysis of Michael Gow's *Away* (1986), Penny Gay alludes to this problem when she asks the rhetorical question: "How can one aspire to write plays when Shakespeare has already, incontrovertibly, written the greatest dramas in the English language?" (1992, 204). For the postcolonial dramatist/critic, this is a politically charged question because the "univocal and monolithic significance of Shakespeare" (Campbell 1993, 2) perpetuates notions of a theatre that is always already constituted within imperial epistemology, and thus closed to Other(ed) knowledges. Decolonizing that theatre must involve the reopening of such closures and the dismantling of Shakespeare's books as a "transcendental signifier" for theatre practice and criticism alike. In this respect, the Bard's function as a cultural shibboleth makes his texts particularly important sites for an "infinite rehearsal" that might bring about the quantum change that postcolonial criticism urges.

The staging of the "intact" Shakespeare play offers one kind of counterdiscourse that might, through a revisionist performance, articulate tensions between the Anglo script and its localized enunciation.[2] Since performing a script is not so much a precise translation as a transformational transcoding from one communicative mode (writing) into a *number* of others, the possibilities for slippage, mimicry, and subversion are almost infinite. Useful here is Patrice Pavis's definition of the mise en scène as "the establishment of a dialectical opposition between [text and performance] which takes the form of a *stage enunciation* . . . according to a *metatext* 'written' by the director and his team and more or less integrated, that is established in the enunciation, in the concrete work of the stage production and the spectators' reception" (1982, 146). This model of an interactive mise en scène, as opposed to earlier models that defined it primarily in terms of the physical elements of a performance (what the spectator sees and hears), already offers a space for negotiation between canonical texts and counter-canonical stagings of them. John Frow argues that since "the social function of the classical text is in the first place to *be* a classical text, to signify its own value as cultural capital," then we can only recuperate heterosignification if we "displace the text from its ideal non-time, restoring a historical distance and strangeness to it" (1993, 216).

There are numerous Australian productions of Shakespeare's plays that have functioned as historicized and politically localized performance events,[3] but it is the actual reworking of the canonical text in and through Australian drama that concerns me here. Along with Gow, playwrights such as Dorothy Hewett and Louis Nowra are well known for their allusions to the "classics," even if some critics regard this intertextuality as little more than "affectionate homage" (Gay 1992, 204). While reshaping Shakespearean narratives and/or Elizabethan theatrical conventions is often a way of contemporizing classical texts (and valorizing contemporary ones), it can also involve a deliberately political act designed to destabilize both the institutional power of the invoked canonical tradition and the currency of its associated discourses. Helen Tiffin has termed this specific reworking of imperialism's tropes "canonical counter-discourse," a process in which "a post-colonial writer takes up a character or characters, or the basic assumptions of a British canonical text, and unveils those assumptions" to "investigate the European textual capture and containment of colonial and post-colonial space" (1987a, 22). While there are a number of contemporary Australian plays that might fruitfully be discussed in this context, one somewhat controversial example—David Malouf's *Blood Relations*[4]—will suffice to demonstrate the ways in which replaying canonical characters, themes, dramaturgy, and representational modes articulates a potentially powerful postcolonial counterdiscourse.

When *Blood Relations* premiered at the Sydney Opera House in 1987, critical response ranged from respect through bemusement to boredom. Most reviewers expressed great disappointment that Malouf's considerable literary talent as a novelist and poet had not been adequately transposed to the stage, and used phrases like "congested," "obscure and tedious," and "static" to describe his first play.[5] Less than half of the reviews mentioned the play's allusions to *The Tempest,* and most of those either failed to discuss the importance of this intertextuality or found the representation of connections between the two unconvincing or merely humorous. Only Ann Nugent, writing for the *Canberra Times,* found Malouf's interweaving of Shakespeare's thematics and dramaturgy politically significant. Focusing on the legacy of imperialism foreshadowed in Shakespeare's *The Tempest,* she saw *Blood Relations* as a "parable of the white settlement of the Australian continent and a powerful image of the spiritual restlessness and cultural isolation of the Australian migrant people" (all those who are not Aboriginal) (1987, 12). This chapter extends Nugent's observation to discuss *Blood Relations* as a postcolonial text/event that writes back specifically to *The Tempest,* not as a narrowly parodic work, but as one that attempts to problematize the power relationships set up in Shakespeare's mythical New World and to question their legitimizing discourses.

Writing back to *The Tempest* is by no means new; in fact, this project has become so widespread in postcolonial literatures that it would seem politically passé were it not for the "bardolatry" that continually revalidates the imperial canon while excluding more local texts. Interpreted as a fable of the colonial experience, Shakespeare's play offers, in the movements of resistance to Prospero's power, several sites for potential intervention in the imperial process through politicized readings and reworkings of the text. The originary site of this potential resistance to imperialism can be found in the text of *The Tempest* itself, which as Paul Brown points out, can be reread as "not simply a reflection of colonialist practices but an intervention in an ambivalent and even contradictory discourse" (1985, 48). Applying Homi Bhabha's theories of the colonial stereotype, Brown argues that Prospero's narrative, which seeks to legitimize a posteriori his usurpation of the island, is continually destabilized by its necessary production of Caliban as the Other who must be mastered in the name of civility.

> Colonialist discourse voices a demand for order and disorder, producing a disruptive other in order to assert the superiority of the coloniser. Yet that production is itself evidence of a struggle to restrict the other's

> disruptiveness to that role. Colonialist discourse does not simply announce a triumph for civility, it must continually produce it and this work involves struggle and risk. (1985, 58)

Hence, in its interpellation of Caliban as a colonial subject, Prospero's discourse opens up the possibility of insurrection and the dispersal of his own power.

Long before the 1950s, when the Prospero-Caliban relationship emerged as one of the key literary paradigms for critics of colonialist discourse,[6] productions of *The Tempest* had demonstrated, albeit sometimes tentatively, that performance is crucial to the counterdiscursive project. In his extensive account of the play's stage history, Trevor Griffiths cites, for example, a nineteenth-century burlesque called *The Enchanted Isle* that featured Caliban as an antislavery campaigner, and an 1838 production in which he was portrayed with sufficient empathy to prompt one reviewer to declare that Prospero was partly to blame for his slave's disruptive behavior (1983, 160–61). Contemporary productions of *The Tempest* that mean to highlight its colonial themes stress Caliban's challenge to his master's power and reveal the inherent instability of Prospero's authority over other characters in the play. In the so-called New World, Caliban has frequently become the quintessential figure of resistance in a local struggle for political and cultural decolonization, while even in the imperial center, some emphasis on colonialism has been expected since Jonathan Miller's influential London revival of the play in 1970, when black actors were cast as Caliban and Ariel to represent differing native responses to European invasion (see T. Griffiths 1983, 177–79). It is this dialogic potential of the power relations between the oppressors and the oppressed in *The Tempest* that accounts for its continued relevance to the decolonizing process, and its popularity as a target for the creative reworkings that have effected potent interrogations of the text's colonialist discourse.

Rewrites of *The Tempest* and critical reactions to them are too numerous to detail here, and there is ongoing debate about how this revisionary project is manifest across various postcolonial regions. However, most authorities agree that Black writers—from Caribbean, African, African-American, or Amerindian societies—tend to focus on the Prospero-Caliban relationship and to suggest that subversion lies in one or more of the following: Caliban's appropriation of the colonizer's language or creation of his own, the redefinition of rape and appetite to implicate the colonizer, and the destruction of a binary system of logic in which black is defined by white, chaos by order, and savagery by civility. Writers from settler cultures such as Anglophone Canada seem more inclined to remodel Miranda as a protest figure,[7] creating a suitable fable for Canada's impulse to reject her role as the dutiful daughter of empire, while Americans concentrate on the legacy of Prospero as artificer, a prototype of the American hero who imposes order in and control over his external world through a domination of nature.[8] Australian responses to Shakespeare's classic text appear to be less numerous and more problematic. *Visitants* (1981), by Randolph Stow, is the only Australian example cited in Diana Brydon's 1984 article on post-colonial reworkings of *The Tempest,* and it remains the best-known local instance of this particular type of canonical counterdiscourse. Stow's novel positions the Australian as Prospero to the Trobriand Islanders in a colonial situation that duplicates the historical relationships between the British colonizers and their indigenous subjects, and Brydon concludes from it that the Australian "Tempest" is external, the result of conflict between two very distinct cultures.

Blood Relations, which was written after Brydon's analysis, clearly falls into a different category, not only in its emphasis on the internal worlds of its characters but also in their hybrid racial and social backgrounds and their complex relations to one another and to a landscape that embodies both the promise and the threat of home and exile. Despite its ambivalences, this play can be seen to contribute to an already substantial body of "*Tempest*-centered" literature that has emerged mostly from former colonies of the British Empire and that is characterized by three specific features: "emphasis on a pastoral setting (some kind of isolation from the outside world); a focus on power relationships involving dominance, subservience, and rebellion (between classes, age groups, or sexes); and a related focus on the role of art in taming nature" (Brydon 1984, 76). Malouf's play, therefore, deserves more serious consideration than reviewers accorded it. Perhaps its allusions to *The Tempest* mystified most critics because they looked for direct parallels between the two texts (with a little local color added of course) and so found, in the Australian version, only insipid imitation or at best parody, whereas a more fruitful approach might have seen *Blood Relations* as a palimpsest containing Derridean traces of past, present, and even future *Tempests,* which would open up the possibilities of transforming its characters, events, and themes. I say "possibilities" because I think Malouf's play could act more transgressively than it does, especially in its examination of power and authority. The women, especially, back away from confrontations with Willy/Prospero at crucial moments when it would seem that they are on the brink of eroding his dominance, but perhaps the ambivalent discourses of the play, like that of

The Tempest itself, more appropriately reflect the uncertainties of their times. In *Blood Relations,* postcolonial resistance is further compromised by the contingencies of a reconfigured social structure in which all settler subjects are continually implicated in imperial power.

The most obvious site of counterdiscursivity in *Blood Relations* can be found in the dramatis personae. Reviewers who noted the parallels between Willy and Prospero, Dinny and Caliban, Cathy and Miranda, and Edward and Ferdinand seldom delved into their effects other than to suppose that Malouf tries (sometimes too hard) to achieve a mythic dimension in his work by invoking Shakespeare. The more important function of these parallels, I contend, lies in their imperfect imitations, their contaminations, of the canonical models. The resultant hybridity, which Malouf's play exemplifies both in the complex genealogical connections among its characters and in their dialectical relationships with characters from *The Tempest,* allows for the emergence of postcolonial discourses by *re*acting (to) the tropologies of Shakespeare's master text.

Willy complicates notions of the Prospero figure through his relationships with Dinny, Frank, and Edward and, for that matter, with almost all of the other characters in the play. Like Prospero, Willy has colonized an indigenous Caliban, but because his colonial subject, the part-Aboriginal Dinny, is also his bastard son, this Other is inescapably a part of the self: a de facto acknowledgment of "this thing of darkness" as his own. Whereas Prospero's narrative operates to locate sexual appetite in the savage Other whom he can control by magic, thus averting the threat of miscegenation, Willy's story reveals the appetites of the self and their consequences: the intentional appropriation of indigenous land and culture, enacted metaphorically in *Blood Relations* through Willy's "rape" of Dinny's mother. By confronting Willy about that rape, Dinny, the "bastard" son, appropriates control of his own hybridity, and therefore his/tory, by reversing the roles of perpetrator and victim: "You were an accident, Willy. . . . I used to think *I* was but I've stopped. In my life you're the accident" (1988, 66). Willy/Prospero is thus interpellated back into the ambivalence of his own discourse, over which he no longer has absolute authority. The colonizer, the play seems to suggest, must eventually face the consequences of his actions; washing off the "muck" after the work of empire only belies a certain hypocrisy, a refusal to be implicated in the recursive effects of colonization—its decivilizing of both oppressor and oppressed.

Willy's identity is further "contaminated" by his relationship with Frank. When Frank runs off with Willy's wife Tessa, Willy, like Prospero, is betrayed by a brother, or at least a "best mate" close enough to be a blood relation. But the discourse of recrimination set up in Prospero's narrative proves inoperative in Malouf's play, which reveals ironic links between Antonio and Willy, whose prior seizure of Frank's fortune cross-refers to Antonio's seizure of Prospero's throne. Thus a slippage occurs between the usurper and the usurped, and Antonio/Frank becomes another Other that Willy must own. This slippage is extended through Edward, Frank's son, who poses a threat to the tycoon's empire and his control over his daughter, Cathy/Miranda. Malouf's call for the doubling of the Frank/Edward and Cathy/Tessa parts stresses the open-endedness of such a cycle of betrayal in which past and present merge into future. Role doubling, a specifically performative technique, harnesses the idea of hybridity in ways that fictional rewrites of *The Tempest* cannot approximate. Played by the same actors, the children and their parents display each other's physical traits through the sociocultural inscriptions on the performing body, even while their dramatic functions vary considerably. The refractions and reverberations of identity suggested by this technique are extended through a further layer of irony in the evocation of each character's Shakespearean counterpart. Metatheatrically, role doubling exposes the arbitrariness of all roles and, at the same time, foregrounds the illusionistic nature of representation to make "seeing double" a process by which the audience can follow the multiple movements of the text vis-à-vis its own enunciation and its intertextual interrogations of Shakespeare's theatre.

Willy, then, is both the Australian Prospero and Prospero's Other, which is to say that he not only shares many of the magician's traits and circumstances, but he also enacts precisely those differences that cause Prospero most anxiety—capitalism, sexual appetite, betrayal of trust, and loss of authority—characteristics both despots attempt to locate in their subjects in order to define themselves in opposition to that which they profess to despise. But whereas Prospero's narrative operates to contain difference by discrediting all discourse other than his own, Willy is forced to confront his past, present, and future in dream sequences that operate outside his control. In this sense, *Blood Relations* produces Willy out of the ambivalence of his imperial prototype, a process that draws attention to the fissures in the originary discourse of *The Tempest* and to the transgressive function of Malouf's counterdiscourse.

If relationships among the men in *Blood Relations* compromise the Prospero figure's power, the women's genealogy, both literal and literary, becomes even more problematic. In *The Tempest,* as Stephen Orgel points out, Prospero's anxiety about the virtues of women is evident in his fears over Miranda's virginity and in his frequent construction of Sycorax as antithetical to his daughter (1987, 18). While Prospero attempts to dichotomize the category of woman into "whore" and "virgin" stereotypes, Malouf's play explores the ambivalence of such discourse. Here, Prospero's absent wife emerges (in the ghostly form of Tessa) to challenge the authenticity of her husband's version of the past. Tessa subverts Willy's authority by placing herself outside it, both in her original desertion of him and in her subsequent unbidden appearance in his memory/dreams. Willy's narrative wants to annihilate Tessa, or at least to confine her safely to the margins in the role of virtuous dead wife and mother, but Tessa is also Sycorax, a condition Willy would rather locate in the Aboriginal women he calls "filth." Tessa, then, blurs the distinctions between the traditional identities allowed to women and contaminates Willy's/Prospero's conception of the role of mother. Unlike Miranda's mother, she resists objectification as "a piece of virtue" (Shakespeare 1.2.56), and this cannot but engender doubt about the daughter's legitimacy and, indirectly, the husband's potency: "You think I couldn't be a bastard?" Cathy responds when her father tells her that running a business requires ruthlessness, her pun undercutting Willy's assumption of patrimony (Malouf 1988, 45). Together with Willy's role as adoptive father to Kit, these complex links between the parents and the progeny in *Blood Relations* dismantle epistemologies that attempt to justify oppression through myths of racial purity. As the play demonstrates, discourses of racial purity are self-deconstructing, and colonialism produces the seeds of its own rebellion.

Cathy and Hilda are clearly implicated in this rebellion as well. Both enact further sites of resistance to a Manichaean discourse that seeks to control women by codification. In her relative inexperience of men, Cathy may initially appear to reenact Miranda's naivety, but whereas Prospero locates sexual aggression in Caliban—and its acceptably muted counterpart, enthusiasm, in Ferdinand—thereby excluding Miranda from the carnal and sensual realm, Willy cannot so easily cast his daughter as a prelapserian Eve. As her rapacious appetite and her rapid annexation of Edward as a potential lover suggests, Cathy's sexuality operates to undermine male dominance even before she deliberately chooses to "break her [own] virgin knot" (Shakespeare 4.1.15) without marital rites. Hilda, too, eludes definition. Willy would like to see her as the "saved" woman who now depends on her rescuer (colonizer) not only for the economic means of survival but also for an acceptable identity—in this case as housekeeper, a role with little authority. Hilda's transgressions of the impotent "saved victim" role occur through Ariel-like transformations to other roles: surrogate wife, clown, opera singer, illusionist, mother, acrobat, nurse, and seer.

While her "magic" may be less adept than Ariel's, it is more politically grounded because it is not at Willy's/Prospero's behest. Hilda's changing roles, however, bespeak provisionality, a characteristic that is also enacted in Cathy's reluctance to sever her bonds with Willy/Prospero even though she continually rehearses, or gestures toward, freedom. This "infinite rehearsal," which is partly the result of a dilemma of allegiance linked to the women's complicity in the power structures of their oppressor, shows that decolonization is always "a process, not arrival" (Tiffin 1987a, 17).

It is Kit, however, who poses the greatest threat to Willy's authority and who holds up the mirror in which Willy must eventually see the effects of his quest for power. As suggested by his dealings in fantasy and illusion, Kit also functions as an Ariel figure, forming the masculine counterpart of his mother's role as the female Ariel. The splitting of Ariel's character underlines notions of hybridity and problematizes gender assumptions about Shakespeare's original spirit, who is often played by a male but gendered neutral in productions of *The Tempest.* Kit, however, cannot be rendered asexual and relegated to the margins as ethereal spirit. Instead, his "gay lib" lifestyle undercuts Willy's/Prospero's normalizing discourse of heterosexuality within marital confines, and its project to produce legitimate, racially uncontaminated offspring to continue the work of empire. And, whereas Ariel's magic abets Prospero's imperialist project, Kit's artifice challenges Willy's through a modus operandi that stresses changeability against the rubric of certainty that enables empire-building. Kit further defines himself in opposition to *The Tempest*'s Ariel by refusing co-option into Willy's family as dutiful subject, and by directly challenging the self-reflexivity of the discourse of power legitimized by family relationships in a microcosm of empire, and redoubled in the colonial situation. As Kit points out, Willy's power has no stable center; it is produced by his language, and it functions to mask ultimate powerlessness, just as Prospero's magic compensates for his failing authority.

Compared to Caliban, Ariel features less frequently, and more ambivalently, in postcolonial *Tempest*-centered literature, and most critics regard the airy spirit's transgressive potential as significantly weaker than that of his earthy fellow slave.[9] Roslyn Jolly argues, however, that Ariel "personifies the power of imaginative transformations" and is a figure toward which colonial Calibans may aspire in order to transcend their oppression (1986, 297). The transformations of Caliban into Ariel can be effected, arrested, or forgone, as Jolly demonstrates in her discussion of Malouf's novel, *An Imaginary Life* (1978), along with creative works by Margaret Atwood and Seamus Heaney. Although her analysis is illuminating, Jolly's conceptual framework is flawed by its teleology: the premise that decolonization is effected through the *evolution* of Caliban into Ariel—transcending the system rather than unsettling power structures. Such assumptions devalue the transgressive capacity of postcolonial revisions of both characters and leave the epistemology and ontology of imperialism unquestioned, while also failing to account for the considerable forces that prevent imaginative transformation from becoming a politicized practice. Susan Bennett offers a more satisfying assessment of Ariel's potential "perversity" in her account of Lewis Baumander's productions of *The Tempest* in Toronto in 1987 and 1989: for Bennett, the performative recalcitrance of Monique Mojica's trickster-inspired Ariel—marked by the signs of both woman and native—"laid bare in Prospero his otherwise uncontested assumptions of symbolic legitimacy and intelligibility" (1996, 140).

In drawing attention to the relationship between Ariel and Caliban, Jolly's model is nonetheless useful because it illustrates the inadequacies of postcolonial methodologies that theorize only the Caliban-Prospero dyad. The white settler Australian, with a history of convictism and colonization of Aborigines, has possibly much more in common with Ariel than with Prospero: both are subservient prisoners to powerful masters and complicit in the oppression of less powerful subjects. To a certain extent, this situation also applies to Willy in *Blood Relations:* he is both colonizer and colonized, emblematic of the nonindigenous Australian who occupies the ambiguous settler role in a triadic rather than dyadic model of colonization. According to Allan Gardiner, "the triadic model for conceiving the antagonists within colonisation . . . allows a re-constitution of the world that takes into account the issues that pit settler-colonialists against metropolitan centres" (1990, 133). Although a Prospero to the other characters in the play, Willy's role as colonizer is modified by the specter of an imperial (European) power that is explicitly invoked in his memories of an oppressive childhood, and also alluded to in the prison imagery of the dialogue. Moreover, Europe's legacy to the contemporary Australian is rendered insistently visible through the play's semiotics, which feature huge crates of (mill)stones from Willy's birthplace as a prominent part of the set. Even while liberating him, Willy's exile from the European center produces a paradoxical constraint—a cognitive disjunction that forces him to create a fresh sense of identity in a linguistically and geographically alien landscape. Like Caliban, he "had to learn a whole new language" in order to survive his migration (Malouf 1988, 79). His response to this dislocation has been chameleon-like changes between a series of selves—Spiros Kyriakou, Bill La Farge, and Willy

McGregor—in an attempt to reconstitute a coherent identity despite the fractures of his personal history.

This diffused subjectivity also arises in contemporary plays by Louis Nowra, Stephen Sewell, Janis Balodis, Alma De Groen, Michael Gow, and others. "Radical instability" of the white Australian subject, Veronica Kelly discerns, is closely linked to the discourse of convictism, which, from colonial melodramas to the present, remains central in Australian theatre. Kelly points to "sharp confrontation scenes and strong formal attempts at tragic closure [as] the generic response which endeavors to stabilise the centrifugal energies" of such narratives (1990a, 133). Though not ultimately tragic, *The Tempest*'s closure moves to contain the disruptive energies that have threatened Prospero's rule and thus his identity throughout the play. *Blood Relations*, on the other hand, shows that a dispersal of power is inevitable and necessary. Willy's self-created subject position as unimpeachable patriarch is firstly "rendered provisional" by satire and direct interrogation, then "suspended" via death (Kelly 1990a, 133). Malouf's semiotics further suggest that a unified sense of self is not possible: in a potent expression of hybridity, a triple figure composed of Willy/Prospero, Dinny/Caliban, and Kit/Ariel emerges to represent, visually, the Australian postcolonial subject (see fig. 1). And finally, Willy becomes the objectified Other, his presence palpable only through scattered ashes and the inscrutable crates of stones.

An unambiguous representation of nature is similarly eschewed by Malouf. Whereas Shakespeare constructs Prospero's banishment in terms of a fortunate fall onto a bountiful island that, once "civilized," will provide for all his needs and wants, nature in *Blood Relations* is neither sympathetic nor controllable, although it also operates ideologically. In *The Tempest*, images of circumscription characterize the geographical discourse of the imagination and have frequently featured in the physical design of productions. Like the magic circle Prospero draws around his antagonists, the island's shores act as a hermetic seal separating one set of sociotopographical features from another except when he himself engineers a violation of the boundaries. Willy's "island" operates dialogically to Prospero's, resisting the Virgilian myth of the pastoral in its typology and its insistent links with society despite an isolated location.[10] This Australian New World is not, strictly speaking, an island,[11] but rather a strip of coastline in the remote North West between two seemingly infinite voids: the desert and the sea. Here, the only operable topography of the psyche pertains to notions of the edge: a place/condition that is an *ultima thule*, a margin, a boundary that speaks through its violation. In contrast to the easy appropriation of nature

Fig. 1. Hybrid subjectivity: Willy, Dinny, and Kit in *Blood Relations*, Sydney Theatre Company, 1987. (Photo: Hugh Hamilton.)

on Shakespeare's mythical isle, *Blood Relations* represents attempts to circumscribe a retreat amid benevolent natural forces as futile, if not dishonest. The harvest vision of the New World portrayed in the masque scene of *The Tempest*, with the colonizer as husbandman, never comes to fruition. The land remains obdurate and yields little sustenance; consequently, the croissants still come from Sydney and links with a metropolis are essential for survival. The edge is thus irrevocably tied to the center, and, as Malouf himself has said, polarity between the two is both inevitable and most sharply felt at the edge (qtd. in Leer 1985, 11). Dinny articulates this polarity when he points to the disjunction between the land and the European (centrist) celebrations of Christmas: "It's bloody ninety-six in the shade out there. And they're singing about a White Christmas" (Malouf 1988, 43). Similar tensions between center and edge are evident throughout the play: we find them in Cathy's yearning for the city, in Kit's feelings of inadequacy when he returns to the edge, in Willy's position at a distance yet not divorced from the center of power, and, most potently, in Dinny's imperialist education at a boarding school miles from his tribal origins.

The edge, however, also offers a site of negotiation that is barred from Prospero's circle. Martin Leer, discussing Malouf's prose and poetry, sees the edge motif as a movable locus of rearrangement and redefinition.

> The edge is where things happen; where sudden discoveries illuminate hidden memories; where revelations and metamorphoses occur. It is where our consciousness is at now, this moment, in that continual process of change (in space and time) which is also the subject of Malouf's work. The edge is also the edge of the self where inside and outside meet and sometimes interpenetrate by a process of osmosis; it is where opposites meet, where we begin to make comparisons, indeed where all the intellectual and creative functions of our consciousness are performed. (1985, 11)

As geographical maps of the psyche, the structures of the edge in *Blood Relations* enact a space in question. Although a metaphorical prison for the colonized settler/convict, Willy's "island" is not only quite penetrable, as demonstrated by the intrusion of McClucky and Dash (the comic buffoons), but it also embodies the idea of flux. Despite Willy's effort to colonize the landscape, nature in its various guises shapes the contours of the performance text so that he loses control of his carefully staged drama as the weird musical sounds of place and the vagaries of the weather (the tempest) intervene. And as the characters move between indoors and outdoors, past and present, dreams and reality, the set, an open living room flanked by verandahs[12] and bits of bushland, allows a reinscription of colonial space in the nexus of culture and nature, breaking down the dichotomy between the two that lies at the heart of imperialism, and that justifies the colonizers' use of "a little force" (or magic) when nature does not comply with their wishes of its own accord. Specifically described as "a place without definition," this setting is itself an outcrop, an edge, and at the same time, a series of places from which to speak and perform difference. It evokes something of the Queensland subtropics transposed onto an Aboriginal heartland and then distanced further westward. Such a heterotopic site, composed of nomadic/relocated places that are themselves transposed onto the stage space, fosters an exchange of views and the breaking down of orthodoxies. It is a place not only befitting the (mardi gras) "magic" of Kit but also one that is essential to the resulting transformations and experimentations that his "fantasy nights" encourage in other characters. However, what emerges from the interaction of culture and nature in the play is radically unstable, moving between extremes from Kit's antimasque, an apocalyptic vision with "flames lighting the rim of the earth" (1988, 62), to the final tableau of Dinny as heir to a future that sees nature and space respond to their piper's call. Hence Malouf's dramaturgy only partially addresses what Dennis Lee cites as the primary problem of the postcolonial writer: "to find words [or in this case dramatic images] for our spacelessness" (1974, 163). His construction of the edge's volatility represents a somewhat ambivalent response to the spatial appropriation of nature enacted by Prospero's usurpation of Caliban's island, and to the colonialist discourse of Gonzalo's utopian fantasy.

In his introduction to *The Tempest,* Orgel points out that Gonzalo's speech (2.1.145–62) enacts "a whole range of Renaissance thought about the relation of Europeans to newly discovered lands and to their native populations" (1987, 31–32), thought that constructs cannibalism, utopia, and free love as defining elements of New World societies, and that, as Brown asserts, mystifies relationships of power and naturalizes subjugation of the "native" as part of the landscape (1985, 60). By interrogating this iconography and its concomitant notions of authenticity, *Blood Relations* further problematizes the representation of nature in *The Tempest.* McClucky and Dash, for example, are set up as comic characters whose quest for authenticity only reveals the schism between wo/man and nature. Their attempt to appropriate the land, with Dinny as its human voice, is portrayed as even more farcical than that of their Shakespearean counterparts, Stephano and Trinculo, who at least manage to co-opt the native Caliban into their plot. McClucky's efforts to construct the indigene as a conduit to nature, however, are frustrated and ridiculed.

> *McClucky:* [I'm] looking for a place that's still authentic, where the traditional owners—
> *Willy:* Abos, you mean. Is that what you're after?
> *McClucky:* Well blacks, yes—if there are any left . . .
> *Willy:* Goannas?

> *McClucky:* Lizards, certainly. My husband photographs them. He's at Flinders Univer—
>
> *Willy:* Blowies? We got some great blowies up here. They're pretty authentic. Get Hilda to take you round by the dunny and introduce you. Maybe Flinders University would like your hubby to photograph *them.*
>
> (1988, 32)

Willy's language cuts through the polite terminology of the tourist-as-anthropologist and undermines the cult of authenticity inherent in his/her colonizing project. This antipodean island does not offer a Brave New World for the enactment of utopian myths but rather a dystopia built on racial tensions, where the despised "blowie" is as good a representation of the "real" as any other icon.

In their bogus roles as tourist and photographer, McClucky and Dash are emblematic of the colonizer who exhibits an "intense and voyeuristic fascination for the other" (Brown 1985, 53) and whose intentional gaze seeks to exercise power over an alien landscape and its native occupants. Susan Sontag argues that photographic "images transfix and anaesthetise" so that the camera becomes "a kind of passport" that annihilates moral responsibility (1973, 20, 41), giving photography its exemplary imperial scope. This is certainly evident in McClucky's and Dash's behavior, but Malouf parodies their scopophilia by blatantly undercutting any idea of essence that would define the "real" Australia and render it accessible to textual/visual capture. So, when McClucky asks to see the beach and the bush, the landscapes that have traditionally defined the quintessentially Australian experience of nature, Dinny replies with contempt: "You can *watch* me feed the chooks" (Malouf 1988, 46; emphasis added). Dinny's neat subversion of the voyeuristic gaze and his refusal to be conflated with the landscape, a stance that is denied Caliban by Prospero's insistent positioning of him within nature (as diametrically opposed to nurture in the play's binary systems), operates counterdiscursively to Shakespeare's text as well as to a much wider body of Australian literature that has conventionalized the use of Aborigines "as a metonym for the indigenous version of nature" (Turner 1986, 26).

Aboriginality, however, remains a problematic concept in *Blood Relations.* Deracinated and alienated from nature by his position within Willy's empire, Dinny operates on the margins of two epistemologies: one, Black, constructs the natural as contiguous with the human realm; the other, white, creates a difference that allows subject-object relations to be set up, naturalizing the appropriation of the land for human purposes. Dinny can ironize other people's attempts to elide the landscape and the indigene, but his feigned cynicism toward nature belies a deep sense of loss, and the need for a tenable speaking position vis-à-vis nature. The way out of this predicament, Malouf seems to suggest rather obliquely, lies in reestablishing a metaphysical communion with the land through dreaming and listening: tuning into nature's languages. This isle is also "full of voices," but, unlike Caliban's "sweet airs that give delight and hurt not" (3.2.133–41), nature in *Blood Relations* articulates itself through a polyphony of sounds that includes the uncomfortable ring of termites boring or insects buzzing. And nature's broadcast is subject to interference by the noises of culture and history; nothing is natural, innocent, or unspoiled. Dinny feels the urgency to listen, to set up a dialogue with the land, but what he hears is never clarified in the play. Authenticity, if it resides in the Aboriginal version of nature, remains a "sacred site" closed to the audience, and Dinny occupies a position where he can listen, sometimes speak, albeit in his colonizer's code, but seldom act. Hence his limitation is not only linguistic but also dramatic: compared to the other characters in the play, he is less able to change roles/positions. This tragedy he shares with Caliban, who, unlike Ariel, is denied access to the transformative magic of representation.

Language is similarly a site of ideological struggle in *Blood Relations.* Malouf dramatizes this struggle in past, present, and mythological contexts to create a text that resonates with many voices but gives ultimate authority to none. In an ongoing verbal battle, positions of dominance and subservience are continually negotiated: no sooner does one character claim to be "in charge" than that power is questioned or destabilized by another. Structurally, the play dislocates language and perception by cross-cutting scenes, shifting focus from one interaction to another, avoiding closure of conversations, and overlaying past, present, and dream spaces. Such devices confound notions of chronology and the internal coherence of speech, exemplifying Mikhail Bakhtin's theory of heteroglossia by creating a multiplicity of languages in dialogic struggle with one another (1981). The resultant drama "replaces temporal lineality with spatial plurality" (Ashcroft, Griffiths, and Tiffin 1989, 36), dispersing the centrality of Willy's narrative and refusing its monocentric perspective of history. As Edward says, when he attempts to conjure the past solely through his own memory, "one voice can't sing it" (Malouf 1988, 51).

Whereas Prospero justifies his control of Caliban's island and its dissenting voices by constructing a historical narrative that silences all accounts of reality other than his own, Willy loses control as his version of history is scrutinized and found fraudulent in its process of strategic forgetting. When the ghosts of Frank and Tessa emerge to challenge Willy's self-legitimizing discourse, history is redefined in the present rather than fixed in the past. Tessa, in particular, draws attention to both the bias in Willy's story and the ways in which language and power interconnect. From the beginning of their dialogue, Tessa contests Willy's authority over language: first, in a move equally subversive but directly opposite to Caliban's refusal to come when called, she resists interpellation as linguistic subject by appearing against Willy's explicit wishes; then she goes on to accuse him of having denied her an identity by treating her like a "dumb and yielding" child who needed *his* education to "grow up," or, to put it more blatantly, to grow into the subservient role that Willy as colonizer assigned her. This teacher-student motif, a key concept in imperialist discourse and one that relies principally on the imposition of the colonizer's language code for its success, breaks down when Tessa learns just enough to resist her oppressor and his educative mission.

Similarly, Dinny breaks out of his ascribed role as pupil, "cursing" his first-class private-school education and refusing to valorize its epistemologies. "Learning to curse," Stephen Greenblatt suggests, is the inevitable outcome of the "poisoned relationship between master and slave" (1976, 575). Prospero's interpellation of Caliban as the "linguistic subject of the master language" (Brown 1985, 61) forms a central concern of much postcolonial criticism, which notes a resultant sense of linguistic deprivation or dislocation between reality and the terms available to interpret it. Although Dinny enacts a linguistic rebellion when he refuses not only to "keep a civil tongue in [his] head" (Malouf 1988, 68) but also to apologize for his incivility, he is confined ultimately to the "prison house" of his colonizer's language. Thus, on the one hand, his recitation of Caliban's "This island's mine" speech (Malouf 1988, 64–65) is a political act that subverts Willy's colonizing project by using Shakespeare's dialogue to make an articulate claim on the Aboriginal land Willy has appropriated. At the same time, Dinny's claim for land rights is compromised because he uses both the language code and the literature of his colonizer to voice resistance. So, despite Malouf's desire to "let an Aboriginal voice take control of a major stage" in Australia (qtd. in Heath 1987, 11), language remains a strategy of containment in the play, no doubt partly because of the playwright's limitations as an articulator of Aboriginal speech registers. Unlike some of the characters in works by Jack Davis and other Aboriginal playwrights that I will discuss in chapter 2,

Dinny's attempts to escape linguistic capture are frustrated by his lack of access to a more localized language, or a pidgin dialect, which could abrogate the privilege of standard English.

The concept of theatricality in Malouf's play also bears further analysis in a comparative context. Self-referentially, both *The Tempest* and *Blood Relations* foreground performance and its related arts, illusion and magic. Performance is the less serious side of Prospero's art; however, it nonetheless confirms his power over representation and, hence, over constructions of meaning. The betrothal masque representing his version of Utopia, for example, dispels the disruptive antimasque forces like those of the storm and the harpies' banquet, enacting a movement from conflict to order (Orgel 1987, 47). Thus the dance of the nymphs and the reapers in this "performance" functions as a representation of ritualized social harmony, while its portent of a bounteous harvest appropriates the New World as a pastoral retreat. Furthermore, the dance desexualizes the body by linking the forthcoming union of Miranda and Ferdinand with images of the fruition of nature, while denying illegitimate sexual desire by excluding Caliban from the spectacle. By refiguring Shakespeare's dance as part of a carnivalesque magic show layered with ironic and apocalyptic overtones, Malouf exposes the ideological assumptions that traverse the dancing body in *The Tempest*'s masque. *Blood Relation*'s dance is framed within a very different kind of metatheatrical moment, a performance that is neither at the behest nor under the control of Willy and that clearly expresses conflict rather than harmony. Kit engineers his magic show despite Willy's opposition; then he foregrounds the dance as homosexual display when he dances in an exaggerated fashion with Dash/Trinculo, eclipsing the performance of Cathy/Miranda and Edward/Ferdinand as the "happy couple." Kit's multiple roles and representations, along with his apocalyptic vision of the future and his prediction of "stormy weather" for Edward and Cathy, upstage Willy's performance with Hilda, aligning the performative motifs of the play with the darker side of Prospero's necromancy by conjuring an antimasque inimical to the magician's orderly presentation of the harvest and civil union. During their movements, the characters' dialogue also operates as a running metacommentary on the dancing itself, stressing its theatricality, which provides the spectator with a method for deconstructing the illusionistic devices of representation. Meanwhile, Dinny makes a potent statement of political autonomy when he abruptly declines an invitation to join the dance, refusing the inscriptions of white ritual movement on his body and holding the whole performance, as well as its Shakespearean prototype, up to scrutiny.

In his role as director of the spectacle and artificer of nature, Prospero can effectively contain the dissenting voices in the play. It is this figure of Prospero as the artist/magician who imposes rather than discerns order that, according to Joan Kirkby, becomes a paradigm for American "frontier" literature (1985, 90). Malouf's Australian Prospero, on the other hand, finds that his attempts to preserve the myth he has created only reveal his role as illusionist and, ultimately, undermine his authority over representation itself. This process, the salient point of the magic show, is also evident in the dream sequences, which together constitute a miniplay recasting Willy as actor and/or passive spectator in, rather than director of, the drama of colonization. Whereas Prospero clearly commands and directs all performances with his omniscient gaze, appropriating the island and its inhabitants in the process, *Blood Relations* constructs the act of looking as an anxious response to uncertainty, a bid for control that is not always successful. Hence Willy can enjoy the circus act he engineers for McClucky's and Dash's benefit, but he is disgusted and disturbed when positioned as an onlooker for Kit's show, which in its admixture of Greek ritual, burlesque, music, and recitation cross-refers to a whole history of drama, demonstrating the play's "blood" ties with its own cultural progenitors. By interrogating its own performance conventions as well as Willy's role as director, the text reuses theatre to replay several perspectives of (theatre) history rather than narrating one.

The end of Shakespeare's play, Brown discerns, displays a profoundly ambivalent attitude toward performance itself (1985, 67–68). Although Prospero expounds upon the illusory nature—"the baseless fabric"—of all representation and even collapses his vision into the "stuff of dreams" (4.1.151–58), momentarily revealing "the forging of [the] colonialist narrative" as "a forgery" (Brown 1985, 67), he extends the civilizing vision of the masque by quelling Caliban's rebellion and representing reconciliation as the natural telos of the play. By comparison, *Blood Relations* more clearly delineates performance as a construction rather than a mimetic representation of some essential reality but nonetheless recognizes the power that validates performance as "real." This process is evident in the self-conscious artificiality of Malouf's characters, most of whom are not what they pretend to be but rather the doubles and split selves that, as I have already argued, are characteristic of the postcolonial subject.

A reunification of split subjectivities, contrary to the opinion of most reviewers, does not necessarily anchor the mythopoeic impulse of *Blood Relations.* And whether a paradigmatic figure of resistance emerges from this text is questionable because it tends to present a movable rather than a fixed locus of counterdiscursivity. Read as an oppositional reworking of *The Tempest,* Malouf's play enacts reconciliation, if at all, in the acceptance of diverse truths rather than the formulation of an integrated narrative. Its mythic project, I would argue, is to articulate a series of Australian selves from a conceptual space fractured by colonialist ideologies and a sense of alienation from the constitutive structures of history and canon. The complex "blood relations" between the two texts also impel a thorough reconsideration of the political imperatives of Shakespeare's play. By reentering the text of *The Tempest,* a postcolonial, countercanonical reading of *Blood Relations* politicizes its intertextuality as a mode of literary decolonization while at the same time suggesting the limits of that project.

That *Blood Relations* resists being read as a celebratory treatment of Shakespearean themes and tropes possibly accounts for its failure to enter the Australian theatre canon, despite Malouf's considerable reputation as a novelist, poet, and essayist. In contrast, Gow's *Away,* which alludes to *The Tempest* in apparently less critical ways, seems to have become an "instant classic" that is routinely included in Australian high school curricula, and periodically produced by amateur and professional companies throughout the country. Arguably, this play also disrupts the authority of the imperial canon, but its narrative and performative allusions to various Shakespearean texts—including *Midsummer Night's Dream, Twelfth Night,* and *King Lear,* as well as *The Tempest*—have generally been read as affectionate homage rather than potential points of counterdiscursivity.[13] Tony Mitchell reveals how Gow's drama about three troubled families on holiday in the late 1960s fits neatly with expectations of the "well-made play": "it is traditional in its form, setting and concerns, reinforces the great ennobling, redemptive and transcendental themes [reviewers] see in Shakespeare, and treats its characters with humane warmth and feeling while poking gentle fun at their foibles" (1989, 20). *Away's* critical reception indicates that the play's vestigial intertexts have been used simultaneously to authenticate the local product and to reaffirm Shakespeare's enduring centrality to Australian culture. Even though Gow himself has protested the ways in which his text has been used to serve hegemonic interests—anecdotally, he remarks that *Away* has even been used to get school students to read Shakespeare[14]—critical enthusiasm for the play remains based on its ability to duplicate the immense symbolic capital of the imperial canon. This would seem to confirm Frow's contention that Shakespearean texts, or in this case, *intertexts,* "have only uses, not inherent meanings and functions" (1993, 216).

The facile critical and institutional co-option of *Away* demonstrates, contrary to Joanne Tompkins's implicit suggestion (1996, 19–20), that postcolonial appropriations of the canon are seldom consolidated at the level of the script alone. What becomes necessary, once again, is a politicized performance practice/process that is always aware of how a play's multiple sites of meaning articulate its relationships with the valorized signs of its culture. A good example here is the 1996 University of Queensland student production of *Away*,[15] which staged Shakespeare's fairies not as the mischievous sprites of *Midsummer Night's Dream* (in its normative versions at least) but rather as malevolent furies. In the play's set piece—a farcical depiction of a typical Australian Christmas at the beach—the fairies invaded the stage to collectively voice the complaints of a chorus of campers who harass newcomers (and the audience) with a litany of complaints (see fig. 2). Their overt menace departed from the more common convention of presenting the campers as a grotesque parody of 1960s kitsch (see fig. 3), itself an effective mockery of any pretense to high art. Shortly after the campground scene, the fairies staged the tempest as an orgy of violence backlit by slide projections of the Vietnam War. Such strategies were designed to unsettle simplistic constructions of Gow's spectacular tempest as merely a mythic force or an artful fabrication following Shakespeare's tropologies, and to stress instead that the play's tempest indicates Coral's personal crisis in response to her son's death, as well as a national crisis of faith in a senseless war. As a further and more local point of counterdiscourse, the University of Queensland production incorporated a scene from Gow's more recent play, *Furious* (1990), which implicitly refers back to the critical reception of *Away* by satirizing schoolteachers (and critics) who are compelled to imbue Australian theatre with so-called universal (Shakespearean) themes. Selective cross-gender casting also "queered" the text while referring to Gow's increasingly ambivalent positioning between mainstream and gay theatre. The play's intertextual field was thus envisaged as highly unstable, rather than firmly embedded in a distant canon.

To facilitate understanding of both the possibilities and the limitations of performative counterdiscourse as it is articulated in, through, and around Shakespeare's canon, we need better (and less text-centered) models of Shakespearean criticism, especially in postcolonial contexts. In Denis Salter's words,

> What about similarly detailed and feisty theoretical studies of actual *theatrical practice?*—of audience-reception, of acting, directing, and design interpretations and styles, of theatrical architecture and public

Fig. 2. The Furies/Campers, *Away,* University of Queensland Student Production, 1996. (Photo: Penny Wilkinson.)

> space, of the social, ideological, cultural, economic, and practical contexts of specific performances for specific communities, and of the kinds of training that theatre workers have received (and not received) when struggling not only with individual texts but with the ideological baggage that the very name, SHAKESPEARE, brings with it? (1996, 7)

Although such detailed examination is beyond the scope of my study, Salter's project should be wholeheartedly endorsed, for it seems to envision

Fig. 3. The Campers' scene, *Away,* Playbox Production, 1990. (Photo: Jeff Busby.)

a corrective to the critical myopia that determines which reworkings of the canon can be tolerated, even celebrated, and which ones stage an affront to the traditions of mainstream Australian theatre, and indeed to broadly held cultural values.

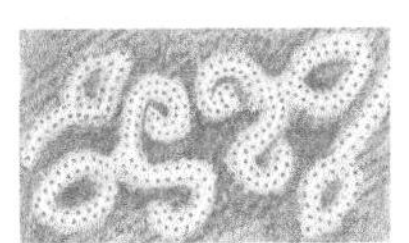

Chapter 2

Contemporary Aboriginal Theatre

Wetjala cunning fella alright. When they come here they had the Bible and we had the land [now] they've got the land and we've got the Bible.
—*Uncle Herbie, from* **In Our Town,** *by Jack Davis*

Aboriginal theatre, developed over the past two decades, poses the Australian stage's most trenchant challenge to the hegemony of imperialism. As a body, this theatre is not only growing rapidly but also becoming increasingly difficult to define. It is one thing to exclude those plays, however well researched, that are written by whites about Aborigines and then handed over to theatre directors to cast and produce, but what of those developed processually through intensive collaboration between the two groups?[1] Referring to literary production, critics such as Mudrooroo express reservations about the Aboriginality of any text that is not wholly produced—written, published, and presented—under Aboriginal control (1985, 1990), but this kind of categorization is problematic even while strategically desirable. In view of the diverse technical and conceptual input that goes into creating a performance text, theatre is only rarely a site of the kind of individual writing that conventional notions of authorship validate, and it clearly involves mediation at a number of levels. More often than not, the plays under discussion have undergone lengthy workshopping processes involving non-Aboriginal as well as Aboriginal actors, directors, writers, and technicians. The notion of authorship thus becomes even more complex than in other narrative genres, as does the concept of text, especially given the potential variance of each enactment of a play.

That the performance text is difficult to define and radically unstable, however, need not always be as problematic as it appears. Within a postcolonial framework that promotes "hybridization" and "literary contamination" as weapons of cultural transformation, delimiting notions of an authentic indigenous text becomes a far less useful task than examining how the multiplicity of *indigenized* elements of a text might be deployed. My use of *hybridization* in this context is not intended to supply a model of reconciliation that merely celebrates diversity or cultural fusion, but rather to suggest that markers of Aboriginality are never pure or "authentic" but rather continually contested by various societal groups. According to Aboriginal sociologist and film critic Marcia Langton, "Aboriginality is remade over and over again in a process of dialogue, imagination, representation and interpretation" (1993, 33). Langton identifies three broad categories of "intersubjectivity" that constitute an "infinite array" of Aboriginalities: interactions between Aboriginal peoples within their own cultural contexts; representations by white people of stereotyped/mythologized Aborigines; and dialogue situations in which "individuals test and adapt imagined models of each other to find satisfactory forms of mutual comprehension" (1993, 33). This complex process of continual becoming is particularly useful because it does not seek to locate an authentic culture but instead recognizes the specificity of various representations of Aboriginality as a cultural construct.

My analysis, then, while concentrating on plays whose authorship has been attributed to Aborigines, is not so much concerned with developing a poetics and aesthetics of Aboriginal drama as with outlining the strategic possibilities of performance for the production and consumption of this body of work as an expression of indigenous culture. Although varied in theme, form, style, tone, and genre, all Aboriginal plays engage in counter-discursive projects that destabilize the power-knowledge axis of imperialism. Prominent on their political agenda is a concern to problematize axiomatic ways of viewing Aborigines and Aboriginal ways of knowing and hence to intervene in the object-signifying processes that have circumscribed representations of native peoples in settler cultures since "history awarded semiotic control to the invaders" (Goldie 1988, 60). In many of these plays, the most overt postcolonial discourses emerge in the substantive content of the dialogue, often through direct commentary by Aboriginal characters on the depredations their cultures have endured since European invasion. As a way of rupturing the authoritative and essentialist "truths" that have buttressed imperial history, these dialogues are both anodyne and necessary but, in themselves, not necessarily the most theatrically enabling discourses available. In fact, it could be argued that the more radical expressions of Aboriginality are often located in the extralinguistic signifiers of these texts as performance pieces. This is not to discount the considerable importance of verbal protests against imperialism and its legacy, but to focus on theatre as an artistic medium that offers particular opportunities (and some specific limitations) for decolonizing Aboriginal cultures.

Not surprisingly, Aboriginal drama has recently attracted more varied critical attention than any of the other fields analyzed here, a situation that reflects not only its intrinsic value as a force with considerable power to reshape the face of contemporary Australian theatre, but also its timeliness in relation to changing perceptions of indigenous peoples and their relationships with wider Australian society. A number of critics have already engaged with postcolonial theory in their attempts to outline the political project of various Aboriginal plays or playwrights,[2] but, in general, this framework has been less fully applied than it might be, especially in the analysis of performative structures and strategies,[3] a critical gap I aim to address in this chapter by looking at space-time, body politics, and orality.

Spatial Histories

Despite the passing of the Commonwealth Native Title Act in 1993, Aboriginal land rights remain Australia's most important unresolved political issue. At a time when there is much debate throughout the nation on whether the federal government can and should overturn the High Court's 1996 Wik decision that native title can coexist with settler title on pastoral leases, it seems appropriate to begin my discussion of contemporary Aboriginal theatre with a focus on its treatment of the relationships between place, history, and Aboriginality. Revisionist historians such as Paul Carter have argued that the colonization of Australia was, above all, a spatial process: linguistic, economic, and cultural domination by Europeans depended on their conquest of the land as a place from which to articulate power over its original inhabitants. All plays examined in this chapter depict, in some way, the historical *dis*placement of Aborigines and their associated loss of identity as a consequence of two centuries of colonization. But while Aboriginal playwrights detail the catastrophic effects for indigenous peoples of the European *landnama* of Australia, they often propose methods of deconstructing Eurocentric epistemological and ontological systems, of reconceptualizing place and space in order to undermine the legitimacy of white settlement and assert Other(ed) versions of history.

An initial examination of Aboriginal drama reveals a central preoccupation with the past as present, and a concerted attempt to enact, often by specifically theatrical means, a symbolic reclamation of space/place by and for Aboriginal culture. In this historiographic project, temporality includes a mythical time constructed through recurrent images and legends from the Dreamtime, which occupies a discursive and spatial field characterized by timelessness. Most Aboriginal playwrights categorically reject the view that the past is irredeemable, at best contiguous with the present but not enacted in it, and assert, instead, a notion of time in which the boundaries between past and present, and ultimately future, are permeable: the past constitutes the present at the same time as it is *constituted by* the present. The dialectic created between past and present ruptures the fixity of historical representation and creates spaces from which the marginalized can speak and act. By challenging notions of linear time and neutral space, Aboriginal plays refuse complicity with the kind of historical consciousness that claims objectivity and by which, as Hayden White points out, "the presumed superiority of modern, industrial society can be retroactively substantiated" (1973, 1–2). Constructions of nonlinear time take different forms in various plays: juxtaposition, elision, and overlaying of different time frames; repetition of visual and aural images; representations of Dreamtime time; and the incorporation of historical documents into the enacted texts. All of these techniques have implications for the representation of historical space and will be discussed, as far as possible, in terms of the theatrical dialectic between space and time.

In many ways, Jack Davis's first full-length play, *Kullark* (1979), an epic narrative of cultural encounter, is the paradigmatic example of a work that interrogates traditional European concepts of time on many levels. Summing up the play, as Ronald Berndt does, as a "review of the present plight of the Nyungar [*sic*] seen in historical perspective" (1982, xiv), is to simplify the themes and virtually ignore the challenge the play poses to imperial methods of historical construction. Similarly, critics who praise or condemn *Kullark* for its naturalism or documentary realism (Shoemaker 1989, 251; O'Brien 1983, 125) fail to note that the structure of the play and the representations of time within its framework undercut these dramatic modes. Although Davis does rely heavily on historical documents as source material for his play and even incorporates some of them into the dramatic text, *Kullark* nonetheless speaks the incompleteness of such documents by presenting, in juxtaposition, many different fragments of a possible past. This kind of narrative depends on what Robert Kroetsch calls an archaeological sense of history, in that "every unearthing is problematic, tentative, subject to a story-making act that is itself subject to further change as the 'dig' goes on" (1989, 24). Thus *Kullark* does not attempt "historical verisimilitude" in its account of colonization. Such a venture, as Adam Shoemaker points out, is doomed to failure anyway because the available documentary material is generally amassed by whites, controlled by whites, and housed in white Australian institutions (1989, 251). Instead, the play contextualizes white versions of a monologic history within a wider concept of the past that portrays the historical, mythological, and political meaning of that past for Aborigines in the present.

The dramatic framework of *Kullark* constructs empirical time-space as elliptical, often nonlinear, fragmented, and even unpredictable. Theatre lends itself particularly well to the representation of this temporal and spatial ambiguity because "all performances create a here which is not 'here,' a now which is not 'now,' restlessly slicing time and space into layers of 'difference'" (D. George 1989a, 74). In *Kullark,* scenes from different time periods, ranging from the moment of colonization to 1979, are enacted in both present, past, and mythological spaces. The set, which comprises "a huge painting in neo-traditional style of Warrgul the Rainbow Serpent in the shape of a map of the Swan River" (1982, 6), establishes, from the beginning of the play, the coexistence of these three time frames. That the painting of Warrgul, a potent symbol of the Dreamtime and creative spirit of the Swan River, is in neotraditional style suggests elision of time periods: Dreamtime mythology informs and shapes contemporary Aboriginal art and vice versa. The serpent's shape as a map also creates a discursive space with implications for temporality. While the Swan River map points indexically to an intentional act of appropriation of Nyoongah land and culture, begun in the past and continued into the present, the map is contained within the figure of Warrgul, which recontextualizes the stage action to follow, asserting an Aboriginal worldview of time and space. This worldview is then challenged, fractured, and continually reasserted as the play progresses, a process made visually apparent through changes to the Rainbow Serpent image, so that the play creates an overall notion of time in space that is both static and fluid, synchronic and diachronic, fractured but not sundered. A final point stresses this: although the fracturing of the serpent image metaphorically outlines the imposition of European culture on the indigene, it also creates an important space from which the colonized can act. In this instance, that space is the kitchen, symbol of the Nyoongah word for home, *kullark.* By framing the contemporary Aboriginal family with a revolving screen that depicts the kitchen also cutting the serpent image, the semiotic network of the play positions the family within the very fractures that compromise the integrity of Aboriginality, allowing them to interrogate the historical processes enacted from a more powerful (insider) position.

Challenges to linear notions of time that underlie the master narrative of history are evident in other structural aspects of *Kullark,* which collapses, through a cinematic montage, over 150 years of lived experience into a few hours of stage time but does not construct events as strictly chronological. Instead, disparate images and brief scenarios show moments from the past juxtaposed to those of the present, while slippages of time frames occur frequently, eliding or overlaying settings so that there is no clear delineation between the spaces claimed by whites during the invasion process and the spaces occupied by Blacks in the contemporary narrative. This is a deliberate technique on Davis's part and one that balances the decimation of Aboriginal culture in the historical narrative with a focus on its survival (in whatever form) in the contemporary moment. Moreover, characters often step outside theatrical time, Brechtian fashion, to comment on the stage action, so that the play's metaphysics continually interrogate imposed European epistemological systems. This is particularly evident at the end of act 1 when Stirling and a soldier narrate, in past tense, their official "story" of the battle of Pinjarra at the same time as they enact the conflict, creating a dual perspective that is impossible in linear constructions of time. The ambiguity of this time/space is further complicated by the intermittent commentary of the actress who played Alice (one of the Irish settlers), now in modern dress, presenting a perspective of the past conflict drawn from historical documents and filtered through contemporary reality. Two additional factors stress the multivalent representation of the past: the Aboriginal men are shot dead in the discursive time-space delineated by the painted emblem of the Western Australian sesquicentennial celebrations on the revolving screens, creating yet another time frame; then the battle is retold from an Aboriginal perspective in ballad verse that demythologizes the white colonizers' popular accounts of outback survival and pioneering—the Australian "myths of origin"—and repositions the indigene as subject rather than object in accounts of the past. The concept of theatrical space is crucial in this scene because it underlies drama's potential to represent narrative elements that can only be alluded to, metonymically, in other creative forms such as fiction and poetry. And even though European-style cause-and-effect logic is at times suggested thematically in *Kullark* through the plight of the contemporary Aborigines, the play's structure resists this narrative trope, giving an impression of time as cyclical and the world as both a synchronic and diachronic totality. The dramatic potential for using time in space this way would seem, then, to modify Kateryna Arthur's argument that "it is impossible to reproduce [a] cyclical understanding of time in a language whose grammar operates out of a different system" (1985, 59). A cyclical notion of time *can* be reproduced in Western texts provided that the discursive space in which the language is utilized is itself nonlinear: stage rather than page space.

The predominantly naturalistic narratives of Davis's related plays, *The Dreamers* (1982) and *Barungin* (1988), also unfold through dramatic structures that evoke spatial and temporal circularity. *The Dreamers* presents a 1980s family whose vestigial links with traditional Aboriginal culture proffer the only antidote to urban hopelessness. Poetry recitals in the play's opening and closing passages construct the past as a "re-occurring dream" that frames the present, while dream sequences occur regularly throughout the play, eliding present, past, and mythic time through spatial links between the deracinated Aborigine, Worru, his dead friend Milbart, and the Dancer. Milbart's dramatic presence is established as an absence that nonetheless occupies stage space whenever his imagined form is conjured up in response to Worru's invocations of his spirit. In this sense, Milbart exemplifies the indigene who has been written out of history (read memory) and rendered invisible in colonialist narrative. However, Aboriginal memory, as Cliff Watego explains, consists of historical recall *plus* the Dreaming, a "psychic transmission of oneself into a spiritual time and place" (1989, 3). The Dancer, who establishes points of overlap and contact between this spiritual world and the more mundane time-space of the naturalistic action, marks the centrality to Aboriginal culture of a Dreamtime realm that continually informs contemporary experience. This realm is intimately associated with the land, as Davis shows through the Dancer's mimed actions—finding water, lighting a fire, making hunting tools—and through the framing of the lounge room setting with a backdrop featuring an escarpment on which a tribal family periodically appears. Within the overall framework of the play, the Dancer can be seen as an alter ego figure who connects Worru spatially with the land/time of his Dreaming by punctuating his passage toward death with the reenactment of scenes from his past and the representation of mythic figures such as the death spirit, Featherfoot. These ritualized moments tend to represent timelessness or the state of being outside the dominant society's temporalities so that a ceremonial catharsis of oppression is possible. When the Dancer appears to complete the dance that Worru, drunken and stumbling, can only half remember, his pounding feet remap and reclaim stage space, symbolically recuperating the tribal dance from a position of marginality in an urban culture, and reasserting the validity of Aboriginal memory by transmogrifying Milbart's imaginary form from absence into a tangible presence. That the three figures occupy the same discursive space suggests that the historical past with its legacy of alcoholism can be obliterated at the same time as it is emphasized through the pathos of Worru's drunkenness (see fig. 4).

Davis's most polemical interrogation of official history occurs in his

Fig. 4. Jack Davis as Uncle Worru, *The Dreamers,* National Theatre Company on Tour, 1983. (Photo: Geoffrey Lovell.)

(counter)bicentennial play, *Barungin,* which uses death as a savagely ironic symbol of the "birthday" of the Australian nation. That the play begins and ends with a funeral service stresses, once again, the circular movement of time, though the second service is in many ways a critique of the first and a demonstration of Aboriginal solidarity. *Barungin* commemorates not only the dead explicitly named by Meena but also those other "absent friends" who haunt the theatrical spaces of all Davis's plays: the babies buried in unmarked graves at the Moore River mission settlement, the thousands of Aborigines annihilated during the initial European invasion of Australia, and those who have since died in custody. Like *Kullark*'s remembrance "ceremony" for the Aboriginal dead at the battle of Pinjarra, *Barungin*'s concluding "wake" is enacted in ways that also use the dramatic potential of the stage to construct an event that reclaims historical space and time for the colonized. The appearance of a dancer just before the funeral scene links the graveside gathering temporally and spatially to the Dreamtime and also to the past constructed in Davis's earlier plays. In a sense, this dancer maps out a stage space that the mourners can inhabit, a space that resists appropriation by the fundamentalist preacher (and his ilk) of the opening funeral scene. The mourners then move into this space, claiming it politically, symbolically, and historically for Aboriginal people. Their wreaths of red and yellow flowers tied with black ribbons stand metaphorically for the Aboriginal flag and are therefore potent signifiers of Black nationhood. Having created a position from which to speak and act, the historically disempowered assert their own versions of the past: Meena reads a list of Aboriginal deaths in custody during two centuries of European "occupation," while Shane reads the poem "John Pat," which deals with a specific case. The poem focuses on oppression of contemporary Blacks by using spatial images—the "concrete floor" and the "cell door"—that interweave with Meena's panoramic reframing of the past in terms of the year and place of each Aboriginal death. The simultaneity of the readings/performances reinforces the possibility of a synchronic and intertextual apprehension of historical time-space. In Veronica Kelly's words, "the past, its historical, political and mythological presence, is alive in the present and actively shaping it" (1987b, 119).

Since site has long been a key aspect of narration in Aboriginal cultures (Muecke 1983b, 94), the proxemics of theatres, or spaces co-opted as theatres, significantly affect the temporal discourses of Davis's plays, just as relationships between actors and spectators vary according to spatial evocations of distance, intimacy, and the like. Contemporary Aboriginal theatre, however commercial, establishes particular spaces and occasions for the production and reception of indigenous performance as cultural expression. The choice of the Fitzroy Town Hall as venue for the staging of Davis's epic *The First Born* trilogy[4]—comprised of *The Dreamers* and *Barungin*, along with *No Sugar* (1985)—added a sharp political edge to the performance, which was valorized by its enactment in a public edifice to imperial history, at the same time as that edifice became a site of symbolic reclamation of Aboriginal land when truckloads of sand were poured over large parts of the interior to create a suitable counterbicentennial set. The production also harnessed the proxemic possibilities of that particular building when, during the performances of *No Sugar,* parts of the predominantly non-Aboriginal audience were impelled to move (at times to the basement) as different sections of the theatrical space were annexed by the actors, forming a metaphorical parallel to the forced dislocation of Aborigines that is the narrative focus of the play.[5]

In his later play, *Wahngin Country* (1992),[6] Davis's contemporary Aboriginal protagonist continues the search for an empowering space from which to speak as he performs in promenade style, moving the audience from a campervan-cum-humpie outside the Octagon Theatre at the University of Western Australia to a nearby park bench in its tropical gardens. The title of the play, which translates as "talking country," along with its particular form—a loose mixture of stories, songs, memories, verse extracts, and open harangues punctuated by the music of the didgeridoo and enacted by a strolling player—asserts, once again, the links between the land and the articulation of Aboriginal histories/identities. This point seemed to completely escape critics such as Leonard Radic, who revealed a distinctly imperialist bias by arguing that the play suffered from an "air of formlessness" that might have been corrected if it were "performed indoors or at least in more tightly controlled surroundings" (1992, 53).[7] That the play was designed for performance on university grounds suggests an attempt to counter the scribal authority of book learning, a pedagogy characterized by physical alienation from the subject of inquiry, with a celebration of an oral tradition that is inseparable from its site of enunciation. This point was further emphasized by the particular spot chosen for the play's opening, a park bench backlit at night by a spill of light from the university library. Davis's storyteller claimed territorial priority over this site at the beginning of his performance by urinating against a tree in what was not just a comic moment but also a deliberate inscription of the land. The performance also stressed that Aboriginal (hi)stories are often a forgotten part of the everyday spaces in which Australians live and study. It is the function of theatre, Davis's work suggests, to make these places speak.

Since, as I have argued, theatrical time-space operates in ways that make possible the simultaneous apprehension of more than one representation of reality, it has the potential to reconstitute the structural basis of historical conception, to make space one of performers and no longer a neutral stage on which the drama unfolds. Co-opting quantum theory, David George explains this concept by arguing that empirical space-time has similar qualities to the subatomic worlds; it is plural, indeterminate, simultaneously wavelike and particle-like, potential rather than actual.

> Theatrical space-time is at once material but coded, perceived but imagined, a meeting-ground of matter and creative energy and, as such, precisely what the quantum physicists have discovered about reality: simultaneously objective and subjective—"out there" but known and even created only by human interaction. (1989b, 173)

The potentiality of space-time stressed in this quotation takes us back to Carter's arguments about the spatial forms through which European "settlers" colonized Australia. Carter views space as a "text that had to be written on before it could be interpreted" (1987, 41). In this schema, historical space was constituted by the intentionality of the settlers; its character emerged through language, the naming of the landscape as an object of desire. Imperial histories establish the pioneer myth that sets up spatial relationships between the settler and the land, ignoring the possibility that Aborigines and whites moved in the same historical time-space, or, at best, they move Blacks "about the stage of white History with the ease of stage props, in order to create an effect, to authenticate a particular vision" (Carter 1987, 344). A spatial history, on the other hand, may suggest a dimension where the two cultures interacted, where the pioneer myth can be rewritten—or reenacted—as a dialectic between invader and invaded.

Davis's plays assert just such a dimension. Even when he does not construct his narratives in ways that dismantle imperialist modalities of time and space, he frequently uses proxemic signifiers to demonstrate how indigenous spaces have been invaded and desacralized by the expansion of an alien culture, how Aborigines have been confined spatially under colonization, and how their relationships with non-Aboriginal Australians are still negotiated through spatial structures. *Kullark*'s depiction of first contact recasts a so-called reconnaissance survey as a territorial dispute when Moyarahn marks the ground with her *wahna* (digging stick) not only to cast a death wish on the surveyors, Fraser and Stirling, but also to inscribe her priority over the land. Such spatial gestures refute the concept of *terra nullius*, a doctrine abolished from Australia's legal framework only in 1992 with the *Mabo v. Queensland* case, and counteract the rhetorical power of the "linguistic shout" that has characterized European models of exploration and acquisition of "new" lands. This mode of possession, Stephen Greenblatt argues in his study of Columbus's voyages in the Caribbean, was a series of speech acts—"declaring, witnessing, [and] recording"—that were public and official but "performed entirely *for a world elsewhere*," the explorer's country of origin, so that a scriptural operation of power could be made even in the face of the original inhabitants (usually in a language they could not understand) and be deemed legitimate since the colonizer/performer "was not contradicted" (Greenblatt 1991, 56–58). *Kullark*'s intervention in the discursive economy of first contact rests in its contra/diction of the linguistic shout by a series of actions and speech acts performed for a world *here* rather than elsewhere.

The set's emphasis on the map motif also foregrounds the contestation of space as a crucial component of a revisionist history of the "settlement" of Australia. As Harley reminds us, maps are a form of spatial knowledge that represent a strategic plan, or at least a desire, to occupy and own particular territories. In colonial times, "mapmaking was one of the specialized intellectual weapons by which power could be gained, administered, given legitimacy and codified" (1988, 281). Because maps always mask their interested selectivity, they seem to convey unbiased scientific knowledge when in fact they help to maintain and justify the colonizers' control over alien space by marking out boundaries and then making them seem natural and necessary. The map of the Swan River Colony in *Kullark* shows the extent of the settlers' intended invasion and indicates the ways in which they conceptualize the land as unoccupied and merely awaiting cultivation. By using this map as part of his backdrop, Davis demonstrates how cartography functions as an aid to colonization; however, the play also disrupts the power of the cartographic gaze because the map is never left intact for long and the Rainbow Serpent remains the dominant image of the set. As a different kind of spatial knowledge, the stylized serpent painting foregrounds "the inevitable discrepancy between the 'natural' and the 'imitated' object" (Huggan 1989b, 121) in ways that hold the supposed mimeticism of the Western map up to question. If, as Denis Wood argues, the "*naturalization of the map* occurs at the level of the sign system in which [it] is inscribed" (1992, 2), the epistemic double coding of *Kullark*'s backdrop, along with its theatrical overcoding as part of the mise en scène, ensures that the map of the Swan River Colony invites a deconstructive reading that dismantles the self-privileging authority of the colonizer.

Although *Kullark* details with great clarity the subjugation of the Aborigines and their disenfranchisement in the face of European military power, the authority of the colonizers is never complete or uncontested. Subversions of colonial rule are enacted through events such as Yagan's sheep stealing, which, though seemingly minor, raise important ideological issues and point to the differences between settler and Aboriginal approaches to the landscape. When Yagan defends his actions by arguing that if the native wildlife belongs to everyone, so too should all the produce of the land, including the sheep, he emphasizes the inconsistency of white notions of ownership. Sheep "stealing" as a small but significant act of defiance also features in Davis's fourth "trilogy" play, *In Our Town* (1990),[8] which reintroduces characters from *No Sugar* and takes up the story of their lives in the period following World War II. In both of these plays, the sheep become metonymic of the larger landscape, which has been coded as the property of the settlers. By their theft of the sheep, Aboriginal trickster figures such as Jimmy Munday outwit their adversaries to achieve not only a comic victory over miserliness but also a symbolic reclamation of the land. As Uncle Herbie of *In Our Town* points out, the issue of land ownership remains debatable: "It might be his land," he says of the white grazier, "but it's still my country" (1992, 16).

In *Kullark,* the gunshots and spear thrusts of the first act express the antagonists' fantasies of erasing each other from the contested historical space. The territorial battle established through these spatial gestures then continues in the verbal representations of the past by the White Actor and the Black Actor in the Brechtian-style commentary that opens the second half of the play. As the White Actor reads out written accounts of colonization, this "script" is held up to scrutiny by the interjections of the Black Actor who, for example, restructures the historically constituted "Aboriginal problem" as a "white problem" (1982, 41). That the two actors interpret the historical space of the past differently reinforces the intentional nature of reality that the quantum theorists highlight: "Since any actual world is only one possible manifestation of a whole array of possible worlds . . . it is not a given, but created as much by its inhabitants as by immutable (social or scientific) laws" (D. George 1989b, 176). Similarly, history is multiple, partial, ambiguous, and relative. Nothing but a human construction made coherent by its formulation within narrative, its logic is primarily that of myth (see H. White 1978, 103). The text can no longer claim to represent a putative real world, so reconstructions of the past can only signal our ideas and stereotypes of that past: "We are condemned to seek History by way of our own pop images and simulacra of that history, which itself remains forever out of reach" (Jameson 1984, 71).

On one level, it could be argued that Davis's plays illustrate the success of the imperial venture to appropriate Aboriginal land and confine its occupants to the marginalized spaces assigned to them by the dominant society. But although his theatre depicts the containment of indigenous peoples within institutions—notably missions and jails—designed to segregate them from white society, Davis stresses the idea of survival and resistance. Hence, what we see on stage is a representation of the world in which Aborigines are always the center of focus even while Davis's versions of history feature displacement and dislocation as the defining elements of Black experience. Boundaries designed as markers of hermetically sealed worlds segregating racial groups frequently dissolve and become instead "debatable places" that speak through their violation. A prime example of this occurs in *No Sugar,* where the Aborigines repeatedly break out of the mission compound and refuse to respect other apartheid enclosures created by representatives of white authority. That the Blacks penetrate the structures set up to confine them to the margins clearly obviates the European ideology that attempts to classify them as simply part of the landscape, to be administered by Superintendent Neville through the "Department of Fisheries, Forestry, Wildlife and Aborigines" (1986, 18). The play's spatial counterdiscursivity is most effectively dramatized in act 1, scene 1 in a series of contrapuntal interruptions to a telephone call between Neville (in Perth) and Sergeant Carrol (in Northam). While Neville and Carrol discuss their planned "relocation" of the Northam Aborigines in terms that objectify them as part of simply another environmental-management program, a pest to be removed from white space, representatives of that Aboriginal community—Jimmy, Milly, and Gran—appear on stage as speaking subjects that will not be so easily eradicated. They not only interject throughout the conversation with demands to be heard, but forcefully enter what has been inscribed as white territory, so that Neville's and Carrol's offices appear as spaces under siege. Here, Davis's use of visual and verbal counterpoint undermines the coherence, logic, and authority of white discourse to create a potent image of contestation rather than segregation.

The idea of contested space is emblematic of the play as a whole, and, ironically, it is precisely the colonizers' continued efforts to construct and enforce apartheid structures that emphasize the Aborigine's insistent visibility, allowing them to define themselves spatially by resisting ghettoization to achieve the racial self-retrieval that underlies the postcolonial writer's constant dialogue with history. Jimmy, for example, flaunts his noncompliance with the rules of the spaces assigned to him by venturing out of bounds when confined to the mission and by disrupting proceedings when put in jail. Through his amusing antics as performer and entertainer, he transforms the prison cell and the courtroom into a form of theatre that allows him to assert control over the spaces designed to segregate and punish him. Such subversions of "white man's law" are widespread in Davis's plays and function to question the validity of that law. Recurrent images of imprisonment and containment are frequently framed by an Aboriginal perspective that sees incarceration as one of the vicissitudes of daily life, or, alternatively, as a substitute initiation for Black men and therefore part of a ritual passage into adulthood. Yet, as the events of *Barungin* remind us, the cell door and the concrete floor are nonetheless powerful symbols of oppression for Aborigines, and imprisonment remains part of the institutional brutality of colonialism that has effected the deracination of indigenous peoples and their alienation from the land.

Similarly, the removal of Aborigines from traditional homelands and their "quarantine" in hospitals and missions is shown in several plays as another form of territorial invasion that dispossesses indigenes of their land. *No Sugar* and *Kullark* detail the effects of this dislocation quite graphically and also examine its potential to effect a loss of Aboriginal identity. The missions masquerade as places constructed for the welfare of the colonizers' charges, but Davis demonstrates that they function primarily as part of an overall strategy designed to undermine tribal and familial solidarity, to appropriate land for the white settlers and to achieve the effective destruction of the Aboriginal race. This illustrates Greenblatt's contention that the "rhetorical task of Christian imperialism" is to "bring together commodity conversion and spiritual conversion" (1991, 71).

Davis's concern with the segregation and marginalization of Blacks in Australian society is reiterated from a different angle in the performative text of *In Our Town*. This play is very much about traversing boundaries and dismantling the physical and ideological structures that disempower Aborigines and position them always at the margins of the dominant culture. For the play's premiere production in Perth, these themes were stressed by a setting that featured a diagonal line or path running from the back of the acting area to the forward limits of the thrust stage to mark a boundary between the town's predominantly white cafe-bar area and the fringe-dwellers' bush camp, which occupied the rest of the set (see fig. 5). Apart from bringing into focus the segregation of the town, and of the country as a whole on a broader symbolic level, this setting and the actors' particular use of it foregrounded the boundary itself as a site of meaning. While some interchanges between Blacks and whites were enacted with the boundary line firmly between the antagonists as a glaring barrier to communication, characters like the Aboriginal youth, David, and his "wetjala" (girl)friend, Sue, were quickly established as people who transgressed such barriers, rendering them ineffective. The white townspeople clearly expected David not to exercise the freedom that his "dog tag"—honorary "white" status granted because of his participation in the war—allows him; hence his frequent presence in the bar and the cafe affirmed his right to occupy the dominant society's spaces, while Sue made an explicit gesture of crossing over into marginalized space to visit the Aborigines' camp. At one point, the two also walked precariously along the boundary line, a movement that symbolized their attempts to negotiate the complex spatial structures of their town and society. By framing its love story in this way, the production showed one possible path for future reconciliation between the two cultures.

Over more than a decade, Jack Davis's drama has challenged not only the substance of imperial history but also the temporal and spatial coordinates of an epistemology that has gained its power "through denying, or rendering transparent, the inherent indexicality of all statements or knowl-

Fig. 5. Borderlines: set of *In Our Town,* Marli Byol Company, 1990. (Photo: David Parker.)

edge claims" (Wood 1992, 41). The *story* of colonization is thus replayed in his work as an uneasy dialogue between all interested parties. As Australia moves toward becoming a republic in the new century, it remains to be seen whether this dialogue achieves the reconciliation and restitution that Davis's theatre so passionately urges.

Body Politics
Dance and Costume

According to Elizabeth Ferrier, mapping out history or reviewing it in spatial terms can be seen as an attempt to reauthenticate the local, lived experience of the postcolonial subject in response to the spatial disorientation that results from the imposition of an alien culture. Ferrier points to the most localized site of all—the body—as the site of greatest potential resistance to imperialist structurations of reality (1989, 68). Performance as the verbal and visual articulation of the body in space-time seems the most logical medium for enacting such resistance. Performance can challenge the imperial gaze, which seeks to annihilate the Other in the constitution of the self. It allows the colonized to position themselves as speaking, moving subjects rather than as manipulable objects. And because it does not privilege the written word, performance offers to nonliterate cultures rhetorical spaces in which their versions of history might be represented.

The physicalized stage presence of Aboriginal actors cannot be undervalued in discussing the counterdiscursive possibilities of the body in performance. I do not wish to embrace notions of an essentialized Black body here—what constitutes Aboriginal or non-Aboriginal identity is neither fixed nor objectively measurable—but to argue that since the signifying systems of contemporary Western theatre (which provides the model of reception for most Aboriginal plays) inevitably encode the body with markers of race and gender (in contrast to a number of non-Western performance practices where gender and race are commonly assigned by costume and/or mask), such differences might well be used as part of the arsenal of the oppressed. This would tie in with Spivak's idea of "strategic essentialism" as part of a "scrupulously visible political interest" (1988, 205). When indigenous roles are played by whites, as they have been in earlier periods of Australian theatre, the resistance potential of the fictionalized Aboriginal body is compromised by the "wayward signification" of its whiteness (Goldie 1986, 5), manifest in the actor despite the illusions created by the role. In contrast, the Black actor of the contemporary Australian stage insists on performing the visibility of the indigene, recuperating that Othered "self" for both the character and the actor through a continual process of transformation from role to performance.[9]

In performance, the Aboriginal body has three functions. Firstly, as a physical body, it is a signifier of racial Otherness that resists appropriation through the metaphysics of its insistent presence on stage. As a social body, however, it becomes a site of contestation showing the historical inscriptions of both indigenous and colonizer cultures and their competing ideologies. Finally, as an artistic body, it bridges the gap between physical and social, grounding Aboriginal voices and perspectives in the theatrical subject. If, as Stanton Garner argues, "exploiting the body's centrality within the theatrical medium" allows its refiguring "as a principal site of theatrical and political intervention, establishing (in the process) a contemporary 'body politic' rooted in the individual's sentient presence" (1990, 146), the performative aspects of the body are crucial in freeing Aborigines from the textual capture and containment that have, until recently, marked their representations in theatre and in Australian history.

Costume and movement are the signifiers most effectively used by Aboriginal theatre to mobilize the strategic agency of the decolonizing body and to expose the ways in which Aborigines have been subjugated by the disciplinary regimes of empire. A number of plays first bring costume into focus by scrutinizing its function at the moment of invasion. Robert Merritt's *The Cake Man* (1975) makes an explicit point of showing how images of the indigene have been fixed and framed by the imperial gaze when the protagonist, a tribal Black who has been shot, awakens and literally steps into the shoes of a stereotype after he discovers a pile of European clothes and eventually, with some comic experimentation, puts them on to rename himself "The Australian Aborigine . . . made in England" (1978, 12). The subsequent narrative details just what becomes of this culturally commodified tourist attraction in the modern era. Whereas Merritt's play makes its point through the indigene's self-parody, Davis's *Kullark* levels its satire directly at the colonizer, whose "civilizing" gesture of clothing the natives is presented as an absurd farce when Fraser comes away from first contact looking decidedly outré in his underwear after he is forced to offer his shirt and trousers to Yagan and Mitjitjiroo. At the same time, the affective power of this costume is clearly recognized through the fear and mistrust it evokes in Moyarahn. In each play, European clothing does not bring the particular level of civility (read subjection) desired by the invader but functions instead as a wayward signifier that might provoke white audiences to shift their perspectives—to see themselves as the others of their Others.

As a further subversive tactic, *Kullark* encodes the (near) naked body of the Aborigine as a costume that evokes fear and desire in the whites who, determined to militate against the threat of racial difference, decapitate Yagan, and skin him to souvenir his tribal markings. The stripping metaphor implied here suggests that the mutilated Black body functions in colonial discourse as a fetishized object and a focus for racial paranoia. On one level, it could be argued that the imperial venture to silence or simply annihilate the Other is shown to succeed historically when the invaders clearly win power over the contested body/space, but, significantly, Yagan's mutilation is detailed (by a white man), not enacted, so while exposing the colonizers' barbarity on a narrative level, the play avoids the trap of voyeurism. What we do see on stage represents the ritually marked body quite differently: as a theatrical costume that potently images elements of a recuperated indigenous culture. This motif is most fully developed during Yagan's ceremonial dance, where movement amplifies the body's agency as a site of resistance that unsettles the pageant of imperial history.

Resisting the real and symbolic power of the colonizers' clothes is an ongoing project for many Aboriginal characters. Among the many habits (in both senses of the word) that have marked their field of representation are the costumes of the co-opted Black tracker, the scruffy and drunken vagrant, and the exotic "savage." These are theatrical costumes that the colonized now frequently *inhabit* for the express purpose of deconstructing their ideological textures through mimicry. Equally disempowering is the "cleanliness and godliness" of the uniforms provided by the mission establishments to which Aboriginal families in plays such as *Kullark* and *No Sugar* are forcibly relocated or quarantined—often for diseases they do not have. Both texts' emphasis on the mission as a place that uses clothing to discipline and sanitize the body of the indigene points to the intersecting oppressions of Christianity, Western government, and imperial medicine. That the "body politics" of the mission system are designed to effect the depopulation of indigenous peoples is clearly illustrated in Eva Johnson's *Murras* (1988) through references to the deliberate and systematic sterilization of pubescent Aboriginal girls, who now "carry the scars from the *wudjella's* medicine" (1989, 106). It is not surprising, then, that the garb of the hospital patient, though seldom explicitly iconized—Sally Morgan's *Sistergirl* (1992) is an exception—also haunts other Aboriginal texts, notably *The Dreamers,* where Uncle Worru seems marked for death from the moment he first enters the corridors of the white hospital, an institution that is troped as an anathema to the well-being of Aboriginal culture. In Kooemba Jdarra's recent production of the play, the menace posed by institutionalization (whether in hospitals, missions, or prisons) was immediately evoked when the hospital room was revealed as a claustrophobic white icebox cut into a wall.[10]

Condemnation of the Black body's annexation by the anatomizing gaze of medical science is paralleled in Aboriginal theatre by a critical focus on the actual physical capture and containment of the racial Other, imaged in that most prominent of colonial costumes in Australia: the prisoner's uniform. As a signifier of colonization, the incarcerated "convict" has multiple associations with imperialism, but the specific links between imprisonment and the subjugation of indigenous peoples have become well established since the prolonged inquiries of the late 1980s into Black deaths in custody and recent charges of institutionalized racism in the police forces of most Australian states. In performance texts, an important sartorial response to this oppression has been to mobilize the symbolic agency of the Aboriginal flag by fabricating costumes that foreground its black, red, and gold markings, or, more specifically, by featuring Aborigines dressed in land rights T-shirts to mark the stage as a politically charged space. This was particularly noticeable in 1988 when a number of productions staged express visual protests against two hundred years of colonization by inscribing their actors' costumes with the two main counterbicentennial slogans: "Don't celebrate '88" and "We survived."

As well as harnessing costume as a strategic marker that might resist imposed identities and/or abrogate the privilege of their signifying systems, the theatrical body can function to recuperate postcolonial subjectivity through movement. As Cynthia Novak argues,

> The body and movement are social realities interacting with and interpreting other aspects of the culture. Structured movement systems like social dance, theatre dance, sport, and ritual help to articulate and create images of who people are and what their lives are like, encoding and eliciting ideas and values; they are also part of experience, of performances and actions by which people know themselves. (1988, 103)

The function of movement in creating identity is also highlighted by Ann Daly (1988, 1989). Both theorists reject the Lacanian notion that constitution of individual identity begins with the child's entry into discourse (the male symbolic world) and argue instead that the infant first gains a sense of self through its own bodily experiences.[11] Consequently, movement and language are seen as sharing in the process of producing the self and the culture.

Movement as producer of one's self and one's culture has special significance for reading dance as a text in Aboriginal plays. In imperial historical accounts, Aboriginal dance has been encoded as the expression of savage or exotic Otherness within a discourse that represents Blacks as objects to be looked at, rather than as self-constituting subjects. W. Robertson, for example, writing in 1928, constructs Aboriginal dance during a corroboree as the picturesque signifier of less-than-human behavior: "The whole programme was wonderful in its savage simplicity. The weirdly painted natives, issuing from the dense blackness of the bush to perform the dances, looked more like wraiths than human beings" (1928, 95). He goes on to state that the spectacle resembled "a *picture* that would have suited Dante's *Inferno,* as with gleaming eyes and frenzied movements they approached the fire" (1928, 122; emphasis added). These descriptions, though purportedly historical accounts, clearly use many theatrical conventions to conflate nature and the indigene, marking the dance as a "primitive" performance event designed for consumption by the imperial spectator. Along with some notion of theatrical order (an implied program), Robertson's narrative points to the use of costuming and makeup (the painted bodies), while evoking backstage areas in the "dense blackness of the bush" and a well-lit space by the fire where the compelling stage action occurs. In constructing a bush theatre to frame (read contain) the dance, and by situating himself as the impartial observer of a series of static "pictures," Robertson naturalizes his perspective, renders invisible the appropriative function of the historian's gaze, and militates against the threat of difference that the Aboriginal dance with its "frenzied movements" poses. He can thus categorize the dancers as more wraithlike than human and relegate the corroboree to the realm of the fantastic, the fictional, the infernal, reserving the notion of "real" dance for the dominant culture by marginalizing its variants. Robertson's failure to acknowledge the dancers' subjectivities prevents him from discerning any functional aspects of the corroboree vis-à-vis Aboriginal culture and certainly blinds him to the possibility of resistance politics. Even when he witnesses dances in which the Aborigines mimic European movements, Robertson fails to recognize their parodic intentions and merely classifies the performance as a comic spectacle with no other purpose than to amuse the onlooker.

Such representations of dance as reified spectacle are problematized in contemporary Aboriginal drama if we focus on movement as a part of identity formation/recuperation and spatial reorientation rather than just as the vehicle for an effect. This approach avoids situating dance as a "universal" sign that does not need interpreting and, paradoxically, as an opaque essence that cannot be "read" anyway because it is "intuitive, visceral, and pre-verbal" (Siegel 1988, 30). Dance features in all of Davis's plays, as well as in the works of most other Black Australian playwrights, though its political effects have been little remarked upon.[12] When incorporated into drama as part of the cultural capital of traditional and neotraditional Aboriginal performative arts, dance militates against the compromising effects of using a European narrative form—the play—to revision imperialist history. In the spatial histories of the Aborigines, Carter argues, "the voice enjoys no special privileges. Dancing and drawing are equally important means of spatial telling" (1987, 346). Contextual elements of the dance are crucial here in preventing the reification that occurs in the spectatorship of corroborees performed for the touristic gaze. Hence, Aboriginal playwrights are careful to present the dance as an inherent part of the structure and meaning of their plays, rather than as mere spectacle.

Bob Maza's *The Keepers* (1988), which charts the gradual destruction of tribal culture in the mid–nineteenth century, begins with a scene that foregrounds dance as an integral part of both Aboriginal *and* settler/invader cultures by introducing his two central characters as dancers who produce their identities through a series of movements that share some characteristics but not others. In matching costumes (a black leotard and a white one), the Boandik woman and the Scottish woman alternately perform dances of "home," then ritual courting dances, followed by a symbolic dance of childbirth. Their differing interpretations of the three concepts establish the dancers' movements not as a part of a universal language but rather as cognate discourses that, theoretically at least, have equal access to representation. Because the movements of the two women are clearly related and are performed on common ground (the same stage space), these dances obviate ideologies that seek to situate Aboriginal dance outside the realm of human behavior and white dance firmly within it. At the same time, the movements of the dancers inscribe individual and cultural differences between the two women as each constitutes the "self" in relation to the "other," a process of identity formation that the contrapuntal dances show to be common to each culture, and not just a privilege of the colonizers.

By encoding identity through movement, Maza's dances function as important modes of empowerment for oppressed characters in the play, avoiding the linguistic capture that compromises verbal attempts by colonized peoples to articulate, in a voice that will be acknowledged, resistance to dominant ideologies and epistemologies. Because movement as a signifying system is, in many instances, "less specific (and therefore often more inclusive and ambiguous), than language" (Novak 1988, 102), it can facilitate some degree of cross-cultural communication that neither denies difference nor appropriates representation for the dominant culture. This is not to suggest, however, that Aboriginal dance essentializes an identity that is unaffected by the operations of the spectator whose constructions of race and gender are inescapably inscribed on the performing body. That Maza's dancers are women risks locking them into historically disadvantaged positions as objects of a masculine (and for the Boandik woman, imperial) gaze, but I would argue that textual and contextual aspects of the performance construct viable alternative viewpoints that change the trajectory of scopic desire. When the women dance for each other as a means of communication and not just for the dominant audience, the spectator's gaze must necessarily register a female observer of the dance at the same time as it attempts to read/consume the embodied movements, a process that prevents the unproblematic suturing of the male gaze to the performance. And if, as Angela McRobbie asserts, dance as a channel for bodily self-expression connects autoerotic dimensions with desires for the Other (1984, 144–45), the women's dances allow a transgressive cross-racial, lesbian desire that further subverts imperial and patriarchal ways of looking at the body's signifying practices.

Spatial aspects of the dance in *The Keepers* are perhaps even more crucial to the play's decolonizing project. The ways in which space is inscribed or made visible by the moving body are integrally linked to cultural and historical orientation. Mikhail Bakhtin claims that language "lies on the borderline between oneself and the other" (1981, 293), but the same could be said of space: prior to the moment of appropriation when the dancer adapts it to his/her "own semantic and expressive intention," space "exists in other people's contexts" and serves "other people's intentions" (Bakhtin 1981, 293). In the larger context of Australian theatre practice, Maza's dancers reinscribe the stage space (and thus a cultural space) for the marginalized. Within the play's semiotic systems, the women map out the spatial forms and fantasies by which they declare their individual and cultural presence, illustrating that Aborigines and European invaders not only moved in the same historical spaces (Carter 1987, 325) but also constituted them in relation to one another.

As an important mode of narrative in Aboriginal culture, dancing (or drawing with the body) can also function to restore masculine identity through links with ritual and male initiation ceremonies. By recreating his Aboriginality through dance performance, Nummy, the "local drunk" and trickster figure in Richard Walley's *Coordah* (1987), escapes the fixity of roles that have been formed within—and in response to—the dominant discourses. Likewise, Guna, the Nyoongah trickster/rogue figure alluded to in the title of Walley's more recent play, *Munjong* (1991),[13] is the character most clearly transformed by his dance. In Davis's *No Sugar,* dancing in a corroboree gives Billy Kimberley, the co-opted Black "politjman," the opportunity to shed his costume/uniform, de-sign his body with *wilgi* (specially prepared paint), and join in a communal ceremony, thus transgressing the tracker/informant role assigned to him within the hierarchical structures of the Aboriginal mission. During the corroboree, individual identity is both created by, and subsumed in, group identity as culturally coded movement that strengthens ritual and social bonds between participants and allows them to shed their everyday roles determined within white hierarchies of power. In this sense, the dance acts as a shaman exorcising evil. It is also an occasion that facilitates an exchange of cultural capital between tribes and a challenge to white priority over contested space. Because dance brings the relationship between the performing body and the territory it marks into acute visibility, it can operate as a form of protest and a bid for land rights. The 1990 production of *No Sugar* in Perth featured dance as a potent tool for symbolic reclamation of Aboriginal land when, even after the performers' movements for the corroboree ended, their spatial inscriptions were clearly palpable through footprints on the sand and a visible layer of unsettled red dust. As Auber Octavius Neville, Chief Protector of Aborigines, walked tentatively across this "sacred" ground in his three-piece suit to deliver a speech that situated Aborigines firmly within white historical discourse, traces of the corroboree marked his presence as incongruous, invasive, and ultimately illegitimate.[14]

That *No Sugar* encodes the corroboree as a masculine activity (the female characters are denied participation *and* spectatorship) raises some problematic issues: on the one hand, it gives the dance a higher status as cultural production because most societies deem the occupations of men more important than those of women (Hanna 1987, 22–23); on the other hand, Davis's predominantly white audience will be tempted to read the performance from culturally subjectified standpoints that link dance with female activity, thereby seeing the corroboree as a feminizing practice. The ritual and spatial codings of the performance, however, resist this totalizing impulse by grounding the corroboree firmly in Aboriginal history and epistemology through its links with the Dreamtime, which, Stephen Muecke claims, is the "constant supplementary signified of all Aboriginal narrative" (1983b, 98). The agency of mainstream Australian theatre practice can also function to legitimize Aboriginal performance practices even while it necessarily compromises them. As Penny Van Toorn argues in her analysis of minority texts and majority audiences, hybridized texts "harness the power of valorizing signs recognized by the dominant audience in order to impart prestige to the valorizing signs" of their own marginalized culture (1990, 112).

Yet another function of dance in Aboriginal drama is elucidated in Johnson's *Murras* and Morgan's *Sistergirl*,[15] which utilize a single dancer, not otherwise a character in the play, in transformative roles to signify an Aboriginal spiritual identity that is linked both to the tribal past and the Dreamtime. As in Davis's *The Dreamers*, the solo dancer in each of these works functions at structural, thematic, and mythic levels. S/he[16] not only reconstitutes Aboriginality through a discourse of the body and its performance but also recontextualizes the rest of the dramatic action (structured largely according to European genres) within the temporal and spatial frames of an Aboriginal metaphysics. Morgan's *Birdman*, like Davis's *Featherfoot*, enters the troubled half-sleep of the dying Aboriginal protagonist, in this case a feisty old woman named Rosy, transforming death into a rite of passage by dancing her back to the world of her ancestors, her Dreaming. Similarly, the Aboriginal identity represented by the *Mimi* dancer in *Murras* is firmly grounded in myth. *Mimi*, the caretaker of the dead spirit, begins the play by presenting the birth dance of the Aboriginal Dreaming (see fig. 6), later enacts Granny's death scene as a ritualized dance, and then completes the performance with a slow circular movement, reminiscent, for white spectators, of the danse macabre. In all these plays, the interrelationships between the movement of the dancer and the movement of the other characters produce a hybridized Aboriginal identity that reflects contemporary Black reality but that is, at the same time, also mythic and therefore resistant to the dominant normalizing impulses of that reality. On another level, the dance/dancer intervenes in the mimetic action to allow a mode of Brechtian historicization of the narrative, which is then less compromised by the exigencies of otherwise predominantly naturalistic codes.

While the spirit figures and corroborees I have been discussing generally harness the signifying power of tribal cultures, they are not indicative of a static, precolonized identity. Oodgeroo Noonuccal's *Why the Corroborees,*[17] workshopped at the 1989 National Black Playwrights Conference, illustrates this point through a syncretic dance sequence that presents a corroboree in parallel with a rap routine. In many cases, specific ancestral or traditional dances are simply not reproducible because either the knowledge or the habit of particular movements has been eroded by the epistemic violence of colonialism. Hence Nyoongahs devised new "tribal" dances for the premiere production of Eddie Bennell's *The Silent Years* (1990) to recreate a heritage not easily accessible to the performers involved in the play.[18] The processual development of dance for/in Bennell's play shows how structured movement systems can mobilize embodied knowledges and experiences as a way of shaping as well as interpreting "a shifting cultural landscape" (Novak 1988, 104). In a related maneuver, Davis's first children's play, *Honey Spot* (1985), actually stages the politics of processual production in performance by using dance as its central action and metaphor for the contemporary dialogue between Aboriginal and non-Aboriginal cultures. By teaching each other their respective dances, Peggy and Tim eventually learn to compromise, using the material of their different cultural archives to choreograph a series of movements that revise concepts of both the European ballet form and the corroboree. The performance of this hybrid dance reinscribes the stage, and by implication, the land, as shared space rather than merely the precinct of the white majority.

Those who subscribe to the "male gaze" theories of spectatorship (the possessive gaze is "male" while the passive object is "female," regardless of the sex of either spectator or actor/character)[19] will argue that representations of Aboriginal dance are essentially feminine and therefore doubly susceptible to voyeurism and fetishization because they enact gender as well as

Fig. 6. Stephen Page as the Mimi Spirit, *Murras,* Adelaide Fringe Festival Production, 1988. (Photo: Di Barrett.)

racial differences. But as Daly points out, the gaze paradigm was originally developed as a theory for film, in which the performer is literally a celluloid object who cannot look back at the spectator and is therefore rendered passive with no "presence" (1989, 26). Daly adds that "we must think a lot more about performative presence" in the effort to theorize alternatives.

> Presence is the silent yet screeching excitement of physical vibrancy, of "being there." It is one of the thrills of watching dance, to see someone radiate pure energy, whether it is in stillness or in flight. Questions abound: What constitutes presence? How do we know it when we see it? Is it pan-cultural or highly coded? How is it related to the structure of spectacle? Why is it so seductive? Does that seductiveness demand possession? (1989, 25)

Although I cannot attempt to give satisfactory answers to Daly's probings within the scope of this study, the notion of presence bears examination in moving toward a postcolonial theory of the body in performance. The staging of Aboriginal dance as an act of cultural retrieval establishes a presence that counteracts the historical erasure of Aborigines in Australian narratives. Such codings also attempt to move away from the eroticism of display to the dance's social functions of mapping, and thus repossessing, cultural and physical territory. Racial signification, celebrating the centrality of the Black body as dramatic subject and resisting the dispersal of difference, also constitutes part of this presence. But perhaps the most important aspect of presence is the idea of pure energy radiating from the still body, an effect achieved in the momentary frozen tableaux of a number of Aboriginal plays (see fig. 7). Here again, quantum theory may provide an instructive paradigm for exploring the counterdiscursivity of the body in performance as it posits a liminal realm of "potentiality" in which all possibilities are latent. The physical vibrancy of this realm and the notion of existential choice that underlies the quantum leap from potential to actual imply a political agency that helps to constitute the body's performative presence without recourse to an "authentic," precolonial identity.

The hit musical *Bran Nue Dae* (1990)[20] by Jimmy Chi and Kuckles is the paradigmatic example of a contemporary Aboriginal play that refuses to lock the "native" under the sign of authenticity by privileging so-called pure forms of cultural expression over more syncretic ones.[21] The play charts an Aboriginal road-movie-style search for a physical and spiritual homeland in the "melting pot" of contemporary Australian society. Not only does the performance text present modern disco, rap, and minstrel routines, along with corroboree dances and classical ballet,[22] but it also appropriates and parodies many of these dance forms while fusing styles in ways that multiply the coded articulations of the body in performance and celebrate the sexual/sensual body as a source of creative energy. Chi, who claims Aboriginal, Chinese, Japanese, and European ancestry, proposes a hybridized vision of life and theatre in general, and of postcolonial identity

Fig. 7. Michael Leslie (front) and Djunawong Stanley Mirindo, *Bran Nue Dae,* Black Swan/Melbourne Theatre Company, 1993. (Photo: Jeff Busby.)

in particular. This kind of hybridity is not meant to suggest a simple multiplication of difference but rather to recognize the several and sometimes conflicting identifications that many contemporary Aborigines experience. While critics such as Tony Mitchell assume that the play depoliticizes Australian race relations because it "deals kindly" with colonialism and invites the audience to "join unironically" in its songs (1993, 21), this assessment fails to recognize the oppositional subtext beneath an apparently hegemonic form. For instance, the lyrics of "Nothing I Would Rather Be" express their parodic message quite cogently, and I would argue that few non-Aboriginal spectators could sing along with this song without identifying themselves as its explicit target.

Willie: There's nothing I would rather be
than to be an Aborigine
and watch you take my precious land away.
For nothing gives me greater joy than to
watch you fill each girl and boy

with superficial existential shit.
[*Chorus dance on from the side.*]
Chorus: Now you may think I'm cheeky
but I'd be satisfied
to rebuild your convict ships
and sail you on the tide.

(1991, 15)

In the 1993 production, highly politicized representations of the past were also staged visually by the projection of archival photographs behind the contemporary action (see fig. 8), adding an air of sobriety to the play's generally exuberant action. By providing a more or less constant subtextual story of invasion and oppression in conjunction with more conventional musical forms, *Bran Nue Dae* engages in a self-conscious metatheatricality that often points with urbane wit to the prejudices of the entertainment traditions that inform it, demonstrating, as Jacqueline Lo argues, that the musical form is not "a completely closed dramaturgy whereby a single cultural discourse—that of Anglo-American Hollywood imperialism—predominates" (1997, 3).

Bran Nue Dae's exuberant and highly physical theatricality claims the stage as a flexible space for representing Aboriginal subjectivities through movement/dance. At the same time, it allows for the effective subversion of imperial authority through the visual excesses of the carnivalesque, here vividly drawn through the play's costuming codes and mobilized in opposition to the proselytizing activities of the church and the multiple oppressions of the law. First in line for satirical treatment is the head of the Perth mission school, Father Benedictus, who, while upbraiding the boys for theft and gluttony after they break into the school tuckshop, cuts an excessive, larger-than-life figure in his ridiculous platform shoes, overtall mitre, and cassock embroidered with Cherry Ripe wrappers. Benedictus's expulsion of Willie from the "Garden of Eden" proves to be an ironic release for the young Aboriginal protagonist, who then undertakes an epic journey north to his homeland in the company of his irascible Uncle Tadpole and two "white" hippies, Marijuana Annie and Slippery. The high points of the journey are iconized in further sartorial subversions, notably when Tadpole "whites up" his face and joins a white-gloved chorus in a vigorous song-and-dance routine that mimics a city traffic policeman, and, more pointedly, that exceptionally racist species of entertainment: the (black and white) minstrel show. Shortly afterward, white judicial systems are again the butt of satire as the travelers encounter two khaki-clad northern cops,

Fig. 8. Prison scene, *Bran Nue Dae,* Black Swan/Melbourne Theatre Company, 1993. (Photo: Jeff Busby.)

played by Aborigines in shorts and bare feet with ill-fitting shirts stretched over huge paunches. The authority of these uniforms thus abrogated, they are quickly commandeered by the marginalized for additional comic effects when the police perform a cakewalk-style strut through the chorus, and while the more ominous aspects of incarceration are never entirely absent from this scene, the Aborigines clearly get the better of the law. A final road-stop routine features tribal Blacks who appear in loincloths for the ritual goanna hunt. Although these costumes, along with a corroboree performed by the hunters/dancers (to a rock and roll tune), mark the travelers' entry into Aboriginal territory, they offer less an authentic or essentialized concept of Black identity than a recognition, through self-conscious parody, of the ways in which Aborigines have been looked at in the discourses of theatre, film, and especially tourism.

The multiracial town of Broome, which is the travelers' last port of call, shows that contemporary Aboriginality wears many guises. Willie's young sweetheart, Rosie, lead singer in a country and western band, proves to be literally a knockout when her dazzling white and silver outfit causes him to fall in a faint. Other costumes appropriated from the dominant culture are similarly celebrated *and* lampooned when a congregation of mixed-race Pentecostals led by Willie's mother, Theresa, arrives on the scene to shrive the community of its sins. In the course of the enraptured singing, dancing, and confessing that follows, it is revealed that almost everyone hides a "black" secret: Uncle Tadpole is Theresa's estranged husband and therefore Willie's father, Marijuana Annie has Aboriginal blood that she has not acknowledged, and Slippery is the son of Theresa and none other than Benedictus. This highly theatricalized scene retropes the sin of miscegenation as a sin of omission insofar as Aboriginal identities have either been denied or repressed in some manner by the institutional costumes of imperialism. As a kind of "penance," the play then makes a point of celebrating a "bran nue dae" of reconciliation with further transgressive visual images: Theresa goes off with Tadpole and returns with her religious habit disheveled after their reunion, Willie and Rosie get off their gear behind the mound to consummate their love, and Slippery puts on a land rights T-shirt while the chorus sings "let's multiply the Aboriginal race" (1991, 77). It only remains for Benedictus to reenter, literally cut down to size in a more demure cassock, and to admit his part in the story of hybridization before conducting the final communion rite by distributing the coveted Cherry Ripes of the first scene to all and sundry, including the audience.

Aided and abetted by the rhetorical power of the theatricalized body, Chi thus manages, through a rather clever sleight of hand, to situate a strong vision of harmony within both Aboriginal performance culture and the very Christian ethos that he has undermined. This ambivalent discursive emplacement is less a weakness than a testimony to the creative "contamination" that is one of the major energizing forces of contemporary Aboriginal theatre. Ultimately Chi's text enacts its tensions and contradictions with untrammeled optimism for a future that embraces Aboriginality itself, however it might be defined, as an essential and ideologically enabling costume for the wardrobe of all colonized Australians. In this hope, utopian though it may be, *Bran Nue Dae* is indeed "a play to ease the pain."[23]

De-scribing Orality

A focus on the performative structures of Aboriginal theatre also inevitably opens up the possibility of challenging the tyranny of the written word on which imperial history (and governmentality) depends. Since oral cultures do not have the kinds of archival "documents" or "texts" that European culture privileges with authority, they have been written out of history or at best categorized as underdeveloped and primitive. Such categorization, Craig Tapping argues, "justifies the subordination of non-European peoples wherever literacy has confronted orality, an encounter always already predetermined by the power which literate culture derives from failing to recognize the full humanity of its antagonist" (1989, 89). Theorists have seldom been slow to identify language as a potential site of resistance in post-colonial literary texts, but they have frequently ignored the problematic status of "literature" itself (as opposed to performance) in cultural decolonization. Without wanting to devalue the poetry and prose works that, through their rhetorical and/or linguistic codes, interrogate the hegemony of literate expression and situate themselves outside its conventional discourses, I would argue that even the most carefully transcribed and annotated oral narrative can never fully approximate a preliterate text. Theatre, on the other hand, allows the orality of oral cultures to be partially realized; it restores to the myths and yarns of indigenous cultures their topology as performance pieces, and in doing so dismantles the forms and conventions, and hence the ideologies, of imposed narrative structures.

Indigenous writing in Australia—the term is used here to include the wider body of texts that currently circulate under the sign of Aboriginal "literature"—insists on the validity of nonliterate representation. Most often, the least literate characters are the ones endowed with the most authority. As orators/storytellers in constant dialogue with the past, they establish a counterdiscourse, often inflected by the words and sounds of tribal languages, that ruptures the integrity of the colonizers' linguistic code and recuperates Aboriginal ways of knowing from the margins of white discourse, establishing them as central to the represented worldview. For the "literary" critic, a problem arises in attempting to define or even name this counterdiscourse without subscribing to the limiting binaries that justify the representation of oral cultures as socially and intellectually inferior to literate ones. Walter Ong, among others, decries terms like *oral literature* that stress the preemptive nature of writing by implying that oral narratives are merely variants of written ones (1982, 11). Such theorists favor the terms *orature, verbal art,* and *oral cultural production,* which I support in principle for their attempts to circumvent hierarchies of value that privilege the literate. This terminology, however, does not completely avoid prejudice, nor does it account for the frequent interplay of oral and written forms. Ruth Finnegan makes an important point when she argues that the "supposed cleavage" between the two has blinded theorists to their possibilities as complementary rather than contestatory modes of communication (1976, 17). I cannot suggest a better name for the specific cultural productions under discussion, but I would argue that drama has long enacted the intertextuality of oral and written forms, and that well before Roland Barthes announced the "death of the author," drama praxis clearly recognized the deauthorizing function of performance. Because each performance text defers and deflects the authority of any written version, drama offers the most enabling context for the recuperation of specifically oral forms of communication in the process of forging postcolonial voices. Performance further provides a space in which naming the specificity of oral discourse becomes less important than vocalizing it. This *de*-scripted (performative) model of orality is by no means new, but it does seem to have been largely overlooked in the growing body of criticism on indigenous texts.[24] Such a model refers not to a text that has never been written, but to one that is *unwritable* at its moment of enunciation. This provokes us to consider the idea of orality and the "unwritable" in terms of Jacques Derrida's work. Although Derrida makes an important point in arguing that language "implies an originary writing" in the sense that signification is inscribed through the senses in a space that is exterior to thought (1976, 52), his valorization of the idea of writing does not take into account the differences between visual and aural signs, nor does it consider writing's political and cultural effects on the oral. In claiming that "oral language already belongs" to writing (1976, 53), Derrida is surely speaking from the perspective of the literate for whom speech is irrevocably linked to its hypothetical visual transformations in writing.

Postcolonial critics have speculated much about the ways in which orality informs the narrative structures and discourses of texts written by literate members of Aboriginal cultures. Tapping (1989) and Arthur (1989) focus on narratives that, through linguistic innovation and structural repetition, evoke notions of performed speech or storytelling. In a related endeavor, Muecke and others have been intent on finding an appropriate medium for the packaging of oral texts for consumption in book form. Muecke wisely locates his interest in the "relation between [the] epistemology and conditions of production" of such books (1988, 48) and makes no claim to reproduce a verbal text with "authenticity." While these theorists are careful to acknowledge the problematic status of the *native informant* (Spivak's term, 1986, 229) and the mediating function of the written word, they tend to shy away from closely examining the ephemeral and problematic oral. Most critics writing on Aboriginal drama, on the other hand, seem to take the oral so much for granted that they deem it scarcely worth noting other than to advocate a performative context for its fullest expression, without considering the political effects of this enactment.[25] However, when we listen to what Aborigines themselves say about orality, performance emerges as fundamental to the ongoing process of de-scribing empire. Jack Davis, for example, points to theatre's facility for verbal improvisation, humor, and irony, along with nonverbal narrative techniques such as mime and dancing, all of which have traditionally been part of his culture (see Chesson 1988, 190–211). Mudrooroo stresses as well the social manifestations of theatre for the representation of Aboriginal identities (1990, 117–29), while both artists share a concern with the spatial locations of oral enunciation, and the dislocation of voice that has resulted from European imperialism. To discuss the political effects of the oral in drama, I want to turn to some of these factors in examining who speaks, for whom, and under what sociocultural conditions.

Language itself is obviously paramount in the articulation of hitherto muted[26] indigenous voices, and it is now widely accepted that the appropriation and abrogation of the colonizers' linguistic codes are essential to post-colonial writing. Like their literary counterparts, Aboriginal performance texts have incorporated these processes in varying degrees by using words (indigenous and creolized), syntax, and grammar that differ from those of standard English. Kevin Gilbert's *The Cherry Pickers,* initially performed in 1971 and regarded as the "first Aboriginal play" in the European sense, makes a point of "bastardising" (Gilbert's own term) conventional English beyond the limits of the purely colloquial by using neologisms such as "tremendaciously," "rememberising," "kunstidonus," or "amphiskkulus" to satirize the pretentiousness of "white-speaking" Blacks and to signal the inappropriateness of English to an Aboriginal context. This strategy is not specific to drama; what is specific, and particularly empowering, are the possibilities for enunciating such discourses orally and with recognizably Aboriginal inflections. Aspects of speech like tonality, diction, rhythm, and accent are clearly important performative tools here, as are associated metalinguistic features. *Bran Nue Dae,* for example, makes abundant use of such devices to produce a distinctive oral text that resonates with the sounds of alter/native languages. Opportunities for individual characters to articulate multiple identities abound in this play, which uses different *voices* for dialogue, storytelling, and singing. Some of its most politically humorous moments also arise from the deployment of voice. Willie's aping of Father Benedictus as the mission boys raid the school tuckshop is a case in point: "Yah it is gut to eat at der Lord's table. First ve haff made un inwentory of der spoils. Den ve haff to partake of der fruits ov our labours.

Thankyou Lord!" (Chi and Kuckles 1991, 7). Although I cannot recreate the specificities of the performances I attended, this quote perhaps gives some idea of how accent might be used subversively to produce colonial mimicry, which, as Bhabha has shown, "is at once a mode of appropriation and resistance" that reveals the ambivalence of colonial discourse and turns the "insignia of its authority [into] a mask, a mockery" (1985a, 103).

Plays by Jack Davis, Bob Maza, and others introduce substantial dialogues in Nyoongah and Boandik, with minimal or no glossing, in attempts to recuperate Aboriginal languages as viable codes of communication. Because these languages are performed rather than inscribed, they proclaim radical alterity in a context where non-Aboriginal audience members can neither "look up" the meaning nor quite imagine how such words might be scripted. If, as Ong suggests, the literate mind's "sense of control over language is closely tied to the visual transformations of language" (1982, 14), this alterity, which prevents the seamless lamination of writing to the oral, enacts an important mode of resistance for oral cultures against the hegemony of literate ones. Bill Ashcroft's discussion of unglossed foreign languages in the written text illuminates this point.

> Signifiers of alterity are not necessarily inaccessible; rather they explicitly establish a distance between the writer and reader functions in the text as a cultural gap. The gap of silence reaffirms the parameters of meanability as cultural parameters, and the language use offers its own hybridity as the sign of an absence which cannot be simply traversed by an interpretation. It directly intercepts notions of "infinite transmissibility" to protect its difference from the incorporating universalism of the centre. (1989a, 72)

The oral text, I would argue, politicizes the signs of absence enacted through indigenous language usage even further by intensifying the ambivalent "fear and desire" responses that codes of difference evoke in a majority audience. Whereas a reader will rarely read or sound out each word of an unglossed text, preferring simply to skip over to the familiar, an audience member experiences difference in complicated ways. On the one hand, aural signifiers, along with gesture and facial expression, make meaning more tantalizingly accessible and thus attach a promise of some understanding, and hence control, to the effort required to decipher the foreign. Nevertheless, at the same time, the verbal mode of communication conjures an Other that occupies theatrical time and space through a series of implosive sounds that cannot be ignored or fully appropriated.

The articulation of oppositional voices also raises the problem of translation, which is further complicated when one attempts to describe or enact a performative mode in a written text. As Anne Freadman argues, translation serves to "make a text heard in a language not its own, to represent that text under an alien law" (1992, 264). It is therefore important to ask what this process silences and what it allows to speak. Louis Nowra's *Capricornia* (1988)[27] invalidates the translating of Aboriginal texts by illustrating the comic effect of the reverse process when Tocky, his part-Aboriginal protagonist, "translates" the Bible into an oral performance in pidgin for her classmates while her teacher reads in a flat voice.

> *Mrs Hollower:* "And the Philistine said unto David, 'Am I a dog and thou comest to me with staves?' "
> *Tocky:* The Philistine was a mongrel.
> *Mrs Hollower:* "And the Philistine cursed David by his gods."
> *Tocky:* He told him to fuck off.
> *Mrs Hollower:* "Then said David to the Philistine, 'Thou comest to me with a sword, and with a spear, and with a shield . . .' "
> *Tocky:* He had sword, nulla nulla and woomera.
>
> (1988, 31)

This quote only begins to suggest the subversive possibilities in such a scene; more striking in dramatization are the particular inflections of a pidgin dialect and the rigidity of Mrs Hollower's voice and stance as opposed to the fluidity of Tocky's. As she translates, Tocky incorporates more and more gestures into her narrative until finally it becomes a full-blown carnivalesque performance when she "mimes cutting off [Goliath's] head and shows it to the crowd, strutting as would David" (1988, 31). Mrs Hollower intervenes at this point and her comment that Tocky's translation is "more than sufficient" is an uncomfortable recognition of the subversive power of the mode of excess created in the performance.

What Mrs Hollower objects to most is Tocky's overliteral enactment of a text that largely derives its authority and "truth value" (in the Foucauldian sense) from the historical contingency of its closure in written form. For Tocky, however, translating involves more than simply substituting one linguistic code for another. The differences between the two narratives can be discussed according to Émile Benveniste's notions of *histoire* and *discours* (1970),[28] though these terms should not be set up as absolute binaries. Mrs Hollower's reading, which avoids interpretive nuances, attempts to abstract the narrative from any enunciative context, and to suggest that meaning is fixed in the priority of language. Tocky's performance, in contrast, foregrounds the role of the interlocutor and the specific context of utterance in the creation of meanings unfixed in *discours.* Aware of her audience (both onstage and in the auditorium) and her own position as entertainer, she undermines the agency of Mrs Hollower's *histoire* by refusing to represent the story symbolically or take its supposed message seriously. While Mrs Hollower concludes that "the word of God requires no translation" (Nowra 1988, 31), Nowra's text makes a completely different point: that translation is never a neutral act but a political one that involves operations of power, usually of the translator over the translated.

The proselytizing activities of missionaries are represented in many indigenous plays as similar confrontations between *histoire* and *discours,* the former usually claiming authority through writing, the latter most often pertaining to speech events. Ruby in Merritt's *The Cake Man* also "translates" the Bible's content and reworks its forms so that the word of God is transmitted through oral storytellings rather than liturgical readings. Though less overtly theatrical, this process also establishes what Bhabha calls "partial knowledges" through a splitting and doubling that undermines the authority of colonialist discourse (1985a, 102). While preserving the priority of writing in the Bible's "paradigmatic presence" as truth, Ruby's appropriation of "the word" neatly "empties [that] 'presence' of its syntagmatic supports," in Bhabha's terms (1985a, 102), by replacing the codes, conventions, and cultural associations of a particular written event with those of a distinctively different oral one. The resultant hybrid text, when scrutinized by Ruby's husband, Sweet William, reveals its problematic relationships with the truth value of both "blackfella yarns" and "gubba books." Informed by both modes of communication, Ruby's story resists claiming authenticity or unproblematic origin for either narrative.

In performance contexts, the truth, if any, is in the telling. By offering a wide range of potential articulations, dramatic texts amplify the splitting and hybridization of dominant discourses. The acoustic variability of actors' voices and the specific spaces in which they resonate become significant sites of meaning. In particular, irony, mimicry, and ambivalence, key linguistic strategies in postcolonial texts, can be inflected in diverse ways in performance. Discord, harmony, synchronicity, simultaneity, and other auditory signifiers also offer possible ways of creating a performative heteroglossia that demonstrates the dialogic interactions between voices that Bakhtinian theories outline (see 1981, 262 and passim). Hence, whereas indigenous *writing* has been termed necessarily *double-voiced* since it "must partake of the colonizing discourses in the process of literary decolonization" (Arthur 1990, 24), Aboriginal *drama* could more appropriately be called voluntarily *multivoiced.*

In its multiple dissembling of axiomatic meanings, performance also opens up the possibility of enacting silence as a viable vocal mode of expression. As one of the framing devices for *The Cake Man*'s mission narrative, silence is the Aborigines' audible response to the colonizing moment when three white men attempt to "civilize" a tribal family by proffering the Bible. The Aborigines' mute rejection of the "gift" can be interpreted as an active protest against imposed languages, as can the increasingly frequent Pinteresque pauses in Sweet William's epilogue to the play. In performative contexts, silence enacts more than a problematic absence of voice that marks an untraversable gap between Aboriginal and white discourses. Unlike readers who must imagine silence through the words that evoke it, and who then fill this potential gap with plenitude as they read on, an audience experiences silence as a powerful code of speech with its own illocutionary and perlocutionary effects. These emerge through the length and depth of the silence in the specific spaces of its enunciation, through its tenor in relation to the volume, tone, and intent of the speech that circumscribes or interrupts it, and through the gestures and postures of the silent. And since an audience will normally respond to silence with more of the same, amplifying the initial presence/absence with multiple echoes, this collective silence marks an unusual chiasma, a moment of discursive conjunction of Aboriginal and non-Aboriginal voices that is both democratic and anarchic.

In apposition to the silent voices in the initial scene of *The Cake Man,* Merritt begins the mission narrative by reintroducing the father of the tribal family as the particularly loquacious Sweet William, who, in a long monologue or, more accurately, a series of dialogues, alternately adopts the guises of storyteller, singer, biblical interpreter, drunken yarn-spinner, amateur philosopher, and cultural mediator. The effectiveness of these voices, which articulate the rhetoric of a paradigmatic trickster figure, clearly relies on performative contexts and the vocal virtuosity of the actor to convey diverse subjectivities. Hence, although Sweet William initially sets himself up as a tourist's souvenir—the genuine Australian Aborigine—this identity is a "rort" in more ways than one. As trickster, his adoption of different voices can be seen as a series of verbal rorts that are particularly theatrical in the sense that acting always implies deception in the notion of role-playing. This particular brand of "acting up" creates a sense of continually shifting Aboriginal subjectivities that forestalls attempts to fix the actor or character as the reified object of the viewer's gaze.

As well as facilitating multiple enunciations of silence and voice and showing that they can be complementary rather than oppositional modes, the theatre offers a particular space to the disembodied voice. Voice-overs, radio voices, offstage voices, and voices of the dead have been used effectively to indicate the linguistic disjunction between Aboriginal reality and the means available for its expression in white cultural contexts. Writing, itself a form of disembodiment that separates the speaker from his/her discursive context, translates its own absences into a series of visible signs—the script. In performance, however, the disembodied voice is indexical rather than symbolic, and it is fully present at the same time as it points to its speaker's absence. This situation might be seen as metonymic of many Aborigines' experiences in the sense that indigeneity is the marginalized aural sign in European history, the voice whose absence is inscribed by the colonizers as a lack of subjectivity at the same time as its presence insistently demands recognition.

I have outlined the specifically linguistic functions of a performative orality as the endless deferral of the authority of writing, the political intervention in translating processes, and the deployment of culturally inflected voices with which Aborigines can speak their differences, their partialities, and their silences. The results are a Brechtian defamiliarization of language as a transparent signifier and a focus on "voice" itself as a site of contestation. Also important in the performance of oral discourses are the specificities of their enunciative occasions, which will vary according to the actors involved, the spaces in which they perform, and the audiences with whom they interact. In discussing the psychodynamics of orality, Ong stresses what dramatists and directors have always recognized—the importance of contextual signifiers in creating meaning.

> Words acquire their meanings only from their always insistent actual habitat, which is not, as in a dictionary, simply other words, but includes also gestures, vocal inflections, facial expression and the entire human, existential setting in which the real, spoken word always occurs. (1982, 47)

Ong argues that orality relegates meaning largely to context, whereas writing concentrates meaning in language itself (1982, 106). Communication studies and current reader-response theories clearly show that writing as a signifier is not so unproblematic; however, performance does utilize a wider range of semiotic systems in the production of meaning. Many of these systems, clearly influenced by culturally specific artistic conventions, are far too complex to be discussed here, except insofar as they evoke the oral in ways that an unperformed text cannot approximate.

Aural signifiers other than language make an important contribution to the production of a de-scripted orality. Traditional oral narrative makes particular use of tribal music, ritual incantation, and imitations of animal noises, all of which have no appropriate form of notation in writing. Modern Aboriginal plays frequently incorporate these sounds into their texts as the resuscitated elements of indigenous cultures and/or as markers of contemporary identity. Bird sounds, for example, feature in Davis's *Barungin,* which uses the call of the *walitj* (night hawk) as a narrative trope to signal impending death. If, as Roberto Da Matta claims, to ritualize is "fundamentally to dislocate an object from its place" (1984, 214), the ritual and symbolic codings of the *walitj* are amplified in performance by a double dislocation of the bird's call—it is removed from its natural environment and from the bird itself. Muecke's work on Aboriginal oral narrative suggests further links between ritual and the act of imitating—and therefore momentarily transforming oneself into—a bird or animal. He explains that transformations, which are very important to Aboriginal narrative, are "always reflexive (people transform themselves rather than magicians turning people into frogs)," suggesting a worldview "which sees people as being in a permanent relationship with an otherness which is discursively constructed as 'the dreaming'" (1983b, 91). In *Barungin,* the *walitj* confirms the proximity of the spirit world, particularly for those whose deaths are imminent. Invisible yet insistently present in the play's aural text, and paradoxically visible in the transformed presence of the person who imitates the bird's call, the eerie screech of the *walitj* constructs a contextual framework that demands that "symbolic statement" be read alongside "gritty realism" (Mudrooroo 1989a, viii).

Music, as a cultural signifier, tends to be more open in Aboriginal plays. While clapsticks and the didgeridoo frequently inform the structure of corroborees and other rituals, these instruments can also be used ironically to trap the tourist dollar, as Peegun's busking routine in *Barungin* shows. Music created or consumed in secular life is often depicted as largely syncretic in form. In Davis's *Kullark,* as Christopher Balme has pointed out (1990, 408–9), enculturation is shown to be at work when country and western music forms a dissonant accompaniment to the narration of a Dreamtime story. But it is problematic to assume that musical forms are generally transported from one culture to another with all of their ideological apparatus intact. Using Hugh Webb's concept of ideotones, Mudrooroo argues that Aborigines frequently appropriate non-Aboriginal music and adapt it to their own purposes. Ideotones are audio-narrative units that suggest "conjunctions that occur in the word/music nexus. They affirm or challenge the apparent unity of the dominant ideological discourses playing at any one time" (1990, 67).

Subtitled *A Musical Journey, Bran Nue Dae* voices precisely this kind of ideotonal subversion even while its music seems, on one level, to disarm the oppositional tenor of the text. Using catchy tunes and pleasant rhythms in ironic apposition to lyrics that voice less than mellow protests against European colonization, the play provides a sustained challenge to the hegemony of conventional forms of the Broadway musical. Singing is enacted in Aboriginal dialects, in English, and in a special blend called "Broome kriol," while the musical score draws rhythmic inspiration from such disparate sources as country and western, calypso, reggae, gospel, blues, and tribal chant to articulate a syncretic mixture of song, sound, and music that reflects the complex genealogies of the characters. In short, the play's music is used to carnivalize genre by appropriating borrowed forms, crossing cultural boundaries and fissuring European notions of aural harmony. It also blurs the distinctions between performer and viewer functions when, consistent with forms of traditional oral narrative, the storyteller, Uncle Tadpole, begins a song in the course of narration and this is taken up antiphonally by the audience, who eventually emerge from the theatre still humming its tune. Taking account of the characters' musical journey from Perth to Lombardina and the play's national tour, the dissemination of its music and lyrics among diverse audiences across Australia could be seen as a kind of song cycle wherein a particular form of Aboriginal artistic expression progresses, song by song, along a given track in the country, creating a dialogue between spaces of cultural representation.

The opportunity to build on speech with movement further revivifies oral traditions and aids the production of Aboriginal subjectivities. Dancing, a powerful index of physicality, as I have argued, also functions at times as a contextual adjunct to voice in the production of orality. The circular rhythms of dance—its repetitions and conscious postponements of telos—parallel conventions of traditional oral narratives. Besides movement and gesture, theatre offers a variety of other resources to augment the enactment of voice and/or create an appropriate mood for storytelling. Finnegan stresses the setting and the function of the actual occasion of enunciation in the detailed content and form of oral narratives (1976, 11–12). Roger

Bennett's recent musical, *Funerals and Circuses* (1992),[29] like other promenade-style plays discussed in this chapter, uses a number of different "real" sites—outside steps, the theatre's foyer, the gallery, the aisles, and of course the stage itself—as "tailor-made" spaces appropriate to the various kinds of oral discourses enacted, including an altercation between an Aborigine and a policeman, a wedding service, a bar-room singsong, and a funeral chant. By implicating the audience in the action, these various enunciative occasions add a dramaturgical complexity to the play's treatment of racism in small-town Australia.

Theatre is not only occasional but also temporal; unlike writing, which remains as residue in between readings and thus announces its own historicity, performance is characteristically ephemeral, latent, potential—a liminal realm governed by the principles of quantum physics. This forces a recognition of the role of the present in constructions of the past, which sets up the dialogic processes that postcolonial texts must engage in if they are to operate counterdiscursively. Aboriginal performance has long recognized that the past is remade in every telling. And even though a performance is a linear event in real time, a movement—no matter how circular—from beginning to end, it allows for the representation of different temporal moments simultaneously, thus bringing into question the "narratability" of the world, or at least opening up the possibility of synchronic histories that are not necessarily bound to any notion of telos. Wesley Enoch and Deborah Mailman's *The 7 Stages of Grieving* (1995) exploits the storytelling mode to convey a range of situations, emotions, and moral/cultural lessons that together provide a panoramic view of Aboriginal life. In this text, grief takes many public forms, communicated variously through fables, songs, chants, stories, and, in one of the play's more chilling moments, a documentary-style account of the death in custody of Murri dancer Daniel Yocke. These fragments of past and present history are presented to the audience by the storyteller (performed by Mailman herself) in a fluid and tightly focused narrative that has continued to change over the period since its first staging.[30]

Performance techniques such as improvisation aid the production of an oral discourse that avoids fixing its trajectory in time and/or space. Anecdotally, Davis tells of a performance of *The Dreamers* in the Sydney Opera House in which two of the younger actors laced the stew with chilis, causing actor Ernie Dingo, the butt of the joke, to add several expletives and a few new lines to his dialogue (see Chesson 1988, 200–203). Different versions of the Koolbardi and Wahrdung (magpie and crow) story in Davis's plays also illustrate how important are skills like extemporization and elaboration in oral narrative. Along with verbal variability, new twists to the story's delivery stress guardianship rather than ownership of oral material and problematize ideas of authenticity and original composition. Hence, as Finnegan argues, performance lessens the split, characteristic in writing, between composition and transmission of narrative forms (1976, 7–9).

Self-referentially, storytelling in theatrical contexts foregrounds the role of the audience in de-scribing orality, as it nearly always situates viewers and/or listeners on the stage as well as in the auditorium. The onstage audience often consists of children and usually shares the culture of the storyteller, emphasizing the alienation of the "real" (mostly non-Aboriginal) spectators. Members of fictional audiences in Aboriginal drama are never passive listeners; they ask questions, interject, comment, and make corrections to performers' versions of stories, further deauthorizing the text. Metadramatic emphasis on the audience also occurs when characters deliberately position themselves as speakers to the larger audience. Davis and Maza, among other Aboriginal playwrights, use white speakers ironically to give historical addresses, implying audience collusion in colonization. Black speech-givers, on the other hand, tend to have a more antagonistic relationship with the audience, which is in keeping with certain kinds of traditional oral expression like fliting (the ceremonial exchange of insults) in which speech is a conspicuously aggressive weapon. In such practices, Ong (following Malinowski) argues, language is more obviously a "mode of action" than a "countersign of thought" (1982, 33).

If "rhetoric . . . is essentially antithetical [because] the orator speaks in the face of at least implied adversaries" (Ong 1982, 111), Merritt's Sweet William is undoubtedly the "classic" Aboriginal orator, a figure who uses public discourses—those of the theatre in this case—for partisan purposes. Though quite humorous, his rhetoric is deliberately designed to unsettle audience members, to make them aware of their prejudices, and to intervene in the illusionistic signifying processes of realist theatre. To a certain extent, his oratory "alienates" Aboriginality, thus exposing it as an ideology that is mapped across the body as a system of beliefs and behaviors. This ideology reflects the dominant group's expectations and status quo as much as any essential Aboriginal identity. Sweet William's disingenuous pose as an "authentic" boomerang-throwing Aborigine, for example, makes the audience complicit in the discourses of tourism, at the same time as it *im*plicitly subverts the voyeuristic conventions of both tourism and theatre.

I have frequently referred to "the audience" in this analysis as if it comprised a homogenous group, which is a gross simplification. Responses to indigenous theatre are likely to differ greatly between Aborigines and whites as well as among class, age, gender, and social groups. I cannot speak for the Aboriginal audience, but I will discuss briefly some important issues that arise à propos the nonindigenous viewer and the institutional frames and/or structures affecting the production and consumption of oral discourses in the context of a commercial venture that is always already marked with the traces of print cultures and European theatrical conventions. If the process of "linguistic capture" has limited what can be said by indigenous peoples since Prospero first taught Caliban "how to curse," the agency of a majority audience has also limited what can be heard, where, and within what contexts. Although I have postulated that the temporality of oral performance resists the priority of writing, there are, however, many other written texts—program notes, reviews, photograph captions, advertisements—that act as authoritative mediating devices in the reception of minority-group performances. Following Van Toorn's arguments, these texts could be categorized as "patron discourses," or "metalanguages" that add value to minority texts by referring them to other sign systems operating in the dominant culture (1990, 109–11), in this case those relating to the conventions of commercial theatre. Van Toorn's concern about these patron discourses focuses on their tendency to situate alterity within dominant "interpretive codes and evaluative criteria" (108); but, as she also points out, such framing devices occupy a politically ambiguous position since they also function as possible modes of empowerment if appropriated by the minority to valorize their own texts (112).

The problem of how orality is articulated and received in the nexus of power through which postcolonial theatre operates can be partly understood in terms of the carnivalesque. Kroetsch argues that "the oral tradition is basic to carnival," that social and political protest occurs through violent ruptures of the laws of language (1989, 100). Carnival rejoices in the hybridizing of forms and languages discussed in reference to Aboriginal performance: the bricolage, the trickery, the fragmentation, the mockery, the collapsing of boundaries that occurs when spaces designated as stage and auditorium become interchangeable. But the freedom that carnival implies is by no means complete or permanent. As Stephen Slemon has pointed out, "the practice of Carnival articulates a double movement of obeisance and transgression" (1988b, 68) in that the purchase it seeks to obtain against hegemony also reveals the limits of its possibility. In the context of contemporary Aboriginal theatre, this double movement is indicative not only of how orality resists imperial inscription but also of how it is inevitably circumscribed by the superstructures of Australian society. The political effects of orality will be located in the interrelationships between these two movements until Aborigines have control over their own means of production of such discourses. Within this system, orality should not be relegated to the realm of the archaized preliterate or seen as a defining Aboriginal characteristic, for that naturalizes the dominance of literacy and keeps the grounds for racism intact. Rather, orality is a practice and a knowledge, a strategic device potentially present in recuperating indigenous voices, potentially effective in de-scribing empire.[31]

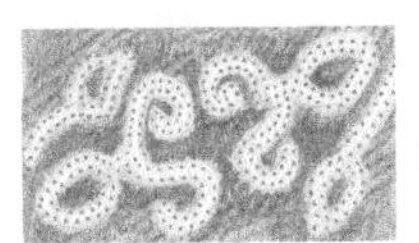

Chapter 3

Settler/Invader Plays

History begins only at the point where things go wrong; history is born only with trouble, with perplexity, with regret.

—*Graham Swift,* ***Waterlands***

For strategic reasons, the idea of a dialectic between colonizer and colonized provides a useful model for banishing imperial history from Australian stages and replacing it with an endless replay of texts and contexts that expresses the imperatives of marginalized cultures. I do not wish to suggest, however, that there is a single colonizing discourse any more than there is a unitary colonized subject. In settler/invader colonies such as Australia, a broad-based application of postcolonial theory must attend not only to the position of indigenous peoples but also to the ambivalent discursive emplacement of the nonindigenous subject who is both colonizer and colonized. Working through Bhabha's concepts of colonial mimicry, Alan Lawson theorizes this settler position as one always already marked by a "dual inscription" of *authority* and *authenticity* that continually frustrates any attempt to formulate a coherent postcolonial subjectivity. In his formulation, the settler experiences colonial authority as a lack of authenticity due to separation from the distant imperial culture that s/he can only mimic. At the same time, the settler exercises authority over the indigene and the land while expressing a desire for native authenticity through a long series of "historical and fictional narratives of psychic encounter and indigenization" (Lawson 1992, 157). This model is very useful for a postcolonial reading of settler/invader theatre since it highlights the epistemological fractures of imperial discourse and calls for the analysis of precisely those ambivalences in and through which settler identity is constituted.

Settler/invader writing is often excluded from the field of postcolonial textuality because, as Stephen Slemon notes, "it is not sufficiently pure in its anti-colonialism, because it does not offer up any experiential grounding in a common 'Third World' aesthetics, [and] because its modalities of *post*-coloniality are too ambivalent, too occasional and uncommon" (1990a, 35). He goes on to argue that this exclusion neglects one of the key projects of postcolonialism: to articulate "the forms—and modes, and tropes, and figures—of anti-colonialist textual resistance, *wherever* they occur, and in *all* their guises" (35). In this respect, writing by subjects ambivalently positioned within and between the binary opposites of colonizer and colonized tends to adopt specific kinds of resistance, and to exert its own particular leverage on the ways in which social and cultural interactions can be conceptualized. However complicit with the discourses of imperialism, the settler/invader subject never acts or speaks with the full authority of the imperial master, nor is s/he located in the same cultural materiality. It is this difference that remains crucial to an understanding of resistance literatures in countries such as Australia, New Zealand, and Canada, where settler and indigenous communities often vie to define the parameters of the recently valorized term, *postcolonial.*

Constructing the postcolonial self can be a fraught process for settler subjects who, having no recourse to alternative systems of knowledge, must nonetheless attempt to recuperate themselves against imperial appropriation or rejection (see Tiffin 1988, 176–77). In the Australian context, escape from the closed narrative of conventional history means reopening windows on a past that is all too often occluded by dominant myths of identity and discourses of nationality. The texts examined in this chapter frequently replay that suppressed past in attempts to come to terms with histories of dislocation, convictism, and oppression of Aborigines. Their historical visions, like David Malouf's revisioned allegory of settlement, tend to be articulated within the semiotic fissures of imperial discourse and are thus marked by the dual inscription characteristic of settler/invader texts. This ontological insecurity should be seen as potentially resistant to, rather than simply complicit with, imperialism's hegemony. Moreover, contra/dictions enable the development of what Slemon calls a "theatre of textual supplementation" (1989, 101) that dislocates old hierarchies without proposing new orders of privilege.

There are, of course, a great number of works in the field of contemporary Australian drama that might come under the very loose descriptor of "settler/invader plays," though many of them are less concerned with postcolonial issues than with articulating nationalist versions of Australian history and culture. John McCallum's list of "history plays" names dozens of such texts, categorized as "Celebrations of the Past" (1987a, 152–53), not to mention the additions to this subset of historical drama in the last ten years. It is worth noting that, David Williamson aside, the playwrights to make a major impact in Australian theatre have tended to be those who have dealt more critically with notions of history and its complex links with subjectivity and discourses about nationhood. This chapter's particular focus texts—by Michael Gow, Stephen Sewell, Louis Nowra, and Janis Balodis—have been chosen to illustrate the broad concerns of a nonindigenous theatre attempting to find stage images for a past/present that reflects the ambivalence of the settler subject. The plays discussed here share with many Aboriginal texts an intense interest in undermining imperial authority, but they articulate that interest in distinct ways. The following analysis outlines some characteristics of the performance and reception of these "mainstream" plays by focusing on their (re)constructions of history, landscape, and the postcolonial body.

Monumental Moments
The Bicentennial Plays

Australia's 1988 Bicentenary represented a specific drive toward historicity insofar as it attempted to fix origins (in 1788) for the ideological construct of "Australia" and to celebrate a sheer passage of time (two hundred years) as the temporal coordinate of the nation's story of growth and development. Bob Hodge and Vijay Mishra argue that underlying this celebration was an "acute anxiety at the core of the national self-image and an obsession with the issue of legitimacy" (1991, x), an observation that can be amply supported by a study of Australian culture in 1988. But as Simon During notes, despite the "explosion of populist nationalism, commercialism and Eurocentrism," the Bicentenary offered "a chance for *all* Australians to brush history whether just by being there, or by hating it, or by speaking against it" (1988, 179). It is not surprising, then, that the ideological and rhetorical importance of history as a potent and recurring master narrative in mainstream Australian theatre is nowhere more evident than in the discursive field constituted by and around a number of plays and dramatic events produced and consumed during the year officially designated for the "celebration of [our] nation." This slogan, of course, suggests a monolithic version of Australian history and uses the discourses of nationhood to erase difference. In retrospect, however, it seems that the Bicentenary played an important part in provoking a serious analysis of Australian nationhood that has continued into 1990s debates on republicanism and multiculturalism. Such self-scrutiny can have positive effects for the country's cultural and artistic production, as Patrick Buckridge argues: "Despite all the consensual rhetoric generated by the Bicentenary, and perhaps because of it, the institution of Australian literature [or theatre] may actually in the course of the year have become more sharply aware of its internal conflicts and hierarchies" (1992, 85).

While Jack Davis's *Barungin* represented Aboriginal theatre's critique of the kind of history endorsed by the slogan "Let's celebrate in '88," the most notable non-Aboriginal plays circulated under the sign of the Bicentennial logo included Michael Gow's *1841,* Stephen Sewell's *Hate,* and Louis Nowra's *Capricornia.*[1] These three plays share *Barungin*'s revisionist project in their determination to reveal that Australian history and much of its attendant mythology are founded on a complex web of lies, but Gow and Sewell shift the focus from Aboriginal peoples to colonialism's production of a dystopian settler culture, while Nowra primarily investigates the development of specific racial identities within such cultures at a particular historical moment. The versions of the past presented by these Bicentennial plays are in themselves important countertexts, but as my discussion of Aboriginal theatre has already outlined the ways in which a replaying of marginalized, muted, or silenced histories radically undermines colonial discourse, it is perhaps more instructive to consider some of the contradictions that inhere in dominant histories as well as the metadiscursive features of the plays themselves as dramatic events. This approach involves analysis not only of methods of constructing historical narratives but also of ways of reading them; moreover, it assumes that the "stories" designated as artifacts of the Government's Bicentennial largesse will inevitably be marked by sharper than usual critical response and, more crucially, particular critical expectations.

Of the mainstage plays commissioned for the Bicentenary, *1841,* which roundly condemns utopian myths of nationhood by dramatizing an imagined moment in Australia's suppressed convict history, provoked the most controversy. As Tony Mitchell details in his article "Great White Hope or Great White Hype? The Critical Construction (and Demolition) of Michael Gow" (1989), this was partly due to the ways in which Gow himself had been lionized since the runaway success of *Away* as the most exciting young voice in Australian theatre. If critics anticipated stringent social comment from Sewell and Nowra, they did not expect it from Gow.[2] In the terms of this analysis, however, the more telling reasons for the play's critical failure can be traced to the kind of attitudes expressed by Peter Ward's assessment that *1841* was "definitely not a Bicentennial occasion" (1988, 7) and Michael Morley's implication that Gow had failed to uphold theatrical tradition: "If the aim is to look to the past, why not mount major productions of Louis Esson or the Doll Trilogy?" (1988, 8). At issue here is the "proper" relation between the playwright and history where history encompasses not only a broad narrative of a perceived communal past but, more specifically, constructions of that past perpetuated within particular institutional frameworks—in this case those of theatre itself.

While many reviewers' anxiety about *1841*'s affront to history manifested in disapproval of Gow's subject and style, few seemed willing to examine their own biases or reckon with the political weight of the Bicentenary as a discursive framework. The minority who lauded the play's staging in the Bicentennial year as a subversive act tended, however, to claim that the content itself was not manifestly political,[3] an approach that is equally limiting because it neatly annexes the narrative substance of the theatrical event from all other constitutive frameworks and suggests that meaning is unmediated by modes of presentation and reception. Gow, on the other hand, is quite explicit about how *1841* situates itself within larger debates about history and historiography, and about theatre's role in politicizing relationships between the two. He deliberately wrote "a pageant play gone wrong" (Gow 1992, 125) to attack both Bicentennial discourses and their manifestation through the Adelaide Festival as a premier cultural event targeted toward the "middle of the middle of the middle" of Australian society (1992, 120–21). His project was to challenge history, to present it as a process of selective filtering, and to foreground that he could find nothing "worth theatrically celebrating" at that specific time and place (1992, 123). Like Davis in *Barungin,* Gow was clearly using the occasional nature of theatre to deconstruct, from within, a particular historical occasion—the Bicentenary itself as a form of theatrical pageant or spectacle. This can be a particularly potent strategy, for, as Derrida notes, "the movements of deconstruction do not destroy structures from the outside. They are not possible and effective, nor can they take accurate aim, except by inhabiting those structures" (1976, 24).

On a thematic level, *1841*'s subversiveness seems to stem less from its grim picture of Australia's convict past—after all, a number of Australian narratives have used the iniquities of convictism to establish the innocence and endurance of their protagonists—than from Gow's failure to provide an alibi for white society's willing participation in the brutalities of that past. His antihistorical pageant is clearly about choice as it attempts to locate moments of existential possibility when the march of imperial history might have been brought to a grinding halt: moments when there could have been a revolution, when white Australia could have made different choices. Aside from his message, Gow's antirealist mode is also distinctly subversive, a direct challenge to expectations and disconcerting for critics and audiences accustomed to reading his work according to the conventions of naturalism. Such reading strategies risk textual overdetermination and have the effect of naturalizing particular hegemonies. The play's mode, then, clearly impacts on its subject matter since, as Veronica Kelly stresses, "constructs of the past are complicit with and informed by generic choice" and "cannot be separated from [their] tropes or codes of formal emplotment" (1990a, 132). The few reviewers who recognized the importance of genre approached *1841* as fairy tale or allegory, while Kelly herself makes a convincing argument about its points of generic overlap with early Australian melodrama. Notwithstanding the cogency of these readings, perhaps the most enabling postcolonial discourses of the play stem from its insistent presentation as metatheatre. In their operational modalities, melodrama and metadrama have much in common, for although specific devices such as plays within plays were much more rare during the Romantic era than they have been since modernism pronounced a profound skepticism about the nature of reality, each type of play implies self-conscious theatricality and the active engagement of the audience, something that Gow's play did not get during its initial production in Adelaide.

Within the theatrical infrastructure of the Bicentenary as an overarching event, *1841* institutes multiple theatrical frames designed to subvert or at least to draw attention to Australian history's characteristic tropes. In Aurora's opening address,[4] the play explicitly acknowledges audience expectations, its intention to leave them unfulfilled, and the constructedness of the (alternative) history about to be presented.

> All I have to offer you is a story of defeat. Failure is the only prize I have for you, the only trophy. How can I tell you? Should I give you a list of names, a list of places, of dates? Should I produce a map and point landmarks out to you? How can I explain to you all, sitting here waiting for a story of triumph, a parade of glory, a victorious spectacle? (1988, 1)

Through her emphasis on inventories of names, places, and dates, Aurora points to imperial history's coordinates as the classification of objects, the conquest of space, and the segmenting of time. Moreover, she reveals Australian settlers' complicity with this kind of historiography by speaking in second person to a "you" who is both the audience *at* the play/event *and* the audience *in* the play—a fictional construct (or character). As the muse of history, it is Aurora's task to create a framework that demonstrates that *1841* is as much about 1988 as about the past. Gow forestalls any attempt on behalf of the audience to neatly partition these two temporal moments or read her speech as merely a prologue. Hence, the muse's narrative is interrupted by a soldier who interacts with her on a purely fictional level at precisely the moment when the metafictional frame has become firmly established. This is a technique used throughout the play as Aurora moves between commentator on, facilitator of, and participant in the action. Its implications for the play's reception as a metatheatrical event that problematizes the nature of both reality and illusion (and therefore history) are quite clear, but in case the audience does not recognize his intent, Gow endows the text with numerous other self-reflexive moments when the analogies between theatre and life are explicitly drawn. A case in point is Aurora's comment on a "performance" (not named but understood as the French Revolution) where the world becomes a stage for political acting/action.

> The stage was as big as a battlefield. All the streets were empty because everyone came to see, to take part. Everyone was an actor. Great men played themselves, the crowd played the masses of France. . . . The city was our stage, our country was our play. (1988, 10)

Clichéd though this metaphor might seem, it points to the audience as inevitably implicated in the action; seeing means taking a part, whether in assent or dissent, and the spectator cannot be meaningfully separated from the spectacle. Along with the former actor Knowles's assertion that successful theatre needs "great cities where crowds press and argue, [and] fight to change their histories" (1988, 17), references to the stage as the arena of political action are designed to impress upon us that the revolutionary call—"Aux armes, citoyens"—in the "walkdown" at the end of act 1 is in fact a challenge to the 1988 audience to use the occasion of the Bicentenary to struggle for historical change. *1841* is, as McCallum argues, "a serious play about the 1980s—about the roots of the new materialism and the individualistic cult of greed and the virtue of self-interest" (1989–90, 200).

To demonstrate the limitations as well as the possibilities of the stage as a terrain on which alternative histories might be mapped, Gow inserts another metatheatrical frame into his text: the play within the play. The plot of this internal play signals by satire the repressive ideology of the convict system and thus seems to call for intervention. However, when Aurora abandons her role and transgresses the framework separating the internal play from the external to convert the action into a cry for justice, she finds her performance censored by Knowles.[5] Knowles's betrayal of the ideal of theatre as a site of struggle and his determination to feed his audience "happy lies" or whatever they want (1988, 33–34) reflects once again white Australia's penchant for "strategic forgetting" and the tendency toward a Gramscian hegemony by consent, a process that Gow suggests is endemic to Australian theatre and to nationalist constructions of history. Although Aurora's revolt does attract one convert in Mercy, the external play's action subsequently shows how the forces of pragmatism and/or despair win out. Thus the play within the play functions self-reflexively as a pivotal point when society as a whole in both 1841 and 1988 failed to choose a more humanitarian future.

That Australians have positioned themselves as the passive witnesses of a pageant that unfolds inevitably toward its telos on a neutral stage—the kind of historiographic process Paul Carter takes issue with in *The Road to Botany Bay*—is made abundantly clear during a scene in which three modern tourists enter the narrative, look at gravestones, take pictures, and then dash off to watch the flogging before the convict village closes. These three exemplify Baudrillard's idea of the tourist, who "consume[s] in ritual form" a past that is "necessarily re-enacted as legend" (1990, 63). Yet another metatheatrical frame is invoked here through an emphasis on looking and spectacle. What Gow suggests is that the play of history risks being framed and contained by the photographic image and the kind of theatre (the flogging) that endlessly reenacts convictism's brutalities for the tourist/voyeur. In juxtaposition to the imperial gaze and its historicizing impulses, he presents a different kind of metatext: the never-ending story. This narrative represents Gow's alternative history-as-process (rather than event), not so much in its content as in its form. It shows a way of remembering forgotten and marginalized experiences and a way of exercising choice. As it spreads temporally and spatially into the past and future through its collective construction by characters who are quite aware of their mythmaking, this other metatext suggests that responsibility for the outcomes of the play, and the story/history of the times, rests firmly with the audience.

Although I have privileged a metatheatrical reading of *1841* in order to place emphasis on the spectatorly functions of the play within the context of the Bicentenary, Gow's text can also be read as a neatly developed allegory that presents the journey through the past as a journey into the present (McCallum 1989–90, 201). These two modes of reading the play are complementary, but whereas its metatheatre works largely through metonymic structures, *1841*'s allegory inheres in metaphorical themes. Similarly, the thematics of *Hate,* Stephen Sewell's account of one family's history of betrayal, bitterness, and constant internal conflict invite the application of a much broader parabolic framework, although most reviewers seemed to miss this entirely or were unable to apprehend resonances that reached beyond a political arena grounded in the play's contemporary setting. Peter Fitzpatrick's detailed analysis of Sewell's penchant for metaphor and grand archetype does gesture toward an allegorical reading, but Fitzpatrick locates the Gothic as the primary context for *Hate*'s "confrontation of Innocence with Predatory Evil" (1991, 125) and stops short of examining the prickly question of history, an issue I want to broach using Slemon's pioneering work on allegory as a potentially enabling mode of discourse for the postcolonial writer (and reader).

Slemon argues that in allegory

> signifiers from the world "out there" are semantically fixed to a culturally positioned and historically grounded "master code" or "pretext" that is inherent in the tradition and is capable of acting as a matrix for a shared typology between the sign and its interpreters. In allegory, signs are interpreted as modalities of preceding signs which are already deeply embedded in a specific cultural thematics, and they work to transform free-floating objects into positively identified and "known" units of knowledge. (1987, 7)

Hence, because it reads present events not within their specific context but according to an already given system of knowledge, allegory has functioned within the discourses of colonialism as a mode of appropriation: in Slemon's terms, "if allegory literally means 'other speaking,' it has historically meant a way of speaking *for* the subjugated Others of the European colonial enterprise—a way of subordinating the colonised, that is, through the politics of representation" (1987, 8). This would seem to rule out allegory as a postcolonial reading/writing strategy; however, Slemon goes on to explain that it can become an especially charged site of contestation and counter-discourse. Following Bhabha's theories about the menacing difference implied in the repetition of mimicry, he asserts that because allegory "in saying one thing also says some 'other' thing," it "marks a bifurcation or division in the directionality of the interpretive process" that cuts across imperial tropes (Slemon 1987, 4). In colonized countries, allegories of nationhood (whether expressed as present or past) tend to relocate the received shibboleths of history and to open up new discursive spaces.

Reading *Hate* as a national allegory requires a close examination not only of relationships between personal and public spheres of action but also of how these impact on, and are situated by, a historical matrix. As Sewell himself says of much Australian drama, particularly David Williamson's satiric portraits, when "those accurate, cutting slices of modern Aussie life [are] not integrated into [a] broader notion of history," they become simply "snapshots suspended in air" (qtd. in S. Morley 1980, 19). That the story of Australia's past is the constant supplementary signified of *Hate*'s contemporary narrative is suggested at a number of points. However, I want to begin an allegorical reading of this narrative/history with an analysis of the *meta*historical aspects of the text as explicitly expressed in the final scene when the Truscotts[6] gather for a memorial service to unveil a bust of the family patriarch. In his eulogy to his father, Raymond characterizes John Truscott as someone who upheld the "great pioneering traditions" both in his commitment to his family and to the country as a whole (1988, 104). John is thus worthily labeled "Australian" and inserted into a particular construction of national history that valorizes the various myths attached to that label. But as the play has already given lie to such myths by revealing hatred, self-interest, betrayal, and violence as the structural basis of Australian culture, Raymond's speech becomes remarkable for its blatant fabrications and highly visible absences. The parodic tone established here, a shift in style from the rest of the play, also strengthens the suggestion that the memorial service should be looked at critically. As a discursive event, this service is deeply implicated in the historiographic project because it uses the *processes* of (highly selective) memory, troped as the *facts* of history, to construct a memorial that is then troped as a historical monument. The slippage here from memory to monumental moment (which of course is the building block of conquest narratives) is subtle but clear. The bust of John Truscott thus functions primarily in the allegorical mode because it is a signifier that refers to an anterior method of signification. Such monuments, Slemon argues, work to "legitimise a particular *concept* of history: that is, history as the record of signal events, the actuations of great men upon the groundwork of time and space" (1987, 5). Whereas Raymond's speech reduces history to a system wherein only a "few privileged monuments of achievement, those events and figures measurable in bronze and stone, have the capacity to signify" (Slemon 1987, 5), Sewell's text makes visible this process and so invites our intervention. The great irony is of course that while the bust commemorates John Truscott (or inflates his importance), it also diminishes his physical presence, a point particularly notable within the context of theatre. On another level, the memorial (as event and object) can be seen as a metaphor for the Bicentenary, which was also very much about making monuments to history. Sewell's implication that the viewer should be wary of this process is reinforced by the fact that the memorial service, like Aurora's opening address in *1841,* explicitly constructs the audience as its assembly.

Hate's main action is less overt in its mode of address but equally emphatic in its criticism of Australian society. That the events preceding John's death might also be read as an allegory of empire is hinted at early in the play when Raymond draws Celia's attention to the family's latest acquisition.

> A specially commissioned painting showing the wonders of Ravenswood in all its nineteenth-century glory. Complete with pebbled driveway and horse-drawn chaise. Even the cracks in the oil are fake. It's wonderful, isn't it, what money and vanity will do to give themselves a history they never had. (1988, 4)

Possibly, the painting forms an analogue for the "specially commissioned" Bicentennial play—what the audience seemed to expect from Gow is certainly consistent with this picture—but since Sewell does not extend that metaphor in any significant way during the main action of his text, I will concentrate on the idea, as suggested by Raymond's comment, that Australian history is the intentional narrative of the rich and powerful. In its focus on unveiling the workings of patriarchal power within the family as a correlative of the larger society, *Hate* has much in common with Malouf's *Blood Relations.* Both plays emphasize that the patriarch's will to power is exercised through acquisition of land and property, the surveillance of colonizable Others—in *Hate,* John's hiring of a private detective to report on Celia is a case in point—and the silencing of oppositional voices. Women and Aborigines figure as the most important marginalized groups to be recuperated, but their efforts to speak or act are repeatedly frustrated by the discourses that buttress imperial and patriarchal systems. As Celia says, "I want to live in a country where you're not fed bullshit from morning to night by people who think they know what's good for you" (Sewell 1988, 44). Exposing the lies—the bullshit—at the heart of family relationships is a major project of *Blood Relations* and *Hate,* and each text destabilizes the power of the patriarch by presenting conflicting versions of the truth and showing how it is subjectively constructed to legitimize past action and present intent. But whereas Malouf's text ends with the dispersal of Willy's power, symbolically represented by the scattering of his ashes, Sewell's memorial service "demonstrates how smoothly hierarchies close ranks to preserve themselves" (Fitzpatrick 1991, 132).

The parallels between John Truscott's exploitation of his family and the wider society's exploitation of the land and its Aboriginal people are clearly drawn on a number of occasions by a process of rapid enlargement of the dialogue/sphere of action from the private to the public domain. This is evident in Celia's remark that her father's power stretches from "here" (meaning the family house and even the theatre) "across the land" (1988, 61), and in the implicit rape metaphor that shapes her reply to Michael's question, "What did he do to you?" (83).

> Look at him through the windows: his dark land; his anger. Look at how he scoured his soul, razed it to the ground and scorched it, possessed it like an animal and ridden [*sic*] it till it screamed in anguish. (83)

Here Celia links her own experience of incest (suggested but never confirmed by the text) with the colonizer's violation of the land, an event that is made much more explicit in John's own comments about the imperial enterprise he euphemistically describes as "the job of building a nation" (100).

> Could love have won this land, Celia? Seized it, cleared it, torn a living from it? Could love have butchered its inhabitants and driven its convicts with cudgel and bayonet into the mines and factories it spawned across the land? Hate, Celia, hate is the only constructive emotion. (100)

Ironically, the hatred and violence John initiates through his conquest of woman/the land lead to his own destruction when the hitherto gentle Michael seizes an ax and chops his father to pieces. Through Sewell's choice of weapon and the sounds of chopping that punctuate the action, this grisly murder scene, like the brutal attack on Sullivan in *1841,* resonates with the echo of the settler's ax. John's dying words, "My country . . ." (103), reinforce this allegorical level and present death as his most *public* private moment. By eliding the country's fate with that of its violator, the scene harnesses what Fitzpatrick calls "the horrors of Grand Guignol" (1989–90, 204) to express the trauma of Australian history. The play's dramatic climax illustrates, once again, the thesis that the violence of colonization is apt to recoil on itself.

Within the family/society that is "forced into existence" by the will of people like John Truscott (1988, 101), Aborigines function at worst as the objects of violence and hatred—as exemplified by John's racial slur about "drunken Neanderthals" (64)—and at best as a palpable absence that makes the colonizer's monuments to "progress" (for example, the Truscott family house) a "debauch" of history (96). Like Gow, Sewell is probably wise to inscribe indigenous "presence" in his text through the sign of absence rather than risking tokenism by introducing an Aboriginal figure into what is above all a story of invasion rather than resistance. And although this strategy does not allow Aborigines themselves to speak, other than through silence, Sewell is careful to remind us that the history of Australia resembles a palimpsest written over rather than a blank slate freshly inscribed. He does this by locating the family estate where all the action occurs on the site of an Aboriginal massacre and then using Gothic tropes such as creaking doors, portentous storms, and suggestive shadows to stress that this edifice of white culture has become a "graveyard of dreams" (73) haunted by the ghosts of the slaughtered. If one of the submerged traumas of *1841* is the settlers' destruction of the environment as represented pictorially by the hacked stumps in the loggers' camp of act 2, genocide of the Aborigines is the unspeakable crime that *Hate*'s semiotics seek to foreground. A culture developed through such brutalities inevitably becomes, in Celia's words, "a nation split in two" (65), a political judgment that had particular resonances during 1988 as the pro- and anti-Bicentennial forces were marshaled to debate the meaning of "Australia."

Although Sewell tends to express evil "in terms of grand absolutes" as evidenced by characters like John Truscott (Fitzpatrick 1991, 130), *Hate* presents a complex treatment of polarities and shows that Michael and Celia, though oppressed by imperial patriarchy, are also complicit with some of its discourses. Like Lynch and Mercy in *1841*, they occupy the ambivalent settler position and should not be identified as spokespersons for the Aborigines despite their sympathetic perspectives and their own experiences of victimization. Reading Sewell's play through a second allegorical urtext, Christ's betrayal by Judas in the biblical story of Passover—a framework established at several points in the dialogue and through the action's Easter setting—stresses the idea that a simple Manichaean approach to the question of morality is problematic. *Hate* dismantles Christian mythology, or at least questions its categories by refusing to affirm who is the Christ figure and who the Judas. As Fitzpatrick has already discussed at length the reasons why various characters can and cannot be comfortably cast in such roles (1991, 126–29), I do not intend to speculate on this further; what is important, however, is that everyone in the play has at least the potential for betrayal, and that temptation is the precinct of those with power because those without it have nothing to offer that might seduce virtue. If Christian mythology is an accessory to imperial discourses, as Sewell's overlapping allegorical frames suggest (and as my discussion of Aboriginal texts in chapter 2 illustrates), then *Hate*'s interrogation of biblical tropes contributes to the postcolonial counterdiscursive project by opening "a space on which false clarities of received tradition can be transformed into the uncertain ground of cognitive resistance and dialectical reiteration" (Slemon 1987, 13).

The critics' reception of *Hate* was generally one of cautious praise, and it received much more approbation than many of Sewell's other works. Some reviewers read it as a political play but few of these bothered to comment on its relation to the Bicentenary although, like *1841,* it was especially commissioned for the occasion. Jim Waites is a notable exception here.

> We had to wait until November for someone to create a decent play for the Bicentenary—or at least a gutsy one, that looks the celebrating hordes square in the eye and challenges any presumption that a pat on the back is correctly deserved. (1988, 8)

Others called *Hate* Sewell's "most commercial play to date" (Lateo 1988, 7), an assessment that usually went hand in hand with the label "least political." In fact, Mick Barnes argued that the play was not really political at all, unless the word politics "is taken at its broadest, the manipulation of those around you for personal advancement" (1988, 3). Quite apart from the extraordinary disavowal expressed in this statement, it is difficult to assess how much of the general critical acceptance of *Hate* had to do with its presentation as primarily a straightforward narrative of a family dynasty in crisis, though in my opinion the allegorical frameworks are quite clear. The more recalcitrant critics could thus read the play within naturalist conventions despite the various aspects of the text/production that attempted to militate against such approaches. The role of specific Bicentennial politics in all this becomes even more difficult to define. One can speculate that *Hate* proved much more palatable than *1841* partly because it could be depoliticized to some extent and because most people expected Sewell to criticize the establishment on such an occasion anyway. Perhaps more crucially, since *Hate* premiered late in the year (19 November) and not at a salutary event such as the Adelaide festival, much of the Bicentennial hype that contextualized Gow's play had dissipated from a bang to a whimper, and so it is primarily only with hindsight that Sewell's play has been adequately assessed in that context. But, as Fitzpatrick argues, *Hate* "contributes to the period of national self-assessment not only a disconcerting perception of the motive force which settled the land, but also a complex view of the guilt which might accompany such a perception" (1991, 138). All characters in the text (and by implication each member of the audience as well) must bear the guilt of "walking on the bones that litter this land" because, as Celia argues, although we might not have made such a world, "[our] presence approves it!" (1988, 81).

The imperative to avoid such guilt, one of history's most prominent psychological legacies in the settler/invader cultures, seems the key to understanding why Louis Nowra's *Capricornia* was received as the "brightest star of the Bicentennial" and "a landmark in Australian theatre"[7] that, according to critics like Tim Lloyd, "almost [made] up for the disappointment of those other Bicentennial plays" (1989, 248).[8] Susan Bredow's review is revealing in this respect: "*Capricornia* captures the essence of the white colonization of Australia without being entangled or bogged down in guilt or apology" (1989, 241). Whether or not this is an accurate assessment of the play is arguable; it is clear from a number of critics' comments, however, that *Capricornia* was actively showcased to demonstrate that the effects of colonization could be represented on Australian stages with regret rather than recrimination. Moreover, the play's success was used to justify the special funding given to the arts in 1988 and beyond that to legitimize the Bicentennial Authority itself as a fair and just cultural arbiter. Bob Evans's review reveals this process of co-option quite plainly: "The Bicentennial Authority has finally scored a much needed hit after some of the *theatrical squibs* it has (to its credit) invested in" (1989, 240; emphasis added). What is also evident in Evans's statement is an anxiety about the "maturity" of Australian theatre itself: if a monumental moment could not be found in 1988 to demonstrate that this theatre deserved to be recorded for posterity in the annals of the Bicentenary, then it could be (mis)construed as still locked in some Oedipal struggle and therefore not firmly inserted into postindependence culture or history.

Although I do not wish to detract from the considerable merits of Nowra's play and its engaging production, it seems that the patron discourses of both the Bicentenary and the critical establishment produced a climate ripe to receive a theatrical giant that would relegate the "squibs" to backstage. But why does *Capricornia* allow such co-option, given that Nowra has delivered Australian theatre's most insistent anticolonial critiques in plays such as *Inside the Island* (1980) and *The Golden Age* (1985), and that *Capricornia*'s thematics are quite in line with his overall theatrical project to expose the processes of cultural domination? The answer to this question, I suspect, lies partly in the fact that Nowra was commissioned to adapt Xavier Herbert's prize-winning 1938 novel, and so the play was inevitably constructed as a monument *to* history, especially in a year when numbers had more than the usual quotient of magic.[9] The canonical status of Herbert's novel and the fact that its author was widely seen as a "pioneer" of antiracist literature undoubtedly cemented this process. Reworked for the stage, *Capricornia*'s depiction of an educated Aboriginal man's confrontation with the racist society of Australia's "top end" in the 1930s could silence some of the Bicentenary's critics by presenting marginalized perspectives while at the same time paying tribute to white literary history. It thus fitted very neatly into Belvoir Street Theatre's "Radical Classics" season and into a larger agenda of liberal humanitarian politics.

As Gareth Griffiths suggests, the more subtle reasons for *Capricornia*'s success may stem from the audiences' perceptions that they are confronting racism when in fact they are distanced from it by the play's historical frameworks: "perhaps . . . the theme of *Capricornia*—of *overt* public prejudice against black Australians is now sufficiently dated to be comfortable fare for a 'liberal' theatre audience geared up to indulge in a kind of holier than thou-ism to Australia's past" (1989, 33). This perception is certainly backed by critical commentary, which categorizes the play as a compelling "outback saga" (Barnes 1989, 243) or the portrait of a "barbaric frontier town" (Evans 1989, 240). In other words, the atrocities the play depicts are "out there," distanced by time and space from a metropolitan audience that can thus congratulate itself for having progressed well beyond such barbarism. (This form of dissociation is tellingly absent from reviews of the production in Darwin.) The audience's ability to construct history as "out there" is aided and abetted in Nowra's text by generic factors: despite its episodic structure and satirical dialogue, the play *does* present its Aboriginal protagonists, Tocky and Norman, through predominantly realist modes, and, unlike most of the texts discussed in this study, Nowra's does not explicitly incorporate a metahistorical frame that shows the interpenetrations of past and present. If, as Bhabha argues, "the discourses of historicism and realism manifestly deny their own material and historical construction" (1984b, 97), then *Capricornia*'s theatrical modes can militate against a deconstructive reading. The foregrounding of Tocky and Norman's romance also makes possible a (mis)reading of the play as an Australian version of star-crossed love—Australia's own, albeit rather quirky, *Romeo and Juliet.*

Where then can the more empowering postcolonial discourses of Nowra's play be located? I would argue that *Capricornia*'s emphasis on hybridity produces a theatrical event that celebrates miscegenation to the point of dislodging racism as its central subject. Hybridity, as Bhabha argues,

> displays the necessary deformation and displacement of all sites of discrimination and domination. It unsettles the mimetic or narcissistic demands of colonial power, but re-implicates its identifications in strategies of subversion that turn the gaze of the discriminated back upon the eye of power. (1985a, 97)

This movement diminishes the authority of the colonizers (including the mostly white audience) and augments the power of the colonized by subverting processes that would merely situate Aborigines as *objects* of a plea for racial tolerance. Thematically, the issue of miscegenation permeates the play from the opening scenes, which show passengers on the boat to Port Zodiac determined to sequester Veronica (the "pretty" white girl) from Norman's advances, to the closing moments when Norman himself pontificates about the invalidity of categories such as "quadroon" to describe the products of interracial sex. That miscegenation threatens to radically destabilize imperial order is reinforced by the fact that fears of racial impurity—particularly of white men "going combo" (having sex with black women)—are reiterated at almost every level of the settler society while such discourses are markedly absent elsewhere. If, as postcolonial criticism argues, imperial government was in many ways a government of the self so that *self-control* was a metonym for and the basis of control of the colony, "going combo" points to a crisis in imperialism's regulatory mechanisms. At the same time, a space is opened up for the marginalized to claim some sort of subjectivity within imperial discourse. An entertaining example of this process occurs when Fat Anna reappropriates miscegenation by using Sergeant O'Crimnell's lust for "black velvet" as a way to earn money and obtain privileges. Fat Anna clearly has the upper hand in this sexual economy because she can withhold favors and/or disclose the sergeant's indiscretions if he refuses her the liberties she demands.

The most persuasive argument for foregrounding miscegenation and hybridity as the locus of *Capricornia*'s political engagement with imperialism must, however, refer to the effect of the text in performance.[10] In this context, skin color as a valorized signifier becomes both deeply problematic and at times even ridiculous, especially since the part-Aboriginal protagonist initially presents as the arch-imperialist in his stylish white 1930s suit. Here, Nowra's masterstroke is to use theatre's resources—in this case costume—to invert the usual stereotypes, a process that is paralleled in the dialogue when Norman expresses the worst racial epithets. By dressing Norman to cut an entirely incongruous figure, Nowra ensures that the rhetorical power of costume becomes quite clear while its inferred meaning is, by contrast, muddied. Similar visual ironies that hybridize racial stereotypes result from other instances of "cross-dressing," for example when Tobias smears himself with red ochre or when Tocky dresses up in Marigold's clothes. Such scenes not only challenge our expectations but also widen the disjunctive gap between race and behavior to denaturalize racism by revealing that it is often based on differences that are discursively constructed rather than simply given.

Not only is the stage consistently peopled with characters (and actors) of diverse and "impure" racial lineages, but these characters often appear to be directing the "show." The most obvious example of this occurs when Tocky and Christobel, who are supposed to behave as docile maids at the Mission Compound tea party, hijack the genteel "performance" of Doctor Aintee and his guests with disparaging remarks and a running metacommentary designed to counteract the racist discourses of the diners. Two distinct levels of performance are established here, and through a metatheatrical sleight of hand the good doctor and his proselytizing friend, Mrs Hollower, become objects of an Aboriginal gaze at the precise moment when their conversation on eugenics reveals an intense desire for control over the indigenous body. Tocky's translation of the Bible for Mrs Hollower, which I have already discussed in my analysis of orality, is another such moment that derives its subversive energies from performance. The overall effect of such a dominant Aboriginal presence in a play written by a non-Aborigine for the consumption of mostly white middle-class audiences is the formation of a reconstituted semiotic field in which Aborigines need no longer function as signifiers that refer only to previously constructed theatrical images, a paradigm that Terry Goldie claims is the informing mode of colonial theatre in settler/invader cultures (1988, 60). Here, as elsewhere in Nowra's work, representation of marginalized peoples is complex and eclectic, resulting in characters who seem legitimate speakers for their societies. And while Norman might bemoan being "made out of bits" like "the monster in Doctor Frankenstein" (1988, 91), Nowra's dramaturgy ultimately celebrates the existence of such hybrids. In this respect, *Capricornia* may well have been the "landmark" in Australian theatre history that the Bicentenary and its pundits sought, not because it seemed to do justice to a classic text but precisely because it went some distance toward interrogating the processes of textual containment implicit in two hundred years of literary and theatrical tradition.

Cartographies
Stagescape/Landscape

While the Bicentennial plays expose a national amnesia characterizing attitudes toward the past, they also suggest that landscape can function as an aid to mnemonics. This idea is powerfully expressed in *Hate* by Sewell's image of Australian society as an uneasy alliance of people destined to bear the guilt of walking over a country littered with bones (1988, 81). The specter of a haunted (and haunting) landscape emerges even more clearly in Louis Nowra's *Inside the Island* and Janis Balodis's *Too Young for Ghosts* (1985),[11] two earlier plays that detail settler responses to an alien land and its indigenous inhabitants. Like David Malouf's *Blood Relations,* these works can be seen to enact a version of the Haitian Ceremony of the Souls, which, as George Lamming explains, entails a dialogue between the living and the dead whereby revenge, guilt, and forgiveness actively reform the present and make possible a redemptive future (1960, 9–10). In the Australian context, this "ceremony" necessarily involves opening up a dialogue with suppressed Aboriginal voices, a process, as Nowra and Balodis suggest, that begins with rethinking dominant conceptions of nature and land ownership. Hence both plays reject the Romantic impulse toward pathetic fallacy and present the landscape not as a metaphor for human attitudes or psychological states but as a palpable force that shapes human experience. This is a common feature of Australian literature and film, as Graeme Turner has amply demonstrated, but whereas most of the writers Turner examines proscribe versions of nature—usually hostile and intransigent—that function to limit personal endeavor and celebrate mere survival as the authentic national myth (1986, 36–37), Nowra and Balodis directly interrogate such myths and the alternative histories thus occulted. Their plays effect a postcolonial deconstruction of imperial history (and geography) by revealing that the land is "an object of discursive and territorial contention" (Seaton 1991, 87) as well as an "accumulative text" that records in multiple inscriptions the spatial forms and fantasies of both settler and indigenous cultures.

Since space is the grammar not only of landscape (Butler-Adam 1986, 24) but also of the mise en scène, a focus on the spatial structures of *Inside the Island* and *Too Young for Ghosts* reveals aspects of each playwright's approach to theatrical representation itself. Both Nowra and Balodis have indicated an explicit interest in the interrelatedness of character, landscape, and stagescape,[12] which suggests a conception of space consistent with Darko Suvin's model of heterogeneity as the topological paradigm of theatrical representation (1987, 322). The following analysis identifies strategies used by each dramatist to intervene in the segmentation and hierarchization of space that facilitates colonial appropriation of the landscape. Extending Michael Issacharoff's account of space and reference in theatre, a theory that relates dramatic meaning to the tension between *per*ceived (mimetic) and *con*ceived (diegetic) space, I focus on ways in which the dismantling of boundaries and frames allows the production of fractal spaces that are multidirectional and unbounded by time. In Nowra's version of settler society, this effect is achieved primarily through an irruption onto center stage of spaces and actions previously confined to areas beyond the frame of imperial history. Balodis, following a slightly different tack, envisions settlement as always already implicated in a continuum of overlaid and interactive spaces that dissolve all such frames.[13]

Using Macherey's theories of literary production, Veronica Kelly describes Nowra's imagistic theatre as making explicit the idea of the text as a "haunted work" that leads back to the histories informing it (1992b, 51–52). For the purposes of this analysis, it is possible to regard the landscape as a haunting device that renders visible the European inscription of colonial space. In such a model, rather than simply indicating a reality that might be decoded in structuralist terms, the semiotics of the stagescape function as part of a system of mnemonic representation through which are negotiated signifiers of past and present, of person and place, and by implication, of self and Other. As Kelly notes,

> All Nowra's plays "remember" by allusion and by revisionary reenactment. It is as though the survivors of historical cataclysms are enforced to replay, as an eternal consequence, fragmented versions of the repressed originary trauma until these can be incorporated into some new kind of future—a future containing the potential of creative reassembly and appropriation of the inherited imperial codes into enabling rather than disabling metaphors. (1992b, 55)

That *Inside the Island* "remembers" Australia's participation in a number of imperial wars, notably Gallipoli and Vietnam, is already well established.[14] Kelly's detailed reading of the play alongside the "Pozière's" chapter of Gavin Souter's *Lion and Kangaroo* (Kelly 1987a, 101–5) reveals many close similarities between the apocalyptic landscape described in Souter's account of the 1916 Somme offensives and that created by Nowra's dramaturgy, so I do not intend to follow that tack here. What I will take up through an analysis of the spatial structures of the play is her suggestion that perhaps the play's most vividly remembered war is the only one not fought elsewhere: "the war for the land itself" (1987a, 105).

The title of *Inside the Island* points to encirclement as the play's central spatial metaphor, a concept that is embedded in the performance text by Nowra's use of the offstage area—what Hanna Scolnicov calls "the theatrical space without" (1987, 14)—to construct a realm of disruptive forces that percolate through the visible action and eventually engulf the onstage area to create a savage and confrontational portrait of settler society. The overall effect is that of a garrison under siege with the characters, and indeed the spectators, inside looking out, trapped within systems of enclosure that show a spatial congruence with the structures of convict society: "The garrison and the prison articulate, at the furthest reach of empire, a concept of power and authority that can only be understood in terms of the whole system of historical reference" (McDougall and Whitlock 1987, 22). In *Inside the Island,* this system operates on a number of levels so that the island-garrison is not only a remote settlement grafted onto land previously owned by tribal Blacks but also "metaphorically Australia" and "the island of individual consciousness" (Kelly 1992b, 52). At all levels, the island as a geographical, historical, and psychological space resonates with the ambivalences of the settler/invader culture, demonstrating the "dialectic of place and displacement" that is a feature of postcolonial societies (Ashcroft, Griffiths, and Tiffin 1989, 9). If David Malouf's "edge" is Prospero's island refigured by hybridity and creative contamination, Nowra's garrison is the island *dis*figured by solipsism and violence. It seems inevitable, then, that the structures designed to keep at bay the landscape and its associated (counter)texts will eventually implode from within and/or be dismantled from without. Kelly views this fate as the consequence of an "incursion [of history] which must necessarily be catastrophic in order to counteract the energy required for its suppression" (1992b, 52).

Mrs Dawson's description of the "pioneer" moment illustrates quite lucidly that the garrison mentality is linked to settler imperatives to annihilate all signs of difference.

> My father built [this house] forty years ago. He was a great man. When he first came here it was just bush—a huge plain of Aboriginals and gum trees. He got rid of the blacks, except for those whom he converted; removed the gum trees. (Nowra 1981, 24)

In one smooth gesture, the Aborigines and the landscape are constructed as a composite threat, a wilderness in need of order via the "cultured" hand of

Europe. Similar rhetorical tropes are evident in David Collins's record of the First Fleet's settlement at Port Jackson.

> After a time order gradually prevailed everywhere. As the woods were opened and the ground cleared, the various encampments were extended, and all wore the appearance of regularity. (Qtd. in Gibson 1992, 6)

It is this sense of colonial droit du seigneur toward the landscape and its inhabitants that *Inside the Island,* like Gow's *1841,* aims to question. While Mrs Dawson dismisses any notion of resistance to the European *landnama,* Nowra's theatre shows quite a different story when the feared dissipation associated with the bush erupts among the soldiers on the cricket ground—a space that has functioned for centuries in far-flung reaches of the British Empire to inculcate "civilized" values through rituals related to gentlemanly demeanor, particular attire (white and well-covering), and good sportsmanship. Significantly, the cricket pitch, a key site of spatial conflict, is not directly shown, which makes its subversion all the more uncanny. The incursion of disruptive forces into an arena of visible action is signaled theatrically by a shift in focus from conceived to perceived space so that what is discursively constructed as offstage, "out there," beyond the spectator's view, and mediated by dialogue, rapidly moves onstage, "in here," and sensually accessible. This phase of the action is marked by the complete breakdown of social, spatial, and temporal boundaries. Even the river proves ineffective as a natural barrier to the bushfire's spread. As the inferno rages and the soldiers wander, spiritlike, over the blazing land, their fate is elided with that of the Aborigines whose camp ground was usurped to build the cricket pitch. Gareth Griffiths lucidly interprets this overlaying of space and time as the compression of time/history into one apocalyptic moment: "Like manic spirits released into a Dreamtime of nightmare, [the soldiers] create a startling image of a past, present and future merging into a single continuous action" (1984, 47).

Tensions between indoor, outdoor, and transitional spaces are also a crucial element of *Inside the Island*'s setting. Aside from the opening scene, which is tonally congruent with the Gothic nightscapes of the latter half of the play, the action moves in a broad sweep from the relatively safe confines of the Dawsons' living room through a number of ambiguous spaces that I term *verandahs*—the verandah itself, the *rear* of the church, *outside* the mill, and the *edge* of the cricket ground—before becoming concentrated in the open fields. Like the boundaries that Paul Carter identifies as corridors of possible dialogue with their own significant narratives (1987, 165), these verandahs are perhaps the most enabling sites of negotiation because they mark the interface of nature and "civilised" culture. On the verandah, anything can happen, as Nowra's text illustrates on numerous occasions with contained but significant undercuts of imperialism's civilizing mission. These occur, for example, when Lillian is forced to abandon her croquet game with the Rector because the cows have broken into the churchyard and left a mess, and when her reading lesson with Andy is abruptly curtailed after her recalcitrant pupil climbs a tree and sheds his clothes.

The strictly hierarchized areas of the Dawson homestead reveal the settler's persistent and futile effort to exert control over alien space and keep indigenous forms of nature safely "out there." This concern with space as a marker of difference is a common characteristic of colonial society, as Gail Ching-Liang Low argues in her analysis of nineteenth-century Anglo-Indian urban development.

> The obsession with walls, detachment and spaces-in-between signals a fear, an imagined pressure from the native quarters, whose bodily secretions and metaphoric productivity threaten to run riot, and spill over established boundaries. Lines of demarcation were also lines of defence. Compounds and walls in Anglo-Indian residences function both as a picturesque frame and as a visual bulwark against undesirable outsiders. Dress, language, behaviour, the collection of objects in the house, and the cultivation of a garden offer the occupants a comforting set of references which help secure the community's links with their cultural origins. English gardens, for example, were a sustained attempt to inscribe a leisured pastoral ideal of Englishness in a foreign land. (1996, 163)

Low's description fits the Dawson homestead only too well. Reference to Lillian's conservatory, which houses the "famous" indoor fuschia garden, outlines the controlling gesture of settlement quite clearly and also undercuts it through satire. Nowra introduces the conservatory to present a critique of Lillian's sanitized and boundaried lifestyle[15] and to foreshadow a fear of contagion, which emerges as her salient concern later in the play. Significantly, the indoor garden, like the tidy green landscape of England that Lillian so admires and the cool white snow of the Victorian border country that captures George's fancy, remains in the realm of diegetic or imagined space. What we do see on stage most often is the dense yellow heat of the wheat fields, which is eventually dissipated only to be replaced by a blackened landscape and charred ruins. This particular visual composition strikes a much more familiar, if unsettling, chord in an Australian audience. The Anglophile Mrs Dawson, in contrast, presents a highly incongruous spectacle most of the time, a point underlined by the play's costuming codes when she insists on dressing herself and her daughter in clothes entirely unsuitable for the local landscape and climate (see fig. 9).

While *Inside the Island* seems on the surface to imply that either conquest or capitulation is the necessary outcome of the settler's confrontation with alien space, there is in fact a third option, accommodation, hinted at through characters like Peter. This option, however, is predicated on alternative spatial epistemologies and a recognition of the landscape's potential to resist the imperial gaze, a facility established early in the play and intensified as events unfold. In the opening scene, for example, George draws attention to the horizon to impress upon Peter the expanses of his empire, but his panoptic and totalizing gaze is immediately undermined by a number of textual and spatial ironies. The horizon, as Foucault notes, is a strategic as well as a pictorial notion (1980, 68); it produces a framework that delimits space and thus renders it under control. At the same time, however, the horizon is an unstable marker of proximity or distance since it is always produced in relation to a movable viewpoint positioned outside the landscape surveyed. George's gesture of appropriation is therefore ambivalent and even impotent, a point underlined by his own disorientation vis-à-vis the landscape/stagescape and by Peter's hitherto undetected hut, a powerful sign of trespass. But the most telling challenge to George's authority over the land emerges in performance, where the diegetic space created by his invitation to look as "as far as [the eye] can see" is modified by the mimetic space of a stage in near darkness where perception is actually quite limited. Nowra's technique of producing a dramatic space radically in question becomes even more pronounced in the latter half of the play when the soldiers become deranged after eating ergot-infected flour. Some present as threatening figures that seem to fade in and out of a darkness that refuses enclosure and frustrates clear spatial perception, while others are thrown into visual relief by the light of background fires. These silhouettes actually contract the perceived depth of field by eliding foreground figures with the horizon to suggest a two-dimensional image. Then in the final moments of the bushfire, the play completely dispenses with the Cartesian separation of the spectatorial subject and the distant object of its sight—the usual paradigm of theatrical as well as imperial looking—when sounds of fire engulf both stage and auditorium.

Fig. 9. Mrs Dawson and the rector, *Inside the Island,* Nimrod Theatre, 1980. (Photo: Peter Holderness.)

> A sudden brilliance is seen, then a sudden blackout. The noise of the fire grows unbearably loud in the darkness as if the audience is going to be swallowed up by it; then it stops abruptly. (Nowra 1981, 87)

In this environment, imperial methods of "reading the country" (and the performance) are continually undermined because the viewing subject is no longer "discretely positioned at a central and superior vantage point, separate from and having command over the totality that is observed" (Ferrier 1990, 38).

To counterbalance the foreshortened horizon created through the night scenes and threatening fires, Nowra often elongates space by using the offstage area to extend the dramatic action well beyond the boundaries of the visible stage. This technique also disrupts the imperial gaze by conjuring vast reaches of landscape in excess of what can be framed and contained by the roving eye. Ironically, colonization itself is partly responsible for the strong feelings of isolation and even agoraphobia induced in many of the characters by the seemingly endless wheat fields, "an export monoculture displacing the original landscape" (Kelly 1992b, 50). In the face of such monotonous stretches of land, the structures designed to make settler society cohere are easily broken down. A case in point is the dwindling church attendance, which Mrs Dawson suggests is a result of sheer distance: "There's so much space out here that it's very easy to lose a sense of proportion" (Nowra 1981, 47). Overwhelmed by space, the settlers experience increasing disorientation when civil disorder erupts and all sense of proportion is indeed lost. Nowra employs a haunting soundscape to intensify this spatial vertigo when, as various characters continue their frenzied search for loved ones amid the carnage, their cries commingle to form a chorus of repeated names that only illustrates a futile attempt to counteract the nightmarish landscape with an assertive human presence. The penultimate scenes of *Inside the Island* chart the disintegration of the colonial body, whereby alien space is internalized as madness and boundaries between the self and the land are interrupted and broken down, movements potently imaged through Private Higgs's hallucination of roots growing through his body and red flowers sprouting from his chest. Death by nature, as opposed to a natural death, is pictured as the landscape's revenge on the colonizer, a fate adumbrated earlier in the play by an account of a mill-hand being drowned in the wheat bin.

Although apocalypse is the telos of empire imaged by *Inside the Island* and theatricalized through its spatial grammar, Nowra's text need not be construed as unrelentingly bleak. Frank Kermode's assertion that the modern apocalypse is "immanent rather than imminent" seems applicable here and I would argue that the play's eschatological anxiety should be read "in terms of crisis rather than temporal ends" (Kermode 1967, 30). Implicit in crisis is a cycle of transition and renovation, enacted in *Inside the Island* through the ritual purgation of the landscape. The catastrophic effects of the bushfires are thus leavened by a promise of regeneration, which is strengthened by the Australian context where some native flora depend on intense heat for germination. Gerry Turcotte's assessment that Nowra's plays "espouse a philosophy of the end of things but can suggest no alternative" (1987, 79) stops short of recognizing the real iconoclastic import of his work. From a postcolonial perspective, the destruction of the Dawsons' wheat fields, house, and mill figures a final dismantling of the deceptively innocuous pastoral myth of settlement (read invasion) and opens up the possibility of imagining new, different, and more enabling relationships between the self, the landscape, and its past inhabitants. There is a strong element of desire attached to the prospect of rejuvenation through fire, a point illustrated by the fact that some of the soldiers experience a kind of ecstatic madness in their encounter with the bushfires. This fascination/desire is reiterated in Nowra's later plays, *Summer of the Aliens* (1992), when the narrator remembers actively willing the flames to jump the road to his side of the street, and *Radiance* (1993), when the three half sisters deliberately incinerate the family home in a gleeful exorcism of their past oppressions. In this respect, the surviving soldiers' horrific experiences in *Inside the Island* seem less abortive and may even be edifying. And if they never "see the world the same way they saw it before" (1981, 90), this, I contend, is a prerequisite of change. If the play as a whole invites a parallel change in the audience's apperception of Australian (spatial) history, then Nowra's evocation of the bushfire as an image "burned" into the psyche of all Australians provides a powerful lens for this revisionary process by tapping into collective memories and perennial fears.[16]

Janis Balodis's treatment of space in *Too Young for Ghosts* is similarly complex and multifaceted, a factor that led Malouf, in his role as sometime theatre critic, to praise the play as visually "unforgettable" (1985b, 12).[17] The most obvious and sustained spatial structure is an overlaying effect that permits three distinct narratives to unfold in separate minimalist settings conjured sequentially and even simultaneously in one loosely mimetic place. As Balodis notes in his preface to the published version of the play, this design is intended to facilitate "rapid switches in time and location" instead of hampering the "flow of action from scene to scene with unnecessary blackouts or set devices" (1985, 4). The visual effect of these superimposed spaces is a dissolution of edges, frames, and boundaries so that distinctions between the various landscapes and time periods represented become quite blurred. In this uncertain universe, quantum potential is once again the enabling paradigm and it is just as possible to perceive a past haunted by the future as a present haunted by the past, a concept Balodis explores through characters who watch and sometimes enter other narratives that are temporally and spatially distinct from their own. The "in between" spaces thus created represent a shifting and debatable realm where some of Balodis's most subversive action occurs. The spatial structures of *Too Young for Ghosts* recall Jorge Luis Borges's model for an alternative worldview as expressed in his short story, "The Garden of Forking Paths." Borges's work is worth quoting at length here, not only because it provides an apt analogue for Balodis's experimental dramaturgy but also because it affirms, through metaphor, the inherent spatiality of time.

> *The Garden of Forking Paths* is an image, incomplete yet not false, of the universe as Ts'ui Pên conceived it. In contrast to Newton and Schopenhauer, your ancestor did not think of time as uniform and absolute. He believed in an infinite series of times, in a dizzily growing, ever spreading network of diverging, converging and parallel times. This web of time—the strands of which approach one another, fork, intersect, break off, or ignore one another for centuries—embraces all possibilities. We do not exist in the majority of these times. In some you exist and not I; in others, I and not you; in yet others both of us exist. In the present one, in which chance has favored me, you have come to my gate; in another, while crossing the garden, you found me dead; in yet another, I utter these same words, but I am a mistake, a phantom. (Borges 1970, 53)

Like Borges, Balodis constructs time-space as phantasmic, reticulated, unbounded, and nonlinear, a direct contradiction of imperial (and empirical) models. His allusive theatricality is further strengthened by the doubling of characters, which, as Kelly notes, is an important part of an overall "thematic doubling [that] aids in foregrounding the relativity of personality and history as the 'ghosts' of past and present encounter each other in the unmapped 'territories' of displacement and migration" (1992a, 123).

Although the three spaces overlaid in *Too Young for Ghosts* are *conceived* as very different—the North Queensland cane fields in the late 1940s, a postwar refugee compound in Stuttgart, and the vast north Queensland interior encountered by explorer Ludwig Leichhardt in 1845—the mise en scène remains quite constant. Tensions between imagined and perceived space have the effect of modifying discursive inscriptions of the landscape/stagescape to enhance a pattern of transference among the various narratives. The wide open land of the explorer's expedition, for example, permeates the displaced person's compound and the corrugated iron huts of the cane barracks, bounded spaces that initially mark the Latvians' experience of exile and that, on a broader historical scale, also "remember" the enclosures of convictism. To some extent, this process undermines the split between nature and culture that undergirds imperial approaches to the landscape. At the same time, the overlaid settings show that how we interpret the past is also a function of where we stand in the present. Hence the European war and American postwar imperialism portrayed by the Stuttgart plot provide an *interactive* context not only for the Latvians' continued "internment" in Australia but also for Leichhardt's journey, a resonance that reminds us that exploration is in fact invasion. A potent example of this technique occurs during one of the play's many "crossover" moments, a rape scene that figures clear parallels between the American soldiers' exploitation of the Latvian women in Europe and the explorers' subjugation of the Aborigines. Balodis's critique of imperialism's rape mentality redoubles as characters are elided and imagined spaces intersect when the Aboriginal women being assaulted by Murphy and Phillips emerge from the bush as Ruth and Ilse, effectively transforming the explorers into the American GIs (played by the same actors) and strengthening the invasion motif. On the whole, although *Too Young for Ghosts* is not as insistently informed by the thematics of war as is *Inside the Island,* Balodis's dramaturgy also positions the exploration and settlement of Australia within the context of the invaders' first war for the land.

Implicit in exploration and settlement is the making of maps, a process I discussed in reference to Aboriginal theatre as always implicated in the deployment of power. Harley makes an important point in this respect: "The surveyor, whether consciously or otherwise, replicates not just the 'environment' in some abstract sense but equally the territorial imperatives of a particular political system" (1988, 279). In effect, what a map inevitably presents is the mapmaker's own values in the guise of scientific disinterestedness. Moreover, as a number of critics have noted, cartographic discourse is one of the more subtle but pervasive tactics by which imperialism establishes, maintains, and justifies control over alien space.[18] According to Graham Huggan,

> The exemplary role of cartography in the demonstration of colonial discursive practices can be identified in a series of key rhetorical strategies implemented in the production of the map, such as the reinscription, enclosure and hierarchization of space, which provide an analogue for the acquisition, management and reinforcement of colonial power. (1989b, 115)

Maps, then, are a form of spatial knowledge that naturalize conquest and empire; hence their construction and usage are of particular interest to a postcolonial critique that seeks to identify potential sites of discursive rupture in imperial history. Elizabeth Ferrier maintains that decolonizing the map involves first identifying and deconstructing its hegemonic tropes, then finding a different spatial logic. Against conventional positivist constructions, she proposes two "other" spatial systems: ruptured, discontinuous or "holey space," as outlined by Deleuze and Guattari; and also the conception of "phenomenological space," which is similar to Bourdieu's idea of "traveled space" insofar as it is felt or experienced rather than simply seen (Ferrier 1990, 45–46). Such alternative models are in fact intrinsic to Balodis's text, not only in the overall design of its dramaturgy, as I have outlined, but also in the specifics of its dialogue and action.

The explorers' narrative in *Too Young for Ghosts* is very much about cartography—about how spaces are perceived and inscribed. The Latvians participate in this cognitive and spatial mapping, although they are more ambivalently placed as dislocated subjects in one imperial regime and potential colonizers in another. Balodis states in an interview with Kelly that his play attempts to explore "ways of seeing" (1990, 24), a focus he returns to in its sequel, *No Going Back* (1992),[19] the second play in *The Ghosts Trilogy.* The Melbourne Theatre Company's production of this sequel explicitly theatricalized cartography as a metaphor for the central action by shaping the backdrop into a huge map of Queensland. Another smaller, tilted map of the northern cape provided both a clump of tree leaves and, where it had been cut out of the main set, an irregularly shaped doorway/entrance point. Commenting on his evocations of the landscape, Balodis explains that both the Latvians' and the explorers' responses to Australia are deeply affected by "what they expected to see" and "what they chose not to see" (1990, 24). This intentional gaze is central to cartography's coercive power as a brief examination of Leichhardt's activities in *Too Young for Ghosts* indicates. When the explorers are first introduced, it seems that the mapping process has broken down, for the sextant reading suggests that they have gone backward and/or become lost. Leichhardt, however, determines to ignore any evidence that does not accord with his projected journey and so happily goes off with book, pen, and ink to extend his daily map. The other explorers, Gilbert and Murphy, lack their leader's peremptory confidence and decide that they are truly lost because they cannot "read" where they are. Here, Balodis ironizes both the map and its coordinates—the book and the sextant—as well as the explorers themselves, a tactic repeated toward the end of the play when Leichhardt envisages returning to Sydney with "a heap of mountain ranges and rivers in [his] pockets" (1985, 46).

This scene also sets up an important opposition between the ways in which Leichhardt and Gilbert perceive and deal with space/landscape. While they share a strong need to feel oriented in the face of a continuing dislocation, Leichhardt is aligned more obviously with the imperialist. His is the panoptic gaze that appropriates and totalizes as he urges Gilbert to "look to the horizon [and] have some vision" (1985, 17). Clearly, the trajectory of Leichhardt's gaze is the settlement/invasion and cultivation of the landscape by Europeans; hence he reads and maps the land according to his own projected desire, declaring Australia an Eden and himself the guide for a new civilization. His claim that "there are no ghosts in her closets" (1985, 18) refuses to acknowledge prior occupation of Australia by Aborigines and fosters instead "the notion of a socially empty space" that "lessens the burden of conscience about people in the landscape" (Harley 1988, 303). Gilbert, on the other hand, is critical of the cartographer's grand vision, which sees all and yet nothing. Arguably, he posits a phenomenological view of space insofar as he locates himself *within* the landscape, albeit in a series of perceived clearings, sitting still a moment to experience in microscopic detail the workings of nature—how a tree grows in the soil or how a bird feeds on its berries (Balodis 1985, 18). Gilbert "travels" most actively *between* the spaces of the two Australian narratives, simultaneously interacting with figures in his present and future, and he also *feels* the indigenous spirits of place that undermine the explorers' journey even before these "ghosts" materialize to attack their camp. But Gilbert ultimately remains a somewhat ambiguous figure, for although he explicitly refutes Leichhardt's conceptions of the landscape as a *terra nullius,* he is deeply imbricated in related imperial discourses. His anatomization of the landscape, for example, figured primarily through the careful collection and dissection of specimens together with their diagrammatic reinscription in his notebook, can be seen as an aggressive complement to Leichhardt's appropriative gaze/map.

That writing or graphic inscription is the authorizing mode of Western cartographic discourse is emphasized in *Too Young for Ghosts* by reference to the diary, the map, and the notebook. Paul Carter argues that the continuity of the journal, for example, leaves "no spaces unrelated and [brings] even the most distant objects into the uniform, continuous world of the text" (1987, 69). Leichhardt's habit of carving his initials on trees to form a meridian of sorts that leads back to "civilization" has a similar textual drive but, as Huggan notes, such markers "do not *describe* the environment; they *deface* and *deform* it" (1989a, 7). It seems fitting, then, that after his death, Leichhardt is doomed to haunt the landscape looking for some sign of his previous existence, eventually finding the tree he initialed only to witness it being chopped down by his Latvian double, Edvards. Meanwhile, Gilbert's ghost searches in vain for his own bones. No tombstones mark the site of either explorer's death, nor can a grave be properly constructed and marked at any future point because nature has completely disseminated their remains. If the marking of a grave serves as a signature certifying ownership of the land, the impossibility of fixed and recognizable (European-style) burial sites represents a form of resistance to imperialism's scribal authority. Through reference to Aboriginal burial customs, the play suggests, moreover, that tabular (graphic) knowledges can never fully erase nonwritten (graphemic) models.[20] Imperial space, whether scripted via the map, the tombstone or the book, is thus exposed as a palimpsest that covers up alternative spatial configurations, a point stressed earlier by Leichhardt's effort to overwrite the priority of Aboriginal habitation of Australia because, in his opinion, their dreaming tracks (a form of traveled space) left no significant mark on the landscape.

Like Nowra, Balodis strengthens the counterdiscursive energies of his play by charting a paradoxical disembodiment of the colonial subject—paradoxical because it is counteracted in performance through *embodiment,* in this case by the "real" presence of the ghosts of Gilbert and Leichhardt. As these two ghosts detail their respective fates, Balodis reiterates Nowra's concern with fire and flood[21] as the agents that actuate "death by nature," imaged once again as the predictable outcome of settlement/invasion. In their progressive disembodiment, the explorers suffer precisely those degradations that subvert their particular responses to the landscape: hence Leichhardt, whose authority relied on specular experience, is blinded by dust and condemned to listen to "[his] own bones sing," whereas Gilbert, the specimen collector, is "scoured out by flood" and dissected by natives (Balodis 1985, 38). In each case, the emplacement of the body within the semiotics of the landscape dismantles Cartesian models of perceiving space, an effect that is enhanced by the mutability of the ghosts as they slip in and out of the Latvians' narrative, thwarting their own repeated efforts to "log" or "map" each other's position or otherwise attenuate movement. An alternative cartography that approximates Deleuze and Guattari's conception of "holey space" (1987, 413–15) is thus produced. It impacts on mimetic and diegetic formulations of theatrical space through its ruptures, gaps, and overlapping fields and requires/produces alternative responses from the audience who must willingly suspend their *belief* in neutral space to reconceive mapping itself as constitutive (and therefore biased) rather than simply representational.

Although dislocation and displacement seem to be the controlling metaphors of all three narratives in *Too Young for Ghosts,* transformation remains a possibility for those migrants willing to acknowledge and deal with the "ghosts" of their individual and collective pasts—what Balodis has called "a kind of mental baggage" (1990, 33). In his play, this movement is enacted not through an apocalyptic resurgence of occulted histories, as in Nowra's text, but through a series of more minor conflicts that continually disrupt the apparent seamlessness of imperial history. While both texts reveal disaffection and instability as characteristic outcomes of colonial encounters with alien space, they also call for a rapprochement of the antagonists involved in Australian (spatial) history: the Aborigines, the settlers, and the landscape itself. Balodis foreshadows this reconciliation more lucidly than Nowra when Edvards/Leichhardt shoulders the guilt of murder—figured visually by Leichhardt carrying Gilbert on his back—in contrast to Lillian Dawson, who refuses responsibility for her part in the cataclysmic violence of empire portrayed in *Inside the Island.* Balodis's final image of promised regeneration is the birth of Ilse's baby, but this is shadowed by the death of Ruth and Leonids, which, along with a continued haunting of the present by the near and distant past, ensures that the narrative of migration remains open. Clearly, the remaining Latvians, like Nowra's surviving soldiers, must continue their struggle "to embrace 'exile' and rename it 'home,'"[22] before the ghosts in their respective landscapes can be laid to rest.

Postcolonial Grotesques
Re-membering the Body

Thus far, this chapter's analysis foregrounds temporal and spatial modalities that encode alternative versions of colonization and traduce the fulsome certainties of imperial history and conventional cartography. The third discursive axis I wish to investigate in depth pivots on representations of the body but also extends to enactments of verbal language wherever the instrumental trajectories of linguistic and corporeal texts and textures intersect or overlap. Michael Dash's argument that the body is "an endlessly suggestive sign" through which are mediated tensions between imperial subjectification and postcolonial recuperation—"dis-membering" and "re-membering" (1989, 20)—holds true for the texts examined here despite the fact that Aboriginal and feminist plays may seem more obvious foci for politicized readings of the (colonized) body. My discussion of the body returns to Louis Nowra's work not only because his theatre is thoroughly imbued with an insistent corporeality but also because it constantly rehearses variant versions of colonization as a primal scene where the body, like landscape, functions mnemonically. Nowra himself links this interest in the body to a fascination with horror movies, which have provided a model for his attempts to "physicalize metaphor" and so appeal to an audience on a visceral level (1987b, 58). Of the critics who have commented on his penchant for the Gothic, only Kelly penetrates its dramatic vitality. Following Rosemary Jackson's study of fantastic literature, she identifies his characters' "excessive somatic states" and deformed, grotesque, and mutilated bodies as "the projections of lost selves" whose energies erupt from the imaginary into the symbolic realm (1992b, 61). Turcotte also draws on Jackson's theoretical frameworks to explain such hybrid identities but is inclined to suggest that Nowra *speaks* the formula of abjection through more conventional linguistic discourses. Although Turcotte's emphasis on verbal discourses can be linked to his focus on Nowra's fiction, drama is included in the analysis, which implies a uniformity of approach that tends to ignore the specificity of performance (see Turcotte 1991, 61–72). A third and somewhat more problematic approach rests on the assumption that the transgressive energies of Nowra's Gothicism reside primarily *hors de là* in an extracorporeal realm expressed through scenic allusion. Jim Davidson evinces precisely this reading of *The Golden Age* when he argues that "the whole piece is posited on a gothic view of Tasmania" that ensures that the play's forest people remain "exotics" in a neo-Georgian setting that is troped as the functional Other of mainland Australian landscapes (1989, 313–14). While Davidson rightly points out that exoticism risks exciting the voyeuristic gaze, his analysis dismisses the subversive agency of the performing (de-formed and re-formed) body and diminishes the dramatic impact of its alterity.

Nowra's plays abound with a great variety of Gothic tropes—the nightmarish figures of *Inside the Island* discussed earlier in this chapter are a case in point—but tend not to replicate that absolutist version of the Gothic world in which all possibilities for ontological change are blocked. On the conventional Gothic stage, there are only two roles: victim and tyrant, and although these roles are often exchanged in a dramatic turnaround of events (Inverso 1990, 61–62), the binary structure of their relationship remains intact. Nowra's work, however, tends to ironize such character positions, to lean toward a more fracturing version of the Gothic, which mobilizes its weird and decentering images without necessarily buying into a politics of impossibility. This calls for a more radical reading of the body in his theatre, one that might go beyond the usual versions of Gothicism to account for that insistent sense of comedy and farce, of parody, or carnival irony that even his most shockingly grotesque figures elicit, and that often gives them some kind of agency despite their oppressions.

An alternative reading framework, the carnivalesque, foregrounds precisely this element of parodic resistance and seems apposite for postcolonial readings of the body politic that seek to dismantle the hierarchized corpus of imperial culture without simply perpetuating the victim/victimizer cycle. The conservative view of carnival as a licensed inversion that can be righted with relative ease has only limited uses for this project; what is much more enabling is the idea of carnival as a subversion that undermines categories of social privilege and thus prevents their unproblematic reassemblage. In postcolonial contexts, Russell McDougall argues, carnival perspectives undermine "the self-determining (im)postures of colonialism by activating that play of difference which is the principle of heterogeneous community" (1990a, 8). Such heterogeneity "sets carnival apart from the merely oppositional and reactive" so that it can operate as a "site of insurgency, and not merely withdrawal" (Russo 1986, 218).

Since both Gothic and carnivalesque identities problematize what Kelly calls the "closed and perfected bodily ego-ideal of Western civilisation" (1992b, 61), I do not wish to implement a rigid distinction between the characteristic corporeal figurations of each genre. Further close parallels between the two traditions are suggested by their common origins in Menippean satire[23] and their shared interest in popular culture as a repository of powerful narrative tropes. What emerge as important differences pertain primarily to the tonal ascriptions of each discourse. According to Bakhtin, the folk grotesque that is essential to carnival enacts a "gay relativity" via regenerative laughter associated with images of bodily life presented through parody, caricature, and other comic gestures derived from the mask (1984, 39–40). The romantic grotesque of Gothicism, on the other hand, dispenses with the ludic forms of the folk grotesque to create an alien and somewhat terrifying world where laughter loses its cognitive value.

Nowra's most pointed deployments of the carnivalesque as a decolonizing strategy can be found in *The Golden Age* and *Visions* (1978), both of which anticipate *Capricornia*'s more direct recuperation of Aboriginal subjectivities by dismantling textual constructions of the docile (colonized) body in favor of an unruly (resisting) body that threatens to loosen institutionalized authority's grasp on representation. In both plays, there is a powerful link between verbal and physical self-assertion, or what Dash terms "*cri* and *corps*" (1989, 21),[24] so that subversive language—including debased and obscure dialogue, silence, and preverbal enunciation—augments the effects of subversive corporeality. *Visions,* like Nowra's earlier work *Inner Voices* (1977), presents a savagely parodic view of the ways in which imperialism produces dystopian societies where power is exercised (and countered) through corporeal inscription. *The Golden Age,* which stages the relocation of a tribe of exiles from their isolated forest home to an urban asylum, reiterates this deauthorizing perspective through a similar repertoire of carnivalesque images. This later play balances dystopian forces with utopian energies that suggest a tentative optimism largely absent from Nowra's prior work. Although he ultimately chooses not to provide an enabling version of postcolonial identity in either play, Nowra illustrates quite clearly here Stallybrass and White's contention that "the body cannot be thought separately from the social formation" (1986, 192).

Juxtapositions of classical and grotesque bodies are prominent in each play and usually function to expose and ridicule the colonizing culture's representational motifs. *The Golden Age,* for example, introduces the dominant ego-ideal through the statuesque bodies of Elizabeth and William Archer as they perform *Iphigenia in Taurus* within the confines of a convict-built Greek temple in their garden. The audience is then rapidly transported to the bizarre and excessively corporeal world of the forest people who, mostly misshapen, mute, and genetically deformed, nonetheless convey a tremendous vitality that carnivalizes classical *form* with grotesque *formlessness.* These people, as Kelly notes, represent the "lost tribes" of modern Australia, the Aborigines and convicts expelled from imperial society and "deformed physically and linguistically by the colonizing ascriptions of alterity" (1992b, 63). Their species of (meta)theatre, Nahum Tate's folk version of *King Lear*—enacted in précis and further bastardized through pastiche and parody—stands in sharp contrast to the Archers' charity concert and stresses populist over imperial interpretations of the theatrical canon. In style, each playlet reveals not only its participants' approaches to the body in performance but also the modus vivendi of the culture that produces and consumes such narratives. The Archers' somewhat static *recitation* points to a regulated and rational society, whereas the forest people's energetic and even histrionic *improvisation* foregrounds their unrestrained physicality. The epistemic split suggested here is further underlined by a marked contrast in the linguistic codes of the two performances, the second enacted in a syncretic patois that carnivalizes the formal English of the first.

The subversive potential of metatheatre, often a feature of Nowra's texts, as my discussion of *Capricornia* has illustrated, is extended when Betsheb stages her pantomime for Francis. This scene from *The Golden Age* illustrates not only the exuberant kinesis of the grotesque body but also its tendency to both beguile and unnerve the viewer.

> [BETSHEB] *throws herself on the ground and rolls over and over down to him like a log rolling down a hill, then jumps up, pretending to be* MELORNE *asking for his hat to take up a collection.* FRANCIS *laughs at her*

> *imitation.* BETSHEB *then squats and pretends to piss, making groaning, pissing noises; a broad grin of contentment passes over her face. She does a parody of a high-born woman. She pretends to sit and sip tea at an exclusive dinner party. She speaks as if delivering bon mots to imaginary guests. . . .* BETSHEB *is extremely happy showing off to* FRANCIS. *She prowls around him like a wild, vicious dog sniffing its prey, and then she turns into a snarling, spitting Tasmanian devil, an act which slightly unnerves* FRANCIS. *Abruptly, she changes again and begins to walk like a grande dame taking a promenade. She motions to convicts nearby and gives them orders. . . . Then the grande dame farts. She discretely* [sic] *waves her hand behind her to get rid of the smell.* (1989, 29–30)

Betsheb's scatalogical humor is not the only carnivalesque gesture here. What is unsettling for Francis is her ability to traverse the divide between human and animal and to violate the space that normally positions the onlooker at a safe distance from the spectacle. Her parodic "play" can be seen to enact precisely that movement which shows the instability of colonial authority: a turning "from mimicry—a difference that is almost nothing but not quite—to menace—a difference that is almost total but not quite" (Bhabha 1984a, 132). Betsheb's telekinesis is also part of this menacing difference. Through it, she carnivalizes the authority of the *founding objects* of imperial cartography—the map, the book, and the compass—turning them instead into objets trouvés that she keeps in a bag with a large lizard.

Through all of its strange "misfits," *The Golden Age* presents the unfinished, protean, and anarchic body and language extolled by Bakhtin (see fig. 10), decentering hegemonic tropes with a corporeal semiotic that promotes unruliness as the rule. Within such a paradigm, Stef's spasticity and Betsheb's epileptic attacks, along with other highly theatricalized moments such as Melorne's fight with Francis, bring images of disorder into acute visibility via bodies that refuse subjection to the rigid control of the rational mind. Angel's muteness is also a form of refusal, even while it points to a powerful personal tragedy. The sharp opposition between form and formlessness developed in the first act of the play can be read through the politics of transgression as expressed by Stallybrass and White in a model that pits "costume" against "statue." Following Bakhtin, they argue that the inert statue, which has no openings or orifices and is usually raised on a pedestal, encapsulates the "transcendent individualism" of the bourgeois body while it also positions us as eternal latecomers to a history that has always already happened, usually elsewhere. Costume, on the other hand, is open, multiple, split, and transformative; it "takes pleasure in processes of exchange and is never closed off from its social or ecosystemic context" (1986, 22). It is important not to elide this figurative use of costume with the literal sense of the term, for although the Archers are emblematic of the statue, they do of course achieve this effect partly through their clothes, a paradox that situates Stallybrass and White's model of costume as a metaphorical conceit that relies upon, but does not replicate, the usual sartorial codes of theatre. The forest people, in contrast, express the polysemic and mutable body of costume. On a literal level, their colorfully patchworked clothes augment this trope and function as part of a carnival masquerade that beguiles and reworks the dominant discourses (see fig. 11). What happens after their return to "civilization" figures, in many respects, the (hi)story of a colonial society's effort to forge statues out of costumes, to suppress carnivalesque energies so that imperial order and (self-)control can be safely maintained.[25] This is partly achieved through costume itself as the forest people are "dressed up" for their new roles; although the reformation of the grotesque body is revealed as a complete farce during the dinner party scene when Betsheb deflates the Archers' pretentiousness by repeating her "vulgar" parody, the subsequent action affirms the agency of the empire's (new) clothes to signify and effect corporeal oppression and disempowerment.

If *The Golden Age* attempts to retrieve the grotesque body from its constitution as "the eternally deformed Other within imperial discourses" (Kelly 1992b, 63), *Visions,* which enacts the tale of Australia's colonial history somewhat more elliptically, stops short of such recuperative projects and deploys carnivalesque imagery primarily to show how regimes of power self-deconstruct. Set in Paraguay in the 1860s, *Visions* details the catastrophic effects of cultural imperialism when Madame Lynch, a Parisian courtesan married to President Lopez, determines to impose her version of "civilized" culture on the country. That this incursion amounts to cultural rape is clearly indicated by an opening image of the peasant, Juana, in a bloodied and mud-bespattered white dress. But Nowra is just as concerned to intervene in the processes of imperialism as to locate them; hence, as the superstructure for domination is put in place through a series of "cultural" events and military maneuvers, so too are mechanisms of subversion activated, in this case primarily through three carnival motifs: dance, costume, and eating.

A brief examination of the *bal masqué* scene of *Visions* shows how dance, which is normally intrinsic to carnival, can be deployed to foreground a disruptive corporeality that resists imperial government. Almost

Fig. 10. Carnivalesque bodies: Stef and Betsheb in *The Golden Age*, Playbox Production, 1985. (Photo: David Simmonds.)

all of Nowra's plays include some kind of dance, most of which enact a struggle for power and authority in tense, uneasy relationships between individuals and groups. In *Visions*, as Lynch and Lopez vie for control over the dance, which, in symbolic terms can be seen as Paraguayan culture and even the country itself, Lynch attempts to assert her mode, the waltz, as the essence of "civilized" movement by establishing herself as the teacher and Lopez as her pupil. This is a common paradigm of colonialist discourse, as I argued in my discussion of Malouf's play, and one repeated in *The Golden Age*, where, despite their romantic codings, the dances between Betsheb and Francis also function as appropriative gestures that attempt to fashion Betsheb's body in the classic mold by dispelling the energies of the whirling-dervish-like dances she has previously performed. But Betsheb carnivalizes the waltz by biting Francis on one occasion and stopping to "squat and piss" on another. In *Visions*, similarly, the self-privileging assumptions of the colonizer's code of dance are quickly dismantled. Notably, the raucous mardi gras music and the excessively literal costumes of the other guests, not to mention the dance of the grotesquely fat sisters, Corina and Adelaide, subvert Lynch's ideal of a "refined" (read European) masked ball, establishing

Fig. 11. Forest people, *The Golden Age,* Playbox Production, 1985. (Photo: David Simmonds.)

instead an atmosphere in which everyday sociocultural boundaries can be, and are, transgressed. As the *bal masqué* devolves into Latin-American street carnival, Lynch herself begins to look somewhat ridiculous, especially when she is obliged to dance with a local militia man dressed as a seven-foot rabbit, an event that undermines, by its diminutive images, her sociopolitical stature and ridicules her identity as harbinger of "culture." Further, Lynch's attempted encoding of the dance scene as "soft and gentle" is ruptured by Lopez's deliberate staging of what he terms a "different kind . . . of entertainment" (Nowra 1979, 33): a bloody fight between two men armed with stones and tied together so that neither can avoid the other's blows. Apart from reasserting the power of the grotesque body, this representation of violence in the dance scene enacts, metonymically, the tension between Lynch and Lopez as each struggles to assert his or her individual and cultural identity over the other.

In *Visions,* the thematics and metatheatrics of costume are even more pronounced than in *The Golden Age,* and Nowra is quite specific in his construction of costume as a colonizing tool when he presents the magnificently attired Lynch as "dressed to kill" in more ways than one (see fig. 12). Put simply, she sets out to refurbish Paraguay's unpretentious wardrobe with Parisian haute couture, but carnivalesque disruptions of her sartorial power redouble as the play progresses, and her obsession with clothes proves not only selfish and stupid but self-destructive. Ironically, only the *bal masqué* costumes get packed when Lynch and Lopez flee the city in panic as their military adversaries close in. Although we never actually see what happens to her finery, the mix-up of luggage wagons adumbrates what Lynch most abhors: the spectacle of "those barbarians parading around in [her] clothes" (Nowra 1979, 49). Even her attempt to maintain a thin veneer of "civilization" by staging a play in the swamps to lift the troops' morale is undercut. With solely the *bal masqué* wardrobe to dress the actors from, the performance is inevitably coded as a burlesque circus featuring clowns, acrobats, strongmen, sword swallowers, and jugglers, and of course the colonized Juana (standing by metaphorical extension for the country itself) as the mouthpiece/puppet of the colonizer. As a vision of Paraguay's future should the Lynch-Lopez coalition win, this antimasque not only exposes Lynch's quest to bring culture to the "barbarians" as a not-so-elegant farce but also replays the tropologies of the New World vision enacted in the masque scenes of *The Tempest.* What Lynch does not sufficiently attend to, here and throughout the action, is costume's potential for subversion: the paradox of its specificity *and* versatility make it an extremely unstable power base because it threatens to become absurd when unsuited to the body or the occasion, and counteractive if seized by the colonized and worn differently. Nor does Lynch realize that her power, like Prospero's, is inherently theatrical: having the key to the costume cupboard gives her some control over representation but by no means accounts for the complex negotiations that occur between actors, audiences, and the mise en scène.

Frequently, Nowra's manipulation of the grotesque body as a particularly theatrical site of resistance to colonization extends beyond an emphasis on form and costume to incorporate those carnivalesque images that pertain to the "lower bodily stratum," Bakhtin's collective term for the digestive and reproductive systems including the orifices and protuberances through which the body maintains its connection to the outside world (see 1984, 21–27 and passim). Through motifs such as eating, *Visions* reveals the rapacious greed of empire and constructs imperialism as little better than an act of savage cannibalism. As well as providing a symbolic framework, eating as metaphor and dramatic action draws attention, once again, to the physical body and shows how even its most basic functions are deeply inflected by discourses of power. The manifestations of this power in

Fig. 12. Dressed to kill: Lynch and Lopez in *Visions,* Paris Theatre, 1978. (Photo: Branco Gaica.)

its more and less overt forms are evident early in the play in two consecutive scenes—the leech scene and the first tea party—that place performative emphasis on eating. Lopez reveals his brutal aspirations quite clearly when he orders the leeches to be applied to his father in what Kelly interprets as the projection of his own recurrent nightmare of engulfment: being eaten alive by a giant snake (1981, 444). Lynch's humiliation of Corina and Adelaide at the tea party that follows is only marginally less pernicious;

although she exerts mastery over the sisters through trickery rather than brute force, her actions effect a similar capture of the derogated subject, as stressed by paralleled images of despoliation. As a realm in which social and indeed physical power is exercised in the interests of imperialism, the tea party features in an even more sinister light shortly afterward when Lynch and Lopez deliberately humiliate the American ambassador over dinner and then poison him. During the meal, Nowra effectively elides the discourses of war with the rituals of elegant dining to stress the ways in which astonishingly trivial regulations of behavior nonetheless territorialize the body. In the subsequent action, however, as Lynch and Lopez lose control over the butchery of war/dinner, poetic justice reasserts itself, inverting the corporeal hierarchies established earlier through the eating motif. Appropriately, Lynch finds no rules of etiquette to safeguard her body when she is eventually shot in the head while poised over her cup and saucer at a solitary tea party in the festering swamps. Lopez's death befits his more explicitly violent exercise of power and replays the tropologies of the leech scene through a focus on his grotesque body, glutted to the point of impotence with the "hearts and eyeballs and bones from [his] victims" (Nowra 1979, 70) but literally unable to vomit up what it has ingested. Although not figuring in exact detail the fate Lopez foreshadows—being "paraded through the streets" in mardi gras costume, "tied to the stake, spat on [and] pissed on" (Nowra 1979, 67)—these carnivalesque death scenes nonetheless enact a ritual degradation that aligns Lynch and Lopez with the mardi gras effigy and presages, in Bakhtinian terms, at least the possibility of a new material order or body politic.

In *The Golden Age*, eating functions less as a metaphor for colonization than as a corporeal activity that is inevitably influenced by social praxis. More importantly, it is a site of contestation through which the forest people assert their difference and thus question the behavioral norms and bourgeois table manners of the dominant group. Surely Betsheb's birdlike feeding of Stef by passing chewed meat directly from her mouth to his remains one of the most striking and subversive images in Nowra's theatre, for it collapses the rigid hierarchies through which distinctions between human actions and animal instincts are constructed and maintained, postulating instead the existence of a "neither/nor" and even "both" creature that simultaneously repels and fascinates. The growls, yelps, groans, and bird calls that punctuate the language of the lost tribe similarly deauthorize the discursive norms—or verbal manners—of "civilized" society. When they move from their own milieu to the Archers' stately mansion, the forest people's destabilizing alterity appears even more pronounced, as the carnivalesque dinner party clearly demonstrates through Betsheb's mimicry and Stef's comic attack-dog assaults on the ankles of a federal politician. Here, as in the many tea party scenes of *Visions,* Nowra's highly parodic mode of theatre deploys the force of the colonizing discourse/body against itself through a "transgression of the high-low domains [that] creates a grotesque hybrid right at the social threshold" (Stallybrass and White 1986, 113).

Like Lynch's attempts at tutelage, Mrs Archer's effort to regulate her guests' manners discloses not only the arbitrariness of her own bourgeois code of etiquette but also its insidious application. According to Pierre Bourdieu, the reformation of manners, though seemingly superficial, is tantamount to a deliberate and strategic colonization of the body that inculcates in the subordinated culture not only the acceptable corporeal forms but also their associated ideologies.

> [Societies] that seek to produce a new man through a process of "deculturation" and "reculturation" set such store on the seemingly most insignificant details of *dress, bearing,* physical and verbal *manners* [because], treating the body as a memory, they entrust to it in abbreviated and practical, i.e. mnemonic, form the fundamental principles of the arbitrary content of the culture. The principles em-bodied in this way are placed beyond the grasp of consciousness, and hence cannot be touched by voluntary, deliberate transformation, cannot even be made explicit. (1977, 94)

The Archers' "civilizing" project enacts precisely this trickery because, in Bourdieu's words, it "extorts the essential while seeming to demand the insignificant" (1977, 95). As the subsequent action reveals, the dinner party is in fact a prelude to incarceration and hence the first in a series of lessons designed to obliterate alterity through the production of corporeal obedience. Although not intended as punishment, the forest people's internment in the asylum nonetheless replays the disciplinary regimes of convict society and also makes parabolic reference not only to the extirpation of Aboriginal tribes in Tasmania during the colonial period but also to their ongoing subjection in the contemporary moment.

Imperialism's disciplinary inscription of the body also targets for reform the lost tribe's transgressive sexuality. On one level, genetic mutation and genital deformity mark their sexual difference, but while these aberrations convey the threat of sterility, that menace is effectively neutralized by imperial medicine's diagnostic eye. More disruptive is Betsheb's excessive libidinal energy as embodied and performed through her animalistic play, her assertive female corporeality, and her unrestrained masturbation. Her particular menace is grounded in her unself-conscious violation of those bodily taboos, including the fantasy of incest, that define "normal" sexuality and expel unacceptable desires. When she desperately attempts to seduce Mac, Francis is shocked and embarrassed by the vehemence of her concupiscence precisely because she enacts *and* activates his own repressed sexual drives. Later, within the context of the Archers' society, Betsheb's sexual overtures toward Francis and her autoerotic gestures are equally unsettling; however, it is perhaps her overly *general* sense of eroticism that mystifies her guardians most, for it presents the body as "a *locus* of sensory interchange with its natural and social environments" (Garner 1990, 148), refusing the Western genital fetish and redistributing pleasure across the entire body to posit a paratactic view of sexuality that is sharply at odds with the dictates of the classical, rational body. Paratactic sexuality, according to Robert Stam's reading of Bakhtin, is "a broad, multi-centred canvas" where sexual pleasure always exists in close relation to other sensual pleasures, particularly those of the lower bodily stratum (1989, 161). Hence Betsheb's is the carnival body par excellence, the active, eating, farting, eliminating, menstruating, and orgasmic alter-body that emphasizes Eros and the life force. It is also the relatively undifferentiated body that deprivileges the phallic signifier and is consonant with Cixous's notion of a body without beginning and without end (1981, 259).

Emphasis on sexuality and other functions of the lower bodily stratum is reiterated verbally in the dialogue of the forest people. As Fitzpatrick notes, their language "is rich in suggestions of sensuality and fertility which establish their freedom from the repressions and indirections of socially-approved sexual dealings" (1985b, 141). Through a process of joyful repetition and reassociation, words like *tarse* and *quim,* along with *cunty, spoon-fuckin',* and even *shit,* are retrieved from negative and obscene contexts and reintegrated with a corporeal semiotic that restores to language the colloquialisms of the marketplace, the profanities and scatological references that Bakhtin regards as valorizing unofficial modes of cultural expression. The outcasts' grammar is similarly heteroclite, a feature that further enlivens the dialogue and augments its counterdiscursivity vis-à-vis the strictures of official language. As Stam argues, the

> linguistic corollary of carnivalization entails the liberation of language from the norms of good sense and etiquette. The rules of grammar are

> suspended in what Rabelais called a *gramatica jocosa,* in which grammatical categories, cases and verb forms are ludically undermined. (1989, 99)

That the arcane creole of the forest people carnivalizes the socially approved language is clearly evident when William Archer attempts to translate Betsheb's dialogue, reducing the figurative energy of her phrases to their functional equivalents so that "windwhistlin'," for example, is paraphrased as "it went quickly," while "voice in a stick" is abridged to "telephone" (1989, 38). This translation, the inverse of Tocky's parodic précis of the Bible in *Capricornia,* also establishes an expressive gap that functions as an index of social difference, intercepting notions of the "infinite transmissibility" of language, and drawing attention, once again, to the incorporating universalism of standard English (Ashcroft 1989a, 72).

The affiliation between the body and word as a form of resistance to imperialism is figured in reverse in *Visions,* where Nowra focuses on the ways in which words actually enter and colonize bodies. Helen Tiffin identifies this process as typical of colonialist education.

> The texts of Europe were both deliberately (and sometimes adventitiously) deployed in the repression of the local and the concomitant reproduction and valorisation of Anglo-European culture at the colonised site, within and through not just the minds but the very bodies of the colonised. (1993b, 909)

Juana, in particular, is a figure profoundly and quite visibly marked by imperialism. Her interpellation is dramatized in potent visual images during the play within the play when, like the ventriloquist's doll, she functions as a literal mouthpiece for Lynch's propaganda. That her stomach pours sand and her mouth spits diamonds illustrates the ingestion and processing of the dominant discourse, enacting in graphic detail the disembodiment of the colonial subject. These are, however, ambiguous images that also carnivalize Lynch's little play, suggesting that Juana is not entirely powerless, especially since she exercises considerable mystical power over her captors. Hence, after she regains her "normal" speech at the end of the performance proper, her articulation of Paraguay's future shows her capture within imperialism's (corporeal) text at the same time as it subverts that text. On one level, recitation or learning "by heart" is a "ritual act of obedience" (Tiffin 1993b, 913); it is not merely a metaphor of instruction but, as Tiffin argues, a "technology of bodily absorption and cultural reproduction" that erases local subjectivities and produces instead a body that "ventriloquizes" the imperial voice at the colonial site (913–14). But while this internalization and embodiment of the European text produces a paradoxical disembodiment of the colonial subject (914), it also sets up the conditions for that imperfect imitation that leads to subversion. In this case, Juana's replication of Lynch's words is both a duplication and, possibly, a form of *duplicity* that might re-form the colonizer's version of the future, even though the durability of Lynch's visions seems to obscure all others.

In *The Golden Age*, the strategic capture of the body is imaged not through ventriloquism but through its visual counterpart: photography. Whereas recitation tells of a disembodied voice, photography shows the disembodied body, the subject split from the image and made obsolescent (McDougall 1990b, 104). Susan Sontag's argument that "to photograph people is to violate them" (1973, 14) seems particularly relevant here, for Nowra clearly indicates that photography is one of imperialism's more insidious instruments. In the asylum, Mac can refuse other institutional procedures designed to render his body docile—his opposition to the manual-skills test is a case in point—but he cannot escape Dr Simon's obsessive and voyeuristic interest in photographing his deformed genitals. Even before he castrates himself in protest, the camera's eye severs and segments his body, producing an anatomized figure whose difference is framed and contained in the *snapshot* image. In the short scene that pictures Mac's mutilated body, Dr Simon repeats this objectification quite overtly as she focuses her camera on his bloodied crotch and then rearranges the corpse with her foot until she has composed the "perfect" photo. The sequence vividly illustrates Gary Boire's point, made in reference to anticolonial trial plays, that the institutionalized body "inevitably appears as the site of aggressive sexual fragmentation and cajoled transformation" (1991, 14). When Dr Simon later defends her callous actions by claiming that "photographs are a legitimate record of a patient's condition" (Nowra 1989, 59), she only highlights the ways in which the documentation of the medicalized body functions as a covert disciplinary regime.

Since Nowra charts the disintegration of the lost tribe almost to the point of extinction but does not suggest that their colonization is ever complete or effected without resistance, it is possible, and even desirable in postcolonial terms, to read much of the asylum narrative not only through Foucault's analysis of the body's construction within power/knowledge systems but also in terms of the Bakhtinian theories already applied to earlier parts of the play. Within the latter framework, Mac's self-mutilation can be interpreted as a transgressive gesture: because his congenital deformity has rendered him infertile since birth, his castration effects not sterilization but a grotesque dismemberment that fractures Dr Simon's gaze and exposes the violence/violation implicit in her photographic surveillance. Betsheb's urinary and menstrual incontinence signals a similar corporeal unruliness, while the tubercular infections of the other forest people always threaten to invade and contaminate the "healthy" society. As in *Visions* and *Inside the Island,* contagion is particularly feared because it dissolves those boundaries constructed by imperialism's tendency to equate illness with Otherness (Tiffin 1993a, 47). If, as Bakhtin claims, dismemberment, degradation, and disease are closely associated with the transformative functions of the grotesque body, even the asylum scenes anticipate a utopian rupture of imperial power. In Bakhtinian terms, these scenes link "the grave [with] the generating womb, the receding past [with] the advancing future" (1984, 193–94), so that the lost bodies of the past—of the convicts and Aborigines—can be reunited with their contemporary counterparts. Nowra hints at the possibility of such a re-membered future when Francis frees Betsheb from the asylum and leads her back to the forest, but this future remains inconceivable within the play's dramatic moment. As Kelly argues, the final image of the two lovers suspends closure, ending instead with a moment of "dynamic stasis" (1988, 107).

Through their emphatic focus on the transgressive potential of the grotesque body in performance, both plays demonstrate Stam's theory that the body is "not a rigid *langue* but a *parole* in constant semiosis" (1989, 159). In its utopian drives, *The Golden Age* ultimately enacts a carnivalesque revision of national identity with more hope than does *Visions.* Each text deploys the grotesque body against colonization—figured in the experiences of both Juana and Betsheb as a form of "shock therapy" that attempts to render the body docile and compliant—but only Betsheb completely regains her (tele)kinetic powers. It is through this recuperation of the female body as emblematic of the Australian nation that Nowra rehearses most fully his version of an alternative and empowering postcolonial subjectivity.

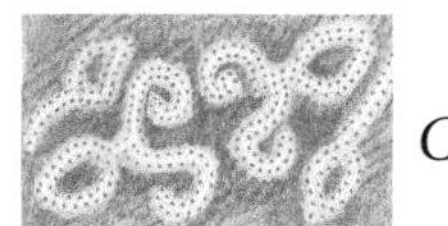

Chapter 4

Feminist Postcolonial Drama

Every journey conceals another journey within its lines: the path not taken and the forgotten angle. These are journeys I wish to record. Not the ones I made, but the ones I might have made, or perhaps did make in some other place or time.

—*Jeanette Winterson,* ***Sexing the Cherry***

A specific focus on the position of women on history's stage adds yet another player to the colonist/settler/indigene triad already outlined and calls for a closer look at the complex relationships between imperialism and patriarchy. Anne McClintock argues that the process and full import of imperialism cannot be fully understood without a theory of gender power: "Gender was not the superficial patina of empire, an ephemeral gloss over the more decisive mechanics of class or race. Rather gender dynamics were, from the outset, fundamental to the securing and maintenance of the imperial enterprise" (1995, 6–7). This argument refers not only to the discursive gendering of various peoples and subject positions, a topic taken up in detail in my next chapter, but also to the material effects of gender power in domestic and public realms at a time when there was a strong imperative to populate colonies with a legitimate settler elite to oversee and perpetuate colonial rule. In Australia, as in most other colonized countries, various forms of gender power have been integral to, and deeply inflected by, the imperial project. Few would question the assertion that gender is as central as race to the Australian imaginary,[1] or that these two sites of difference are the main discursive axes on which cultural nationalism has been constructed, but this does not mean that they can be analogized unproblematically. As the work of theorists such as Jenny Sharpe clearly illustrates, race and gender, like social class, should be delineated as categories of "difference for designating the relation between colonizer and colonized" (1993, 12),[2] rather than elided under the umbrella of marginality. While it might be tempting to simply focus on parallels between the experiences of women interpellated by patriarchy and those of indigenous subjects marginalized within the imperial situation, we cannot assume, as Helen Carr does, that women and non-Europeans "occupy the same symbolic space" in colonialist discourse (1985, 50). Rather, gender complicates the positioning of a range of colonized subjects, albeit in different ways. By foregrounding the role of gender as a category that cuts across the discursive field of colonialism, this chapter attempts to map out some of the "intersecting marginalities"[3] in and through which the contours of a feminist postcolonial theatre might be traced.

To avoid the dangers of collapsing specific subject positions into a single site of gender oppression, a self-critical feminist postcolonial analysis must begin "with difference and dislocation rather than identity and correspondence" (Sharpe 1993, 11). In this respect, I wish to clarify a few terms that traverse current debates about the position of women in postcolonial societies. Most importantly, a distinction must be made between indigenous and nonindigenous women, to prevent what Gayatri Spivak (1985) and Caren Kaplan (1987), among others,[4] rightly criticize as the homogenizing impulse of Eurocentric feminist theories that fail to account for the differential effects of race (and other specific differences) on the oppressions experienced by women. In attempting to make this distinction, some theorists have argued that Black women are doubly colonized while white women are only half colonized (see Visel 1988, 39), but such terminology is problematic, for it quantifies what should be qualified and also considers oppressions and privileges to be summative (hence one adds to or takes away from the other) rather than dynamically interacting. Moreover, this formulation tends to suggest that white women were the hapless onlookers of empire rather than ambiguously complicit with many of its discourses and its practices. A more appropriate model for understanding the differences *between* women might follow Chris Prentice's assertion that "any individual is interpellated by multiple discourses and multiple social formations" (1991, 64). It follows, then, that colonization should be conceptualized less as a fixed state than as a complex process informed by a continually self-constituting hegemony that is always under threat from competing discourses.

While the representational paradigms used to (re)construct images of Aboriginal women may seem the natural focus for a feminist postcolonial study of Australian theatre, that area of analysis is not my chief concern here. For a number of interrelated reasons, much of this chapter concentrates on the figure of the female settler as presented in plays written by white women, so that race is discussed primarily as a marker of Otherness against which colonial definitions of Anglo-European femininity are drawn and/or critiqued. In particular, I explore the ways in which gender expectations position many colonial women as intrinsic to the proliferation of settler culture while often denying them access to that culture's formal power structures and material profits. Such positioning is characteristically linked to anxieties about female sexuality, since, as McClintock explains, imperialism made special demands on women's reproductive labors.

> Controlling women's sexuality, exalting maternity and breeding a virile race of empire-builders were widely perceived as the paramount means for controlling the health of the male imperial body politic, so that by the turn of the century, sexual purity emerged as the controlling metaphor for racial, economic and political power. (1995, 47)

When white women evaded their imperial "duties" or refused to comply with the normative gender conventions of their era, this frequently became the moment at which Aboriginality was invoked, whether as a site of gender solidarity or a yardstick for measuring the colonial woman's recalcitrance.

This chapter's focus on settler writing supposes that race eclipses gender as the salient issue in the relatively few plays that have been devised by Aboriginal women—hence my positioning of Eva Johnson's *Murras* and Sally Morgan's *Sistergirl* within the field of Aboriginal rather than feminist theatre.[5] Johnson's own work explicitly warns against notions of a feminist sisterhood between Aboriginal and white women when race still operates as a site of fetishized difference that replicates colonial relations, albeit in a more muted fashion. In *What Do They Call Me?* (1990), her quasi-autobiographical play about asserting an identity as a Black lesbian, Johnson points to the hypocrisy of many of her "white sisters," feminists whose theoretical commitment to racial equality dissolves in the face of actual interracial contact (1991, 250–51). In contrast, *Sistergirl* seems to suggest Morgan's investment in "female bonding" across racial and cultural boundaries, thus inviting a universalist interpretation; but, as Rachel Hennessy points out, the play also takes pains to present the specificities of Aboriginal women's experiences as gendered subjects of imperial rule (1995, 50–52), especially in the scenes that detail Rosy's anguish at having had her infant daughter removed from her care by the so-called Protector of Aborigines. Among more recent indigenous plays, *Ningali* (1994) focuses entirely on the experiences of an Aboriginal woman using an eclectic mix of storytelling techniques to convey the protagonist's particular historical experiences. While this monodrama suggests an instance of cross-cultural feminist practice in so far as it was developed by the collaborative efforts of Josie Ningali

Lawford, Robyn Archer, and Angela Chaplin, the fact that *Ningali* depends on Lawford's input as sole actor and narrative subject tends to situate performances of the play in relation to the kinds of Aboriginal theatre already examined.

Whereas the plays discussed in the previous chapter often concern themselves directly or indirectly with Aboriginal issues and/or with Australia's history of race relations, Aborigines appear only infrequently in contemporary plays by settler women writers. This is a curious phenomenon in some respects, given that plays by a similar cohort in the 1920s–1950s abound with representations of indigenous Others. While the reasons for this trend are not entirely clear, I would suggest that the particular genre of "bush realism" theatre that was prominent local fare in the earlier part of this century more easily accommodated reference to Aboriginal women, even if, as in plays such as Katharine Susannah Prichard's *Brumby Innes* (written in 1927),[6] Henrietta Drake-Brockman's *Men Without Wives* (1938), and Mona Brand's *Here Under Heaven* (1948) they are troped primarily as sites of illicit desire and miscegenation that threaten orthodox relations between white men and women. The generally urban focus of the 1970s new-wave theatre seemed to provide fewer opportunities for such characterization, and, of course, there had been a significant shift in public attitudes toward Aborigines and other racially marked groups by this time. But perhaps the most plausible explanation for the declining interest in racial issues is that feminist theatre of the period was fully occupied with the struggle to find an audible voice and presence, given the aggressively masculinist definitions of nationalism that converged in the figure of the Ocker as the dominant theatrical (anti)hero of a revitalized urban dramatic tradition.

A major objective of feminist postcolonial writing is to map out "the areas of women's subjugation and invisibility in the colonial situation" and to formulate a language that is capable of expressing women's experiences when they have been "denied a place in the imagination" (Petersen and Rutherford 1985, 9–10). Bill Ashcroft proposes a creative cross-fertilization of *écriture féminine* with creolization as the linguistic strategy that might most effectively be adopted to create an imaginary space from which postcolonial women can write or speak.[7] But what he does not consider in his otherwise very useful model is the possibility that such a language, through performance, might be grounded in the body itself rather than in verbal signifiers, so that reconceiving identity, or "writing the body" out of a sense of spacelessness, also becomes writing *with* the body in space. It is primarily this relationship between women's bodies and space, particularly the spaces allocated to them in colonialist structures, that I wish to pursue in this chapter by considering how colonial women's emplacement within, or displacement from, the domestic realm reveals the workings of gender power within imperialism. The first section demonstrates the difficulties faced by convict women in their attempts to come to terms with displacement and exile and to establish some kind of autonomy despite the limitations of their expected gender roles. My ensuing discussion of Alma De Groen's *The Rivers of China* (1987) deals with a more psychological form of displacement, figured metaphorically by a focus on the positioning of the woman writer/artist within colonial space. The final part of this chapter is devoted to an analysis of the ways in which feminist performance aesthetics have been used to deflect the gaze of imperial patriarchy, thus fostering heterodoxies rather than orthodoxies.

Convict Women and Gender Power

While the texts discussed under the category of settler/invader drama do offer women prominent roles in a counterdiscursive replay of history, they tend not to explore issues that are specifically linked to gender and/or what might be termed loosely as "female experience." Their sphere of action is public and broadly referential even when, as in Stephen Sewell's *Hate,* the narrative is tightly focused on the family. The two plays examined here, Jill Shearer's *Catherine* (1978) and Hilary Bell's *Fortune* (1993), follow a different tack, each showing how gender oppression, although experienced primarily in domestic spaces, is nonetheless deeply inflected by the structural hierarchies of imperialism.

A brief analysis of *Catherine,* which details the deportation of convict women to Australia on the second fleet, reveals that Australian society is based on a long history of class and gender conflicts that were intrinsic to the social structures of imperial England, and amplified in the colonial situation. The play imaginatively recreates the history of Catherine Crowley, a transportee whose son became one of the so-called founding fathers of settler society in Australia. During the voyage from England, Catherine ameliorates her position as a lower-class convict by becoming mistress to the ship's surgeon, Wentworth, but she is quickly reassigned to the margins of the dominant society on arrival in the new country and written out of its official history. Like Gow's *1841,* Shearer's text illustrates how Australia has been conceived within imperial discourse in both dystopian and utopian terms as an unattractive outpost fit only for Europe's criminal dross, or, alternatively, as a place/space promising freedom, wealth, and a regenerated social order. What is worth noting in *Catherine* are the gender-specific articulations of this vision as foregrounded not only through contrasts between Wentworth's expressed hopes and Catherine's explicit fears, but also in the narrative construction of the relationship between the two during a journey that replays familiar oppressions and thus presages a settler society bound by the same social strictures as those operative in the "old country." Privileged by his sex and social class, Wentworth is in a position to "fancy a new life . . . free of the mould and decay of England" (1977, 14), while Catherine clearly is not. Put crudely, she must choose between rape or prostitution, the only difference between the two being the degree of agency the latter option affords her as Wentworth's mistress. The play suggests, then, that men can look forward to sexual, social, and economic opportunities in the new colony, while women face physical exploitation, social marginalization, and, at best, economic dependence. In this schema, the journey refigures displacement as possibility for the male settler but only enacts *mis*placement and *im*possibility for the female convict, who experiences mostly what Brian Matthews identifies in his study of colonial women's autobiographies as "dislocation": a "suspicion that [one] is at the mercy of events . . . in the wrong place at the wrong time" (1985, 44). Catherine articulates this dislocation simply but with great clarity when, to the shout of "land ahoy" at the end of their voyage, she says, flatly, "I see only . . . blackness" (1977, 76).

If the females in Shearer's text seem to have little sense of their role to play in colonial expansion, the men are not slow to harness the women's sexual, social, and reproductive labor for their own purposes. Gayle Rubin's phrase "the traffic in women"[8] can be applied quite literally here to describe a series of commodifications and exchanges designed to ensure that imperial patriarchy is not imperiled by the contingencies of settlement in an "empty" land. The convict women are shipped as cargo, described as objects—comfortable, smooth, compliant—and utilized to "balance the imbalance" of the colony (Shearer 1977, 40), or, put more blatantly, to mask the colonizer's deviant "sexual" behavior (with indigenous women or other men) and to provide acceptable progeny for the successful peopling of the nation. As opposed to the Aboriginal woman, whose sexuality was invariably aligned with nature, the Victorian woman's sexuality could be sanitized in the service of culture. The colonial woman's necessary subjugation to the generational tasks of empire is nowhere more obviously figured than in the prospective management of Catherine's pregnancy: Wentworth declares that he will acknowledge the child (a male of course) as his own, and in his great benevolence, make sure that its mother is looked after, at least until she can deliver it safely into his hands. Ketu Katrak's argument that "the traditions most oppressive for women [in colonized societies] are specifically located within the arena of female sexuality: fertility/infertility, motherhood, and the sexual division of labour" (1989, 168) seems particularly relevant here. What is really being safeguarded by the emphasis on bringing women to the colony is of course the double standard that relegates male sexuality to the private sphere while female sexuality is publicly structured (Loomba 1989, 109). Provided he is reasonably discreet, the colonizer's peccadilloes can be excused as personal weaknesses, while the body of the woman/Other becomes the physical terrain on which colonial expansion is mapped symbolically and literally through reproduction of the imperial self. This manipulation of gender hierarchies neatly illustrates Sara Mills's point that imperialism "seem[s] to be as much about constructing the masculine British identity as constructing a national identity *per se*" (1991, 3).

Pointing out discrepancies between male and female "realities" is only one way to insert the dimension of gender more fully into accounts of colonial experience, and Shearer does this quite effectively, but perhaps the more radically destabilizing counterdiscourses of *Catherine* arise less from the somewhat predictable conflicts enacted by its main characters and more from the insistent presence of the other female convicts. Though never actually appearing on stage, they refuse erasure by suffusing the narrative with their voices, their curses, and their cries, to the extent that the play's central action is often disrupted, even distorted. As opposed to Catherine, who becomes the "domesticated Other,"[9] these women resist appropriation more vigorously by embracing precisely those roles designed to disempower them. In seeming to live up to class and gender stereotypes, they also threaten to realize imperialism's worst fear: fecund sexuality unmediated by social (read patriarchal) control. Thus the cargo of women displaced to provide comfort for the men and balance in the new settlement ironically *un*settles the integrity of constructions that rationalize the voyage as a humanist enterprise.

The story's general containment within the narrative spaces of a sea journey has important resonances for my argument that women's displacement poses a threat to the stability of colonial space/society. Although the boundaries between the dominant and the deviant are policed as carefully as usual during the voyage, these boundaries are much more vulnerable for being constructed on a boat, a space that Foucault identifies as the paradigmatic heterotopia.

> The boat is a floating piece of space, a place without a place, that exists by itself, that is closed in on itself and at the same time is given over to the infinity of the sea. . . . The boat has not only been the great instrument of economic development but . . . simultaneously the greatest reserve of the imagination. (1986, 27)

Viewed in these terms, the convict ship/heterotopia destabilizes the authority of the dominant discourse's spatial organization and exposes the unequal power deftly inscribed in its spatial relationships (Rowlands 1989, 80). Hence, while threatening to implode with the pressures of conflicting discourses, a threat that in itself casts the imperial project in a doubtful light, this ship also provides a space for the "counter culture of the imagination"[10] that postcolonial theory identifies as a crucial step toward decolonizing settler literatures. And since the signifier "woman" becomes interchangeable with "ocean" and "boat" in the rhetoric of the typical sailor—Captain Traill, for example, talks about the ocean's "tricks and tantrums" (1977, 15)—the heterotopian spaces imaged by the convict boat in *Catherine* can be utilized to trace that concealed journey, those other histories, that forgotten angle, which in turn foster a feminist critique of the official imperial voyage.

Catherine's emphasis on untold histories is especially facilitated by the metatheatrical framework of the play. To trace the trajectory of imperialism's impact on Australian society, Shearer presents the voyage as a play/rehearsal within a play, using the framing text to create a critical distance between the audience proper and the action of the inner narrative. The idea of a rehearsal structure rather than a performance is important here as it leaves a number of possibilities open, including the suggestion that the actors' interpretation of the convict voyage is neither finished nor final. Together with the text's emphasis that only selected parts of the story will be rehearsed on that particular night, the actors' arguments about how Catherine and the other characters will be played maintain a constant self-reflexive focus on the role of art in mediating history. And since the stage itself can be conceptualized as a heterotopia par excellence, characterized by a "*removal from* and *extension into* social space" (Loomba 1989, 134), these debates also function as interventions into representation. The play's structure thus historicizes Catherine's story while providing a contemporary reference point that situates the political and social effects of the historical narrative firmly in the present as well as in the past.

Hilary Bell's *Fortune,* written some fifteen years after Shearer's text, also reflects the thesis that the colonial sphere was constructed as a sexualized space, while the "vast, fissured architecture of imperialism was gendered throughout by the fact that it was white men who made and enforced laws and policies in their own interests" (McClintock 1995, 6). Set in the goldfields of small-town Australia in the 1860s, this play stages the "fortunes" of an Irish ex-convict, Kathleen, and her unlikely companion, Chang, an eleven-year-old Chinese giant whom she exhibits as a freak in order to earn enough money to survive in a savage society where the dictum "flog or be flogged" seems to summarize the constant dilemma of the oppressed classes. The particular historical moment that Fortune stages records a meeting of migrants and exiles from all over the world, the bulk of them searching for an elusive dream of wealth and power. Through her emphasis on such Others, Bell presents a vision of Australia's colonial diversity in ways that aim to complicate celebrated myths of a frontier forged by heroic men, and to question accounts of nation building as the precinct of white settlers.

Kathleen is positioned within the depicted milieu as a tenacious survivor whose pragmatic outlook belies a history of pain and betrayal. Although she speaks lightly of her past, the odd references to her grim voyage from Ireland, to the child she buried at sea, to time she spent in the female factory, and to months when she lived on vermin because the supply ship failed to arrive all record the abject realities of convictism and its particular effect on those whom the dominant society casts as its Others. When the play opens in the windswept and desolate town of Cold Bath Creek, Kathleen has just been deserted by her male companion and left with no money; then, over the course of the narrative, she is bullied, raped, and robbed of her modest savings. Her vulnerability is doubly stressed by the fact that she must depend on Chang, himself only a child, for her livelihood and even her safety. This representation of the convict woman's typical experiences in a cutthroat colonial society draws to some extent on gender stereotypes, but Bell is careful not to construct her female protagonist as a helpless victim. That Kathleen refuses to be intimidated by the men who exploit her, to give way to despair, or to wallow in self-pity attests to an indomitable will to survive and move beyond some of the constraints she faces.

In many respects, Kathleen typifies the unruly woman whose refusal to comply with gender expectations unsettles various power relations on which the stability of the colonial settler society depends. Her potential for physical aggression is revealed, almost casually, when she tells Reinhardt, "I was sent here for murder, sir, and if I had a good reason I'd do it again. So hop back on your horse and piss off home" (1995, 36). At this point, the play demythologizes the oft-vaunted idea that most convicts (especially women) were in fact only petty criminals whose misdemeanors amounted to "stealing a loaf of bread." Kathleen is thus situated as unfeminine and imminently dangerous, a subject position reinforced by her coarse language and by the fact that she actively avoids marriage, child rearing, and the domestic responsibilities that would have fallen to most women of her era, including ex-convicts. If, as McClintock argues, "domesticity denotes both a *space* (a geographic and architectural alignment) and a *social relation to power*" (1995, 34), Kathleen's ability to exist and act outside the domestic realm, however contingently, represents an important subversion of patriarchal power. Her sexual history is also thoroughly at odds with the morally sanitized ideal of Victorian femininity, a point stressed when, after the freak show loses its ability to pull in customers, she plans to "try [her] hand as a lady of pleasure" (1995, 31). Such sexual "misconduct" confirms her position as one of empire's "nonproductive" subjects: those, such as prostitutes, unmarried mothers, spinsters, and homosexual men, who received special opprobrium for failing to produce *proper* stock to secure and uphold the imperial system.

Within imperialist regimes, unruly women become particular sites of anxiety because their failure to control wanton sexual urges threatens to actualize the possibility of miscegenation. Colonial discourse commonly links interracial sex to social Darwinist ideas about contagion and the degeneration of the human species, which, in turn, suggest the tenuousness of white masculinity and potency. In reference to Victorian social life (in Britain and in the colonies), McClintock argues that panic about blood, contiguity, and *métissage* focused on the female body as a point of racial instability.

> Body boundaries were felt to be dangerously permeable and demanding continual purification, so that sexuality, in particular women's sexuality, was cordoned off as the central transmitter of racial and hence cultural contagion. Increasingly vigilant efforts to control women's bodies, especially in the face of feminist resistance, were suffused with acute anxiety about the desecration of sexual boundaries and the consequences that racial contamination had for white male control of progeny, property and power. (1995, 47)

In *Fortune,* Duck's repeated insinuations that Kathleen is Chang's whore attests to the white male's anxiety about miscegenation and female desire. Because the play clearly shows that Duck's accusations are unfounded, the focus remains firmly on his paranoia, suggesting that the patriarchal system constantly reproduces constructions of female sexuality as a product of its own disciplinary processes. In this respect, Duck's savage rape of Kathleen can be seen as an attempt to confirm his own power, to control her sexuality, and to punish her for apparently taking up with a "Chink."

That *Fortune* relates many of Kathleen's hardships to the brutal system in which she is enmeshed does not mean that she becomes a secret sharer in the oppressions of the more obviously marginalized characters depicted. In fact, the play clearly shows her complicity with certain aspects of the imperial project, especially its denigration of nonwhite races, when she vilifies Chang, calls him offensive names, neglects his emotional needs, and readily exploits his Otherness to earn a living. Although she treats Chang more humanely than does Reinhardt, this is partly because she needs to protect her source of income; hence, the maternal feelings she eventually develops for her charge are complicated by economic dependency as well as racial prejudice. Similarly, Kathleen's general contempt for Iris Mackinnon, a Chinese woman whose dress, speech, and manner mimic those of a Victorian Englishwoman, reveals a deeply ingrained racism that is exacerbated by her perception that Iris has grossly overstepped the boundaries implicit in the community's racial (and therefore social) hierarchy: "I love it. A Chink telling me this is sacred land. A Chink who thinks she's the Queen of England! I should be wearing them dresses" (1995, 41).

Although Kathleen's gender and her Irish heritage suggest that she might have a "natural" affinity with imperialism's racial Others—British colonial discourse tended to stereotype the Irish as a simianized and degenerate race—the play shows that the axes of race, gender, and class are linked through their differences as much as their similarities. It is only at the end of the narrative, when Kathleen positions herself as Chang's equal rather than his exploiter, that any real cross-cultural understanding between them can occur. She tells Chang, "I'll do more than spruik. I'll be an exhibit. Lock myself in a cage, shave my head, throw on my convict rags—they'll pay fourpence for a photograph" (1995, 89). In the bizarre, carnivalesque world of the play, this abrogation of power marks a turning point that imagines more equal relations between races. Chang's final reluctance to completely turn the tables on his erstwhile oppressors, even though he clearly has the power to do so, solidifies Bell's vision for a multicultural Australia in which difference does not necessarily translate into division.

Whereas *Fortune*'s representation of the convict woman functions to make visible some of the connections between imperialism and gender, the play's treatment of Chang as its male protagonist is designed to highlight the ways in which race intersects with various categories of Otherness in colonial discourse. Deliberately constructed as a freakish Chinese giant, Chang reflects back to Australian audiences their own xenophobic images of the "Mongolian Octopus" that characterized many local nineteenth-century depictions of China (and indeed of a monolithic Asia) in both visual and verbal media. At the same time, the fact that Chang is still a child tends to evoke sympathy, especially when he is cruelly treated, and to align him with the women characters, his "femininity" stressed by the fact that he wears long gowns and braids. In an attempt to theorize discursive constructions of childhood, Jo-Ann Wallace argues that "the category of 'the child' remains caught in [a] tension between what one might call the empty and the full, between lack (of personality, attributes, and history) and excess (full natural presence)" (1995, 291). This statement seems true of Chang, who initially appears to Kathleen as a mute absence—a tabula rasa in the Lockean sense—and, simultaneously, as a threatening hulk whose mere presence intimidates those around him. His position as both child and racial Other seems to confirm Wallace's point that the child-subject is a common site for the convergence of imperialist anxieties about subjectivity and citizenship: "'The child' is the subject yet to come—*not yet* literate, *not yet* capable of reason, *not yet* fully agential—but also the subject before now—the primitive, the prehistoric, the presymbolic, the presocial" (1995, 97–98). Thus, Chang's struggle to assert his full humanity can be seen as partly due to his positioning within a society that produces "childhood" as always already marked with signs of alterity.

As a freak, Chang is further marginalized by his community, whose members mostly view him with disgust and even horror. The fact that he is repulsed by his own body, and that he curses himself using the dominant society's racial epithets, shows how easily the colonized subject is interpellated by discourses that denigrate difference. Semiotically, Chang represents the empire's abject: that which is repudiated, cast off, expelled. But the play makes the explicit point that Chang is Australian and also cites his birthplace as Gulgong, a town known for its association with Henry Lawson, who is generally regarded as one of the "founding fathers" of nationalist writing in Australia. Chang's citizenship therefore locates his grotesqueness as internal rather than external to the nation, problematizing not only his own sense of identity but also the myths of nationhood through which racism accrues its normative power. At a slightly different level, Chang's freakishness—as manifest by his huge bulk, his androgynous appearance, and his voracious appetite—can be seen as another figuration of the carnivalesque tropologies that dramatists such as Nowra have explored so fruitfully in their attempts to construct a theatrical body that suggests the complex, and often contradictory, subject positions produced by and within imperial regimes. In this respect, the human circus/freak show depicted in *Fortune* also functions as a heterotopian space where it becomes possible to break down singular accounts of Australian history and its associated myths of identity.

The deconstructive agenda of the play is actually introduced in the opening scene, which uses photography to stage the visual commodification of Chang as "freak," only to show how he subverts the process of textual capture. The actual mechanics of the portrait session—Reinhardt's incessant fussing about Kathleen's appearance and, in turn, her reluctance to approach Chang to have her photograph taken—reveal the constructedness of the camera's image (see fig. 13). While the imperialist habit of voyeuristic looking is here temporarily reenacted, it is clear from Chang's bored compliance with the whole procedure that he exerts a certain recalcitrance as object of the imperial gaze. Much later, Chang reappropriates power over his own body and takes control of its commodification, deciding when, how, and to whom he will exhibit his monstrosity. Moreover, his appearance as an actor in the Chinese theatre involves a performative presentation of grotesqueness that suggests the ways in which the freak is constructed by and within social relations. The performance also gives Chang a new sense of agency so that he is able to finally see himself as a person rather than a freak-show exhibit. As in a number of plays discussed in this book, metatheatre provides an arena in which postcolonial subjectivities and positions of empowerment are realized. The use of Chinese theatre traditions also has a recuperative function for the Chinese community in the imagined world of the play, and, beyond that, in contemporary Australia as a whole. By contextualizing these traditions within a narrative that dramatizes aspects of the community from which they are drawn, Bell's dramaturgy avoids the common trap of theatrical appropriation. At the same time, spectacular cultural symbols can be used to assert difference and even to trick the oppressors, for instance when the Chinese dragon appears to Duck as a phantasmal creature seeking revenge for the desecration of graves in the Chinese cemetery.

At the very end of *Fortune*, Duck is reduced to a helpless idiot who depends on Chang for his livelihood, putting paid to the masculine myth of the white frontiersman as primary nation-builder. The final image of Duck, Kathleen, Iris, and Chang as a rather bizarre colonial family presents an alternative myth of origin through which to consider current conceptions of Australian nationhood. The social unit of "the family" is of particular

Fig. 13. Portrait session, *Fortune,* La Boite Production, 1996. (Photo: Melanie Gray.)

interest to postcolonial theory because it has figured prominently in imperialist discourse as a trope that marshals various cultures into a single narrative of progress ordered and managed by Europeans. Again, McClintock's work on the connections between imperialism and gender power are most illuminating.

> The family offered an indispensable figure for sanctioning social hierarchy within a putative organic unity of interests. Because the subordination of woman to man and child to adult were deemed natural facts, other forms of social hierarchy could be depicted in familial terms to guarantee social *difference* as a category of nature. The family image came to figure *hierarchy within unity* as an organic element of historical progress, and thus became indispensable for legitimizing exclusion and hierarchy within nonfamilial social forms such as nationalism, liberal individualism and imperialism. (1995, 45)

If the trope of the organic family *re*forms (as in reshapes and disciplines) difference in order to incorporate it, through various forms of paternalistic domination, into a normative social unit, *Fortune*'s family of freaks and social misfits represents a breakdown of "natural" order. In this respect, the various subversions of race and gender hierarchies that are enacted in the course of the narrative can be seen as part of a larger project to dismantle the epistemological framework of imperialism. It must be noted, however, that the play's emphasis on assertive Otherness as a way out of the imperial bind means that the colonized subject remains to some extent enmeshed in a binary system even while dismantling its claim to authority. While various levels of political subversiveness *are* facilitated by the freak-show motif, the use of tropologies that highlight difference as a marketable commodity tends to support Jonathan Dollimore's point that the "marginal may not only be repressed by the dominant (coercively and ideologically) but actually produced by it" (1986, 181). Although Bell is obviously aware of this dialectical relationship—indeed, the play demonstrates the ways in which deviance or freakishness is constructed in order to sustain hegemonic social structures—*Fortune*'s failure to imagine a postcolonial subject position beyond that of Otherness suggests the difficulty of articulating unmediated forms of resistance.

Travel, Exile, and the (Post)Colonial Woman

Whereas Shearer and Bell examine convict women in order to foreground gender bias in Australian historiography, Alma De Groen's *The Rivers of China* concentrates on the figure of the colonial woman writer/artist. At its simplest level, this award-winning play speaks to conventional literary history by *re*presenting Katherine Mansfield's final few months of life in ways that draw attention to her positioning within the territorialized spaces of the imperial patriarchal canon. As a public figure, Katherine is caught up in a complex textual web, not least because she is an expatriate colonial subject writing in and from the imperial center while living with her English editor-husband. Hence, whereas the project of Shearer's Catherine is to emerge from the critical silence of narrative erasure, De Groen's Katherine must be recreated against critical co-option into a hegemonic tradition. *The Rivers of China,* especially in performance, gives its historical protagonist voice and presence to resist the disempowerment marking her role as woman, colonial subject, wife, and invalid. The play also questions the constitutive framework that has colored discussions of Mansfield's work, reminding us that her writing might more properly be considered in its historical specificity alongside that of other Antipodean expatriates, rather than assigned to the homogenizing universal (read British) canon.

De Groen's play fuses its quasi-historical portrait of the colonial woman artist with a contemporary narrative about a young Sydney man who, after therapeutic hypnosis following a suicide attempt, wakes up in hospital believing he is Mansfield. This strand of the play explores the implications of gender power in a feminist dystopia in which women have appropriated the Medusa's power (the ability to kill with a look) in order to reverse the workings of patriarchal rule. Although the figure of the Man becomes a paradoxical site for the recuperation of Mansfield's subjectivity, De Groen resists the temptation to effect an unproblematic *re*patriation of the colonial subject to the present-day Australian society.[11] Rather, she suggests, through the discomfort Katherine/the Man experiences with her/his new body and locale, that alienation for the postcolonial artist is located not in a global proliferation of the image, but in the nexus of gender and nation.

Postcolonial criticism has long recognized the ambivalent positioning of the colonial writer, poised on the cusp between home and exile whether s/he remains in the colonies (alienated from the valorized centrist literary institutions and often working in a language that fails to fit the local experience) or migrates, as many have done, to the metropolitan center. For the expatriate artist who has chosen exile, the dislocation from cultural roots can offer certain advantages even while it complicates notions of identity. Edward Said, for example, finds great merit in "stand[ing] away from home in order to look at it with the exile's detachment."

> The exile knows that in a secular and contingent world, homes are always provisional. Borders and barriers, which enclose us within the safety of familiar territory, can also become prisons, and are often

> defended beyond reason or necessity. Exiles cross borders, break barriers of thought and experience. (1990, 365)

Similarly, feminist critics such as Kaplan advocate the advantages of exile and warn against a partisan approach to the idea of home.

> We must leave home as it were since our homes are often the sites of racism, sexism, and other damaging social practices. Where we come to locate ourselves in terms of our specific histories and differences must be a place with room for what can be salvaged from the past and what can be made new. (1987, 195–96)

The importance of these arguments to an analysis of colonial women's subjectivities lies in the assessment of the exile's potential to destabilize a range of comfortable orthodoxies that are frequently naturalized in concepts of home. We should keep in mind, however, that exile and migrancy are never sites of transhistorical experience; hence Revathi Krishnaswamy's recent critique of the postmodern tendency to create a deterritorialized consciousness as the privileged site of imaginative experience: "By decontaminating the migrant of all territorial affiliations and social affinities, the mythology of migrancy ironically re-invents, in the very process of destabilizing subjectivity, a postmodernist avatar of the free-floating bourgeois subject" (1995, 143). These reservations about migrancy or exile as an appropriate metaphor for postcolonial subjectivity—or indeed as an actual locus of that subjectivity—can only be addressed by giving attention to the specific and the local.

The complexity of exile as an ideological site from which to speak calls for a politicized reading of place in *The Rivers of China,* which, as De Groen reminds us, continually puts "the audience in the position of having to say to themselves: 'Where are we?'" (1989–90, 15). This question is articulated in the play's theatrical images and dialogue and expanded through the dislocating effect of its narrative forms. Records of the premiere production, for example, show a minimalist set—Eamon D'Arcy's spiral floor design with only freestanding French mirror windows behind it—that resists emplacement within recognizable social and historical contexts, so that questions of location arise even before the characters enter the stage. This slightly futuristic setting and the rapid transpositions of place and time are deliberate components of a form that aims to keep the audience aware of the need to be oriented, and while it is the Man who actually gives voice to this need when he wakes up after his operation asking, "Where am I?" his question is always implicit in Katherine's experience of exile, and in Wayne's alienation from a dystopian social order that limits his ability to transcend the role of hospital orderly.

The play balances the pain of dislocation with "the pleasures of exile"—to use the title of Lamming's celebrated book about his own exile in Britain—in a number of ways. Insofar as it allows her to eschew the confines of the "tower" that Middleton Murry has chosen as her work space for the summer, Katherine's departure from England is an important move toward autonomy in both feminist and postcolonial readings of the play since it distances her self and her art from the well-meaning but appropriative grasp of her husband. Of course, Gurdjieff's institute proves to be an even more repressive bastion of sexism (masquerading as philosophical truth), but, ironically, the discursive power of his ideology recoils on itself as his program for self-development eventually provokes Katherine to undertake a more sustained examination of her position. Their frequent heated exchanges highlight her attempts to delineate herself as an artist, not defined passively in relation to men but rather by the *activity* of her writing. While it is undoubtedly empowering to view Katherine's exile as a crucial step toward recuperated subjectivity, we are never allowed to become complacent about the stability of this recuperation. As the dystopian narrative shows, her attempts to defend a space for the colonial woman artist fail to prevent Middleton Murry from packaging her work and her private life for consumption by the literati after her death. His actions exemplify a kind of paternalism easily exercised in imperial and patriarchal systems, wherein the difference of the never wholly assimilated Other is harnessed in the production of the imperial self—in this case to construct Murry as "the romantic lover of a doomed woman" (Perkins 1987b, 17).

Even though Katherine is given an opportunity to voice her protest about being turned into an industry, that form of dissent cannot fully unravel the complex matrix of intertextual dialogue that surrounds the real-life figure of Mansfield nor completely free the subject from textual capture. In this respect, the fluid form of *The Rivers of China* is crucial if the contemporary characters, and the viewers, are to mobilize exile as a position from which to speak, act, and react. While the historical scenes directly question the ideological biases of imperial patriarchy, the more radical postcolonial moments of the play are often located in the interstices of interwoven and fractured narratives that transform each other while leading the audience through what Elizabeth Perkins calls a "process of multiple empathy and sympathy" (1987b, 19). As Katherine's spirit is reborn in the Man, her/story coalesces with his/tory, producing a number of slippages between places, between past and present, between masculine and feminine, and between sickness and health. Perkins is surely right when she argues that this "form is a political concept" (1987a, 39), for De Groen's arrangement of the scenes and action in both narratives disrupts the logic of chronology, and hence that of imperial history, while her blurring of the ontological categories of male and female ruptures the binary gender system that forms the constitutive basis of patriarchy.

Through this form, the integrity of Katherine Mansfield as a unitary character, constructed in and through the literary canon, is questioned in multiple dissemblings of her image, which has strong resonances in three of the present-day characters. Rahel, the plastic surgeon, is clearly the modern female artist figure, but Katherine's identity is grafted almost seamlessly onto the Man through hypnosis, while her problems as a deracinated artist in the early part of the century are echoed in Wayne's struggle to become a writer. Situated within a feminist dystopia that reverses the historical oppressions of patriarchy so that women are the makers of history and culture and men are not recognized as writers or artists, Wayne's story is to some extent a mirror image of Mansfield's. But De Groen does not suggest that an inversion of the valorized pole of the male/female and center/margin binaries constitutes a solution to the dislocation experienced by the colonial woman. Clearly Katherine/the Man feels just as alienated in her Antipodean context as she did in Paris, and before that in England. And although never quite at home in either sense of the word in England, s/he nonetheless exhibits the colonial writer's characteristic internalization of (literary) England as the locus of "real" experience.

> *Man:* Get me [some books]. . . . When [D. H. Lawrence] mentions gooseberries these are real, red, ripe gooseberries that the gardener is rolling on a tray. When he bites into an apple it is a sharp, sweet, fresh apple from the growing tree—
>
> *Wayne:* Gooseberries, eh? Apples. What about a truckload of pineapples from north Queensland? Or some oranges from the Murrumbidgee?
>
> *Man:* [*Indicating the* Collected Stories] If you can get me this you can get me some Shakespeare.
>
> (1988, 45)

The Man's stalwart refusal to respond to Wayne's deliberately localized sense of place attests to the interpellative power of the British canon. Wayne's pointed invocation of pineapples and oranges as more appropriate literary icons for the Australian context can of course be read as a rebuke of precisely this kind of hegemony, as can his rather bemused "Who?" in reply to the request for Shakespeare's (Prospero's) books.

Positive transvaluations of the condition of exile do nonetheless emerge in such moments, primarily from the play's conscious nomadic movement between perspectives. Said sees this habit of "dissimulation" as unavoidable and even political if mobilized against orthodoxy.

> For an exile, habits of life, expression or activity in the new environment inevitably occur against the memory of these things in another environment. Thus both the new and the old environments are vivid, actual, occurring together contrapuntally. There is a unique pleasure in this sort of apprehension, especially if the exile is conscious of other contrapuntal juxtapositions that diminish orthodox judgment and elevate appreciative sympathy. (1990, 366)

The contrapuntal effect Said advocates emerges most fully in performance through the simultaneous onstage presence of Katherine as historical figure *and* contemporary Man, and through their polylogue of interlarded words and actions, particularly toward the end of the play when slippages among the living, the dying, and the dead become most prominent. This role sharing—two actors playing one character bifurcated into two different bodies, positioned narratively in diverse places and times—though differing in concept to role doubling, has a similar deauthorizing effect. Consistent with postcolonial and feminist aesthetics, the performative text constructs the self as fluid, adaptable, discursive, continually gesturing toward a recuperated subjectivity for the female artist, but suspending any notion of identity as something fixed in the confluences of time, place, and physical being.

Closely related to exile is of course the concept of travel, a common motif in postcolonial feminist writing, where the attempt to move through and beyond the strictures of imperial patriarchy can be effectively emblematized by a notional or actual journey that persuades the colonized subject to jettison at least some of the ideological baggage of oppression. For this analysis, I am less interested in Katherine's literal journey to France, although I have argued the importance of its repercussions, than in the play's conceptualization of travel in thematic and structural terms. The title, reiterated in Katherine's explicit reference to her mother's fantasy of exploring the rivers of China, is but one of the departure points for the textual development of travel as a strategic theme. Others include literary signifiers such as the opening poem by Emily Dickinson, which images the liberation of the soul "abroad"; John Keats's verse, which depicts a poet traveling in "realms of gold"; and the music, "Journey to Inaccessible Places." The latter provides an analogue for Katherine's symbolic movement toward selfhood, and in a sense for the play as a whole. Such images posit a journey away from the quiescence of the tower into a kinetic space that promises freedom through the *act* of traveling rather than in the condition of arrival. What Katherine must confront is the difficulty of reaching this somewhat utopian conceptual space when men patrol the borders, as she finds out in one of her many confrontations with Gurdjieff.

> *Gurdjieff:* Only way for woman to evolve—go to what you call "Heaven"—is with man.
> *Katherine:* If one happens to have misplaced one's man?
> *Gurdjieff:* She does not go anywhere.
> *Katherine:* We don't cross the border without you? You provide the passport? Password? Maps?
>
> (1988, 52)

Although Katherine is categorical in her rejection of Gurdjieff's self-privileging philosophy, she is nonetheless enmeshed in its totalizing system by dint of her position within patriarchy and imperialism, systems that "invest women's stability with moral values" and posit her stillness as "crucial for social, familial, [and] cosmic harmony" (Loomba 1989, 74). But the concept of mapping introduced here provides an important key to the recuperation of female subjectivity because it articulates the need for a feminist cartography that can "dissociate itself from the 'oversignifying spaces' of patriarchal representation [to] produce an alternative map characterized not by the containment or regimentation of space but by a series of centrifugal displacements" (Huggan 1989b, 125–26).

The lack of access to an epistemological system that militates against the gendering of travel and exploration as male activities surely accounts for the inevitable containment of Katherine's journey toward autonomy. For the audience, however, the play's intersecting narratives and overlaid fictional spaces construct a series of "centrifugal displacements" that map the terrain of travel and exploration quite differently. De Groen has used the term *wrongfootedness* to explain this deliberate emplotment, which, though it might sound awkward, is crucial to the effect of the text in performance, as she explains.

> The play isn't clumsy at all; it's very calculated. I need the audience to go on the journey that Katherine was going on, and that all women go on from the time that they are born, never quite being at home in the

> universe, and not having any maps and being told to look to the male for a passport and guidance when the boundaries within this world and the next all have a male sentry. The notion of wrongfooted ties into never quite knowing what's around the next bend in the river. . . . At the same time, the journey has been very carefully calculated, especially the rhythms, and if these are too dissimilar to the original intention, then the journey is incorrectly plotted. (1989–90, 15)

By inviting the audience to undertake this journey, De Groen does not imply that we should simply identify with Katherine as the naturalistic subject of the play. In fact, the dynamic of "wrongfootedness" and the Brechtian emphasis on alienation that it implies demand that such identification is continually disrupted, or to use the metaphor of the river evoked by the play's title, that the boat is kept rocking. As in Shearer's play, destabilization of the kind of travel motivated and oriented by the intentional gaze of the (male) colonizer provides the necessary yet uncomfortable condition for change. As Katherine herself says,

> If we set out on a journey we must submit to the journey. We're afraid. We resist. The little boat enters the dark gulf and our only wish is to escape: "Put me on land again." But it's no use. The shadowy figure rows on. One ought to sit still and uncover one's eyes. (De Groen 1988, 40)

Metatheatrically, this motion within stillness—sitting quietly with uncovered eyes as the boat moves on—is constructed as the spectator function within De Groen's play, which aims to produce a moment of "theatrical quietism"[12] that transforms the concept of exploration by rupturing the binaries—active/passive and subject/object—that direct conventional looking relations. The metaphor suggested by the boat can also be aptly applied to the structural organization of the performance text because river travel is always inflected by the double, often oppositional, movement of the river *and* the vessel so that the vector of the journey remains somewhat unpredictable.[13] Similarly, the characters of *The Rivers of China* inhabit a volatile stage in the sense that its continual fluid transmutations both produce and result from the contingencies of particular narratives. In the play's premiere production in Sydney,[14] these narratives were visually integrated in the spiral design of the set, demonstrating what Perkins calls a "constructivist interest in sculptural movement in space" (1987b, 19). Once again, it is the theatrically realized structural apparatus of the play that proffers the most significant opportunities for a feminist postcolonial reading by foregrounding performance as a way of resisting the "enclosure and hierarchization of space" that have been identified as "key rhetorical strategies implemented in the production of the map" (Huggan 1989b, 115).

The idea of a journey through time itself is also crucial to *The Rivers of China*'s representation of history as a fiction that can be repeatedly challenged and reformulated. As chapter 2's examination of Aboriginal texts has already revealed the ways in which disrupted chronologies and interwoven narratives problematize the assumptions of a linear history, I do not intend to labor that point here, although De Groen uses these techniques with equal effectiveness. What is interesting and different about her interrogation of history's discursive foundation is the paradigm shift to spiral rather than circular movements of time in space. While constructing in the dystopian narrative a present that looks backward to recuperate some aspects of the past, the play also creates a past that looks forward into the present/future so that events in different time frames inflect each other. Unlike Aboriginal playwrights whose access to an indigenous metaphysics might posit the possibility of timelessness, De Groen must conceive a structure that, in its emphasis on double and split perspectives, confounds the logic of linear time while nevertheless accepting some notion of teleology, or, to return to the idea of the vector, a structure in which the trajectory of time is influenced by a number of coordinates (see fig. 14). Within this spiral concept of time, the Man's actions and dialogue are frequently retroactive—his castigation of Murry for publishing all of Mansfield's writings is a case in point—while Katherine's can be seen as proactive when, for instance, she foreshadows the mutation of her body into the Man.

> It's funny—I feel older than Jack now. As if I'd somehow skipped decades, become very old and everyone I knew had died, and I think of them, remember them as they are now, but I've become utterly changed. (1988, 14)

Through her multidirectional narrative, De Groen clears a space for the colonial woman artist to speak through time, making an irrefutable claim to representation in history. At the very moment when Katherine declares her own death, she asserts a subjectivity that cannot be nullified post mortem: "Time is not. I *am,* January the ninth, 1923, a dead woman" (1988, 54; emphasis added). It is this partly recuperated self that allows her to articulate her artistic vision at the very end of the play and to forestall a sense of finality.

What *The Rivers of China* attempts to establish, then, is a performative cartography that addresses both feminist and postcolonial concerns in its determination to decolonize the map/stage, reconceptualize travel, and

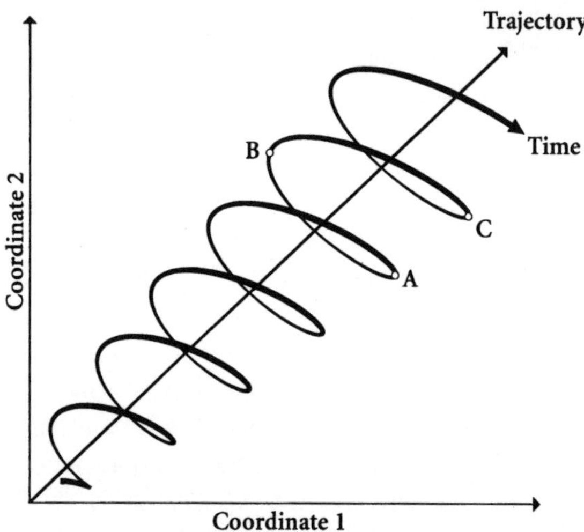

Fig. 14. Vector representation of the spiral concept of time. Note the spatial proximity of points A and C despite their temporal distance. (Graphics: Cameron Browne.)

sever the "cartographic connection" between imperialism and its associated forms of patriarchy. The modalities of travel (both thematic and theatrical) enacted here open up a series of questions that Paul Carter never confronts in his effort to formulate a spatial narrative as an alternative to imperial history. We might ask, for example, "Did women imagine their movements in and through colonial space differently, and if so, did these other journeys constitute a critique of imperialism even while they were imbricated in its discourses?" De Groen's text, like Shearer's *Catherine* and Bell's *Fortune,* suggests that some women "traveled" in heterotopian landscapes, and that their split and splintered histories complicate the broader picture of colonial society. This, in itself, is a movement through spaces in question, places of debate, boundaries, and margins.

Reframing the Gaze
Metatheatre/Feminist Performance

Thematizing the oppressions of women in colonial contexts and recuperating their muted or suppressed histories represents an important intervention into the ideological frameworks of imperialism. All three plays discussed in the previous sections of this chapter demonstrate how fiction is troped as history in order to authenticate a particular present and, conversely, how some histories are dismissed as fiction at the whim of the dominant society. At issue here, as elsewhere in this study, is the coercive power of narrative, a central concern for feminist and postcolonial theorists alike. As Elin Diamond argues,

> To understand history as narrative is a crucial move for feminists, not only because it demystifies the idea of disinterested authorship, but because the traditionally subordinate role of women in history can be seen as the legacy of narrative itself. With its relentless teleology, its ordering of meaning, narrative accrues to itself the power to define and legislate; it is, as Mária Minich Brewer puts it, the "discourse of authority and legitimation." (1990, 95)

The dismantling of narrative and its underlying structures of "authority and legitimation" proceeds not only through a reorganization of relations between the basic content and the form of representation—as illustrated by the fragmenting and resequencing of events, the chronological looping, the overlaying of time frames, the refusal of closure, and the other narrative interventions identified across the categories of drama under discussion in this book—but also through a rethinking of the very nature of theatrical representation itself. This broadly metatheatrical project is by no means new, as the notorious example of Pirandello reminds us, but it does take on particular political inflections in a postcolonial analysis that must reckon with the exercise of power in and through the performance event.

As a method of foregrounding the audience's role in narrativity, and, consequently, the construction of subjectivity in performance, metatheatre has surfaced at a number of points in this study. What I wish to examine now are some of the ways in which performance can subvert the conventions of a medium that would seem to collude in gender subjugation by positioning women as objects of knowledge, part of a spectacle framed and contained by the intentional gaze of the spectator. This inquiry has important implications for postcolonialism insofar as it attempts to expose and rework those scopic regimes that institute and maintain power over the colonizable Other.

One way of reconceptualizing the phallocratic economy is through an emphasis on theatre as a stronghold of presence.

> The very placement of the female body in the context of performance art positions a woman and her sexuality as speaking subject, an action which cuts across numerous sign-systems, not just the discourse of language. The semiotic havoc created by such a strategy combines physical presence, real time, and real women in dissonance with their representations, threatening the patriarchal structure with the revolutionary text of their actual bodies. (Forte 1990, 260)

While such presence—the staging of difference—can destabilize hierarchies of power, as I have argued in reference to Aboriginal performance, it does not fully neutralize those cultural laminations that facilitate the body's appropriation by dominant signifying systems. In other words, politicized theatre cannot simply assume that the emplacement of the "alter-body" on stage effects subversion. This is where the self-conscious performance practices of metatheatre become very useful in reframing the theatrical event. In Barbara Freedman's formulation, if theatre "shows that it knows that it is showing," it fractures the viewer's gaze by forcing an awareness of the complex dialectic between spectatorship and display that is always implicit in the condition of theatricality (1991, 69).

The metaphor of the woman as actress is a familiar feature of contemporary feminist (meta)theatre,[15] and one that draws attention to the performativity of gender itself. In Australia, this particular trope can be traced back to the colonial stage, where acting talent in women was valorized as a sign of authenticity/national identity. Thus, the eponymous heroine of Edward Geoghegan's musical comedy, *The Currency Lass* (1844), establishes her "native" status (in this case, an identity based on differentiation from both the imperial center and the indigenous margin) not through any fixed role, but rather in her uncanny ability to make just about any role fit as she stages a virtuoso performance of "fictitious personages" for the gullible British new chum who must judge her suitability as his nephew's prospective bride. Many of the women playwrights whose work fits within the ambit of my study show a similar interest in the con/texts of performance, but they also extend its subversive potential so that role-playing becomes a way of countervailing imperial history's strictures and/or refusing its characteristic roles. Dorothy Hewett's drama is exemplary in this respect, not only because of her focus on the multiplicity of roles women have played in Australian society, but also because she frequently utilizes theatre as a self-reflexive art form that foregrounds the ideological assumptions traversing representation itself.

Among Hewett's works, *The Man from Mukinupin* (1979) concerns itself most directly with Australia's legacy of imperialism.[16] Set in rural Western Australia around the period of World War I, the play presents an assortment of two-dimensional figures whose comic interactions form a deceptively simple narrative anchored by the age-old motif of thwarted love. Here, metatheatre functions on a number of levels in a text that masquerades as a lighthearted romantic musical but gradually strips itself of that guise while penetrating the respectable veneer of a community that has long obscured from its collective memory an unpalatable history: the genocide of its Aboriginal peoples. Bill Dunstone describes the political effect of the play's self-reflexivity as an intervention into the closures of language-based discourse, an important project in postcolonial theatre.[17]

> The particularly valuable and distinctive perspective which *The Man from Mukinupin* opens on discourses of difference and absence is that while the dramatic discourse defines itself linguistically as post-colonial writing, . . . it also develops a critical metalanguage to interrogate the privileging of written or spoken language over those nonverbal, iconic, gestual and pragmatic characteristics of theatrical relationship. In this way the play radicalises discourses of abrogation and appropriation within the dramatic text, the *mise en scène* and audience reception at the very pragmatic and discursive moment of performance itself. It establishes semiotic "gaps" between linguistic discourse and theatre discourse, and by shifting the emphasis from the text (as encoded meaning or closed internal structure) to reception as the site for interpretation and meaning, it distinctively foregrounds the presence of social, cultural and political forces which traverse the text and the performance. (1990, 74)

Thus, the intense self-scrutiny of the performance text functions to defamiliarize those representational codes that might naturalize theatre as mimesis.

Costume is but one of the signifiers of the play's outrageous theatricality: witness, for example, the fashionable robes of the aging Shakespearean diva, Mercy Montebello (see fig. 15); the black dress and veil of the Dickensian Widow Tuesday; the ever-opening raincoat of the town Flasher; or the colorful garments of the Misses Hummer, presenters of the spectacle and themselves remnants of a bygone era of showbiz. These sartorial excesses, along with Hewett's parodic treatment of the "fabrications" of theatricality, remind us of the constructedness of all roles. An emphasis on dressing and undressing on stage further historicizes costume, alienating it from the body/text even while underlining the arbitrary meanings assigned to certain garment types or styles. In Brechtian terms, this tactic outlines how gender is mapped across the theatrical subject through sociocultural inscriptions on the performing body. Such is the case with Pretty Polly Perkins, who is deemed to have become a woman when Miss Clarry, town dressmaker and ex-wardrobe mistress of the well-known J. C. Williamson's theatre company, overtly constructs the teenager's new (sexualized) status by dressing her up in a beaded pink georgette with a lengthened hem (see fig. 16). Soon afterward, the symbology invoked by this action is questioned when, in a parallel scene, Touch of the Tar, her unacknowledged half-caste sister and sole survivor of the Aboriginal massacre, seizes the costume of the colonizer and, looking just like Polly, sashays down the main street of Mukinupin, all "dressed up to kill" (1979, 92). The threat of miscegenation, which is suppressed by the settler's version of history, is here potently imaged through the play's cross-referencing of performance events. At the same time, Touch of the Tar's mimicry features "dressing up" as empowerment, an oppositional strategy whereby the subjugated woman can appropriate the vestments of authority. This mimicry, in its likeness to *and* difference from the original event, also provokes a sudden awareness of the ways in which authority and authenticity are constructed in the first place.

Role doubling is another of *The Man from Mukinupin*'s specific metatheatrical devices, and one that "subverts the neat polarities on which [the play] is constructed" (Fitzpatrick 1995, 111). The characters are divided into two seemingly separate groups: the daytime townspeople, synonymous with white Australian society; and the nighttime revelers, aligned with the oppressed Aboriginal culture. Although costume is used to signal whether a character belongs to the light or the dark side of town and to distinguish between the two groups since both are played by the same actors, this systematic doubling technique sets up an immediate paradox: despite the differences signified by their clothes, once two characters are introduced by the same actor, each carries traces of the other throughout the action, a process that thwarts the formation of an unproblematically delineated identity. The pairing of Polly and Touch of the Tar provides a particularly complicated instance of such a paradox since the (white) actor playing both roles is required to cross color lines, a theatrical form of miscegenation that has been signaled in some productions by having the actor (lightly) blacked up.[18] On one level, this kind of racial "cross-dressing" tends to erase white as a color, simultaneously positioning the non-Aboriginal as the invisible norm while marking black (Aboriginal) as Other. It could be argued, however, that Hewett foregrounds theatre's artifice in ways that acknowledge

Fig. 15. Shakespearean diva Mercy Montebello in *The Man from Mukinupin,* Royal Queensland Theatre Company, 1989. (Photo: Fiora Sacco.)

the impossible fantasy of wholeness that often drives cultural cross-dressing in contexts where identification with the fetishized Other operates to "make good colonial alienation and lack" (Low 1996, 232). Thus the play hybridizes the dark and light sides of town in order to mediate between their opposing perspectives but still maintains considerable tension across the racial fault lines even while de-essentializing the categories that undergird imperialist constructions of race. Such strategies can be linked, once again, to Bhabha's idea of the ambivalence of the colonial subject: the performance produces characters that are "less than one and double" (1985a, 103), which is to say that representing one always signifies the other's *partial* presence in both senses of the term.

Hewett's doubling of events produces yet another split or multiplication in the process of narrativity, which is further complicated by numerous allusions to both canonical texts and local theatre history. Not surprisingly, Shakespeare figures as a prominent site of theatrical reinscription.

Fig. 16. Dressing up Pretty Polly Perkins, *The Man from Mukinupin,* Royal Queensland Theatre Company, 1989. (Photo: Fiora Sacco.)

When Touch of the Tar marries Harry Tuesday, shell-shocked war hero and twin brother of Polly's sweetheart, Jack, her wedding ceremony foreshadows her sister's but undercuts the ostentatious display of the approved sacrament with simple bush rites shaped from the (mis)appropriated lines of *The Tempest.* This scene enacts another type of antimasque that fractures the utopian vision of its prototype through the insistent presence of racial alterity and also undermines the canonical status of Shakespeare's text by a process of dispersive citation. Thus Hewett's theatre, like that of Malouf and Nowra, can be viewed as "haunted" or shadowed by multiple ghosts, not least of which are those passed on through theatrical traditions themselves.

In drawing attention to its own sites of enunciation, *The Man from Mukinupin* presents identity as ideologically constructed and therefore capable of being changed. That theatre provides such sites of intervention is potently illustrated when, during a performance of "The Strangling of Desdemona" staged by touring thespians, Jack leaps on stage screaming "Murder, bloody murder" and knocks down Othello, evoking a standing ovation from the townspeople (1979, 29). The entire scene displaces the generic markers of Shakespeare's tragedy when the performance becomes a site of slapstick comedy that discursively intervenes in the racial paradigms embedded in the canonical text. Such metatheatricality resists the textual closures of imperial (stage) history and enacts what Dunstone calls a "crisis in reception" that problematizes the audience's role in the production of meaning because a split gaze is required to follow the many overlapping images (1990, 79). And if the text bespeaks a need for reconciliation between the feminine and the masculine, the light and the dark, the Aborigines and white Australians, it also offers performance as a means to rapprochement. "In the theatre," says Miss Clarry, "everything is possible" (Hewett 1979, 19). Whether or not this condition of possibility can always facilitate material rather than simply metaphorical forms of reconciliation remains a moot question.

As Hewett's work demonstrates so clearly, a thorough appropriation of *theatricality*—often a pejorative term connoting feminized behavior—is an important strategy in a theatre that seeks to move beyond imperial and patriarchal patterns of representation. In a related maneuver, feminist performance theory (and practice) advocates metatheatre as a way of radicalizing the avant-garde movement to shift attention "from the mirror's image to the mirror's surface and frame" (Dolan 1992, 3). By looking beyond the framing and staging of the theatrical event to focus on the scopic regimes instituted between the spectator and the spectacle, a self-conscious performance criticism scrutinizes that economy of desire implicit in constructions of the colonizable Other. What is crucial here is finding a model of visual representation that resists or deflects such desire, or, in Freedman's terms, that "play[s] out the fantasy of reflecting a look in such a way as to stare it down" (1991, 67).

At this point, my analysis returns to Alma De Groen's *The Rivers of China* because it stages in mythic detail precisely that refracted gaze forwarded by Freedman, among others, as the appropriate paradigm for a feminist drama.[19] Harnessing the legendary power of the Medusa, the play examines "looking relations" in such a way as to enact a powerful counter-discourse to the patriarchal economy. Although explicitly invoked in only one scene, the Medusa myth is central to the structural framework and political agenda of De Groen's text. Not only does it inform her vision of the present-day world where women maintain political, social, and ideological control through the agency of "the look"—a characteristic specifically linked to the Gorgon and ascribed to all females regardless of their position in society—but it also provides a way of intervening in representation itself.

The primary intervention occurs as a reenactment of a snuff movie that depicts but does not entirely explain the genesis of female ascendancy. Briefly the scene unfolds as follows: two men are setting up ready to film a snuff movie in a makeshift studio while the woman they have captured for the purpose sits gagged, bound and blindfolded on the floor (see fig. 17). The men discuss in graphic detail variant scenarios for filming her rape and death, but when they release the woman's blindfold in preparation for the "shoot," she petrifies first one then the other with her gaze, mysteriously appropriating the Medusa's magical powers to instigate a traumatic breach of patriarchal rule.

In its focus on the Medusa legend, De Groen's text signals a transfer of power from the phallus to its matriarchal equivalent, the look. The danger in this simple transference, as Carolyn Pickett points out, is that the play's particular revisioning of the Medusa myth might be read as a "cautionary tale" that "shows the power of women to be a malignant force" (1991, 12). Hence the central icon of the serpent/Gorgon as emblem of and metonym for the destructive urges of woman remains intact, as does the implied threat of castration. On a purely thematic level, it is hard to argue against this reading of the Medusa's reconstruction in *The Rivers of China*, for the look *is* both brutal and coercive, facilitating methods of surveillance that produce a kind of "big sister" culture that ultimately oppresses women as well as men. The real subversive power of the snuff scene, I contend, arises not so much from what it shows but from how its action engages with and even deflects that much-discussed paradigm of visual representation—the male gaze.

First theorized by Laura Mulvey in her influential article "Visual Pleasure and Narrative Cinema," the male gaze supposes a model of representation, derived from psychoanalytic theory, that turns upon "scopophilia (pleasure in looking at another person as an erotic object)" and "ego libido (forming identification processes)" (1975, 17). Mulvey argues that in conventional representation man is positioned as the bearer of the look, while woman is inevitably its object. Three looks are posited: the look of the camera that records the event, the look of the audience at the film, and the look of the characters at each other, all of which encourage identification with masculine viewpoints and so construct a male viewing position regardless of the spectator's gender (see Mulvey 1975, 11–14). Although developed specifically in relation to cinema, the male-gaze model has been applied to drama, and, more importantly, questioned in performance contexts. According to Freedman, it is inappropriate as a theory of spectatorship for the theatre because the live performer is "aware that she is seen, reflects that awareness and so deflects our look" to effect a "fractured reciprocity of the

Fig. 17. Snuff scene, *The Rivers of China,* Melbourne Theatre Company, 1988. (Photo: Jeff Busby.)

gaze" (1991, 1). The multivectored look implicit in theatre—as opposed to the unidirectional gaze of cinema—is staged by De Groen in mythic proportion through the metatheatrical codings of the snuff scene.

Although the scene is constructed by the characters as a video that Wayne shows to the Man/Catherine to explain the history of the feminist dystopia, this "video clip" is actually acted out for the audience by live performers to achieve precisely that fracturing of the gaze that Freedman consigns to theatrical looking. De Groen's text explicitly foregrounds this fracture in its focus on the eyes of the woman who is about to be raped and murdered in service of that most gendered of cinematic products, the hardcore porn movie. When the would-be victim mysteriously seizes Medusa's power to return the look, the male gaze is split, splintered, and neutralized, while women are reconstituted as *looking* subjects rather than *looked-at* objects, an inversion that is crucial to the feminist agenda of the play. And when Wayne switches on the lights to reveal himself and the Man, and beyond them the audience, as spectators, the scene reinforces, through its multiple self-reflexive frameworks, what Paul Willeman posits as the fourth look (in addition to the three outlined by Mulvey): the sense that the audience is seen in the process of seeing—called the "reverse shot" in filmic terms (1986, 216). What this reversal attempts to provoke is the spectator's awareness that s/he is deeply implicated in the voyeuristic aspect of all theatre, or what has been called the "pornography of representation"—to use the title of Susanne Kappeler's book (1984).

The legend of the Medusa seems the perfect myth to invoke here, not only because of her killing glance, but also because she embodies the logic of the amulet: the ability to turn like against like, as demonstrated by the ancient Greek and Roman practice of using the Medusa mask to neutralize fascination and ward off the evil eye (Siebers 1983, 8)—or, in this case, the male gaze. In some versions of the classical legend, Perseus actually kills Medusa by petrifying her with her own reflected image in his shield, a detail that is also important to *The Rivers of China* insofar as it draws our attention to parallels between the Medusa look and the male gaze and suggests that the look is the gaze turned back on itself, or the return look that feminist theatre aims to privilege. The snuff "video," then, is a primal scene that reconstitutes gender identities and gender relationships and, crucially, interrogates the spectatorial models that have positioned women as objects connoting what Mulvey calls "to-be-looked-at-ness" (1975, 11). The snuff scene also revises the legend of Medusa by means of its focus on a woman who actively appropriates the look to avert rape rather than passively accepting it as punishment for male lust and power, as in classical versions of the myth when Medusa is turned into a Gorgon after Poseidon violates her in Athena's temple.

The central positioning of the snuff scene in both narratives of *The Rivers of China* and a recognition of parallels between patriarchal and imperial looking relations lead us to interpret De Groen's radical expropriation of the male gaze as an essential step toward overthrowing the restrictive social structures that disadvantaged Katherine Mansfield, and questioning the system of exchanges that underwrite her construction as the colonial woman artist in imperial literary histories. But, as the play suggests, a simple inversion of the gaze is problematic, for it reinscribes binary oppositions and leaves the epistemology of oppression intact. The dystopian vision thus created proves unsatisfying even in feminist terms, as illustrated by the dissent of Rahel, the bewilderment of Katherine/the Man, and her/his refusal to embrace this particular "Brave New World." We might well ask, then, what kind of looking position, if any, is sanctioned by the play. I suggest that the answer to this important question lies in at least three different but closely related sites. In the Mansfield narrative, the privileged eye, which constitutes the "I" as subject in self/other paradigms of identity formation, is displaced by the voice when Katherine learns to locate her "self" by articulating "I" as grounded in various parts of her corporeal existence (1988, 32–33). This process is related to creating the self through memory: "Until you can remember yourself you do not exist" (33), Gurdjieff tells Katherine in one of his more instructive moments. Katherine's voiced "I" in this scene is simultaneously echoed and amplified by the Man to create a complex moment of performative "remembering" that establishes the composite Man/sfield figure who then represents the second site of deprivileged "looking."

The Man, as an androgynous figure positioned in the matrix of a number of intersecting discourses, poses the most radical threat to the power dynamics of the imperial and patriarchal gaze. As Lloyd Davis points out, since inscriptions of gender usually function to "reinforce and impose social organizations of the body, of sex, and of sexual identity," then androgyny "disrupts the social narrative of gender's origins and ends" (1992, 132). Hence, Katherine/the Man repeatedly destabilizes the relations s/he designates, a point evident as her/his narrative shifts with great celerity between perspectives—female and male, forward looking and backward, from home to exile. As a floating signifier, the androgynous look exemplifies Ashcroft's reading of Kristeva's "theoretical bisexuality of the unconscious," which he sees as "not simply a union of the maternal and the paternal, but in post-colonial terms [as] an openness to the continuing deferral of cultural identity" (1989b, 33). An important moment of deferral occurs in the play when Katherine/the Man demands a mirror to determine who s/he is and reels in response to the unexpected image of a man in the glass. In addition to the obvious feminist focus on women's erasure in imperial/patriarchal systems, this scene makes a point of exposing the mirror image as a play of surfaces that obscures subject relations and looking mechanisms. Gender identity as a reproducible facsimile constituted through the mirror (through visual representation) is thus undermined.

A third site of radical looking in the play rests in the relationship between the audience and the various dramatic signifiers. I have already discussed the ways in which the form and content of the snuff scene splits our gaze and intervenes in conventional modes of spectatorship, but the idea of the Medusa mirror or shield that reflects the gaze bears further examination in the light of the play's production history in Sydney, where onstage mirror windows were used as part of the set. As Foucault argues, the mirror combines utopian with heterotopian vision.

> The mirror is, after all, a utopia since it is a placeless place. . . . But it is also a heterotopia in so far as the mirror does exist in reality, where it exerts a sort of counteraction on the position that I occupy. From the stand point of the mirror I discover my absence from the place where I am since I see myself over there. (1986, 24)

To the extent that the stage always represents an unreal, virtual space at the same time as it exists in reality, theatre provides a similar kind of utopian/heterotopian experience to that which Foucault describes. Developing the stage's parallels with the mirror along these lines revises traditional readings of Hamlet's famous assertion that performance "hold[s] as t'were, the mirror up to nature." In *The Rivers of China,* the stage provides not a reflection or duplication of what is, but a representation of what *might* be at any given moment, or in Foucauldian terms, a "counteraction on the position I [the viewer] occupy" (1986, 24). Hence the audience is situated in ambiguous spaces indicating distance from *and* proximity to the scene/seen. Furthermore, when a mirror reflects the "look," it "threatens the voyeur's invisibility" (Rowlands 1989, 37), and because the seeing subject is also the seen object, the mirror's specularity breaks down the power relations implied in a unidirectional gaze. Thus the play's mise en scène enhances a particularly theatrical model of looking that entails negotiation between a range of possible subject/object positions, transforming the way dramatic subjects are seen, and enacting multiple refractions of the I/eye through a focus on the "readerly" (spectatorly) functions of the text. "Like the shield held up to view Medusa, [this kind of] theater offers a perspective glass by means of which our look is revealed as always already reflected, defined by the exchange of signifiers that displace [even] as they place us" (Freedman 1991, 72). In this respect, it could be argued that the mirroring aspects of the Medusa, and the process of image fragmentation and multiplication invoked by the teaming mass of wide-eyed serpents on the Gorgonian head, encapsulates the energy and subversiveness behind the mythopoeic project of De Groen's play.

The Serpent's Fall (1987), by Sarah Cathcart and Andrea Lemon, also invokes the legend of the Medusa as part of its performance aesthetics but focuses less on the Gorgon's look than on her creative energies, aspects of the myth that have increasingly influenced the Medusa's literary representation and iconography from the Romantic period to the present. The other mythical figure central to the play is the Aboriginal Rainbow Serpent, which shows something of a Medusa link in its representation in indigenous Australian art, both traditional and contemporary. The Rainbow Serpent shares with Medusa the powers of fascination and petrification and a tremendous potential for destruction, but these are less important to the play than its (re)generative aspects. Drawing freely on both mythical traditions, Cathcart and Lemon illustrate how patriarchal rule has effected the alienation of woman from the snake, and the demonizing of both through a retroping of ancient mythologies centered on worship of the Serpent Goddess. The cleavage between woman and the snake becomes emblematic of her split from the land under imperial patriarchy and, ultimately, of the gap between Aboriginal and Western (read patriarchal) epistemologies. Overall, *The Serpent's Fall* advocates a rapprochement of woman and the serpent as the metaphorical blueprint for a postcolonial Australian society. In terms of the duality of the Medusa figure, illustrated by Euripides' version of the legend, which details how two drops of her blood were taken, one medicinal and one poisonous, we might say that while De Groen shows the Medusa look as the inevitable outcome of a sick society, as underlined by the hospital and sanatorium settings and the disease motifs in *The Rivers of China,* Cathcart and Lemon focus on the healing powers of the Gorgon.

Their play features five main female characters and consists of short and often very witty scenarios depicting aspects of their daily lives, all interlarded to produce a fractured narrative that is loosely stitched together by the actor/artist figure who plays all the various roles. These women face the challenge of rediscovering primal links with the female principle as iconized by the serpent—wisdom, fecundity, sensuality, and spiritual knowledge of the land—in a society where women are deeply interpellated by the patriarchal biases of Western imperial and biblical traditions. The text opens with an interrogation of the Adam and Eve story and then develops this deconstructive project by presenting a number of ancient gynocentered and/or Aboriginal myths that radically revision the serpent's iconography. Much of this material is presented through parody and satire in a dramatic form that questions the narrativity of genres such as myth insofar as the play eschews closure and conventional emplotment while rewriting the tragedy of the "Fall of Man" as "The Serpent's Fall," an event that accounts for the current alienation of humans from the spiritual realm, be it represented by some pre-Christian golden age or by the Aboriginal Dreamtime. The play's dismantling of the Adam and Eve myth thus takes place on a number of fronts: we are alerted to its inherent misogyny by witnessing the lives of women who have internalized its politics; at the same time, various characters present alternative readings of the serpent as icon. Medusa becomes central to the text's deconstructive project when Bernice on one of her archaeological digs at Knossos finds a statue of the Snake

Goddess, Ishtar, and draws a direct parallel between the two, invoking Medusa as the Goddess of Wisdom who will preside over the reconstruction of "herstory" from the artifacts of history.

In terms of spectatorship, one could argue that it is also the performative structures of *The Serpent's Fall* that function to resist the concept of woman as a passive object of the male gaze by dispersing and transforming the images through which she is represented. In this play, the theatrical look splits, redoubles, and multiplies not only on the head of Medusa but also through the multiple transmutations of the Rainbow Serpent, and, more crucially for the reconciliation of cultures and the recuperation of women's histories that the play envisions, through the intertextuality of these reworkings of the various serpent-centered mythologies. Like De Groen, Hewett, and the many other playwrights who use metatheatre to resist the imperial and/or patriarchal gaze, what Cathcart and Lemon offer is a different way of seeing and, consequently, a refracted worldview.

The Serpent's Fall was deliberately written as a monodrama and has been performed most often by Cathcart herself playing Sarah, an Australian actor, who plays, alternately, a young archaeologist, a middle-aged Greek migrant, an urban Aborigine, and a retired schoolteacher. Insofar as it uses images and myths circulating in Australian culture to devise a "tribal" story told by one person through dancing, singing, explication, and impersonation to an audience that is actively included in the tale, the play resembles, in its structure and enactment, an Aboriginal oral narrative. If, as Cathcart and Lemon suggest, Aboriginal culture offers alternative mythologies for Australian society as a whole and for women in particular, the choice of form, which implicitly questions the teleology of Western narrative, is an important one.

While there have been successful amateur productions of *The Serpent's Fall* using separate actors for the different roles, what is missing from this choice is the self-reflexive focus on the transformative powers of the artist/actor/storyteller figure, and subsequently on the notion of theatrical transformation itself. Conceived as a monodrama, the play writes the body in Cixous's terms by writing *with* the body, which is to say that it harnesses the corporeality of a single actor playing multiple characters to produce a fluid concept of gender identity while at the same time conveying sociocultural differences between the characters. As Sarah slips from one character to another without costume changes or breaks, using only mimed props, the performance enacts what Jill Dolan outlines as the two opposing feminist theories of the self, identity politics and poststructural notions of the decentered subject.

> Identity politics claims to define women's subjectivity by their positions within race, class, or sexuality, positions which the dominant culture—and often the dominating voices in feminism—have effectively squelched. Poststructuralist practice suggests that any such coherent conceptions of identity are specious since even race, class, and sexuality, as well as gender, are constructed within discursive fields and changeable within the flux of history. According to poststructuralism, subjectivity is never monolithic or fixed, but decentred, and constantly thrown into process by the very competing discourses through which identity might be claimed. (1989, 59–60)

These theories of self may both be applied to a reading of the play's dance, a sequence that not only showcases the subversive energy of the moving body in performance, but also exemplifies the form of the play as a whole. Initiated by the libidinous energy of the Snake Goddess, this sequence shows Sarah performing the dances of four separate women in rapid succession. She begins by moving to the beat of an urban disco, then adapts her steps to enact a tribal narrative before being possessed in a moment of ecstatic energy that finally transforms into a Greek dance. As she dances, her transitions between characters, and the traces of difference thus enacted by a single but composite body, both produce and simultaneously deconstruct cultural and racial specificity, presenting identity as fluid but not without some sort of grounding in individual sociohistorical circumstances. Accordingly, the dance functions as a mode of empowerment for all of its participants: for Kelly, it forms a link with the land and her Aboriginality; for Sula, a moment of resistance to the drudgery of the cafeteria; for Bernice, the possibility of rewriting the body against the discourses of power engendered in the biblical myth of genesis; and for Sarah herself, further indication that her own performance, and therefore her "self" is, in a sense, intertextual. This shifting, hybridized sense of identity, which is also characteristic of the postcolonial subject, figures as the most important feature of the play's construction of the feminine, and the Australian.

Sarah's occupation as actor/dancer also foregrounds the self-reflexivity that prevents passive consumption of the theatrical event. The audience is always aware of the actor as she plays the different characters; hence, this Brechtian style of "acting in quotation marks" (Willett 1964, 192–94) frames the narrative as a deliberate intervention into representation/history. Nevertheless, the collapsing of a number of culturally marked identities into a composite performative body once again raises some thorny issues about authenticity. While constructing many of the women's stories as embodied knowledges, the play does not seem to question its own authority to present those knowledges via a character (and beyond that, an actor) who signifies as generically white. This failure to fully scrutinize its own site(s) of enunciation makes *The Serpent's Fall* somewhat problematic in political terms even though the impulse to speak for imperial patriarchy's Others seems to result from a well-intentioned effort to circulate stories that might not otherwise be told.

The few plays mentioned in this chapter represent only a small part of a repertoire of recent Australian drama that uses the richly suggestive possibilities of metatheatre to increase women's visibility as narrative subjects, and, simultaneously, to question the conventions through which women are represented. If metatheatre provides a forum for self-conscious constructions of female subjectivity, then it can also usefully extend the political and cultural agenda of feminist theatre. This agenda becomes interwoven with postcolonial concerns at a number of points, notably when discourses of nationhood intersect with ideas about gender and sexuality. As my final chapter suggests, such intersections (manifest explicitly and/or implicitly) pervade contemporary theatre in Australia, giving credence to McClintock's argument that "despite an ideological investment in the idea of popular *unity*, nations have historically amounted to the sanctioned institutionalization of gender difference" (1995, 353).

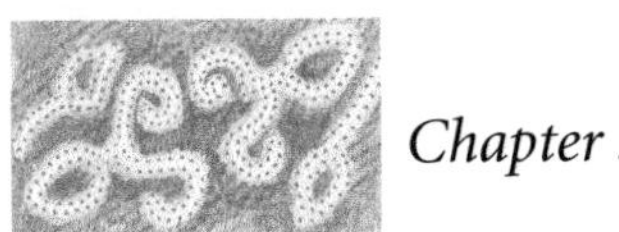

Chapter 5

Neoimperialism

Gender and Nation

If post-modernism is at least partially about how the world dreams itself to be "American," then post-colonialism is about waking from that dream and learning to dream otherwise.

—*Diana Brydon, "The White Inuit Speaks"*

Discovering Asia has been as painful as wearing Europe.

—*Lynne Strahan, "Aussie Still in Search of Self"*

This chapter's focus on neocolonialism extends the model of postcoloniality based on British hegemony and argues that colonial relations are not simply a question of Europe and its imperial periphery. While the discourses of European invasion and settlement remain key sites of interrogation for both Aboriginal and non-Aboriginal dramatists, other forms of imperialism have become increasingly topical subjects in contemporary Australian theatre. The most powerful player on the neoimperial stage, and consequently the most obvious target for counterdiscourse, is, of course, the United States, and there is no shortage of plays that attempt to offer some kind of resistance to what has been aptly termed the *Coca-Colanization* of Australian culture. Equally complex, and often more overtly ambivalent, are the representations of Australia's relationships with various Asian countries, which are sometimes troped as potential or actual aggressors, and at other times portrayed as victims of Australia's own imperial activities in the Pacific region. In plays from the 1970s and early 1980s that figure United States military presence in Asia, Australia's positioning in the neocolonial triangle becomes even more complicated, for while the shouts of protest against America's methods of domination are loud and clear, there is often tacit approval of its basic strategic agenda: to contain the spread of Asian communism and neutralize perceived threats to the "integrity" of Westernized cultures in the region. This geopolitical fixation with communism has not entirely subsided in the 1990s, although many

Australians now consider the invasion of Asian capitalism to be a greater threat, if a necessary evil.

Not surprisingly, war features as a common subject in many Australian plays about neoimperialism and will thus be a focus in my discussion. Gareth Griffiths argues, in relation to John Romeril's work, that war represents "the extreme form of a socioeconomic process in which Australia's involvement has to be seen within the paradigms of her colonial and neocolonial relationship first with Britain, and subsequently with America" (1993, 130). In the plays examined here, war is an especially charged site of discourse not only because it sharpens the conflicts depicted, but also because its implicit gendering often occludes the narratives of female Others whose positioning in the battlefield is problematic. As my analysis of feminist postcolonial drama has demonstrated, a model of counterdiscursivity constituted solely on the colonizer/colonized dialectic does not adequately account for the complicated negotiations of power through which Australians continue to define their sexual, racial, and geographical identities, nor does it recognize their complicity with certain imperial and patriarchal discourses. This final chapter moves further toward a concept of postcolonialism as inevitably hybrid and multidiscursive, an approach flexible enough to posit a speaking position for the various players on the Asia-Pacific stage without co-opting their differences. The first section traces the broad features of contemporary Australian drama's responses to American imperialism, while the second concentrates on two plays that offer particularly interesting representations of Australia's Asian context. In each section, I am concerned to locate the intersections of gender and nation as important sites of postcolonial inquiry.

American Neoimperialism

Many cultural analysts like to pinpoint the moment when Australia began to experience new forms of imperialism as a result of transferring its primary allegiances from the "mother country" to its American "uncle." The pivotal event for these historians is of course World War II, or, more precisely, Prime Minister Curtin's response to the war in a new-year message delivered to the Australian public on 29 December 1941: "Without any inhibitions of any kind, I make it quite clear that Australia looks to America, free of any pangs as to our traditional links or kinship with the United Kingdom" (qtd. in Phillips 1988, 15). Undoubtedly, this statement *was* a watershed event in Australian foreign policy, but colonization does not occur overnight, and it would be naive to suggest that the political, economic, and cultural influence of the United States had not already permeated Australian society in significant ways long before the perceived threat of a Japanese invasion precipitated the call for American military support. That this influence had also been registered in some circles at least as a form of neoimperialism is evident, for example, in the debates of the mid-1920s about Australian importation of American films,[1] and also in P. R. Stephenson's call, in 1936, for the "un-Yankeefying" of Australian culture as well as for its "de-Pommification" (1936, 98, 89).

A critique of American imperialism in its varying forms has been a recurrent motif in Australian theatre for some time, especially since the new-wave period when dramatists such as Romeril staged a number of plays and agitprop protests against Australia's internalization of American hegemony.[2] What I want to trace here is the postwave theatre's reassessment of Australia's historical involvement with the United States in the last half-century, when the influence of British imperialism has waned while American neoimperialism is increasingly regarded as a pressing issue. What the events of World War II highlighted was Australia's profound ambivalence toward its trans-Pacific ally, a feeling catalyzed by the "GI invasion" during the early 1940s (Phillips 1988, 14), when over a million American soldiers passed through Australia. The word *invasion* is significant here: used with equal frequency in a range of popular and scholarly histories focusing on that period,[3] it signals the neoimperial thrust of American strategic interest in Australia and situates the intruders firmly in the enemy camp. There is also an implicit image of rape, which underlines parallels between the GI invasion and the European settlement of Australia, a trope already noted in chapter 3's analysis of Janis Balodis's *Too Young for Ghosts.* For this chapter, however, the significance of the rape metaphor lies not so much in its parabolic reference to the invasion of Aboriginal land in the colonial period as in its suggestion that new forms of cultural domination, like the old, often hover obsessively, if sometimes covertly, around the body/text of "woman" as a site of conquest.

Two contemporary plays that focus directly on the consequences of the GI invasion of Australia are Linda Aronson's musical revue, *Dinkum Assorted* (1988), and Bob Herbert's living room drama, *No Names . . . No Pack Drill* (1979). Neither offers the savage critique of American imperialism evident in plays about subsequent United States military intervention in the Asia-Pacific region, especially in Vietnam, but they do represent Americans as a corrosive influence and suggest that women in particular should be more chary of the GIs who are "over-sexed, over-paid, and over here," to use part of the title of John Moore's book (1981). In both plays,

Australian women function as arbiters of the competing versions of masculinity embodied by the Aussie Digger[4] and the Yankee GI, and they are expected to exercise probity in their choices. At the same time, women are troped as the trouble spots of the nation's defense system. Vulnerable and potentially treacherous, they threaten to compromise the moral fabric of society and to become conduits for a dirty capitalism that trades in sex, nylons, and perfume.

While no males figure directly in *Dinkum Assorted*'s cast of characters—even the goat is female—men are the central reference points in the lives of most of the women workers at the small-town biscuit factory depicted. Forming a feminine version of Dad's Army, these women run the factory while their husbands and brothers are at war; but although the play certainly celebrates their pluck, recuperating women's experiences from the margins of wartime history, it ultimately suggests that their most crucial task is not to keep the economy going but to resist the sexual allure of the stocking-toting American airmen who loom large in the background of the action. This allure is punctured at various points through the play's comic theatricality, most notably when the women perform a highly amusing chorus-line dance routine using stuffed dummies to represent the lascivious GIs. The finale also pokes fun at the airmen in a song about the embarrassment of falling in love with "A Yank Called Marion" (Aronson 1988, 90–91), but elsewhere the Americans function as objects of desire and temptation. By representing them as oversexed and yet paradoxically feminized, the play risks upholding phallocratic discourses through an unintentional sleight of hand: the GIs must *appear* highly virile to explain why some women succumb to their charms, but if this sexual prowess is in fact a myth, the onus is on the women to detect such duplicity. In all this, the masculinity of the conspicuously absent Australian soldier is never contested but rather approved by an implied comparison with his effete counterpart. While the Yanks are aligned with the domestic realm and figured as poachers and/or cowards, the real men, Aronson suggests, are the ones off fighting, or at the very least suffering the privations of a prisoner-of-war camp.

Bob Herbert's treatment of a GI who has deserted ship in Sydney is more sympathetic insofar as he develops a psychologically complex American character, but the narrative of *No Names . . . No Pack Drill* is also shaped as a cautionary tale. Appealing though the GI, Rebel Potter, may be, he is nonetheless a coward who hides behind women's skirts, a point underlined by the play's semiotics when he conceals himself in the bathtub under a pile of Kathy's underwear. That Rebel eventually escapes the military police while Kathy, as his Australian girlfriend, faces a jail sentence for refusing to reveal his plans situates the woman as the appropriate target of disciplinary action and public censure. Herbert's inclusion of an Australian man, Tiger, as the Judas in the story, does not disrupt this paradigm since Tiger is beneath contempt, already marked by cowardice and corrupted by his "business" with the Americans. Once again, the real soldiers are at the front line, and, curiously, it is left to Kathy, acting as proxy for her brother, to uphold their behavioral codes by refusing to "dob" on a mate. Her misdirected loyalty to Rebel is thus lauded while the relationship between the two is neatly desexualized by its emplacement within the masculine ethos of mateship.

In these two plays, seduction, unwanted pregnancy, and abandonment are presented as the likely outcome of Australia's mésalliance with the United States. In metaphorical terms, a naive and feminized Australia is penetrated by her supposed protector and then left with the ill-begotten offspring of that union. Neither play speculates on the nature of this "bastard" child, but it could be argued that Vietnam figures somewhere in the political equation since Australia's military involvement there was partly a result of the shift in foreign policy that brought the GIs to Australian shores in the first place. Herbert and Aronson do develop lines of resistance to the GI invasion, but these are mostly linked to what seems like an urgent imperative to differentiate the Australian soldiers from their Yankee rivals and thus preserve the myths that have undergirded patriarchal versions of nationalism in Australia. The pressing issue is women's fidelity, while the presumed supremacy of the Western male, a notion that lies at the heart of imperialism in its new forms and its old, is never questioned.[5] From a counterdiscursive point of view, neither text is as complex or satisfying as Balodis's *Too Young for Ghosts* because Herbert and Aronson stop short of examining Australia's complicity with American hegemony. Instead, they tend to downplay the ambivalence that characterizes Australian attitudes toward the United States and to construct women as unwitting allies of the smooth-talking roués who peddle American dreams as well as black-market goods. In contrast, Balodis's play depicts women actively resisting sexual exploitation by the GIs, or at least appropriating it for their own purposes. Hence, Ilse refuses to play the aggrieved rape victim and insists that she "traded" with the GIs on *her* terms, not theirs, a claim substantiated when she later refuses to have sex with them and bites one on the lip to make her point. Karl's role in this trade is revealing: rather than defending Ilse, he stands by like a pimp, hoping to profit from the exchange, and then passively watches the GIs attempt to violate her. His positioning as a voyeur in the composite rape scene, along with the elision of the GIs and the explorers, clearly implicates Australian men in the (neo)colonial venture and suggests a tacit bond between them and their American adversaries. In this way, gender is shown to inflect upon national and political allegiances as the men establish a sexual economy designed to facilitate the colonization of women. Ilse, of course, is fully aware of this, as indicated by her riposte to Karl's warning to be friendlier to the GIs.

> *Karl:* Don't go biting any more Americans, they're on our side.
> *Ilse:* They're on *your* side.
>
> (1985a, 21; emphasis added)

Whereas Ilse has no illusions about American imperialism, in this play it is Karl who is seduced by American dreams of the "post-war high life" (Balodis 1990, 25).

The portrayal of the Americans as openly predatory and violent suggests that the World War II narrative in *Too Young for Ghosts* has been adapted to fit the contingencies of the post-Vietnam era. Balodis himself affirms this, saying that he could have used English or Russian soldiers but chose Americans deliberately.

> I grew up through the Vietnam period, and my parents and a lot of Latvian people have right-wing views, in opposition to the communist imperialism in Latvia. So they were always unquestioningly embracing the Americans and their right to be in Vietnam, whereas I wanted to question that. . . . [The play] was actually throwing into relief the notion that the Americans were the saviours. (1990, 25–26)

In this respect, *Too Young for Ghosts* enacts the complex revisioning of history that marks postcolonial texts—a process based not only on recuperating marginalized perspectives but also on interpreting the past through contemporary terms of reference. It could be argued that many recent Australian narratives about World War I are also deeply inflected by the Vietnam conflict, although few show such direct cognizance of its legacy. In particular, attempts to revivify the Anzac legend,[6] as evident in a number of 1980s and 1990s novels and films,[7] can be linked to a deep anxiety about the erosion of the heroic soldier ideal that resulted from Australia's experience of Vietnam. Similar anxieties have energized media coverage of events relating to Australian military history, for example, the seventy-fifth anniversary of Gallipoli in April 1990, and the return of the body of the

Unknown Australian Soldier to the Canberra War Memorial in late 1993. Such celebrations of the soldier figure, as Susan Jeffords has argued in *The Remasculinization of America: Gender and the Vietnam War* (1989), suggests a reordering of the gender relations that feminism has threatened over the last quarter-century. It is important, then, to review briefly the function of the Anzac myth in Australian (theatrical) culture before going on to focus on Vietnam as the crucible of contemporary Australian-American tensions.

During the World War I period, the uniformed (boy) soldier of the Gallipoli myth was ambivalently constructed in the nexus of imperialist and nationalist discourses: on the one hand he represented loyalty to the mother country and a willingness to defend England's interests; on the other, he became the "custodian of nationhood" for a country anxious to give itself a "heroic, legendary core" (R. White 1981, 130). Fetishized since then, on stage and in film, as a national icon, the Digger has been invested with distinct, albeit sometimes contradictory, traits. Costume played a key part in his differentiation from British soldiers as the Digger uniform came to embody Australian versions of masculinity and mateship. Its khaki colors and rakish broad-brimmed hat pinned up on one side showed affinities with the habit of an idealized bush proletariat and suggested a certain larrikinism even while packaging the (white) Australian as an exemplary soldier type—broad-built, strong, skilled at survival, and, crucially, disciplined enough to outgrow the moral turpitude of his convict heritage. The conflicting codes of the Digger myth, as Richard White points out (1981, 136), have long been embodied in Anzac Day celebrations, which feature two very different forms of (theatrical) display: full military dress parades and solemn rituals in the morning, followed by drunken brawls and gambling in the afternoon, the latter functioning to splinter the performative codes[8] of the former in many ways. Particularly interesting about the longevity of the Anzac myth are the ways in which its conflation of imperial and anti-imperial discourses approves the basic military agenda of the British Empire but critiques its specific strategies, thus providing the perfect alibi for Australian defeat: betrayal by the parent culture. This traditional narrative trope, which reached its apotheosis in such films as Peter Weir's *Gallipoli* (1981), also features in plays about Vietnam, only here the neglectful parent has evolved into a malevolent uncle—or bullying big brother. The reluctance of these texts to confront Australia's own colonizing activities in the Asia-Pacific region reflects the dilemma that intervention in Vietnam posed to a country that has "relied all too heavily on a military past for images of national character" (Murphy 1987, 153).

Maurie McNarn's argument that Australia's "involvement in Vietnam was the climax of the shift from dependence upon Britain, as an Imperial appendage, to alliance with America, as a satellite" (1979–80, 73) is now commonplace, and most historians agree that the same colonialist mentality has governed both patterns of allegiance. According to Alison Broinowski, the anti-Americanism that characterized Australia's Vietnam period "was the latest version of post-colonial defiance which was itself the reverse side of Antipodean dependancy" (1992, 119). That Vietnam has since become, in Robin Gerster's terms, a sort of "military pariah" while Gallipoli "remains sacrosanct" (1987a, 30) is less a function of the eventual outcome of these respective conflicts—Australians may have lost the battle at Anzac Cove, but they were on the winning side overall—than of the perception that Australians fought the American way of war in Vietnam and not the Australian way, as they had at Gallipoli. Dennis Phillips argues that this also explains why "Australians as a whole have shown little inclination to remember the Vietnam War, to evaluate the experience, or to try to draw historical lessons from it" (1988, 134). Phillips is both right and wrong, for although this war "has not had the cumulative social impact in Australia that it has had in the United States" (134), it remains a site of rupture in Australian (hi)story and a signal event that continues to inflect upon local constructions of both America and Asia. As far as representations of the United States are concerned, the tendency is to retrope the sexual threat posed by the 1940s GI invasion as a cultural and ideological one that is far more pernicious. Australia, meanwhile, figures ambivalently in many critical reassessments of the period, often exculpated of guilt for its aggression toward Vietnam but at the same time vilified for its status as "lackey" to yet another imperial power.

As an unresolved issue, Vietnam haunts a number of contemporary plays, (dis)appearing in the margins as a site of repressed trauma that frequently attenuates the social and psychological growth of individuals and/or groups. Stephen Sewell's *The Blind Giant Is Dancing* (1983) and Michael Gow's *Away* both feature dysfunctional characters whose guilt at having sent their sons to Vietnam emblematizes a wider psychic stress over Australia's failure to resist the tide of American imperialism. Most notably, Louis Nowra's work exhibits a recurrent and intense interest in the subject of Vietnam, although this is often communicated by visual resonance rather than direct reference. If the apocalyptic landscape of *Inside the Island* remembers Gallipoli, it also conjures the killing fields of Mai Lai, as does the nuclear inferno imaged in *Sunrise* (1983). In this play, Nowra makes the Vietnam link explicit through the figure of the gardener, Ly, a shell-shocked Vietnamese refugee who cowers trembling when the helicopters fly overhead, but it is not until in *Cosi* (1992) that Nowra mentions American imperialism in Vietnam, and then only briefly. Other dramatists take a slightly different tack, seeming to engage directly with the central debates raised by Australian participation in that "dirty capitalist war," but ultimately using Vietnam as a pressurized space to sharpen more personal conflicts. This pattern is evident in Nick Enright's "bildungsdrama," *St James Infirmary* (1992), which situates the emotional and political crises of its rebel schoolboy protagonist within the framework of the 1960s Australian protest movement. In all of these texts, Vietnam is somehow displaced from center stage, included as an unnameable anxiety or referred to in passing but not dwelt on for long.

Sewell's *The Blind Giant Is Dancing* is perhaps the odd play out here, for although it does not foreground Vietnam, it does enact a sustained attack on American neoimperialism and on Australian's tendency to accept the ideologies that have allowed and even encouraged it. From its opening scene, which uses the generic conventions of a B-grade Hollywood detective movie, to its closing moments, when the Australian workers mount a revolutionary challenge to "American control of [their] national life" (1985, 132), Sewell's play draws our attention to the ways in which the cultural, economic, and political influence of the United States pervades Australian society. On a general level, "America" itself is portrayed as a powerful epistemological referent, as evident when Louise uses the example of the Dakota badlands to support her point about degradation of Australian farmland (59), or when her mother cites "those new diseases in America" as one of the sources of global angst (65). More specifically, Sewell conveys the hegemony of capitalism as an omnipresent threat through the character of Carew, the American who oversees the wheeling and dealing that will lead to the multinational takeover of the Australian steel industry. It seems to matter little that the mysterious Carew might not have the power ascribed to him; the fact that he is American is intimidation enough to demand that he be taken seriously. This atmosphere of threat is deepened by a number of direct references to American military and economic aggression, even though some might seem like throwaway lines. Bob's comment that, should the socialist revolution hit, "[he]'ll be on the first Hercules out after the Yanks have bombed shit out of the joint" (21) is but one example of how the United States dictates the direction of Australian politics. Also aligned with the Americans is Rose Draper, seen by some critics as the Mephistopheles who tempts Allen from idealism into corruption and betrayal. Throughout all this, the playwright's warning against cultural, economic, and moral bankruptcy is clear, as is his suggestion that these are the inevitable outcomes of multinational capitalism. But it is Australia's willing compliance with American imperialism that Sewell most deplores and the interruption of that pattern of compliance that his play attempts to effect. This is an important postcolonial agenda if, as Beryl Langer has argued, "our relationship to the imperial power is less formal than the one we used to have with Britain, but no less profound in its capacity to define the material and cultural parameters of everyday life" (1985, 30).

Notwithstanding the probable connections between Vietnam and the attack on American imperialism expressed in *The Blind Giant Is Dancing*, it is curious that playwrights such as Sewell, Nowra, and Gow, who have elsewhere been chroniclers and reinterpreters of the broader canvas of Australian history, and mordant critics of imperialism, have not seized more directly upon Vietnam as a dramatic subject. In a 1983 interview with Jeremy Ridgman, Sewell and Nowra identified it as one of the "central experiences" of Australian culture. Sewell states,

> The interest in Vietnam for me goes back to a sense of shame; about how the crime was committed against the Vietnamese people and how we participated in that crime. No acknowledgment has been made at the level of culture, let alone in reparations, after we participated in the devastation of that country. (Ridgman 1983, 122)

Nowra adds,

> It was a dubious and immoral war, especially from the point of view of Australia. We were a participant, not from ideas of honour or moral commitment or beliefs, but from a cringing necessity to align ourselves with a big boy power. (Ridgman 1983, 122)

Neither playwright shies away from confronting the fact of Australia's willing participation in Vietnam, and together they highlight the complex power relations at issue in the whole conflict. That their planned collaboration on a Vietnam play has not eventuated suggests, nevertheless, the acute difficulty that this subject poses.

Of the few postwave plays that do focus squarely on the significance of the Vietnam experience for the wider Australian community, Rob George's *Sandy Lee Live at Nui Dat* (1981) provides the most thoroughgoing indictment of American imperialism. In his preface to the published text, the playwright claims that the events of the 1960s precipitated the "Americanisation of Australia in a way that had never been known before" (1983, viii).

He explores this phenomenon dramatically on a number of levels by examining those who participated in the Vietnam War, those who protested against it, and those who profited from it. What is most distinctive about this text is its cognition that Australians have become neocolonials—or "Coca-Colonials"—through active consent. As Langer argues in her discussion of American hegemony, "We tend to conceptualize our status as colonized subjects in terms of a discourse of cultural imperialism which constructs our relation to the United States as one of domination/oppression. What this leaves out is the extent of our own complicity" (1991, 31). Rob George's play, like *The Blind Giant Is Dancing,* is very much about this complicity even though it is openly anti-American. Its lines of counterdiscursivity are developed not only in direct debates about neoimperialism but also through a nonnaturalistic mode that uses parody, song, and agitprop theatre to underscore criticism of all factions. The play's overt theatricality is particularly apposite for its subject since to many the war seemed like a badly managed stage production. Gerster describes Australia's participation in these terms.

> This was not the starring role and triumphant curtain call in a drama of clearly demarcated "good" versus "evil" to which Australians—thanks largely to the zeal of mythmakers like the First World War Official Historian C. E. W. Bean—had become accustomed. . . . Australians in Vietnam were "a side show . . . a walk-on part in an expensive production." To use a squib in vogue during the conflict, the whole sorry performance seemed to prove that Australia really was "The Lackey Country." (1987b, 10)

The protest movement, with its carefully orchestrated performances—the public burning of conscription papers is a case in point—was also styled according to theatrical paradigms, albeit of a different kind.

George's play sketches its characters in terms of broad stereotype, and its structure is loosely documentary, developing in juxtaposition three distinct narratives that eventually merge. No Americans or Vietnamese actually appear in the text; the emphasis is on how these Others are constructed and positioned within the neocolonial triangle created by Australian involvement in what is seen as America's war in Vietnam. On the home front, the action revolves around the presentation of a number of pieces of street theatre by the antiwar agitators, university students Peter and Pat, along with a focus on their political ideologies as revealed in less public moments. Using the parlance of the period, these two characters articulate a vehement protest against the American invasion of Southeast Asia. Well-worn slogans such as "Read about American war crimes" and "Smash US imperialism" resonate throughout their rather crudely staged demonstrations, but the playwright is careful to point out that even the theatre of protest has a distinctly American flavor. Hence Peter's (unoriginal) idea to make a show of burning his call-up papers is treated with a degree of cynicism.

> *Peter:* The important thing is the act of defiance that is involved; the symbolic gesture and the stage managing of that gesture. . . . It's a piece of street theatre.
> *Pat:* Right, but based on a script from an American news service.
> (1983, 20)

That Peter's "symbolic gesture" goes entirely unnoticed suggests that mindless emulations of American models of (mis)behavior are both ineffective and anything but revolutionary.

Elsewhere in the play, the use of street theatre reveals something of the mechanisms by which Australians construct themselves vis-à-vis their Yankee allies/enemies. Theatrical signifiers such as costume and accent become important in delineating national identities here, since the Australian-American contrast lacks a paradigm of racial difference to make visible the sense of essential Otherness that aides self-definition. When Peter and Pat perform a routine while decked out as Uncle Sam and Vietnam respectively, the play illustrates, by dint of metatheatrical emphasis on their artifice, how costume grafts particular characteristics onto the performing body rather than simply functioning as a neutral device that "blends straggling physiological signifiers so that they contribute to character" (Gaines 1990, 193). Peter's costume is intended to be highly evocative, suggesting militarism and political coercion, as well as more covert forms of cultural dominance. Uncle Sam is also very much a showbiz figure who reminds us that American hegemony operates through popular culture and the media. Hence his song has the structure and tone of an advertising jingle, as does Vietnam's reply.

> *Peter* [as Uncle Sam]: Howdy doody, hello ma'am
> You can call me Uncle Sam
> I am big and I am strong
> I've come to kill the Viet Cong
> I'll teach you all what's right and wrong

Come to save you Vietnam
So come up here and let's shake hands.

Pat [as Vietnam]: Thank you for your offer, friend,
But on ourselves we will depend.
We know our house is far from calm,
But we want peace and not napalm.
Yes, we want peace for Vietnam.
So give us food and we'll say thanks,
Don't sell us your expensive tanks.
(1983, 10–11)

Punctuated by Uncle Sam's gesture of pointing a revolver straight at Vietnam's head (see fig. 18), Peter and Pat's performance is unequivocal in its positioning of the United States as an imperial power to be resisted at all costs. The gender codes are abundantly clear: male America stands poised to rape and murder a female Vietnam. However, since this scenario also uses visual and aural cues suggestive of an American-style Vietnam protest sketch, its real subversiveness turns on the question of appropriation, that is, on whether the students actively seize upon the (stage) languages of the American protest and Australianize them or whether they simply reproduce borrowed tropes. I would argue that George's careful delineation of Pat, the questioner, from Peter, the mimic man, ensures that such scenes operate counterdiscursively because at least one of the pair seems fully aware of the hegemony of American discourse whether it peddles war or peace. Hence, the overall function of street theatre in this play seems to be to relocate the enemy as rhetoric itself. This move approximates what Peter Pierce terms the *tertiary stage* of Australian representations of the enemy in war literature, the stage wherein "language itself . . . comes to be recognized both as foe and as a major casualty of modern war" (1985, 172).[9]

The war narrative of *Sandy Lee Live at Nui Dat* concentrates on Australian imperialism in Vietnam, avoiding the common temptation to project national guilt over the war onto the Americans. While the Americans' "pacification" of a whole village certainly triggers the events that lead to the final catastrophic murder/suicide, it is clear that at least some of the Australian soldiers not only condone such violence but also (mis)use it for their own purposes. In particular, the play reveals how the (hi)story of Vietnam is shaped by the storytellers in ways that support personal agendas. Hence, the mercenary, Ted, reports the pacification in order to crush Bruce's romantic dreams while the third soldier, Gordon, later appropriates Bruce's

Fig. 18. Uncle Sam and Vietnam, *Sandy Lee Live at Nui Dat,* Stage Company, 1981. (Photo: David Simmonds.)

grief to concoct a credible tale that will convince the protesters of his anti-American stance. Gordon's disingenuous pose is of course radically undermined by the fact that he depends on the GIs to facilitate his drug trafficking, a point that emphasizes how the graft and corruption associated with the Vietnam War is widespread rather than simply confined to the Americans. I do not wish to suggest that this section of the play is any less trenchant in its critique of American imperialism but, rather, to argue that Rob George also directs our focus toward the discursive representation of that imperialism. Here, as in the protest narrative, it is Australia's own complicity with the American way of war/words that is highlighted.

The Vietnam scenes also communicate the Australians' anxiety about their official position as allies of the United States in a war where the antonyms *friend* and *enemy* are no longer polar points in a binary opposition, and where the racial Other refuses simple categorization. The mistrust that ensues in such situations is aptly described by a 1960s news report.

> The Vietnamese hate the Americans. The Americans hate the Vietnamese. Americans hate other Americans. The local Chinese are hated by both the Vietnamese and the Americans. The Australians hate everybody. (Qtd. in Pierce 1991, 262)

This certainly seems applicable to most of the soldiers in Rob George's play. Gordon's comment that the Diggers are "open season for Charlie and Uncle Sam and every slope-eyed bastard [they] come across" (1983, 29) reveals not only his racism but also a deep confusion over how the enemy might be confidently identified. The result is a solipsistic retreat into self-delusion or cynicism. Through the figure of the soldier doubly alienated from both his nominal allies and his fellow Australians, the play dismantles the myth of mateship that undergirds the Digger legend. Like Nowra in *Inside the Island,* George also refuses to present images or myths of a revenant soldiery that will exonerate the Australians, or to sanitize the war narrative by filtering it through the discourses of Gallipoli. Instead, he makes a point of deconstructing the Anzac myth by showing how the "innocent" and youthful bush balladeer, Bruce, is anything but a modern version of his heroic prototype, for he is neither courageous nor self-sacrificing, and, crucially, by his obsessive love/lust for a Vietnamese woman, he calls into question his fealty to his "mates."

While Bruce is the one soldier to draw our empathy, his fetishization and appropriation of his Vietnamese lover is severely criticized. He might profess undying devotion to Lai Dai, but it is quite obviously his own construction of her as a Madonna figure that fuels his love, a point stressed when he reveals that he does not even know her real name. That he simply makes up a new name for her denies her subjectivity and demonstrates, once again, the linguistic interpellation of the racial and sexual Other that is characteristic of imperial patriarchy. Similarly, his plans to bring Lai Dai to Australia suggest that she is merely a commodity to be imported at will. The particularly sexual nature of Australian imperialism in Asia is clearly expressed by Ted's satirical response to Bruce's query about why they are in

Vietnam at all: "It's actually all just a great big lonely hearts club where poor unattached males like you get to meet beautiful Asian girls in the romantic, exotic and colourful Far East" (1983, 25). Thus the play makes explicit the generic links between the war narrative and the traveler's tale,[10] positioning the Australian soldiers as Occidental (sex) tourists whose invasion of Asia is the predictable outcome of a wider desire for self-authentication through conquest of the passive Oriental other.[11] That Bruce's Orientalist fantasy devolves into a "bad trip" that leaves him "travel sick" is one of the major ironies of the Vietnam tour. Where the Americans fit in this paradigm is slightly less clear, but I would argue that a large part of the Australians' antipathy toward them can be traced to the same genital anxieties identified in this chapter's earlier discussion of the GI figure. This view is supported by Ted's aggressively dismissive construction of Lai Dai as a "whore" who "chat[s] up the Yank generals" (27), and by the ways in which the Australians compare themselves repeatedly to the Americans in what could be sexual terms of reference: "Is it true that us Aussies are six times better than the Yank soldiers?" asks Bruce (14). Significantly, Digger Dave and GI Joe never seem to meet in the flesh, or at least this is not detailed by the play. In the complex story of Vietnam, as in representations of the GI invasion of Australia, the female body is the space on and through which competitive national masculinities are contested.

If the war scenes of *Sandy Lee Live at Nui Dat* reveal the sexual imperative of Australia's neoimperialism in Asia, the third narrative thread of the play, which focuses on the pop singer, Sandy Lee, shows another kind of economic exploitation. Sandy Lee's career exemplifies capitalism's most insidious workings, not only because her tours to the military camps in Vietnam take on a progressively opportunistic bent, but also because her music and her public rhetoric justify Australian participation in the war. By setting her nauseatingly patriotic songs in ironic counterpoint to the students' protest ditties, the play strips her form of entertainment of its apolitical masquerade and positions the singer as yet another conduit for American hegemony. A sitting target for parody, Sandy Lee functions as a further site of counterdiscourse, but she is also an ambiguous figure who elicits some sympathy because she is obviously a victim of the very imperial and patriarchal systems she supports. This is particularly evident in the way that she too is situated as the fetishized object of the male gaze, constructed by Bruce as a surrogate for the beautiful Lai Dai, and by Ted as "a pretty round-eyed sheila" who will remind the soldiers "that the army does, after all, care for them" (1983, 9–10). Within the overall scheme of the play, however, Sandy emerges as a callous character and one who practices the worst kind of denial. Even though, in an unguarded moment, she articulates most fully the moral futility of the Vietnam "tour" of duty, it seems she has learned little from her travels. That her closing number is a song stolen from Bruce and introduced by an announcer with a phony American accent reminds us that Sandy Lee shows the ugly face of Australia's neocolonial experience in Vietnam, the pervasive cultural Coca-Colanization that is the enduring legacy of the American dream.

Rob George's honest, complex, and entertaining assessment of Australia's complicity with American imperialism in Asia should have sparked more interest in Australian theatre circles than it did, and it is regrettable that some of the prickly issues he raises have not been fully canvassed in a number of more recent plays about Australia's ongoing and problematic role in Asian-Pacific politics. The major exception here is Peter Copeman's *Hearts and Minds* (1992)[12] project, an intercultural theatre piece that explores the effects of the Vietnam War on two families, using a mixture of Vietnamese water puppetry and actor-based realism. In this play, a relatively simple love affair between an Australian university student and the daughter of a Vietnamese refugee becomes complicated when their respective parents find that the relationship releases suppressed memories of wartime trauma. Much to his credit, Copeman is unflinching in his depiction of the ways in which Australians were implicated in Vietnam atrocities, either by active participation or by a failure to intervene, and he resists the impulse to project a sense of national guilt onto the United States.

A brief analysis of Barry Lowe's *Tokyo Rose* (1989) illustrates how Australia's imperative to distance itself from American neocolonialism can result in a figural displacement of its own economic, military, and sexual aggression toward various Asian countries. Although set during World War II and ostensibly about the trial of a Japanese-American woman suspected by the United States of treason, *Tokyo Rose* has the ambience of a Vietnam protest play. Its quasi-documentary structure and burlesque musical style, along with an extended focus on the figure of Uncle Sam, invites comparisons with *Sandy Lee Live at Nui Dat.* In particular, the savage anti-Americanism of *Tokyo Rose* seems commensurate with a post-Vietnam assessment of the United States imperium, as does the play's portrait of a feminine Japan/Asia victimized by the menacing Uncle Sam. Lowe's inclusion of an Australian soldier as the adventitious "innocent abroad," combined with costume and scene designs that emphasize contrasts between the Aussie khaki and the Yankee red, white, and blue, completes the picture of a refracted and displaced Vietnam narrative.[13]

Like Rob George, Lowe is intensely interested in exploring the rhetorical and theatrical power of American popular entertainment and in showing how its tropes can be deployed to critique imperialism. In the first half of the play, he presents the (hi)story of Iva Toguri, the woman framed as Tokyo Rose, within the framework of a proposed musical being put together by a smooth-talking American, Carroll, who appropriates Iva's experience for his "exotic" new show. Carroll presents himself as the quintessential Broadway entrepreneur, "the body merchant" and "connoisseur of female flesh," who will "turn Iva's life-story into the sensation it should be" (1989, 2). The mutability of this kind of patriarchal history is clearly demonstrated as Carroll experiments with a number of ideas and theatrical images, censoring Iva's tale unless it is contingent with his own vision. That this vision is not only appallingly clichéd but also full of contradictions seems of little import to the entrepreneur as long as he gives the public what it wants. His idea for the jail scene, for example, begins with lights up on Iva as the "poor crushed butterfly" and then unfolds as follows:

> Tokyo Rose [Iva] in her cell at the mercy of her captors. But is she blue? Is she down in the dumps? No Siree! Our Rosie sits at her dressing table in her elegant kimono and keeps herself the glamorous, exotic, demure woman we know her to be. And to keep her spirits up, she sings as she rubs herself with expensive lotions and perfumes. (1989, 34)

While this scenario expresses the Western male fantasy of the fragile Oriental "butterfly" at the mercy of her American captors—an image immortalized by Puccini's opera, *Madame Butterfly,* and more recently deconstructed in David Henry Hwang's *M. Butterfly* (1988)—it also evokes images of the all-American girl unfazed by her traumas, especially since "Our Rosie" will be played by a tall and beautiful Caucasian. Of course, Carroll's blatantly artificial reconstruction of Iva/Tokyo Rose is specifically designed to expose his biases, and on a broader level, to critique the racism and sexism of his society; however, despite the play's metatheatre, or maybe because of it, the audience is easily persuaded that such distortions of history are the precinct of the Americans. What is missing from the performance's self-reflexive focus on the making of history/theatre is the sense that the audience is always implicated in that process. Whereas *Sandy Lee Live at Nui Dat* challenges Australian spectators with uncomfortable reminders of their likeness to the Americans, *Tokyo Rose* reassures them of their difference.

The play's construction of Uncle Sam as Iva's corrupt and malicious prosecutor similarly distances us from the American-style (in)justice meted out by the judges, bureaucrats, and politicians whose prejudices deny her a fair trial. When he brands her a "dastardly slur on the lives of other women" (1989, 37) and a "female Nipponese turncoat" (57), Uncle Sam only reveals his own misogyny, while his accusation that Iva is a "vicious propagandist" has more than a hint of irony (39). Always appearing in full stars-and-stripes regalia and present on stage for most of the action, Uncle Sam is a grotesque parody of American culture, especially when he performs musical routines with the Andrews Sisters, aptly described by one reviewer as "pneumatic, khaki-clad dollies with eyebrow arcs like steel parentheses and lips as puffed and glossy as scarlet gift-wrap ribbon" (Gough 1989, 43). Once again, costume is used as a visible hook that allows the audience's immediate recognition of cultural stereotypes. As in George's play, Uncle Sam is very much the performer, the master of showbiz who weeps theatrically at will, the media hack who "speaks like a TV promo" as he publicizes Iva's court case: "As exciting as a spy thriller, as informative as history. Watch the trial of Tokyo Rose unfold before your very eyes" (Lowe 1989, 43). But because we are never made aware that someone is also playing the part of Uncle Sam, unlike in Rob George's text where Peter's "act" is encoded as an entirely visible piece of (meta)theatre, Lowe's Uncle Sam character, despite his artificiality, is naturalized as the average American. Hollow to the core, a simulacra, a play of surface images, he embodies Australia's postmodern nightmare of a thoroughly globalized (Americanized) local culture, but the reasons behind this *postcolonial* critique of America are rarely examined, when perhaps they should be.

For the purposes of this discussion, I have privileged George's account of American neoimperialism over that of Lowe because the former shows an acute awareness of the complex ambivalence that results from Australia's partial identification with *and* simultaneous disavowal of the colonizing culture. *Tokyo Rose* is, nevertheless, an important countertext insofar as it recognizes and satirizes Orientalist discourses and undermines the disciplinary regimes, both rhetorical and corporeal, through which American neoimperialism attempts to bring the destabilizing difference of the racial/sexual Other under its control. As far as Australian-American relationships are concerned, however, perhaps the real subversion of the play lies in Lowe's deliberate appropriation of American theatrical tropes—the Uncle Sam figure, the Broadway razzmatazz, the musical chorus—to create a strongly anti-American play. This approach not only generates the ironic double vision that is necessary to appreciate fully Lowe's critique of American hegemony—a case in point is when the Andrews Sisters sing "California Here I Come" as Iva returns to San Francisco to be incarcerated—but also enacts the subversive mimicry that postcolonialism lauds. If, as Bhabha posits, "The *menace* of mimicry is its *double* vision which in disclosing the ambivalence of colonial discourse also disrupts its authority" (1984a, 129), *Tokyo Rose*'s replication of American generic conventions surely provides a grotesque mirror that refracts inherited stage traditions even while attempting to emulate them.

That the war dramas of contemporary Australian theatre generally enact their more penetrating critiques of American neoimperialism by examining it in some relation to Asian characters or countries is a result not only of the historical circumstance of United States military intervention in the Asia-Pacific region since World War II but also of Australia's own ambivalences in dealing with the countries of this region. While Australians have long perceived the importance of having Western allies to protect their privileged position in what is essentially a non-Western region, they do not want the dependency, servility, and competition that such a relationship implies. Pierce's argument that Australia's bitter resentment of American neocolonialism (compared to its tolerance of British colonialism) stems from the absence of "countervailing forces of Empire loyalty" (1985, 180), tells only half the story. The other half, as Jeff Doyle avers, is that such anti-Americanism

> betrays the insecurity of Australia's movement from an inward looking, conservative and comfortable nation aspiring to an Anglo-European culture long since passed, to a player of whatever calibre on the world stage and in particular on the stage of Asia-Pacific matters. That move had been and remains troubling and problematic. (1991, 119)

If Australia's ambivalence toward the United States remains unresolved, as its contemporary drama suggests, this attests to the complexity of the neocolonialisms that have impacted upon Australian history and that continue to shape its contours. From a postcolonial perspective, however, Australians might be tempted to agree with Pudd'nhead Wilson that "it was wonderful to find America, but it would have been more wonderful to miss it" (Twain 1969, 224).

Australian/Asian Relationships

If Australian responses to American imperialism betray a fundamental insecurity about various countries' positional power on the Asia-Pacific stage, representations of Asia itself suggest that this insecurity is linked to deep anxieties about Australia's relative economic strength and about its racial, cultural, sexual, and political identities. While a growing, albeit sometimes reluctant, acceptance of geographic links with Asia has precipitated Australia's reassessment of bilateral relations with a number of its northern neighbors, and the concomitant dilution of some of the more paranoid myths of invasion that have colored attitudes toward them, Australia remains, as a nation, ambivalent about moving toward the Asia Pacific Economic Cooperation group's goal for economic integration with Asia by 2020, and generally even less enthusiastic about asserting an Asian identity. Since the election of the Liberal-National Coalition Government in 1996, Asian immigration has become a political football once again, while the generally positive attitudes toward Asia encouraged by Paul Keating's previous Labor Government seem to have declined in some sections of the community. Not least among the reasons for this are fears of military aggression (mostly by Indonesia), and economic imperialism, particularly in the case of Japan, with whom an official politics of cooperation has not entirely dispelled many Australians' postwar hatred and mistrust. Racism also fuels this xenophobia, leading to a widespread concern, perhaps even an obsession, with what Lisa Lowe calls "adamant differentiation" of self and Other (1986, 45). Countering these fears, however, is a desire to embrace certain aspects of Asian cultures, particularly those philosophies and/or practices that might be appropriated to aid the formation of a hybrid Australian identity that reflects Australia's regional location. As Helen Tiffin argues, this interest in Asia, like attempts to synthesize the influences of European and Aboriginal cultures, can be seen as part of a wider process of "indigenization" through which many postcolonial cultures seek to define their distinctiveness (1984b, 469).

As a result of their increasing interest in and knowledge about Asian societies, Australians are now less inclined to trope Asia as a monolithic bloc or to represent its peoples according to a very limited number of undifferentiated stereotypes. Hence, there is a decreasing tendency to follow the pattern of representation identified by Peter Fitzpatrick in the mid-1980s wherein a "one-dimensional Asian stereotype throws into relief the multi-facetedness of the Australians who try to deal with him" (1985a, 39). As Gareth Griffiths argues, playwrights such as John Romeril demonstrate that "Australia's relations with its own history, with Asia and with the rest of the world are far more complex than the myths of national stereotypes suggest and that they cannot be understood outside an analysis of the whole network of contemporary multi-national and international economic and political ties which help bring them into being and to which they are ultimately subjugated" (1992a, 148).[14] At the same time, nevertheless, the ambivalent mixture of fear and desire that characterizes Western responses to racial and cultural Otherness continues to influence Australian constructions of various Asian countries and characters. In theatrical contexts, this ambivalence is further complicated by an active fascination with a wide range of Asian performance styles and an eagerness to adopt their richly evocative semiotic codes to enliven Australia's predominantly naturalistic tradition, as the recent proliferation of plays and productions that experiment with Asian theatre techniques demonstrates.[15] Where such meshing of practices is evidence of a genuine postcolonial hybridization and where it becomes a form of intercultural appropriation remains a perplexing question that can only be broached by examining the hierarchies of power involved in the particular cultural "exchange" at issue, a topic that is beyond the scope of this study, except on a speculative level. In the last few years, plays by Asian Australian writer/performers have also begun to influence characteristic representations of Asian cultures, though the impact of this body of theatre remains at present largely limited to specific festivals and/or targeted fringe groups (see Lo 1998).

My argument for a postcolonial approach to mainstream Australian theatre's "Asian" plays returns to the issue of representation and in particular to the ways in which imperial constructions of self and other are disrupted and/or dismantled by the very differences they seek to marginalize or suppress. In analyzing the structures of racism, counterracism, fear, and desire encoded in and by the texts under discussion, I draw on a number of concepts derived from Edward Said's *Orientalism* and generally follow his theory that European discourse has had a considerable material and political investment in constructions of the Orient during the post-Enlightenment period (1979, 6).[16] I am also concerned, however, to interrogate the implicit binarism of his model of East-West relations. A number of critics otherwise sympathetic to his project have pointed to problems in Said's work—specifically, to his construction of Orientalism as a monolithic discourse that permits no space for subversion, evasion, or contestation. Dennis Porter, for example, suggests that literary works may contain "contra-dictions," and that we need to consider "the feasibility of a textual dialogue between Western and non-Western cultures . . . a dialogue that would cause subject-object relations to alternate, so that we might read ourselves as the others of our others and replace the notion of a place of truth with that of a knowledge which is always relative and provisional" (1983, 181).

I am also concerned to locate the versions of Orientalism under discussion in a particular time and place. As Lisa Lowe suggests in her readings of Flaubert,

> The notions of what constitutes the Occident or the Orient are not constant; nor is the represented relationship of Occident and Orient. . . . The representations, and the means of representation, of the Orient and the oriental, reflect the changing historical circumstances, and the changing proximity and shifts of power, between western and non-western worlds. (1986, 44)

In the Australasian region, the politicized oppositions of East and West, Orient and Occident, are splintered not only by geography and cultural history, but also, as suggested in this chapter's first section, by the neoimperial presence of the United States. Two plays that illustrate extremely well the specificities of Australia's current relationships with individual Asian cultures within the broader context of Asian-Pacific politics are Jill Shearer's *Shimada* (1987), about wartime conflicts and present-day Japanese economic expansionism in Australia, and Michael Gurr's *Sex Diary of an Infidel* (1992), an exposé of Australian sex tours to the Philippines. The United States figures only briefly in Shearer's text as an alternative "imperial master" to Japan (Kelly 1990b, 226), but it is clearly an economic and political power to be reckoned with, as it is in Gurr's play, where a critique of American imperialism is much more visible but ultimately not the primary interest. That the neoimperialisms at issue in each text are based on quite different external circumstances need not preclude comparison, for both plays engage, consciously or not, with the discourses that are central to postcolonial inquiry. More specifically, these plays illustrate the weaknesses of models of imperialism that discount a narrative of resistance against the gendering, distancing, and/or silencing of the colonized Other.

Insofar as they locate Australian-Asian interaction within the contexts of war and/or tourism, *Shimada* and *Sex Diary of an Infidel* revisit the discursive spaces of Romeril's controversial play, *The Floating World*, first produced by the Australian Performance Group (APG) in 1974.[17] Gareth Griffiths's recent reassessment of Romeril's work outlines the limited kinds of representation that result from war and tourism as twin modes of encounter, the former leading to "a demonised reductive vision," while the latter inevitably promulgates "an exoticised reductive vision" (1992a, 144). Though Romeril makes every effort to show that the stereotypical Others presented are the constructs of less than likable Australian characters, this does not necessarily mean he is able to represent Asians (or Australians) unproblematically. There is ample textual evidence to substantiate Tom Burvill's claim that the play enacts an unresolvable narrative of national identity by meshing the "potentially conflicting discourses of counter-racism, working-class masculinity, radical politics and opposition to economic imperialism" in ways that "reveal a major difficulty with the shifting significations of Asia and Asian-ness in relation to Australia and Australian-ness" (1993, 91). In 1995, Playbox undertook a special cross-cultural project with Yuki-za, one of Japan's most famous puppet companies, to stage *The Floating World* in Japanese. As a result, Romeril's play was performed in Tokyo and then in Melbourne (this time subtitled) in repertory with an Australian production of Tanaka Chikao's *The Head of Mary* (first performed in Japanese in 1951), which deals with the aftermath of the bombing of Nagasaki. As well as developing a riveting piece of theatre, the project's political and artistic recontextualizing of *The Floating World* went some way toward transforming the impossible tensions that Burvill describes into a positive cross-cultural dialogue (see Sawada 1996).

As *The Floating World* has already been the subject of considerable critical attention,[18] I do not intend to unravel its complex and contradictory texts here but rather to point to a few areas of overlap that show that this pioneering play, dubbed an "unruly masterpiece" by critics, is a prototype for later plays about Australian-Asian relationships, and that it shares with them precisely the kinds of dialogic "contra-dictions" that Porter advocates in his critique of Said's *Orientalism* (Porter 1983). I also wish to trace the trajectory of these contradictions in an era of postwave Australian theatre, when representations of Asia/Asians can be distanced (though certainly not divorced) from the particular avant-garde politics and performance processes of the Australian Performance Group.[19]

Shimada, which dramatizes current economic tensions and past military conflicts between Australia and Japan, has a number of thematic and structural connections with *The Floating World,* though there is a vast difference in tone and mood between the two texts.[20] Like Romeril, Shearer is interested in the ideological friction between local experience and global economics as played out on a stage that splits *and* merges time frames, places, and identities in complex ways. Her play's dialogue with history also unfolds through a series of juxtaposed images: one thread of the narrative presents the experiences of a group of Australian soldiers interned in a Japanese prisoner-of-war camp during World War II, while the other charts the psychological disintegration of one of these prisoners when, some forty years later, he faces the prospect of working with the "enemy" after a projected Japanese takeover of the small bicycle factory where he works in provincial Queensland. In its dialogic structure, *Shimada* has much in common with *The Floating World* and with a number of "history" plays discussed in this study, but Shearer is somewhat less inclined to fully exploit the counterdiscursive potential of this structure, and overall her play sidesteps the kinds of epistemological challenges posed by Alma De Groen's *The Rivers of China* or Janis Balodis's *Too Young for Ghosts* because it maintains a fairly conventional sense of telos and uses its flashback sequences primarily as a way of explaining rather than problematizing the present. The war scenes, for example, are staged as credible versions of a verifiable past. Consequently, the viewer easily forgets how these flashbacks are filtered through Eric's consciousness and then reproduced in a series of externalized dream/memory fragments that are inevitably shaped by the fears and fantasies of an unreliable narrator. What is also sometimes obscured in Shearer's dramatization of the military conflict between Japan and Australia is the subtle and pervasive gendering of the various discursive fields within which the narrative is constituted: the fields of war, of theatrical representation, and of Orientalism. My reading of *Shimada* thus attempts to combine postcolonialism with feminist deconstruction in an effort to reveal the "contra-dictions" embedded in the text in its written and processual forms.[21]

The parallels between Romeril's protagonist, Les, and Shearer's beleaguered veteran, Eric, suggest that war as a mode of cultural encounter continues to influence not only Australians' images of the Japanese but also their approved self-images. The myth of the Digger, its inviolable code of mateship always shadowed by the possibility of betrayal, surfaces in both texts, even though Shearer is more equivocal in her deconstruction of the Anzac legend. The twin specters of impotence and perfidy—of failing to uphold mythic versions of Australian masculinity—lie at the heart of each character's psychological disintegration, and their respective fates can be read as flip sides of the one coin: Les projects onto others his self-loathing for "scabbing" on his mates (betraying them) and so moves inexorably toward his final violent knife-attack on the Japanese, whereas Eric internalizes his aggressive response to the "enemy," eventually choosing suicide as the only face-saving alternative to what he sees as betrayal of the mateship ethos by doing business with the "enemy."

While Australian audiences might feel more empathy for Eric's confused response to the Japanese than for the overtly xenophobic Ockerism of Romeril's (anti)hero, Shearer's effort to avoid the charge of racism is not entirely successful. The play opens with unglossed Japanese dialogue in what seems an overt attempt to unsettle audience expectations and to clear a speaking space for the Other. Similarly, the inclusion of the largely sympathetic figure of Toshio is designed to balance Eric's reductive vision of the Japanese, as is the use of theatrical tropes from No and Kabuki traditions. But the politics of *inclusion* can become perilously close to the politics of co-option. As I will argue, despite the playwright's best efforts—and maybe because of them—*Shimada*'s Asian characters remain embedded in a web of signification that reflects not only the particular biases of Australian versions of history but also a whole complex of race and gender issues.

The play's images of the Oriental Other of Australia are based not only on perceptions of national and racial difference but also on a long history of intercultural conflict inflected by ambivalent sexual politics. While there are complex intersections and metaphorical transfers between the masculine, the imperialist, and the nationalist, which can compound *and* undercut discrimination in significant ways, the Orientalist and Occidentalist discourses depicted in *Shimada* are complicated by a homoeroticism/homosexuality that offers a threat to the colonizer/colonized and male/female binaries, and a means by which they may be disrupted. It is important, then, to identify the gaps and ambivalences through which constructions of gender and sexuality emerge and to examine how these attributes affect power relations between the antagonists in the play.

The force of "ambivalence" that Bhabha describes as energizing the colonial stereotype is, in the case of Australia's historical representations of Asia, an ambivalence that usually rests on feminization, as Adrian Kiernander argues.

> The Orient is defined as feminine to render it conceptually colonizable; this feminized Asia waits ready to be taken, in marriage or in rape, by an Occident that is male and potent. The oxymorons of a falling Orient and rising Occident are not the only paradoxes at work here—the idea of colonizability depends itself on an elegant series of paradoxes: it is *desirable* to colonize what is portrayed as feminine because it is fascinating, attractive, and weak; it is *necessary* to colonize what seems female because it is powerful, threatening, and different. (1992, 187)

Thus Asia is read as the seductress, the willful temptress, simultaneously alluring and threatening; if the Aborigine offered an encounter with the "barbarian" Other on home ground, Asia is presented as the feminized enemy just beyond Australian shores. The perpetual requisition of the Other through recognition takes place.

A recurrent concern with sexuality—the Orient as a site of exotic/erotic mystique—is by no means new but rather one of the most important concerns of Orientalism as it is defined by Said. The contemporary power and pervasiveness of this discourse in the West can be seen in the Orientalizing of commodities such as perfume, which captivates the West through the capture of the East. But Bhabha's point about the instability of colonial discourse is well illustrated in Shearer's text by the fact that woman becomes a metaphor for both the Orient and, conversely, the Occident, in the subtext of the military confrontation dramatized. As a testing ground for national identity, war is a double-edged sword that simultaneously constructs and destroys the masculine because heroism and cowardice are inextricably linked in the victor/vanquished binary. In the absence of woman as potentially vanquishable Other, each side attempts to feminize its opponents in order to preserve patriarchal power, for the defeated man, even if racially different, testifies to masculine vulnerability. Although "real" women are evacuated from the front lines and visible conflicts of the war depicted in *Shimada,* the figure of *woman*—externalized through images of the transvestite Billy—is insistently present as a free-floating signifier. At the same time, female sexuality is harnessed in the production of a colonizable Other. As a mode of cultural contact, then, war foregrounds common concepts of masculinity in the soldier figure and, metaphorically, enacts a sexualized battle, the outcome of which determines who wears the pants and who the dress. Although the latent power of the feminine emerges in *Shimada*'s contemporary scenes, it is only ever a partial power. The bicycle factory may be owned and predominantly run by women, but the uncertainty over its future is imaged primarily through the conflict between Eric and Toshio. Even here, woman remains the space on and through which the men can be sorted from the boys, the battleground that determines not just the military and economic victors but also the cultural constructions of the masculine. In the context of Orientalism and the historical gendering of the Orient as implicitly feminine, the specter of the Japanese wielding power over the Occidental, be it through war or commerce, involves not just a racial defeat but, more frighteningly, a sexual one.

Shimada's war narrative establishes Australia's encounter with Japan as a catastrophic rout. Eric says,

> You go off and the bands are playing. Girls throw flowers at you. *(Pause)* Then all of a sudden it's a mess. Like a typhoon . . . a hurricane.

> Cutting us down, paring us down . . . to what we really are. The fearful, the mediocre . . . the cowards. (1989, 24)

The metaphorized castration depicted in this passage recalls, once again, the tropologies of *The Floating World.* In Romeril's play, Les Harding's offhand remark about his postwar "fuck" with a Japanese woman images a similar kind of impotence: "I slipped a geisha what was left of my length and she said shagging me was like making love to a bird cage" (1975, 8–9). More often, Les expresses his anxiety over emasculation in aggressive and misogynist tones through "dirty ditties" and all manner of crude language circling endlessly around references to copulation and the female body, both of which appear to be as threatening as they are desirable. A feminizing process is also enacted in each text in slightly different forms: whereas Shearer uses Billy's transvestism to actualize the threat of feminization, Romeril works through the metaphors of disease and sickness as his protagonist relives his shocking experiences as a prisoner of war. Afflicted by "eighteen different diseases at once" (1975, 92), Les's body is pictured as passive, open, swollen, excoriated, subject to all kinds of contagion, and inscribed not only with the indelible mark of the feminine but also with the scars of those "exotic" tropical diseases that are the Others of Western epidemiology.[22] What is activated here is the fear of an atavistic savagery resulting from contact with the racial and sexual Other, a threat figured elsewhere in geographical terms through the apposition of the "virgin rainforest" of Queensland (1975, 5) to the "acres of contaminated Malayan soil" (1975, 67). If, as Tiffin argues, "the trope of illness" is associated with "boundary drawing and boundary erosion" (1993a, 50), Les's "hostile penetration" by disease marks a moment of discursive rupture when race and gender binaries are broken down. The final irony is that he is able to feel a "new man" only by a total retreat into illness and psychosis. That this represents a further feminization—and infantilization—is reinforced in the play's closing image through the costuming codes of the hospital straitjacket that signals his imminent transfer to an institution.

The Australian soldiers in Shearer's text share Les Harding's fear of and contempt for the Oriental Other, and they are similarly disadvantaged in their battle with the Japanese by their position as prisoners, with all the real and symbolic disempowerment that incarceration implies. In such a situation, their fear of feminization becomes pervasive and the need to resist it, paramount. Their relative impotence would seem to modify Said's contention that "Orientalism depends for its strategy on [a] flexible *positional* superiority, which puts the Westerner in a whole series of possible relationships with the Orient without ever losing him the relative upper hand" (1979, 7). That the Japanese have gained the upper hand here is potently demonstrated by Billy's recurrent appearances as the quintessential emasculated soldier: frail and in geisha costume—a hessian kimono and fan—he is visibly marked by the signs of woman/Oriental Other. Forced to play camp singer and entertainer in exchange for food for the prisoners, he acts as prostitute and castrate, but not of his own volition. His lack of control over costuming choices denies him the imperialist power that cross-cultural dressing can imply: "the promise of 'transgressive' pleasure without the penalties of actual change . . . since the cross-dresser may always reveal or revert to the white identity underneath the native clothes" (Low 1989, 93).[23] Clive and Eric are deeply implicated in this symbolic castration; unable to prevent it, they are not only unmanned by their confrontation with the Orient, but they also actively contribute to their own feminization even while trying vehemently to resist it. As the dressmaker and costumier who fits Billy with the clothes for his role, Clive in particular becomes increasingly aligned with the feminine. It is appropriate, then, if ironic, that he must don the geisha costume after Shimada's brutal killing of Billy during a concert performance. The geisha role, overtly constructed and forcibly attached to successive prisoners, foregrounds gender as a costume that functions to signal defeat of the enemy Other while maintaining the masculine warrior ideal intact.[24]

Ironically, it is woman herself who is invoked to dispel the fear of feminization, a practice often evident in colonialist discourse, which tends to mobilize the internal Other—usually female and/or indigenous—to resist the tropologies of the external Other. Though categorically excluded from *Shimada*'s war story, women are insistently present as the absence through which men maintain their tenuous hold on masculine identity. In a more amiable moment, Shimada shows the Australians a photo of his wife, proudly proving his virility by his ownership of a beautiful woman. Similarly, when Eric asks Billy if he has a girl, the Australians invoke the discourses of heterosexuality to lift the young man's flagging courage. This is the first hint we get that Billy might not be gay. On cue, he produces a letter from a girl as tangible evidence of his "normality"; it seems to matter little that he met her only once, and then only for a brief moment on a railway station. Subsequently, "you'll get married Billy" (1989, 30) becomes the platitude designed to stave off his death wish. In war as in contemporary society, woman circulates as the surface and image designed to affirm masculine strength and potency, regardless of national identity; yet, paradoxically, her absence from the scene of battle also renders man impotent because it inevitably entails frustrated desire, which is frequently displaced onto other men.

As Susan White avers, "constructions of the masculine, especially in war, expel anything infantile, female or homoerotic"; however, the infrastructure of the military is formed by "blood and violence and desire for male love, all of which must be externalised onto women and enemy" (1988, 125). Fantasies of cross-dressing expressed in the performance text of *Shimada* are deeply inflected by homoeroticism, which Shearer takes pains to align with the Japanese by stressing Shimada's visual pleasure in Billy's transvestism and highlighting his final cruel attack on this "woman-soldier." The staging of Billy's murder activates another Orientalist fear, that of the savage (sexual) power of the Other. Like the paintings of such nineteenth-century artists as Gérome and Delacroix, the play's depiction of the Oriental tyrant suggests an "erotic fantasy combined with the scenography of despotism to produce a perverse and sadistic visual theatre, which can suggest 'the connection between sexual possession and murder as an assertion of absolute enjoyment'" (Wollen 1987, 17).

Billy's elision with the figure of the geisha further disrupts the already fractured paradigms of desire embedded in the play. Given that the geisha is commonly the object of the Western male imperial gaze, the Orientalized Billy must also be acknowledged as a strong locus of homoerotic desire for his fellow soldiers. The theatrical codes used to represent the composite Billy/geisha character facilitate this dual positioning within the sexual economy depicted. His initial appearance in the shadow box upstage evokes the Oriental woman in all her mystery and eroticism. Technically, the shadow box is an ambiguous space that reveals and conceals the subject, creating surfaces or depths depending on whether it is lit from within or without. Within this box, an area largely delineated in the rest of the play for the projection of reified images of Japan, Billy is framed, contained, and packaged through a cinematic reduction of depth that tends to produce a two-dimensional construct rather than a fully embodied presence that might return or refract the voyeuristic gaze. The resultant "celluloid" image affirms his availability for consumption by either side. Reappearing in the shadow box later in the play, Billy is visually linked to the Wisteria Lady, a Kabuki character, when Toshio brings a doll puppet for his prospective Australian associate. A gift intended for a fellow businessman—Toshio never thought he would be dealing with a woman—the Wisteria Lady functions as a passive object of exchange between men. Such an exchange, Gayle Rubin argues in an article entitled "The Traffic in Women," situates "woman [as] a conduit of a relationship rather than a partner to it," and locates her oppression within social systems rather than in biology (1975, 174). Similarly, Billy as geisha/Wisteria Lady is a desired commodity whose ritual exchange is conducted according to the context of the cultural contact between those who desire ownership. In war, where the rite/right of possession is contested rather than negotiated, woman becomes not the gift but the booty.

Clive and Eric's attraction to Billy cannot be fully disentangled from their relationships with the Japanese. Ironically, the threat of the homosexual rape of Billy by the "enemy Other" is neutralized by the Australians' homosocial bonding. Eve Sedgwick defines male homosocial desire as "the whole spectrum of bonds between men, including friendship, mentorship, rivalry, institutional subordination, homosexual genitality, and economic exchange" (1991, 227), many of which are evident in *Shimada.* The letter reading scene between Billy and Eric is a case in point. Though purportedly conjuring a memory of Billy's girl, this scene becomes a poignant expression of homosocial desire between the two soldiers as they divvy up the woman's words and recite them to each other, erasing her presence except as an alibi for their dialogue and its emotional subtext. That such male bonding is revealed as (psycho)sexual as well as social supports this chapter's earlier assertion about military discourse's strategic erasure of the feminine and impels a more skeptical look at the mateship ethos that has been a cornerstone of Australian military history. More complex metaphorical transfers inform the specific construction of the Anzac legend's *boy* hero, whose function as an idealized figure is predicated as much on sexual innocence as on fighting potential. He can assert his manhood *and* operate as a locus of male homosexual desire only if he remains untouched by woman's castrating Otherness. The real subversion effected by the geisha costume in *Shimada* must then rest on the audience's recognition of its sexual taint. Billy himself is poignantly aware that this costume vitiates the Gallipoli myth, as indicated by his desperate efforts to divest himself of the kimono lest he die, gender-fixed, "done up like some tart" (1989, 20).

Despite a tendency to reinforce some of the prejudices of Orientalism, the play's slippages and excesses of signification demonstrate how gender, race, and sexuality are often unstable markers of Otherness. An emphasis on that other common Asian stereotype of "inscrutability," an emotional and cultural impenetrability that heightens both interest and irritation for the West, also testifies to the difficulty of constructing Asian characters. As Michael Dalby argues, the Japanese are "the fascinating and elusive, yet recalcitrant objects of our scrutiny" (1980, 486). The modern-day meeting of the two cultures in *Shimada* is marked by precisely such frustration and fascination. Toshio's entrance into the offices of the Australian bicycle factory via a *hanamichi,* a ramp extending from the edge of the stage to the back of the auditorium, immediately conjures an air of mystery that deepens in the awkwardness and silence that characterize the workers' responses to him. Confronted by this outsider, Sharyn, director of the company, displays what Bhabha posits as the prominent features of colonialist discourse: a simultaneous recognition and disavowal of racial, cultural, and historical differences (1983, 19). Hence she assumes shared codes of business behavior—"talk helped by tea" (Shearer 1989, 15)—but remains uncomfortably positioned in what develops as a Japanese-Australian tea ceremony.

During this, Toshio's inscrutable difference emerges most clearly through his ritual gift giving, both in the choice of gifts—a Kabuki doll and a samurai mask—and in his emphasis on the wrapping, a cover designed to obscure the gift even while enhancing its aesthetic appeal. The idea of Japan as a culture obsessed with form, with masking and theatre, with appearance and a warrior tradition, is here reinforced. The play links the mask and the doll to the war narrative through its iconography and uses the same actor doubling as Toshio and Shimada but does not confirm or deny that the two are indeed the same character, further deepening the enigma that the Oriental/Other poses. But, in masquerading as the stereotype, constructing himself as the enigmatic Japanese *and* the knowable outsider whose difference can be captured and packaged like a souvenir, Toshio acts as provocateur to the Australians' confusion through a kind of colonial mimicry. In other words, his self-parody/mimicry undermines those colonial stereotypes that seek to fix his identity in recognizable and repeatable images (see Bhabha 1984a, 125–28). Whereas Orientalism generally commodifies the East for consumption by the West, here the Orient commodifies itself or selectively presents to the Occidental gaze those reified images that, removed from their appropriate cultural contexts, merely reflect the West's biases.

The politics of the present-day intercultural encounter are further complicated when Shearer uses the theatrical tropes and styles of one culture to illustrate the psychic processes of the other, positioning the Western audience as outsider in its own narrative, in its own theatrical spaces. Self-referentially, the text claims similarities with a No play, and it also appropriates the geisha and samurai figures that signify the Australian suspicion of, and fascination with, Japanese culture (Kelly 1990b, 225). The Samurai, as an alter ego figure for Eric, forms the masculine counterpart of the geisha. The fear of Asian neoimperialism comes into play here—the power of the Other must obviously be taken seriously and countermanded through co-option. Thus, as well as representing the ghost who stalks Eric in his nightmares of the war, the Samurai also becomes the warrior ideal whose strength and morality expel woman/Other from the contemporary scene through an overarching construction of the masculine. The struggle over the bicycle factory can then be removed from the sphere of woman's influence and redrawn in Eric's mind as a ritual battle in which two samurai fight to defend their honor. As Eric and the Samurai warily circle each other in the final moments of the first act, the play provides a potent metaphor for the current Japan-Australia relationship.

To a certain extent, *Shimada*'s contemporary narrative positions Eric as outsider to a new world order where the Digger code no longer applies to a workplace increasingly hybridized by the influences of women and foreigners. When he commits "honorable" suicide after the contract to merge the bicycle factory with Uchiyama is signed, he is responding not only to defeat and racial hatred but once again to a fear of feminization. His misguided effort to reassert his masculinity by emulating the samurai code of death is, in the Australian cultural context, a nihilistic gesture, though it does accrue some meaning artistically when Toshio points out the parallels between Eric's story and a No play. Even so, Eric functions more as a puppet than as director of his own death because he fails to interrogate the conventions of the (theatrical) narrative—the story of the Samurai—that he has appropriated, thus confusing the chimera with the real. His claim to insider status vis-à-vis Japanese culture reveals his own neoimperializing impulses and also indicates the danger of the intercultural experiment. What is missing from Eric's carefully staged No drama is an insider's understanding of the subtlety of the plot.

Shearer's flirtation with Japanese aesthetic styles risks a similar misunderstanding insofar as the figures and conventions used present only a partial perception of complex and culturally specific performance traditions. It is important, however, to make distinctions between the characters' responses to such items of "semiotica" as the Kabuki doll or the samurai mask and the play's overall engagement with Japanese theatrical tropes. Whereas Eric and even Sharyn seem limited in their capacity to extend the demonized or exoticized versions of the Other as introduced in Romeril's earlier work, the performance text of *Shimada* does offer opportunities for a genuine meshing of styles that enables dialogue between cultures. The scenography of the Brisbane production illustrates this point: following the Kabuki convention of the *hanamichi* as corridor, waterway, or road, Greg Clarke's set design featured a slatted walkway built across water to link areas symbolizing Australia and Japan (see fig. 19). The structural proxemics of the set thus created a heterotopian space open to multiple inscriptions. Similarly, Billy's role as transvestite is underwritten by the Kabuki tradition that reserves the most interesting (and often the most heroic) roles for the *onnagata* (female impersonator). As Veronica Kelly argues, then, Shearer's "Kabuki-inspired imagery" balances Eric's largely paranoid constructions of Japan and its people so that the play can be read within "recent multicultural discourses of cultural rapprochement with our Asian neighbours" (1990b, 227).

If Shearer is somewhat equivocal in her effort to untangle Australia's complex relationship with Japan, Michael Gurr seems more sure of his project, possibly because his best-known play, *Sex Diary of an Infidel,* focuses on Australia's own neoimperializing impulse toward Asia and so raises fewer anxieties about the political correctness of the Oriental figures represented. This is not to suggest that his main Filipino protagonist completely escapes the web of imperial signification, especially in performance,[25] but rather that Gurr is always aware of how Orientalist discourses facilitate an economy of desire that captures and contains difference. Developing the tourism motif established in *The Floating World,* his play aims to deconstruct both the exoticized vision of Asian peoples and, perhaps more crucially, the kinds of looking relations—imperial and patriarchal—that inform and enable this vision. Like playwrights such as De Groen and Hewett, Gurr tackles his subject through a self-conscious inquiry into representational modes and the forms of spectatorship they enhance or disrupt. His attempt to expose the scopophilic pleasures of tourism parallels the feminist project to disrupt the male gaze, while the play's explicit interest in the sexual aspects of Australia's encounter with Asia extends the submerged thematics of texts like *Shimada* and the Vietnam plays discussed in my account of American neoimperialism.

The ostensible subject of *Sex Diary of an Infidel* is the sex trade between Australia and the Philippines, but while Gurr is concerned with the specificities of this particular "exchange," he also uses it as a metaphor for the congress between Western and Third World nations. In this way, coercive sex becomes a trope for other kinds of imperialism—economic, cultural, and even military—so that "the deceit of the sex tourist is just a cartoon of much bigger lies" (1993, 4). Links between sex, tourism, and imperialism are established at the beginning of the text and remain a focus throughout, both thematically and structurally. Since several characters openly vocalize their criticism of the exploitation inherent in all three modes of contact, the play's manifest counterdiscursivity occurs at the level of dialogue, resulting, in some respects, in a highly verbal text that plays out

Fig. 19. Japanese-style *hanamichi* designed for *Shimada,* Royal Queensland Theatre Company, 1990. (Photo: Christopher Ellis.)

(and plays with) its ideas through language. As I will argue, however, the playwright's choice of form also offers a radical critique of the verbal and visual tropes used to construct those stereotypes that naturalize imperial relations.

In his prologue, Gurr introduces journalism as the first of many discourses to be scrutinized. By positioning the audience as the collective "you" of Jean's opening address, a speech accepting a major prize for her news stories, he sets up a framework that implicates all Australians in the narrative conventions of the media and, by dint of metatheatrical allusion, in the performative structures of the theatre. What is thus problematized is the presumed innocence of the reader/viewer/consumer as well as the transparency of the text. Similarly, Jean establishes her function as a simple scribe—"this boy told me about his life [and] I told that to you" (1993, 1)—only to have that role questioned as the action unfolds. That the journalist's craft(iness) relies on fabrication and distortion is evident long before she overtly admits to Tony that she "had to write [him] into credibility" (44), following the stereotype of the destitute street kid whose story would capture public interest and empathy. Gurr's onomastics, which link Tony with

Toni, the Filipino prostitute, along with the play's positioning of these two figures as the recalcitrant objects of the media's gaze, suggest that Jean's purported exposé of the sex tours will merely reinscribe journalistic privilege and reinforce well-worn mythologies. In constructing each case history, the historian/journalist articulates the so-called plight of her subjects by rendering them *inarticulate* so that their own stories can be "fixed"—edited, abbreviated, written over, covered up, and hence packaged for a market economy. This kind of *reportage* is clearly illustrated when Toni describes his interview for Australian television.

> They put me in a chair and they put a light behind me so you couldn't see my face. They asked me about Australians who come to the Philippines to fuck with kids. . . . So I told the truth, but they weren't happy. So I told them some lies and I cried. They liked that better. They gave me one thousand dollars. (1993, 46)

What the journalist does not reckon with is the potential agency of the victim: Toni, like Tony, unabashedly adopts the expected role/pose and so beguiles the victimizers by using his access to victimage as a way of foregrounding exploitation without becoming reduced to it. Bhabha's notion of the "sly civility" of the colonial stereotype is called into play once again (see 1985b, 71–73).

On the whole, Gurr's characters are more analytic, more intelligent, more sophisticated than Shearer's or Romeril's, and they often articulate an acute, if ironic, awareness of the (sexual) politics of their actions. But because they talk to their diaries, to God, to themselves, and to the audience, as well as to and at each other, the result is less a coherent dialogue than a linguistic bricolage that relativizes all points of view. There is also much in the play to suggest that language is not to be trusted as an index to "truth," that words can mask infidelity and confound communication, producing a hermeneutic circle with limited referential frames. The frequent use of phones, answering machines, taping devices, recitation, and prerecorded voice-overs deepens this sense of the linguistic simulacra and encourages the audience to look beyond the content of language to the ways in which it is shaped, packaged, and used by and within ideology. In this respect, the ubiquitous tape recorder functions as a potent visual reminder that the journalist's diary records some fragments of information and not others, that it severs the voice from the body and splits the speaking subject from the site of enunciation to produce a technologized narrative that can be erased, spliced, rewound, or simply silenced at will. That the Australian pimp, Max, also uses his tape recorder as a journal suggests a parallel between his work and Jean's, implicating her in the more sordid aspects of a political economy that clearly trades in words and images as well as in bodies. Their respective "sex diaries" thus reveal more about the diarists' own morality than about the sex trade or the Oriental subject. On another level, the tape recorder as media icon reminds us that the very news-gathering process determines what can be said, when, and how. Such censorship is blatantly obvious when the Western journalist writes the script for the Third World subject, as in the above-cited interview. What is most radical about Gurr's use of the tape recorder, however, is that he often directs its censoring ear toward the colonizers, positioning them as the objects of self-scrutiny and leading them to engage in somewhat farcical dialogues because they are aware of being taped.

Closely aligned with the tropes of narrative journalism are the conventions of photography. Together, these discourses form a seemingly innocuous alliance that finds its analogue in the "words and pictures" team of Jean and Martin, her photographer boyfriend. As the play reveals, however, both modes of recording news are highly selective and therefore highly suspect; the journalist's facts are no more than fictions, and the camera does indeed lie. That the photograph's "rendering of reality must always hide more than it discloses" (Sontag 1973, 23) makes the camera particularly effective as an instrument of imperial representation. Its pretense of disinterest masks an even more insidious kind of partiality: that which operates to preserve the status quo. As Susan Sontag discerns, to take a picture is not passive observation but active participation that affirms "complicity with whatever makes the subject interesting, worth photographing" (1973, 12). Moreover, the photograph multiplies to potential infinity the event it captures, "mechanically repeat[ing] what could never be repeated existentially" (Barthes 1981, 4). The resultant reified vision of the camera's subject is precisely what Gurr critiques through the motif of photography in *Sex Diary of an Infidel.* Martin's tendency to construct people and events as re(pro)ducible images is a case in point. His lack of real interest in the colonized subject's resistance to imperialism is illustrated by the fact that he is only too happy to snap dozens of shots to illustrate the sex tour article but seems paralyzed to record Toni's revolutionary protest against American military bases in the Philippines. Ultimately, as the portrait exhibition at the end of the play suggests, Martin's photographs function less as an exposé—a call for some kind of public intervention—than as an exhibit—a public display of *non*intervention.

Gurr's thematizing of what Sontag calls the "insatiability of the photographic eye" (1973, 3) depicts the voyeur's gaze as Australia's characteristic look toward the Philippines and, by implication, toward other parts of Asia. Like the tape recorder, the camera serves as a substitute phallus mobilized in an attempt to exercise libidinal power over the racial/sexual Other. While the play's semiotics bring the codes of photography into acute visibility so that we are always aware of how the camera positions the Other as the "purloined object of [its] look" (Freedman 1991, 71), Gurr is equally concerned to subvert that look. This is evident in Toni's self-conscious adoption of parodically languid B-grade movie poses, and, in a different way, in Martin's autoerotic self-portraiture, where the photographic/pornographic eye is turned back on itself. The rhetoric of "the pose," as a particular form of response to photoimperialism, is charged with theatricality. In *Sex Diary of an Infidel,* as in Hilary Bell's *Fortune,* discussed in chapter 4, the Asian Other performs for the camera, adopting the expected role or pose so as to reflect the normative codes of the (Western) viewer (see figs. 20, 21). A further subversion of imperial looking relations is enacted in Jean's transformation at the end of the play from journalist to larger-than-life "celluloid" image: frozen in a photo pose,[26] she is repositioned as an object of scopic desire. In terms of Gurr's overall project to dismantle the "words and pictures" construction of Asia depicted through the media, Jean's discursive capture is a decisive victory for the postcolonial subject. I use the word *discursive* here in the sense of discourse as visual *and* verbal: Jean is captured visually in the photograph and turned into a kind of souvenir; she is also silenced in the process.

The play's critique of voyeurism as a mode of power/knowledge is quite explicit elsewhere but perhaps nowhere so effective as in its form, which is designed to dislodge the photographic referent from its moorings and so disrupt the gaze that has "sutured [the audience] into identification with the camera" (Freedman 1991, 67). Structurally, *Sex Diary of an Infidel* draws on the conventions of both photography and film, foregrounding the spectatorial paradigms to be disrupted as the action unfolds in a series of "snapshot" scenes—short, sharp, and imagistic—interspersed with cinematic sequences in which scene segues into scene. While the logic of the camera collocates disparate images into a dramatic album/video, its centripetal energies are countered in a number of ways. First, because the processes of photography are enacted within the viewer's larger field of vision, s/he remains cognizant of the gap between what is being "shot" and what remains outside the frame. Second, Gurr's dramaturgy resists the hermetic closure of the camera's focus-image since all of the characters remain on stage throughout the play even though most scenes directly involve only

Fig. 20. Rhetoric of the pose: Toni in *Sex Diary of an Infidel,* Playbox Production, 1992. (Photo: Jeff Busby.)

one or two (see fig. 22). Their insistent and extraneous presence is rarely contiguous with fictionalized space and action; hence that presence tends to dissolve the photographic frame, substituting instead a metatheatrical one that focuses not merely on the framed subject but more precisely on the interplay between that subject and the acts of framing and staging it—or, in other words, on theatricality itself. Following Barbara Freedman's analysis of the crucial differences between theatre and film, the onstage audience can be seen as part of a critical metalanguage that severs perceptual alignment from the seeing eye of the camera, disperses the possibilities for identification, and splits our gaze to show it always already in motion (1991, 68). The use of a thrust stage enhances this effect, whereas a proscenium arch would structure a point of view akin to that of film. At the same time, the assertive visibility of the fictional audience further inhibits the voyeur's look because it dramatizes the impossibility of seeing without being seen. Extending this idea is a third performative intervention in the discourses of film and photography, the staging of a number of "snapshot" images or freezes that paradoxically emphasize the embodied presence of

Fig. 21. Chang in *Fortune,* La Boite Production, 1996. (Photo: Melanie Gray.)

the character, and beyond that, of the performer. Most notable is Martin's exhibition, which features live actors in photographic poses to produce somewhat unnerving "portraits" that return the observer's look. Thus Gurr presents another version of that "fractured reciprocity" of the gaze which, as argued in chapter 4's analysis of De Groen's *The Rivers of China,* refuses the closure of imperial and patriarchal looking relations.

Although Gurr's radical dismantling of the camera's codes in *Sex Diary of an Infidel* can be read as part of a postmodern intertextual experiment in what Hutcheon might call "fringe interference,"[27] its function is more strategic than playful. If, as John Urry maintains, the photographic image constitutes the grammar of tourism (1990, 138–40), its deconstruction is crucial to the play's larger agenda of unsettling Australia's exoticized vision of Asia, a vision that rests largely on a predominantly Eurocentric tourist gaze. This gaze, it should be noted, is homogenizing but not homogenous: it "varies by society, by social group, and by historical period" (Urry 1990, 1). Guided by Urry's analysis, Graham Huggan elaborates that tourist gazes

> do not just refer to the cognitive processes by which tourists encode and decode their touristic experiences; they also refer to a socially

Fig. 22. Multiple time-space frames, *Sex Diary of an Infidel,* Playbox Production, 1992. (Photo: Jeff Busby.)

> organized system—an apparatus of preconstituted knowledges and beliefs—that underpins, and to some extent determines, the nature of those experiences. Tourist gazes are filters of touristic perception; they provide a medium for what the tourist sees, but also a guideline as to how s/he *ought* to see. So while tourist gazes are instruments of vision, they may also function as screening devices that restrict or impair vision. (1993, 83)

In the case of Australian constructions of the Philippines, the tourist gaze is inflected by a fantasy of licentious, anonymous, interracial sex, of rape without repercussion. As Max puts it, "We somehow believe that these soft brown people won't tell on us. That every muscle, including the soul, will dilate for the fat white god" (Gurr 1993, 53).

Analogies between the sex trade, journalism, and tourism are clearly drawn in the play. In fact, Jean and Martin's sex tour article is an exemplary piece of travel writing, complete with the evocation of an exotic place, the titillation of cultural Otherness, and the invitation to the armchair reader to go and see for him/herself (1993, 57–58). In the same way, Toni's summary of his "cultural exchange" with Max—"he sells the culture and I keep the change" (36)—could apply equally to his dealings with Martin or Jean. This blurring of ontological categories locates all of the Australians as (sex) tourists at some level or other; thus their experience of/in the Philippines is lived within that frame. (Even Max is but a temporary visitor who can catch the first business flight back to Australia if things go wrong.) According to John Frow, tourism is structured around the twin poles of denial and disappointment, both of which are evident in the web of lies created by Gurr's characters: denial because the tourist fantasizes dissociation from tourism itself, which "destroys (in the very process by which it constructs) the authenticity of the tourist object" (1991, 146); and disappointment because the tourist gaze is "suffused with an ideality" that can always be frustrated in the face of the literal (125). Furthermore, representations of the Other are always filtered through the tourist gaze, resulting in a chain of supplementarity that refers endlessly to prior constructions. That Martin and Jean are deeply implicated in this signifying process is suggested near the beginning of the text in a grotesquely parodic image of them sitting on a Qantas jet watching a promotional video that presents the Philippines as "The Land of Smiles" eagerly waiting to welcome the tourist (Gurr 1993, 11). Ironically, in a parallel scene toward the play's end, it is the colonizers themselves who become saturated with the "anachronistic substance" of Baudrillard's tourist (1990, 63) as they fly off into the sunset, their dialogue prerecorded and amplified as in a voice-over video presentation.

The play's depiction of the various exploitative economies perpetuated by the exoticized vision of the Other illustrates Frow's point that "the logic of tourism is that of a relentless extension of commodity relations and the consequent inequalities of power between center and periphery, First and Third Worlds, developed and underdeveloped regions, metropolis and countryside" (1991, 151). What Frow's very useful analysis does not consider, however, is the potential agency of the commodified subject and the possibilities for undermining those unequal relations on which tourism depends. Toni's contribution of part of his prostitution/tourism earnings to fund the communist army's revolt against American imperialism is a case in point, and I have already alluded to a number of other such subversive moments or techniques. So perhaps one final example, as described by Max, will suffice.

> One of our clients was rather creatively "got" this week. Tattooed under Seconal. I believe his prick now sports a colourful local insult in indeli-

> ble ink. Try explaining that to the wife. Somewhere in Australia, in a tiled and floral-towelled bathroom, a man is weeping over a pumice stone. So much sadness for an hour of what isn't always bliss. (1993, 52)

It is not the tattooing as an act of (sexual) violence against the client that I want to focus on here, even though this is a significant act of resistance, but rather the tattoo as a subversion of the souvenir that is part of tourism's stock in trade. Susan Stewart argues, "To have a souvenir of the exotic is to possess both a specimen and a trophy; on the one hand, the object must be marked as exterior and foreign; on the other it must be marked as arising directly out of an immediate experience of its possessor" (1984, 147). Thus the souvenir links the world of past experience to the foreign culture through metonymy and tells a narrative not of the object itself but of the collector who, "through the souvenir, possesses the lost and recovered moment of the past" (Frow 1991, 145). In this particular case, what the client has is certainly a souvenir of sorts—it is marked by both Otherness and direct experience—but it is neither specimen nor trophy in the conventional sense. Instead of a collectible object or specimen that might adorn his floral-toweled bathroom, the man is left with the permanent inscription of the foreign on his own body. This text is a tale of illicit desire rather than sexual conquest. Moreover, the particular siting of the tattoo effects the disempowerment of the sex tourist because it repositions the phallus as a part object, a souvenir, a fetish.

Gurr's incisive attack on tourism and its related epistemological apparatus is guided by an insistent awareness of the ways in which Australia's relationship with and representations of Asia have been shaped by Orientalist discourses. Whereas Shearer's play seems at times to stumble upon a discovery of the imperialist bias implicit in Australian versions of the Orient, *Sex Diary of an Infidel* clearly targets that bias in its deconstruction of Orientalism's frames of reference. Hence the focus on tourism as a sexualized narrative is deliberately engineered to pick up on one of Orientalism's major tropes. In an article entitled "Fashion/Orientalism/the Body," Peter Wollen suggests that

> the Orient is the site of scientific and political fantasy, displaced from the body politic of the west itself, a field of free play for shamelessly paranoid constructions, dreamlike elaborations of western traumas. [It is] a secular, licentious narrative, with almost no trace of moralism . . . but full of tales of deviant, transgressive and fantastic sexuality. (1987, 17)

The opening of the play proper, with its aural evocation of sex between the Western male and the Oriental woman, is designed to play on just such fantasies, but because the scene foregrounds its own commodification as prerecorded "phone sex," it is more parodic than titillating. Gurr follows a similar tack in separate scenes that show Max trying to clear up a client's confusion between Mandy and Sandy, and then Toni reading a children's book to a masturbating client. Here, the patently silly story—complete with Toni's omissions and ad-libbed insertions—encodes the sex tourist's implied pedophilic fantasy as completely ridiculous. In each instance, the object of desire remains invisible to the audience, frustrating the voyeuristic paradigms of Orientalism and drawing attention instead to the Orientalist's fantasy of what Max calls an "illicit multicultural fuck" (1993, 53).

Toni's role as transsexual prostitute requires a much more complex reading. Although it could be argued that Gurr falls into his own trap by constructing his one Asian character as the locus of imperialist desire, this would be to deny the ways in which Toni reappropriates that role, abrogating the colonizer's privilege and unsettling his desire. On one level, Toni *does* personify the deviant and transgressive sexuality that Wollen outlines; thus his is the "intextuated body" mapped according to discourses that focus on the boy/Other as a site of homoerotic desire and the Orient/colony as a place of sexual freedom where fantasies of homosexuality or other kinds of "deviance" might be freely lived.[28] His costuming in "androgynous silk," along with his general effeminacy, is consistent with another familiar rhetorical trope: the West's gendering of the East as feminine. However, since Toni's sexual ambiguity is not merely figural but also literal, it ultimately upsets Orientalism's gender lexicon by insisting on the impossibility of a closed and hierarchized gender binary. As suggested in Max's description of what a client can "do" with Toni, he embodies that play of difference, that excess of signification, which refuses categorization within heterosexual or even homosexual paradigms. Nor does Toni exactly fit the category of transvestite because, unlike Shearer's Billy, he has no stable sexual identity to "cross" in his costuming. This kind of "subjectivity in formation" can posit a "dialectical relationship between the personal and the political without reducing them to each other in a metaphorical embrace" (Pathak, Sengupta, and Purkayastha 1991, 204–5). At the end of the play, Toni's change from prostitute to revolutionary is linked to the embodied knowledges of both sexes as he is acutely aware of both his penis and his breasts when his face is seared by the Molotov cocktail he hurls at the Americans. Gurr's valorization of the transsexual/androgyne[29] as an iconoclastic figure is evident in the thematic and scenographic links between Toni and the angels of

Piero della Francesca. As one reviewer argued, despite his prostitution, Toni "ultimately reveals a purity which is given both a political and religious expression in the end" (Thomson 1992, 24).

Through its sustained focus on Australian neoimperialism in Asia, *Sex Diary of an Infidel* directly addresses an issue that is often downplayed in the agenda of postcolonial inquiry, as this chapter's study of the Vietnam War plays demonstrates. Although interested in the Philippines specifically, Gurr's critique invokes a wider application because he is concerned with precisely those processes that situate the racial, cultural, and/or sexual Others of contemporary Australia as objects of a powerful but unstable imperial gaze that endlessly replays history's folly. There are even ways in which the Philippines situation can be read as a parable—or a warning—of a repeat Vietnam, "a slow motion Saigon," in Martin's terms (1993, 57). While this analogy rests on the fact that American imperialism, both economic and military, facilitates Australian "trade" (read exploitation) in the Philippines, Gurr resists the temptation simply to blame the Americans. As Toni says, "It's bigger than that. Anyone can hate Americans. It's almost too easy" (1993, 65). What Toni is alluding to is a more general First World consciousness that continues to subject the Third World to the demands of a globalized capitalist economy. In its recognition of this dynamic, *Sex Diary of an Infidel* has much in common with a number of 1980s plays dealing with Australia's role in the various colonialisms that have impacted upon specific parts of the Asia-Pacific area. Alexander Buzo's *Marginal Farm* (1981), Tony Strachan's *Eyes of the Whites* (1983), and John Romeril's *Top End* (1988), to name just a few about colonial relations in Fiji, New Guinea, and East Timor respectively, anticipate Gurr's acute cognizance of the privileges that have undergirded Australia's status as a Western nation in a non-Western region. While these earlier plays certainly deserve further analysis, my focus texts adequately show how complicated are the neoimperialisms of the Asia-Pacific region and how, like British colonialism, they spawn narratives of resistance that can splinter and rupture the colonizer's monologue.

I have suggested that the description of Orientalism provided by Said is not entirely appropriate to Australia's circumstances and its representations of the Oriental Other, that Australians (and sometimes Asians) are at once the subjects and objects of colonial scrutiny, a gaze that seeks to encode relations of political power and to hierarchize relations of race, nation, and gender. It is necessary, then, to begin work on a comprehensive archaeology of discourses about Australia and its various Asian neighbors, tracing the "emergence, production and theorization . . . of one culture's representation of another, i.e., the historical beginnings and ruling principles (the arches) which determine the way human societies relate and think of each other, and the role of discourse in the constitution and preservation of this archaeology" (Rasul 1987, 1134). To begin, we might remember that *orient* can indicate not only the East, but the necessary provisionality of perspective. As Richard Terdiman points out in his discussion of Flaubert,

> "Perspective" is a system of relation of elements in the tableau, not only to each other but, crucially, to one privileged element *outside* it; that is to the source of perceiving consciousness (which it can represent only by its absence). . . . Perspective is about *difference as a hierarchical mode of relation,* and about how it can be depicted or managed. (1985, 28)

Perspective is always implied in and by differences of power, differences that emerge in Shearer's *Shimada* both at the level of narrative and also through the incorporation of Japanese performative conventions. *Sex Diary of an Infidel* also plays with the idea of perspective, and there is little or no sense of a coherent version of the racial or sexual Other that Said's concept of Orientalism may imply. By problematizing the positioning of the Other in a complex intertextual "tableau," I have attempted here, and in previous chapters, to unsettle the notion of fixed colonial binaries that refuse a discursive place to the colonized. A focus on the "contra-dictions" implicit in the various imperialisms dramatized opens up opportunities for the marginalized to "reterritorialize the act of narration itself," and to interrogate the complicity of narrative "with the privilege of consciousness" (E. Jackson 1989, 457–58).

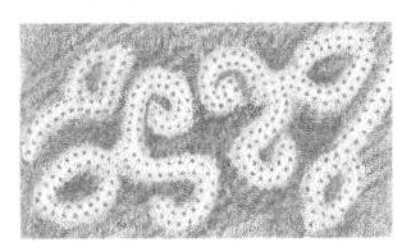

Conclusion

Even as we look towards the horizon or turn away down fixed routes, our gaze sees through the space of history, as if it was never there. In its place, nostalgia for the past, cloudy time, the repetition of facts. The fact that where we stand and how we go is history. This we do not see.

—*Paul Carter,* ***The Road to Botany Bay***

In its application of postcolonial theory to a range of contemporary plays, this study has outlined an interpretive framework that expands current critical discourses on Australian theatre. My program of interference has proceeded through a mapping of the links and tensions between history, subjectivity, and representation, in order to illustrate the potential of theatre as a site of strategic reform in the ongoing and difficult process of decolonization. In contradistinction to models that present imperial history as a bounded theatrical space/event that permits no intervention, I have proposed a model of theatre that replays history to actuate a differential and contestatory semiotics. In one way or another, all of the dramatists discussed here have engaged with this historiographic project and, in doing so, have attempted what Linda Hutcheon calls the "problematized inscribing of subjectivity into history" (1987, 297). Accordingly, my study has treated history as a complex and polysemic text that is continually renegotiated in the processes of representation.

Reconstructing the self in history inevitably leads to a restructuring of national identity. As Bhabha asserts, "Counter-narratives of nation that continually evoke and erase its totalizing boundaries—both actual and conceptual—disturb those ideological manoeuvres through which 'imagined communities' are given essentialist identities" (1990, 300). In this study, I have attempted to outline some characteristic ways in which both indigenous and nonindigenous dramatists challenge the myths of nation that naturalize imperialism in its past and present forms and give rise to normative definitions of the "imagined community" of Australia. At the same time, however, I have sought to remain cognizant of the many different counternarratives that have been articulated in recent years and of how these intersect to form complex and often contradictory histories. As I have moved through my discussion of Aboriginal theatre, settler/invader plays, feminist drama, and plays about neoimperialism, the constant question has *not* been who or what is Australian, but rather who is being represented as Australian, who is marginalized by that representation, and for what purposes? Hence the search for a distinct Australian theatrical subject gives way to the recognition of multiple subjectivities.

In the current conservative political climate where anxiety about native title and Asian immigration continues to fragment communities, the concept of Australia as "one nation" becomes increasingly contentious. As Graeme Turner argues,

> Settler/postcolonial societies face enormous problems in articulating a common identity across competing forms of ethnicity and against a history of occupation and dispossession of the original inhabitants. The more we become aware of these internal differences and ambiguities, the more problematic becomes any simple affirmation of collective identity. (1994, 123)

If Australia's movement toward republicanism is to be more than a populist gesture, it is vital that nostalgic attachments to nationalist myths of origin be replaced by a recognition of heterogeneity and cultural difference. In this respect, the arts play a significant role in reconfiguring the conceptual modalities through which to imagine a range of individual and collective subjectivities.

Ideally, academic analysis should not only interpret shifts in artistic practice but also actively redefine the cognitive structures that underpin particular forms of cultural production. By suggesting that there are ways of watching and performing postcolonialism as well as ways of reading and writing it, this book extends the limits of what has generally been conceived and practiced as a *literary* theory. My theoretical refigurations open up the discursive field of postcolonial criticism to claim a space for theatre and, by implication, for other nonwritten forms of cultural expression. It is important to remember, however, that there are no sites of "pure" resistance to imperialism; counterdiscourses are neither simply there nor always separable from the apparatus they seek to transgress (Sharpe 1989, 143). This is particularly the case in theatre, which must operate within a material culture that depends largely on the patronage of the audience—bourgeois or otherwise—for its survival. Hence, in order to avoid totalized or simplistic readings of all postcolonial texts as inherently subversive, it is necessary to bear in mind their specific sites of reception as well as their specific histories.

In the context of drama and theatre studies, perhaps the most significant aspect of this project lies in its politicizing of the whole semiotic network of visual representation, a project that has important implications for performance theory and practice. By reading some of the key topoi of postcolonial texts through their corresponding theatrical sign systems, I have been moving toward a model of performance (and critical spectatorship) that eschews the overdetermined spaces of naturalism to deliberately ruffle the smooth edges of the staged image and thus challenge its presumed ideological neutrality. This approach demands a constant awareness of the inscriptions of power on the performing body and its spatial frameworks and posits the possibility of staging acts of resistance to that power. More work is needed in the area, however, if we are to develop a fully articulated set of postcolonial performance practices that might radicalize dramatic representation in the ways that feminist theatre and theory have done. What I have provided here is a provisional framework for this particular project, which must necessarily interrogate the visual and conceptual trajectories—the sightlines—of theatrical signification as well as its conventional sites of meaning.

Notes

Introduction

1. Carter is even more specific about the theatrical nature of history making in his recent book, *Living in a New Country: History, Travelling, and Language.* He argues that to uncover the historical meaning of situations, "it will be necessary to rid historical writing of its own implicit theatricality, its tendency to stage events as if these events were not already staged, already performances" (1992, 160).

2. My usage of the capitalized word *Other* indicates a reference to the stereotyped category constructed as the deprivileged term of self/other binary oppositions.

3. This ambivalence has specific inflections for each playwright: critical assessments in the 1980s that saw Gow as Australia's most "promising" (young) playwright have been modified in the light of his failure to produce a "hit" for the Bicentenary in 1988, and because of his increasingly visible interest in homosexual issues; Sewell has repeatedly been castigated by reviewers for flabby dramaturgy, for his didactic approach, and, conversely, for allowing his politics to become diluted in a bid to capture the mainstream audience; meanwhile Nowra's growing popularity with middle-class audiences sits uncomfortably with critics who feel that his recent work makes too many political compromises.

4. Begun in 1978, Sydney's Mardi Gras is now internationally renowned as one of the world's premiere carnivals, though it remains the subject of some controversy among the more conservative populace in Australia.

5. The Currency/Methuen series of critical studies on such playwrights as Jack Hibberd, Stephen Sewell, David Williamson, Alexander Buzo, and Dorothy Hewett all take this approach. See Hainsworth 1987, Fitzpatrick 1987b and 1991, McCallum 1987b, and Williams 1992.

6. Sexist, racist, patriotic, deliberately offensive, highly theatrical, and forever male, the Ocker figured prominently on the new-wave stage and was roundly celebrated for his quintessential "Australianness" even while often functioning as a site of social critique.

7. It is interesting to note that a number of very recent comparative studies still focus largely on the new-wave writers, a situation that seems to confirm that the perceived coherence of this period lends itself more readily to broad analysis than the apparent fragmentation of the postwave era. See, for example, Jacobson 1990, Fitzpatrick 1990, and Radic 1991.

8. The following summary indicates the current state of play in Australian theatre criticism: Fotheringham's edited collection of essays, *Community Theatre in Australia* (1992) provides insights into diverse community practices but is not intended to offer a widely applicable critical framework; Aboriginal theatre has attracted a substantial amount of comparative commentary in the form of articles and short papers (see chap. 2 for further information); outside of Tait's book, broad-based studies of contemporary feminist theatre are scant, although Perkins (1994) and Williams (1992) have

produced studies of individual playwrights. In terms of more general studies, the essays in Peter Holloway's updated edition of *Contemporary Australian Drama* (1987) are designed to reflect the diverse approaches of their authors rather than any consistent perspective. Elizabeth Webby's *Modern Australian Plays* (1993) outlines thematic and stylistic links between the texts under consideration but is primarily intended as a study guide rather than an intervention into ways of examining the field. Dennis Carroll's recently revised version of *Australian Contemporary Drama* (1995) gives scant space to the post-1970s period and, disappointingly, fails to update its original material in any systematic way, effectively erasing the significant movements in Australian theatre since the book's first publication in 1985. Veronica Kelly's forthcoming edited collection of essays, *Our Australian Theatre in the 1990s* (1998), will offer up-to-date criticism on a range of issues including arts policy, community and fringe theatre, experimental performance work, and multicultural theatre.

9. The more obvious alternative (and intersecting) discourse is multiculturalism (see Gunew and Rizvi 1994), but it would also be instructive to assess developments in stylistic features over the period—to analyze, for example, the interest in nonnaturalistic modes including expressionism and epic theatre.

10. See, for example, Hodge and Mishra 1991, Tiffin 1984b, Nettelbeck 1992, Ashcroft 1989c, Lawson 1994, and Gibson 1992.

11. In its more general application, *interculturalism* has been a style of thought characterizing some of the more imperialist work carried out in such fields as anthropology, sociology, and cultural studies; however, the term will be used in this discussion to refer to a particular mode of performance theory and practice. See Marranca 1991, 11–15, for background on the emergence of interculturalism in theatre over the last ten years.

12. See, for instance, Appiah 1991; Ashcroft, Griffiths, and Tiffin 1989, 155–56; During 1987; Hutcheon 1990; and Slemon 1990b.

13. All three have been involved in intercultural productions for some years, but it is mostly Schechner who has written extensively on the subject and who, through his editorship of the *Drama Review,* has encouraged a body of such scholarship. See Schechner 1993, Schechner and Appel 1990, Barba 1982, and Pavis 1992 and 1996, 1–21, for an account of Western intercultural practice, and also Bharucha 1993 for a perceptive critique.

14. Whereas in some settler countries the descriptor *multicultural* is applied to indigenous peoples as well as to various migrant groups, Australia's particular take on multiculturalism most often restricts the term's reference to migrants who are not of Anglo-Celtic descent. Implicit in the exclusion of Aborigines from debates about multiculturalism is a recognition that indigenous Australians face significantly different problems than either postwar European migrants or more recent immigrants from Asian and other countries.

15. See Lo 1998 for an analysis of the fledgling field of Asian-Australian hybrid performance work.

16. See, for instance, Kay Schaffer's *Women and the Bush* (1988) and Graeme Turner's *National Fictions* (1986) for further discussion on the role of nature and the landscape in Australian narratives.

17. The important exception here is Paul Makeham's dissertation on discourses of landscape in Australian drama (1996a). Makeham's broad-ranging study deals with a

variety of scenographic tropes, including the "bush" landscapes common to 1920s nationalist plays and the reimaged rural and urban landscapes of more recent works. See also articles by Hopkins (1987) and Dunstone (1985).

18. Throughout this book, the term *culture* is used variously to describe the characteristics and products of particular human societies, and the normative concept of civilization that informs imperialist discourse, especially in reference to the nature-culture opposition theorized as central to settler countries such as Australia. Robert Young (1995, 42–43) argues that *culture* should not be used as a synonym for *civilization,* but I am following a common usage as befits the topics at issue.

19. According to Deleuze and Guattari, the rhizome is an appropriate model for the multiple connections and disconnections of deconstructive ways of reading (1987, 7). See also Huggan's formulation of a rhizomatic postcolonial cartography (1989b, 125–26) based on Deleuze and Guattari's work.

20. While there is a growing body of literature that attempts to theorize dance itself as an art form with specific cultural inflections (see Foster 1996), the very useful work done in this area seems not to have been taken up by most critics writing on drama.

21. Adapted from the title of Eve Kosofsky Sedgwick's *Epistemology of the Closet* (1991).

22. Lamming takes up this issue at length, arguing that Prospero's gift of language to Caliban is also the very prison that will limit what he can say (1960, 92–95). See also Brydon 1989, 2–3, and Brown 1985, 61, for further discussion of linguistic capture in postcolonial contexts.

23. Trevor Griffiths's article (1983) on the performance history of *The Tempest* discusses in some depth the ways in which representations of Caliban on the British stage were inflected by imperialism.

24. See L. Young (1988), who also identifies explicit signs of emasculation embedded in the style of dress chosen for male convicts.

25. The term *black* is capitalized in this book when it is used as a synonym for Aborigine or as a marker of cultural or political identity. Parallel capitalization is not used for *white* since this term is more commonly used as a form of categorization rather than a sign of identity.

26. Harris's novel, *The Infinite Rehearsal* (1988), both theorizes and practices this idea. See also his critical article (1992).

Chapter 1

1. This issue has inspired a great deal of academic criticism. See Viswanathan 1990 as an outstanding example, and, specific to Australian contexts, Philip Mead and Marion Campbell's edited collection of essays, *Shakespeare's Books: Contemporary Cultural Politics and the Persistence of Empire* (1993).

2. Such performances can also have the effect of emphasizing the racial/cultural biases of the canonical play. A good example of this is David George's staging of *The Tempest* in Bali, which cast Australian actors in the major roles while the Balinese provided the "magical" background for a production that seems to have largely side-stepped the imperialist motifs of the play despite George's avowed efforts to avoid the "cultural rape" that is often the result of the intercultural experiment (see D. George 1989–90).

3. Examples include Black Swan's production of *Twelfth Night* (directed by Andrew Ross, Octagon Theatre, Perth, 1991), Grin and Tonic's *The Merchant of Venice* (directed by Bryan Nason, Van Gogh's Earlobe, Brisbane, 1995), *The Taming of the Shrew* (directed by Sue Rider, La Boite, Brisbane, 1994), and *Hamlet* (directed by Sue Rider, La Boite, Brisbane, 1995), all of which were noted for their cross-cultural casting as well as other revisionary strategies.

4. Chapters 3 and 4 briefly treat other instances of canonical counterdiscourse in Louis Nowra's *The Golden Age* (1985) and Dorothy Hewett's *The Man from Mukinupin* (1979). Malouf's *Blood Relations* provides the most appropriate focus text for this chapter's analysis because the play clearly articulates some of the colonial themes central to my overall study.

5. See, for example, Bennie 1987, 13; Bramwell 1987, 30; and McGillick 1987, 26. Similar responses greeted the play's subsequent season in Adelaide. A few of these critics blamed Jim Sharman's direction for "overloading" the play with Gothic and symbolic effects and allowing little room for the "audience's collective imaginative contribution" (Bennie 1987, 13), but it was mostly the playwright's attempts to dramatize the inner worlds of his characters that came under fire.

6. Lengthy discussions by O. Mannoni in *Prospero and Caliban: The Psychology of Colonization* (1950; trans. 1964) and Frantz Fanon in *Black Skins, White Masks* (1952; trans. 1967) initiated this interest in *The Tempest* as a colonialist text. In the wake of Mannoni's and Fanon's work, other critical studies, most notably George Lamming's *The Pleasures of Exile* (1960) and Max Dorsinville's *Caliban without Prospero* (1974), emerged to explore the dialectical nature of the Caliban/Prospero relationship and to argue for a more interactive model of colonial relations. More recently, feminist scholars have also problematized the tendency to situate Miranda as bipolar opposite to Caliban. See Donaldson 1988 and S. Bennett 1996, 119–29.

7. Francophone rewrites, on the other hand, choose a Calibanic model of resistance that highlights dissension between Quebeçois and Anglophone Canadians. See Zabus 1985 or Dorsinville 1974 for further discussion.

8. For a further brief survey of this whole body of literature, see Ashcroft, Griffiths, and Tiffin 1989, 189–91, and Salter 1996, 4–7.

9. For example, Aimé Césaire's play, *Une tempête d'après "La Tempête" de Shakespeare: Adaptation pour une théâtre nègre* (1969), locates subversiveness in a bellicose Caliban, the rebel slave, as opposed to the obsequious Ariel, who borders on capitulation to colonialist values. Dorsinville (1974) and Zabus (1985) also argue that a "Calibanic" discourse that resists the rape of identity and language will be most effective in severing the colonial "bond between oppressor and oppressed" (Zabus 1985, 49).

10. Graeme Turner points out that the pastoral mode, widely used in Australian narrative, functions ideologically to appropriate an alien landscape: "The longevity of the pastoral ideal, surviving as it does Australia's urbanization and suburbanization, suggests that its survival is due to its ideological and mythic function rather than to its close relation to historical conditions at any point or series of points in Australia's past or present" (1986, 32).

11. Most reviewers, however, refer to the play's island setting—Bramwell even concludes that this island is in Queensland (1987, 30)—which attests to the strength of the island mythology invoked in *The Tempest.*

12. See Malouf's essay, "A First Place: The Mapping of a World" (1985a, 7), for a discussion of the verandah as an uncertain space where nature and culture intersect.

13. See Gay 1992 as an illustration of this argument, and D'Cruz 1993, 168–74, for a discussion of the ways in which *Away*'s intertextual references to Shakespeare have facilitated its positioning within critical discourse.

14. See Evans 1994. In an attempt to encourage less idealized readings of *Away* as a quintessential study of regeneration, Gow also rewrote the play's ending for the 1992 Sydney Theatre Company production that he directed himself, showing that the protagonist, Tom, had obviously died before the rehearsals of *King Lear* in the closing scene.

15. Directed by Helen Gilbert (Avalon Theatre, Brisbane, 12 September 1996) as an experimental project designed to investigate intertextuality, canonicity, and nationality in Australian theatre.

Chapter 2

1. Here I would include not only plays by Aboriginal authors that have been shaped by white directors and advisers but also those performance texts originally written by whites yet substantially shaped by Aboriginal actors and consultants. Tony Strachan's *State of Shock* (1986) appears to fit this latter category, along with very recent plays such as *Radiance* (1993) and *Crow* (1994) by Louis Nowra, *One Woman's Song* (1993) by Peta Murray, and the award-winning *Dead Heart* (1993) by Nicholas Parsons.

2. The most sustained and successful applications of such theory can be found in Dibble and Macintyre 1992, Tompkins 1993, and Lo 1997.

3. Exceptions here are analyses of Davis's work by Balme (1990) and Webby (1993, 65–79). Neither critic adopts a specifically postcolonial approach, but both underline the political contexts in which Aboriginal performance must be "read." Webby highlights theatre history while Balme focuses on theatrical form.

4. Directed by Andrew Ross, Marli Biyol Company, Fitzroy Town Hall, Melbourne, 8 May 1988. See Suzanne Olb's excellent description/analysis of the spatial aspects of this production, which, she argues, positions the "first born" at the center, while whites are relegated to the periphery, boxed and separated by the set (1988).

5. See Webby 1993, 74–75, for details of the proxemic structures of *No Sugar*'s first production at the Maltings in North Perth (1985) and of the play's 1988 London run. The formal proscenium-arched venue of the 1990 Perth production (directed by Neil Armfield and Lynette Narkle, Marli Biyol and Belvoir Street Companies, The Playhouse, Perth, 22 October 1990) situated the performance within more conventionally delineated actor/audience spaces. Unless otherwise specified, all subsequent analyses of *No Sugar* refer to the latter production together with the published text.

6. I am grateful to Jacqueline Lo, who provided me with details of the performance of *Wahngin Country* (directed by Michael Leslie, Black Swan Theatre Company, University of Western Australia, Perth, 21 February 1992).

7. See also Gibbs, who classified *Wahngin Country* as "a surprisingly reactionary piece" and saw "no particular dramatic purpose" in the "set" or style of production (1992, 52–53).

8. Initially performed under the title *Our Town* (directed by Phil Thomson,

Marli Biyol Company, The Playhouse, Perth, 22 October 1990). Subsequent analysis of the play is based on this production together with the published text.

9. Transformation, as Muecke explains, is a key trope in traditional Aboriginal narrative and tends to be reflexive rather than transitive; thus tribal dancers/storytellers frequently enact their stories by firstly transforming themselves into mythic figures (1983b, 90–91). Contemporary performance, as an analogous process, provides specific possibilities for decolonizing the body.

10. Directed by Wesley Enoch, Festival Space, Brisbane, 28 August 1996.

11. See Daly's response (1988, 46) to Daniel Sterne's theories of behavior and Dolan (1988, 41–43) for an extended discussion of psychoanalytic theories of identity formation.

12. Balme, for instance, classifies dance in Davis's drama as one of the markers of its syncretism but tends overall to posit the syncretic model as adaptive rather than politically exigent (1990, 406–7).

13. Directed by Vivian Walker, Aboriginal National Theatre Trust, George Fairfax Studio, Melbourne, 7 March 1990.

14. The published text of *No Sugar* does not place the scenes depicting the corroboree and Neville's speech in adjacency; however, the directors worked closely with Jack Davis on this production.

15. My analysis of *Murras* refers to the published text; comments on *Sistergirl* are based on a performance attended during the play's premiere season (directed by Andrew Ross and Sally Morgan, Black Swan Theatre Company, Arts Theatre, Adelaide, 17 March 1992).

16. Although this single dancer is referred to in the stage directions of *Murras* and *The Dreamers* as "he," it is assigned no gender in the character lists and appears as gender neutral in the photographs from the opening performance of *Murras* (see fig. 6). The representation of this dancer as not specifically male or female offers possibilities for performances that resist eliding issues of gender with issues of race. *Sistergirl*'s dancer, on the other hand, calls specifically for a male character to emphasize the (hetero)sexual desire he embodies.

17. No script is available for this piece; see Mudrooroo 1989b for a full report of the conference.

18. Details on the dance are from personal conversations with Eddie Bennell and Phil Thompson, Perth, 21 September, 1990.

19. Mulvey 1975, 6–18, and Dolan 1988, 41–58, explain most clearly the properties and problems of the "male gaze" models of spectatorship. For a convincing analysis of the inapplicability of such paradigms to theatre, see Freedman 1991, 48–56. This is a topic I will be taking up in greater depth in subsequent chapters, particularly in my discussion of feminist postcolonial theatre.

20. Analysis of this play is based on the published script, and on performances attended during the play's initial national tour (directed by Andrew Ross, Bran Nue Dae Productions, Lyric Theatre, Brisbane, 12 December 1990) and during its 1993 remount (directed by Andrew Ross, Black Swan Theatre Company, The Playhouse, Melbourne, 2 July 1993). Performance details specific to only one of these productions are indicated in footnotes.

21. Among non-Aboriginal critics, *Bran Nue Dae* has been the subject of some controversy, with a minority insisting that the play is compromised by its failure to

deliver a hard-hitting political message. In response, critics such as Makeham (1996b) and Lo (1997) offer detailed analyses of the ways in which *Bran Nue Dae* encodes various modes of resistance within its apparently conventional form.

22. Classical ballet, complete with the usual costumes of that genre, was added to the 1993 production.

23. As advertised in the program notes.

24. Scott 1990, Balme 1990, and Tompkins 1993 do examine orality to some extent but tend to locate it almost wholly in the figure of the storyteller or in the actual words used. What is thus overlooked is the materiality of the voice and its associated articulating systems.

25. Goldie 1988, 72; Shoemaker 1989, 132–33; and Scott 1990, 127, for example, all argue for the mobilization of drama as enabling the expression of an "authentic" Aboriginal voice, but they do not deal substantially with the theoretical aspects of the oral or of performance.

26. I use *muted* in Elaine Showalter's sense to suggest mediation rather than full silencing. Showalter explains that the term suggests "problems both of language and of power" because "dominant groups control the forms or structures in which consciousness can be articulated" (1981, 200).

27. Although Nowra is not Aboriginal, he collaborated with Justine Saunders and other Aborigines in the adaptation of the novel *Capricornia* to develop a text that uses orality as a political strategy. By leaving it up to the actors to provide an eclectic mixture of languages that "translate" the scripted English, the play provides significant sites of resistance for Aboriginal voices.

28. See Elam (1980, 144–48) for a discussion of these distinctions in dramatic discourse, and Muecke (1983a, 72–73), who applies Benveniste's theories to Aboriginal oral narrative.

29. First performed at the 1992 Adelaide Festival. My analysis refers to Magpie Theatre's subsequent touring production (directed by Steven Gration, Universal Theatre, Melbourne, 16 October 1993).

30. The 1996 remount of the play, for example, changed considerably to incorporate political satire directed at parliamentary member, Pauline Hanson, whose racist comments have mobilized yet another long-running "race debate" in Australia.

31. This description of orality relates to Arthur's idea of nomadic reading that "roams randomly *between* positions . . . causing multiple fractures and disruptions" to existing orders (1989, 39).

Chapter 3

1. The following are the production premiere details for these plays. *Barungin:* Directed by Andrew Ross, Marli Biyol Company, The Playhouse, Perth, 10 February 1988; *1841:* Directed by John Gaden and Michael Gow, State Theatre Company of South Australia, The Playhouse, Adelaide, 3 March 1988; *Capricornia:* Directed by Kingston Anderson, Company B, Belvoir St. Theatre, Sydney, 23 April 1988; *Hate:* Directed by Neil Armfield, Playbox Theatre Company and Belvoir St. Theatre, Belvoir St. Theatre, Sydney, 19 November 1988.

2. The politics of *Barungin,* while confrontational and uncomfortable for many reviewers, could however be accepted because of their emplacement within a broader Aboriginal critique of white society.

3. See Nugent's review of the Adelaide production (1988, 6) and Gow's interview with Pearson (1992, 122).

4. Although this address begins the published text and appears to have been included in the Sydney production of *1841,* it was cut during the play's initial run in Adelaide. McCallum argues that Gow's instinct to include it was correct because it warns us that Aurora is not "simply another ordinary migrant on the last convict ship" (1989–90, 200).

5. My analysis here is indebted to Kelly's account of the play within the play, although her discussion focuses on its intertextual references and generic links with Romantic and early modern German drama (1990a, 138–39).

6. Although the family is named the Gleasons in the published text, this represents a version of the play printed during the rehearsal period and does not include subsequent revisions by the author. As critics have noted, the change to the name Truscott, with its connotations of both trust and mistrust (trust not) adds another small irony to the text.

7. See Bredow 1989, 241, and Barnes 1989, 243, for these specific comments that are also echoed by reviewers such as Kruger (1989, 247).

8. Here Lloyd (1989) is referring to *1841* and to what he calls the "musical lemon" by Tim Robertson and Don Watson (with John Romeril): *History of Australia: The Musical* (directed by John Bell, Princess Theatre, Melbourne, 16 January 1988). Evans 1989 and Kruger 1989 also specifically cite *Capricornia* as a fitting showpiece for Australian theatre in 1988.

9. It is worth noting here that Nowra was not originally offered this commission but stepped in to write *Capricornia* after some members of the original team abandoned the project just six weeks before the premiere of the play was scheduled. (See Turcotte 1989–90, 189.)

10. This section of my discussion is based on a performance of the original production witnessed in Canberra during the play's 1988 tour.

11. Other plays that also foreground the role of the landscape (and climate) in creating Australian subjectivities include Balodis's *Wet and Dry* (1986), Gordon Francis's *God's Best Country* (1987), Elaine Acworth's *Composing Venus* (1994), and Louis Nowra's *The Incorruptible* (1995), which posits Queensland as Australia's version of the American Deep South.

12. Nowra states that when he writes a play, he sees his "figures in relation to the landscape" and argues that Aboriginal culture is rooted in the land, whereas whites have taken over Australia but not become part of it (1987a, 141). Balodis is also interested in the idea of putting down roots but generally seems more optimistic about white Australia's ability to develop a symbiotic rather than parasitic relationship with the land. He explains that in *Too Young for Ghosts* he wanted to explore "the character in a physical landscape," while others of his plays such as *Heart for the Future* (1989) attempt to take an "internal landscape and externalise it" (1990, 6).

13. Although some critics have tended to see Balodis's play as a study of exotics in the Australian landscape and therefore not representative of settler society, I would argue that his concerns about exile and the encounter with alien space are common

across ethnic and cultural boundaries. See Kelly 1992a for an in-depth discussion of how the discourses of multiculturalism impact upon Balodis's work.

14. See Kelly 1987a, 101–5, and McCallum 1984, 290. Nowra also points to these intended connections both in his preface to the published version of the play and in a subsequent interview (Nowra 1987a, 139).

15. Particularly relevant here is Low's argument that "English gardens were fetishized for their ability to counter the polluting influences of what was reinscribed as *foreign*" (1989, 85).

16. Nowra explains his interest in bushfires and argues their particular suitability in Australian narrative. He also tropes these bushfires in terms of crises: "Notice how we mark our epochs by saying 'It was around the time of "Black Friday" or "Black Tuesday" or "Black Wednesday."' Bushfires, for Australians, are both horrendously real and apocalyptic metaphors" (1987a, 143).

17. Malouf refers to the Sydney Theatre Company production (directed by Phillip Kier, Drama Theatre, Sydney Opera House, 16 September 1985); similar comments are expressed by other reviewers.

18. Ferrier 1990, Foucault 1980, Huggan 1989a and 1989b, and Harley 1988 all take up this issue at length.

19. Directed by Roger Hodgman, designed by Tony Tripp, Melbourne Theatre Company, Russell Street Theatre, Melbourne, 16 July 1992.

20. Huggan explores contrasts between graphemic and graphic models of space, arguing that oral cultures create maps as a form of spoken expression, while Western preference for graphic representation can be traced to the perceived supremacy of the written over the spoken word (1991, 58–59).

21. The flood motif is also relevant to Nowra's *Inside the Island,* although this play primarily figures nature's destructive energies through fire. Lillian points out that the floods have in fact only recently receded; Julie's drowning and George's close escape from the same fate are also significant in this respect.

22. Kelly (1988, 107) uses these terms to discuss the "possibility of homecoming" as the utopian project of Louis Nowra's *The Golden Age.*

23. See R. Jackson 1981, 15–16, and Bakhtin 1984, 186–87. In her study of the origins of Gothic literature, Jackson argues that the *menippea* was a traditional form of fantastic art that influenced both carnivalesque and modern Gothic narratives.

24. Here Dash is working through Edouard Glissant's dual focus on the verbal (the frantic shout) and the carnal (the frenzied body).

25. That the world represented by the "statue" is a civilization in decay is suggested through the play's semiotics by the crumbling temple in the Archers' garden and later by the shattered and bullet-riddled statue of Frederick the Great that Francis encounters in Berlin during the war.

Chapter 4

1. Although class has also played a fundamental role in formulations of Australian myths of identity, it tends to be ignored in popular discourse, giving way to the myth of a classless society despite the fact that convictism was absolutely predicated on hierarchies of social privilege.

2. This approach characterizes much recent feminist scholarship in the field of postcolonialism and would seem then to modify Ashcroft's argument that "the amount of genuine cross-fertilisation between the two [theoretical approaches] is scant" (1989b, 23). As well as McClintock's very important work (1995) see, for example, Loomba 1989, Trinh T. Minh-ha 1989, and Suleri 1992.

3. The title of Ashcroft's article: "Intersecting Marginalities: Post-colonialism and Feminism" (1989b).

4. See also Suleri 1992 and Sharpe 1993, 11–15.

5. Hennessy 1995 offers a detailed and valuable reading of the ways in which Aboriginal and non-Aboriginal women playwrights have represented indigenous women in recent times.

6. Although it won an important prize, *Brumby Innes* was not performed until 1972, apparently because its depiction of interracial rape was considered too shocking for the times. Compared with *Men Without Wives,* Prichard's play is much more liberal in its approach to Aborigines, and it positions them more centrally in narrative terms than does *Here Under Heaven.* Yet, despite her interest in exposing the brutalities Aboriginal women suffered at the hands of men such as Brumby, Prichard's overall depiction of race relations tends to endorse romanticized views of "natural" sexuality as the precinct of the native Other. According to this equation, the young Aboriginal girl, Wylba, is ultimately presented as a more appropriate partner for Brumby than his white, city-bred wife, May, and the two females are cast as adversaries even though they share a common fate as the exploited objects of male lust and power.

7. For further discussion see Ashcroft (1989b, 27–33), who argues that the postcolonial artist must construct a sense of place from which s/he can then speak; this process is equivalent to Cixous's notion of "writing the body." Creolization, or hybridization, a theory of writing developed originally in the Caribbean, focuses on the complexity of cultures and pushes cultural/sexual identity beyond limiting essentialisms.

8. Rubin posits that in patriarchal systems women function in a symbolic exchange that cements the relationships between men (1975, 174–75).

9. Spivak's term (1985, 253). The implication here is that Catherine will become the colonizer's help-mate, internalizing the discourses of imperialism.

10. This term, coined by Michael Dash, is elaborated by Tiffin (1987b, 29–31).

11. Geographical proximity and related histories of colonization, combined with the extensive migration of New Zealanders to Australia, tend to complicate the formulation of entirely separate national identities, and this too is reflected in the play's positioning of the Mansfield figure as Australian in the contemporary narrative. In some respects, this slippage of identities illustrates a productively political hybridity, but within the framework of a postcolonial inquiry, we might also ask if the transmigration of Katherine's soul implicates Australia itself as an imperial center to New Zealand, and to what extent Mansfield is reappropriated through the material effects of the play's circulation within the canon of Australian drama.

12. Perkins uses this term to describe the play's potential for radically transforming concepts of woman (1987b, 20), but I feel it applies equally well to my discussion of travel and exploration.

13. I use the term *vector* here in the mathematical sense of a variable quantity that

has magnitude and direction and can be resolved into components that are odd functions of the coordinates (Collins English Dictionary).

14. Directed by Peter Kingston, Sydney Theatre Company, Wharf Theatre, 9 September 1987.

15. Apart from plays discussed in this chapter, other contemporary Australian texts that feature the woman as actress include Dorothy Hewett's *The Tatty Hollow Story* (1977), Alma De Groen's *Vocations* (1983), Dina Panozzo's *Varda Che Bruta . . . Poretta* (1991).

16. This play has attracted a number of critiques that pay attention to its treatment of colonialist discourse, particularly in reference to the landscape. See Hopkins 1987 and Fitzpatrick 1995.

17. Dunstone's entire article, "Performance and Difference in Dorothy Hewett's *The Man from Mukinupin,*" (1990) focuses on the play's multiple metatheatrical codings and covers that subject extremely well. To avoid simply repeating his argument, I have limited my discussion to points that link with the focus motifs of this book.

18. Most productions of *The Man from Mukinupin* have followed Hewett's directions for the roles of Polly and Touch of the Tar to be doubled, and the script implies that a non-Aboriginal actor would be the most appropriate casting choice. As part of its program for Australia's Bicentenary, the Western Australia Theatre Company mounted a production (directed by Kingston Anderson, The Playhouse, Perth, 8 November 1988) that split the roles, featuring Aboriginal actor Jedda Cole as Touch of the Tar. This seems to have politicized the play in different ways while giving Touch of the Tar a poignant fragility, although some critics argued that such casting posed problems of dramatic balance (see Britton 1988).

19. See also Forte 1990, 262–63, and Dolan 1988, 48–50.

Chapter 5

1. See Walker, who argues that the monopoly of the American film industry "was seen as a threat to the continuity of civilized values as these were expressed in literature, drama and education," and also to "the economic and cultural future of Australia" (1976, 143–45).

2. Dennis Carroll comments at length on what he calls Romeril's "anti-Americanism" (1993), but I would argue, with Gareth Griffiths, that Romeril is more concerned "with the negative impact of multi-national corporate capital" on Australia than with demonizing any particular nation (Griffiths 1993, 3). Many other "anti-American" plays of the period were direct responses to the politics of the Vietnam War, which I will take up shortly.

3. See, for instance, Dennis Phillips's *Ambivalent Allies: Myth and Reality in the Australian-American Relationship* (1988), and also Libby Connors et al., *Australia's Frontline: Remembering the 1939–45 War* (1992). The latter has a separate chapter entitled "The Friendly Invasion of GIs" that deals specifically with the effects of the American presence on the "femininity and morality" of Australian women during the war (1992, 140–88).

4. I use *Digger* and *Anzac* interchangeably as colloquial terms that represent the Australian version of the idealized war hero, although the former suggests more the legendary construction than the actual soldier of the Australian and New Zealand Army Corps (ANZAC).

5. Since some historical accounts of the GI invasion argue that the presence of large numbers of African American soldiers disrupted the racial discourses of the time (see Connors et al. 1992, chap. 7), the absence of Black characters in these texts points to another suppressed site of anxiety about American imperialism.

6. Constructed around the purported heroism of Australian soldiers in the face of impossible odds during World War I battles in southern Europe, the Anzac legend has played a major part in nationalist versions of Australian identity.

7. See, for example, the Channel Nine television series, *ANZACs* (directed by John Dixon, George Miller, and Pino Amata, Burrowes Dixon Co., 1985), along with David Malouf's *Fly Away Peter* (1983) and the film *Gallipoli* (directed by Peter Weir, Associated R & R Films, 1981). Recent films about Australians in the Boer War, for example, *The Light Horseman* (directed by Simon Wincer, RKO Pictures, 1987), can also be seen to express concerns about the contemporary status of the war hero.

8. I am using *performative* here in its broader sense of behavior that is staged or ritualized, though not necessarily in the context of theatre art.

9. According to Pierce, the first stage confidently locates the enemy "in the opposing battlelines," while in the second, he is also "discovered elsewhere," mainly as a cowardly profiteer (1985, 172). Loosely speaking, this schema fits representations of the enemy in the unrevised Gallipoli legend (stage one), and in accounts of World War II that focus on the GI invasion (stage two) discussed earlier in this chapter.

10. Gerster (1991) explores this link in detail by examining the history of Australia's involvement in overseas wars that offered not only the chance of heroism but also the attraction of foreign travel. His recently published collection of Australian "literary traveling" to the East, *Hotel Asia* (1995) extends this motif. I will be taking up the idea of Asia as a gendered "travel" destination in the second section of this chapter.

11. Capitals are used to indicate that the reference is to the stereotypical meaning of the terms *Orient* and *Occident.*

12. No script is available for this play; see Copeman 1994 for a detailed description of the project.

13. My discussion of *Tokyo Rose* is largely based on its premiere production (directed by Jim Vile, La Boite Theatre, Brisbane, 11 October 1989).

14. Two recent plays that attempt to historicize Australian-Asian relationships in this way are Anna Broinowski's *The Gap* (1993) and Virginia Baxter and Keith Gallasch's *Tokyo Two: A Tourist Thriller* (1992).

15. For instance, *wayang kulit* was used in the Brisbane production of Graham Shiel's *Bali: Adat* (directed by Jim Vile, La Boite Theatre, 22 April 1987); *bunraku* in the Sydney version of Daniel Keene's *Cho Cho San* (directed by Geoff Hooke, Belvoir Street Theatre, 22 April 1987); and a combination of *butoh* and the Suzuki technique in Zen Zen Zo's *The Cult of Dionysus* (directed by Simon Woods, Princess Theatre, Brisbane, 6 November 1996). The interest in Asian theatre styles is also evident in festival programming, which has recently featured a number of specifically Asian events including Tadashi Suzuki's *The Chronicles of Macbeth* (1993) and performances by the Bejing Opera (1995).

16. Much of the following conceptual material on Orientalism is based on work done jointly with Leigh Dale (Dale and Gilbert 1993). I have rewritten this section of my analysis, but it was, in the end, neither possible nor desirable to separate my ideas from Dr Dale's. I wish to acknowledge the great debt I owe her in this respect.

17. The version of *The Floating World* produced in the 1970s (which is the basis of the published text) was very much the result of a collective process. For further information on the politics and processes of the group vis-à-vis this play, see Varney 1989 and Burvill 1993.

18. See, for example, G. Griffiths 1992a and Webby 1993, 34–44.

19. Some of Romeril's more recent work—*Top End* (1988) for example—certainly falls within the ambit of this section's inquiry, but I have chosen the texts by Shearer and Gurr as case studies because they offer greater opportunities to effect the feminist postcolonial critique that the historical gendering of the Orient calls for.

20. Other recent Australian plays dealing in some way with Japan include Michael Gurr's *The Hundred Year Ambush* (directed by Bruce Myles, George Fairfax Studio, Melbourne, 6 June 1990) and John Misto's *The Shoe Horn Sonata* (1995).

21. The following analysis is based on the published text together with the Queensland Theatre Company production of *Shimada* (directed by David Bell, designed by Greg Clarke, Cremorne Theatre, Brisbane, 5 July 1990).

22. This and the following analysis of disease/illness is indebted to Helen Tiffin's work on the metaphorizing of malaria as a culturally freighted trope in colonialist discourse (1993a). Incidentally, malaria is mentioned in *The Floating World* as one of the very worst illnesses threatening the Australian soldiers at Changi.

23. Low argues that the colonizer's donning of his/her subject's clothes does not indicate the disruption of power hierarchies but rather reinforces them by presenting the Oriental world for consumption. Cross-cultural dressing, then, is a fantasy available to the colonizer but not often to the colonized. See also Garber 1992, 304–52, for a discussion of transvestism and the erotics of cultural appropriation.

24. On one level, gender as an imposed costume gives the Australians an alibi for their demasculinization—they are, after all, only playing a role—but on another level, it also poses questions about the relationship between the self and the role played. The notion of gender fluidity that this masking raises accounts for the Australians' intense need to resist feminine roles lest they prove to be self-actualizing.

25. The following discussion is based on the Playbox production (directed by Bruce Myles, designed by Judith Cobb, Melbourne, 4 October 1993) together with the published text. This production used the same set design and most of the same actors as the 1992 production, also at Playbox. It was enacted on a largely bare thrust stage and featured an oversize mobile of Piero della Francesca's angels hanging from the ceiling.

26. The published text suggests that an oversize photo of Jean be used, but the Playbox production actually simulated this effect with the live actor in a freeze.

27. Hutcheon is interested in those constructions that combine the visual and the verbal in ways that interfere with the characteristic codes of particular art forms (1989, 118–24).

28. For homosexual writers and travelers, the colonies have been represented as an ideal world in which homosexuality might be freely lived, both with the indigenous population and with those fleeing metropolitan puritanism. See Kiernander 1992 and Dollimore 1991, 3–18, for further discussion.

29. I do not wish to conflate these two categories but to pick up on Gurr's representation of Toni as both transsexual and androgynous, the latter conferring a kind of mythical status.

Bibliography

Acworth, Elaine. 1995. *Composing Venus.* Sydney: Currency.

Ang, Ien. 1993. "Migrations of Chineseness: Ethnicity in the Postmodern World." In *Cultural Studies: Pluralism and Theory,* ed. David Bennett, 32–50. Melbourne: University of Melbourne English Department.

Appiah, Kwame Anthony. 1991. "Is the Post- in Postmodernism the Post- in Postcolonial?" *Critical Inquiry* 17:336–57.

Aronson, Linda. 1989. *Dinkum Assorted.* Sydney: Currency.

Arthur, Kateryna. 1985. "Fiction and the Rewriting of History: A Reading of Colin Johnson." *Westerly* 30 (1): 55–60.

———. 1989. "Neither Here nor There: Towards Nomadic Reading." *New Literatures Review* 17:31–42.

———. 1990. "Beyond Orality: Canada and Australia." *ARIEL* 21 (3): 23–36.

Ashcroft, W. D. [Bill]. 1989a. "Constitutive Graphonomy: A Post-Colonial Theory of Literary Writing." *Kunapipi* 11 (1): 58–73.

———. 1989b. "Intersecting Marginalities: Post-colonialism and Feminism." *Kunapipi* 11 (2): 23–35.

———. 1989c. "The Post-Colonial Revision of Australian Literature." *New Literatures Review* 18:1–9.

Ashcroft, W. D. [Bill], Gareth Griffiths, and Helen Tiffin. 1989. *The Empire Writes Back: Theory and Practice in Post-Colonial Literatures.* London: Routledge.

Attwood, Bain. 1992. Introduction to *Power, Knowledge, and Aborigines,* ed. Bain Attwood and John Arnold, i–xvi. Melbourne: La Trobe University Press.

Auslander, Philip. 1988. "Embodiment: The Politics of Postmodern Dance." *Drama Review* 32 (4): 7–23.

Bakhtin, Mikhail. 1981. *The Dialogic Imagination: Four Essays.* Ed. Michael Holquist. Trans. Caryl Emerson and Michael Holquist. Austin: University of Texas Press.

———. 1984. *Rabelais and His World.* Trans. Hélène Iswolsky. Bloomington: Indiana University Press.

Balme, Christopher. 1990. "The Aboriginal Theatre of Jack Davis: Prolegomena to a Theory of Syncretic Theatre." In *Crisis and Creativity in the New Literatures in English,* ed. Geoffrey Davis and Hena Maes-Jelinek, 401–17. Amsterdam: Rodopi.

Balodis, Janis. 1985. *Too Young for Ghosts.* Sydney: Currency.

———. 1989. *Heart for the Future.* Unpublished playscript.

———. 1990. "Projecting the Inner World onto an Existing Landscape." Interview by Veronica Kelly. *Australasian Drama Studies* 17:5–39.

———. 1991. *Wet and Dry.* Sydney: Currency.

———. 1992. *No Going Back.* Unpublished playscript.

Banting, Pamela. 1993. "The Phantom Limb Syndrome: Writing the Postcolonial Body in Daphne Marlett's *Touch to My Tongue.*" *ARIEL* 24 (3): 7–30.

Barba, Eugenio. 1982. "Theatre Anthropology." Trans. Richard Fowler. *Drama Review* 26 (2): 5–32.

Barnes, Mick. 1988. Review of *Hate,* by Stephen Sewell. *Australian and New Zealand Theatre Record* 2 (11): 3.

———. 1989. Review of *Capricornia,* by Louis Nowra. In *Reviews: Australia's Bicentennial Arts Program, 1988,* ed. Sarah Overton, 243. Sydney: Mead and Beckett.

Barthes, Roland. 1981. *Camera Lucida: Reflections on Photography.* Trans. Richard Howard. New York: Farrar, Straus and Giroux.

———. 1986. *The Rustle of Language.* Trans. Richard Howard. Oxford: Blackwell.

Baudrillard, Jean. 1990. "Mass Media Culture." In *Revenge of the Crystal: Selected Writings on the Modern Object and Its Destiny, 1968–1983,* ed. and trans. Paul Foss and Julian Pfanis, 63–97. Sydney: Pluto.

Baxter, Virginia, and Keith Gallasch. 1993. *Tokyo Two: A Tourist Thriller. Canadian Theatre Review* 74:54–72.

Bell, Hilary. 1995. *Fortune.* Sydney: Currency.

Bennell, Eddie. 1990. *The Silent Years.* Unpublished script.

Bennett, Roger. 1995. *Funerals and Circuses.* Sydney: Currency.

Bennett, Susan. 1996. *Performing Nostalgia: Shifting Shakespeare and the Contemporary Past.* London: Routledge.

Bennie, Angela. 1987. "Malouf's Dreamtime Prods the Unconscious." Review of *Blood Relations,* by David Malouf. *Australian,* 26 June, 13.

Benveniste, Émile. 1970. *Problems in General Linguistics.* Trans. Mary Elizabeth Meek. Coral Gables, Fla.: University of Miami Press.

Berndt, Ronald. 1982. "The Aboriginal Heritage." In *Kullark* and *The Dreamers,* by Jack Davis, xiii–xxi. Sydney: Currency.

Bhabha, Homi. 1983. "The Other Question . . ." *Screen* 24 (6): 18–36.

———. 1984a. "Of Mimicry and Man: The Ambivalence of Colonial Discourse." *October* 28:125–33.

———. 1984b. "Representation and the Colonial Text: A Critical Exploration of Some Forms of Mimeticism." In *The Theory of Reading,* ed. Frank Gloversmith, 93–122. Brighton: Harvester.

———. 1985a. "Signs Taken for Wonders: Questions of Ambivalence and Authority under a Tree outside Delhi, May 1817." In *Europe and Its Others: Proceedings of the Essex Conference on the Sociology of Literature, July 1984.* Vol. 1, ed. Francis Barker et al., 89–106. Colchester: University of Essex Press.

———. 1985b. "Sly Civility." *October* 34:71–80.

———. 1990. "DissemiNation: Time, Narrative, and the Margins of the Modern Nation." In *Nation and Narration,* ed. Homi Bhabha, 291–322. London: Routledge.

Bharucha, Rustom. 1993. *Theatre and the World: Performance and the Politics of Culture.* London: Routledge.

Boire, Gary. 1991. "Tribunalations: George Ryga's Post-Colonial Trial 'Play.'" *ARIEL* 22 (2): 5–20.

Borges, Jorge Luis. 1970. "The Garden of Forking Paths." Trans. Donald A. Yates. In *Labyrinths: Selected Stories and Other Writings.* Harmondsworth: Penguin.

Bourdieu, Pierre. 1977. *Outline of a Theory of Practice.* Trans. Richard Nice. Cambridge: Cambridge University Press.

Bramwell, Murray. 1987. "Pale Intimations." Review of *Blood Relations,* by David Malouf. *Adelaide Review* 42:30.

Brand, Mona. 1969. *Here under Heaven, Our Dear Relations,* and *Barbara.* Sydney: Wentworth Press.

Bredow, Susan. 1989. Review of *Capricornia,* by Louis Nowra. In *Reviews: Australia's Bicentennial Arts Program, 1988,* ed. Sarah Overton, 241. Sydney: Mead and Beckett.

Britton, David. 1988. Review of *The Man from Mukinupin,* by Dorothy Hewett. *Australian and New Zealand Theatre Record* 2 (11): 38.

Broinowski, Alison. 1992. *The Yellow Lady: Australian Impressions of Asia.* Melbourne: Oxford University Press.

Broinowski, Anna. 1995. *The Gap.* Sydney: Currency.

Brown, Paul. 1985. "'This Thing of Darkness I Acknowledge Mine': *The Tempest* and the Discourse of Colonialism." In *Political Shakespeare: New Essays in Cultural Materialism,* ed. Jonathan Dollimore and Alan Sinfield, 48–71. Ithaca, N.Y.: Cornell University Press.

Brydon, Diana. 1984. "Re-writing *The Tempest.*" *World Literature Written in English* 23 (1): 75–88.

———. 1989. "Commonwealth or Common Poverty? The New Literatures in English and the New Discourse of Marginality." *Kunapipi* 11 (1): 1–16.

———. 1990. "The White Inuit Speaks: Contamination as Literary Strategy." In *Past the Last Post: Theorising Post-Colonialism and Post-Modernism,* ed. Ian Adam and Helen Tiffin, 191–203. Calgary: University of Calgary Press.

———. 1994. "'Empire's Bloomers': Cross-Dressing's Double Cross." *Essays on Canadian Writing* 54:23–45.

Buckridge, Patrick. 1992. "Canon, Culture, and Consensus: Australian Literature and the Bicentenary." In *Celebrating the Nation: A Critical Study of Australia's Bicentenary,* ed. Tony Bennett, Patrick Buckridge, David Carter, and Colin Mercer, 69–86. Sydney: Allen and Unwin.

Burvill, Tom. 1993. "Romeril's Work with Race, Class, and Ethnicity." In *John Romeril,* ed. Gareth Griffiths, 86–102. Amsterdam: Rodopi.

Butler-Adam, John. 1986. "Reading Landscapes as Texts: Grammatology, Hermeneutics, and the Spatial Imagination." Draft Text for Discussion. Institute for Social and Economic Research, University of Durban-Westville.

Buzo, Alexander. 1985. *Big River* and *Marginal Farm.* Sydney: Currency.

Campbell, Marion. 1993. Introduction to *Shakespeare's Books: Contemporary Cultural Politics and the Persistence of Empire,* ed. Philip Mead and Marion Campbell, 1–5. Melbourne: University of Melbourne English Department.

Carr, Helen. 1985. "Woman/Indian: 'The American' and His Others." In *Europe and Its Others: Proceedings of the Essex Conference on the Sociology of Literature, July 1984.* Vol. 2, ed. Francis Barker et al., 46–60. Colchester: University of Essex Press.

Carroll, Dennis. 1993. "John Romeril and the APG." In *John Romeril,* ed. Gareth Griffiths, 35–54. Amsterdam: Rodopi.

———. 1995. *Australian Contemporary Drama.* Rev. ed. Sydney: Currency.

Carter, Paul. 1987. *The Road to Botany Bay: An Essay in Spatial History.* London: Faber.

———. 1992. *Living in a New Country: History, Travelling, and Language.* London: Faber.

Cathcart, Sarah, and Andrea Lemon. 1988. *The Serpent's Fall.* Sydney: Currency.

Césaire, Aimé. 1974. *Une tempête d'après "La Tempête" de Shakespeare: Adaptation pour un théâtre nègre.* Paris: Éditions du Seuil.

Chesson, Keith. 1988. *Jack Davis: A Life Story.* Melbourne: Dent.

Chi, Jimmy, and Kuckles. 1991. *Bran Nue Dae.* Sydney: Currency; Broome: Magabala Books.

Chikao, Tanaka. 1995. *The Head of Mary.* Trans. David Goodman. Sydney: Currency.

Childs, Peter, and Patrick Williams. 1997. *An Introduction to Post-Colonial Theory.* London: Prentice Hall/Harvester Wheatsheaf.

Chin, Daryl. 1991. "Interculturalism, Postmodernism, Pluralism." In *Interculturalism and Performance: Writings from PAJ,* ed. Bonnie Marranca and Gautam Dasgupta, 83–95. New York: Performing Arts Journal Publications.

Cixous, Hélène. 1981. "The Laugh of the Medusa." Trans. Keith Cohen and Paula Cohen. In *New French Feminisms: An Anthology,* ed. Elaine Marks and Isabelle de Courtivron, 245–64. New York: Schocken.

Connors, Libby, Lynette Finch, Kay Saunders, and Helen Taylor. 1992. *Australia's Frontline: Remembering the 1939–45 War.* St. Lucia: University of Queensland Press.

Copeman, Peter. 1994. "The *Hearts and Minds* Project: Towards an Austral/Asian Theatre." *Australasian Drama Studies* 25:166–76.

Cranny-Francis, Anne. 1988. "The Moving Image: Film and Television." In *Communication and Culture,* ed. Gunther Kress, 158–80. Kensington: New South Wales University Press.

D'Cruz, Glenn. 1993. "A 'Dark' Ariel? Shakespeare and Australian Theatre Criticism." In *Shakespeare's Books: Contemporary Cultural Politics and the Persistence of Empire,* ed. Philip Mead and Marion Campbell, 165–74. Melbourne: University of Melbourne English Department.

Da Matta, Roberto. 1984. "Carnival in Multiple Planes." In *Rite, Drama, Festival, Spectacle: Rehearsals towards a Theory of Cultural Performance,* ed. John MacAloon, 208–40. Philadelphia: Institute for the Study of Human Issues.

Dalby, Michael. 1980. "Nocturnal Labors in the Light of Day." *Journal of Asian Studies* 39 (3): 485–93.

Dale, Leigh, and Helen Gilbert. 1993. "Looking the Same? A Preliminary (Post-colonial) Discussion of Orientalism and Occidentalism in Australia and Japan." *Yearbook of Comparative and General Literature* 41:35–50.

Daly, Ann. 1988. "Movement Analysis: Piecing Together the Puzzle." *Drama Review* 32 (4): 40–52.

———. 1989. "To Dance Is 'Female.'" *Drama Review* 33 (4): 23–27.

Dash, Michael. 1989. "In Search of the Lost Body: Redefining the Subject in Caribbean Literature." *Kunapipi* 11 (1): 17–26.

Davidson, Jim. 1989. "Tasmanian Gothic." *Meanjin* 48 (2): 307–24.

Davis, Jack. 1982. *Kullark* and *The Dreamers.* Sydney: Currency.

———. 1986. *No Sugar.* Sydney: Currency.

———. 1987. *Honey Spot.* Sydney: Currency.

———. 1989. *Barungin.* Sydney: Currency.

———. 1992. *In Our Town.* Sydney: Currency.

Davis, Lloyd. 1992. "Discursive Androgyny/Androgynous Discourse." In *Signifying Others: Selected Papers from the Second Cultural Studies Association of Australia Confer-*

ence, ed. Brian Musgrove and Rebecca Snow-McLean, 130–35. Toowoomba: University of Southern Queensland Press.

De Groen, Alma. 1983. *Going Home* and *Vocations.* Sydney: Currency.

———. 1988. *The Rivers of China.* Sydney: Currency.

———. 1989–90. "Walking Around in Other Times." Interview by Helen Gilbert. *Australasian Drama Studies* 15–16:11–20.

Deleuze, Gilles, and Félix Guattari. 1987. *A Thousand Plateaus: Capitalism and Schizophrenia.* Trans. Brian Massumi. Minneapolis: University of Minnesota Press.

Derrida, Jacques. 1976. *Of Grammatology.* Trans. Gayatri Chakravorty Spivak. Baltimore: Johns Hopkins University Press.

Diamond, Elin. 1990. "Refusing the Romanticism of Identity: Narrative Interventions in Churchill, Benmussa, Duras." In *Performing Feminisms: Feminist Critical Theory and Theatre,* ed. Sue-Ellen Case, 92–105. Baltimore: Johns Hopkins University Press.

Dibble, Brian, and Margaret Macintyre. 1992. "Hybridity in Jack Davis' *No Sugar.*" *Westerly* 37 (4): 93–97.

Dolan, Jill. 1988. *The Feminist Spectator as Critic.* Ann Arbor, Mich.: UMI.

———. 1989. "In Defence of the Discourse: Materialist Feminism, Postmodernism, Poststructuralism . . . and Theory." *Drama Review* 33 (3): 58–71.

———. 1992. "Gender Impersonation Onstage: Destroying or Maintaining the Mirror of Gender Roles?" In *Gender in Performance: The Presentation of Difference in the Performing Arts,* ed. Laurence Senelick, 3–13. Hanover, N.H.: University Press of New England.

Dollimore, Jonathan. 1986. "The Dominant and the Deviant: A Violent Dialectic." *Critical Quarterly* 28 (1–2): 179–92.

———. 1991. *Sexual Dissidence: Augustine to Wilde, Freud to Foucault.* Oxford: Clarendon.

Donaldson, Laura. 1988. "The Miranda Complex: Colonialism and the Question of a Feminist Reading." *Diacritics* 18 (3): 65–77.

Dorsinville, Max. 1974. *Caliban without Prospero.* Erin, Ont.: Porcépic.

Doyle, Jeff. 1991. "Dismembering the Anzac Legend: Australian Popular Culture and the Vietnam War." *Vietnam Generation* 3 (2): 109–25.

Drake-Brockman, Henrietta. 1955. *Men without Wives and Other Plays.* Sydney: Angus and Robertson.

Dunstone, Bill. 1985. "'Another Planet': Landscape as Metaphor in Western Australian Theatre." In *European Relations: Essays for Helen Watson-Williams,* ed. Bruce Bennett and John Hay, 67–79. Perth: Centre for Studies in Australian Literature, University of Western Australia.

———. 1990. "Performance and Difference in Dorothy Hewett's *The Man from Mukinupin.*" *New Literatures Review* 19:72–81.

During, Simon. 1987. "Postmodernism or Post-Colonialism Today." *Textual Practice* 1 (1): 32–47.

———. 1988. "Australia 1788(?)—Foundling of the Enlightenment?" *Meanjin* 47 (2): 179–93.

Edwards, Brian. 1992. "Australian Literature and Post-Colonial Comparisons." *Australian-Canadian Studies* 10 (2): 142–46.

Elam, Kier. 1980. *The Semiotics of Theatre and Drama.* London: Methuen.

Enoch, Wesley, and Deborah Mailman. 1996. *The 7 Stages of Grieving.* Brisbane: Playlab.

Enright, Nick. 1993. *St James Infirmary.* Sydney: Currency.

Evans, Bob. 1989. Review of *Capricornia,* by Louis Nowra. In *Reviews: Australia's Bicentennial Arts Program, 1988,* ed. Sarah Overton, 240. Sydney: Mead and Beckett.

———. 1994. "The Trial That Won't Go Away." *Sydney Morning Herald,* 5 August, 20.

Fanon, Frantz. 1967. *Black Skin, White Masks.* Trans. Charles Lam Markmann. New York: Grove.

Ferrier, Elizabeth. 1989. "Mapping the Local in the Unreal City." *Island* 41:65–69.

———. 1990. "Mapping Power: Cartography and Contemporary Cultural Theory." *Antithesis* 4 (1): 35–49.

Filewod, Alan. 1992. "Between Empires: Post-Imperialism and Canadian Theatre." *Essays in Theatre* 11 (1): 3–15.

Finnegan, Ruth. 1976. *Oral Literature in Africa.* London: Oxford University Press.

Fischer, Gerhard, ed. 1993. *The Mudrooroo/Müller Project: A Theatrical Casebook.* Sydney: New South Wales University Press.

Fitzpatrick, Peter. 1985a. "Asian Stereotypes in Recent Australian Plays." *Australian Literary Studies* 12 (1): 35–46.

———. 1985b. Review of *The Golden Age,* by Louis Nowra. *Australasian Drama Studies* 7:139–44.

———. 1987a. "After the Wave: Australian Drama since 1975." In *Contemporary Australian Drama,* rev. ed., ed. Peter Holloway, 161–80. Sydney: Currency.

———. 1987b. *Williamson.* Sydney: Methuen.

———. 1989–90. Review of *Hate,* by Stephen Sewell. *Australasian Drama Studies* 15–16:202–5.

———. 1990. "Staging Australia: Models of Cultural Identity in the Theatre." *Australian Studies* 13:53–62.

———. 1991. *Stephen Sewell: The Playwright as Revolutionary.* Sydney: Currency.

———. 1995. "Dorothy Hewett and Contemporary Australian Drama." In *Dorothy Hewett: Selected Critical Essays,* ed. Bruce Bennett, 95–114. Fremantle: Fremantle Arts Centre.

Fitzpatrick, Peter, and Helen Thomson. 1993. "Developments in Recent Australian Drama." *World Literature Today* 67 (3): 489–93.

Forsee, Aylesa. 1963. *Albert Einstein: Theoretical Physicist.* New York: Macmillan.

Forte, Jeanie. 1990. "Women's Performance Art: Feminism and Postmodernism." In *Performing Feminisms: Feminist Critical Theory and Theatre,* ed. Sue-Ellen Case, 251–69. Baltimore: Johns Hopkins University Press.

Foster, Susan Leigh. 1996. *Corporealities: Dancing Knowledge, Culture, and Power.* London: Routledge.

Fotheringham, Richard. 1992. *Community Theatre in Australia.* Rev. ed. Sydney: Currency.

Foucault, Michel. 1979. *Discipline and Punish: The Birth of the Prison.* Trans. Alan Sheridan. New York: Vintage.

———. 1980. "Questions on Geography." In *Power/Knowledge: Selected Interviews and Other Writings,* ed. and trans. Colin Gordon, 63–77. Brighton: Harvester.

———. 1986. "Of Other Spaces." Trans. Jay Miskowiec. *Diacritics* 16 (1): 22–27.

Francis, Gordon. 1987. *God's Best Country.* Sydney: Currency.

Freadman, Anne. 1992. "Ramus against Quintilian: A Civil War, Some Readings, and a Couple of Allegorical Diversions." *Southern Review* 25 (3): 252–67.

Freedman, Barbara. 1991. *Staging the Gaze: Postmodernism, Psychoanalysis, and Shakespearean Comedy.* Ithaca, N.Y.: Cornell University Press.

Frow, John. 1991. "Tourism and the Semiotics of Nostalgia." *October* 57:123–51.

———. 1993. "Regimes of Value." In *Shakespeare's Books: Contemporary Cultural Politics and the Persistence of Empire,* ed. Philip Mead and Marion Campbell, 207–18. Melbourne: University of Melbourne English Department.

Gaines, Jane. 1990. "Costume and Narrative: How Dress Tells the Woman's Story." In *Fabrications: Costume and the Female Body,* ed. Jane Gaines and Charlotte Herzog, 180–211. New York: Routledge.

Garber, Marjorie. 1992. *Vested Interests: Cross-Dressing and Cultural Anxiety.* London: Routledge.

Gardiner, Allan. 1990. "Discourses of Settlement and the Works of George Lamming and J. M. Coetzee." M.A. thesis, University of Queensland.

Garner, Stanton B., Jr. 1990. "Post-Brechtian Anatomies: Weiss, Bond, and the Politics of Embodiment." *Theatre Journal* 42 (2): 145–64.

Gay, Penny. 1992. "Michael Gow's *Away:* The Shakespeare Connection." In *Reconnoitres: Essays in Australian Literature in Honour of G. A. Wilkes,* ed. Margaret Harris and Elizabeth Webby, 204–13. Sydney: Oxford University Press.

Geoghegan, Edward. 1976. *The Currency Lass.* Ed. Roger Covell. Sydney: Currency.

George, David. 1989a. "On Ambiguity: Towards a Post-Modern Performance Theory." *Theatre Research International* 14 (1): 71–85.

———. 1989b. "Quantum Theatre—Potential Theatre: A New Paradigm?" *New Theatre Quarterly* 18 (5): 171–79.

———. 1989–90. "Casebook: *The Tempest* in Bali—a Director's Log." *Australasian Drama Studies* 15–16:21–46.

George, Rob. 1983. *Sandy Lee Live at Nui Dat.* Sydney: Currency.

Gerster, Robin. 1987a. "The Gallipoli Glut." Review of *Gallipoli: One Long Grave,* by Kit Denton. *Australian Book Review* 90:29–30.

———. 1987b. "The Least Popular War." Review of *Australia's War in Vietnam,* by Frank Frost. *Australian Book Review* 95:10–12.

———. 1991. "Occidental Tourists: The 'Ugly Australian' in Vietnam War Narrative." In *Vietnam Days: Australia and the Impact of Vietnam,* ed. Peter Pierce et al., 191–235. Ringwood: Penguin.

———, ed. 1995. *Hotel Asia: An Anthology of Australian Literary Travelling to the "East".* Ringwood: Penguin.

Gibbs, Geoff. 1992. Review of *Wahngin Country,* by Jack Davis. *Australian and New Zealand Theatre Record* 6 (2): 52–53.

Gibson, Ross. 1992. *South of the West: Postcolonialism and the Narrative Construction of Australia.* Bloomington: Indiana University Press.

Gilbert, Helen, and Joanne Tompkins. 1996. *Post-colonial Drama: Theory, Practice, Politics.* London: Routledge.

Gilbert, Kevin. 1988. *The Cherry Pickers.* Canberra: Burrambinga.

Goldie, Terry. 1986. "Indigenous Stages: The Indigene in Canadian, New Zealand, and Australian Drama." *Australasian Drama Studies* 9:5–20.

———. 1988. "Signifier Resignified: Aborigines in Australian Literature." *Kunapipi* 10 (1–2): 59–75.

Gough, Sue. 1989. Review of *Tokyo Rose,* by Barry Lowe. *Australian and New Zealand Theatre Record* 3 (10): 43.

Gow, Michael. 1983. *The Kid.* Sydney: Currency.

———. 1987. *Europe* and *On Top of the World.* Sydney: Currency.

———. 1986. *Away.* Sydney: Currency.

———. 1988. *1841.* Sydney: Currency.

———. 1992. Interview by John Pearson. *Southerly* 52 (2): 116–31.

———. 1994. *Furious.* Sydney: Currency.

Greenblatt, Stephen. 1976. "Learning to Curse: Aspects of Linguistic Colonialism in the Sixteenth Century." In *First Images of America: The Impact of the New World on the Old,* ed. Fredi Chiapelli, 561–80. Berkeley and Los Angeles: University of California Press.

———. 1991. *Marvelous Possessions: The Wonder of the New World.* Oxford: Clarendon.

Griffiths, Gareth. 1984. "Australian Subjects and Australian Style: The Plays of Louis Nowra." *Commonwealth: Essays and Studies* 6 (2): 42–48.

———. 1989. Review of *Capricornia,* by Louis Nowra. *New Theatre: Australia* 11:33.

———. 1992a. "'Unhappy the Land That Has a Need of Heroes': John Romeril's Asian Plays." In *Myths, Heroes, and Anti-Heroes: Essays on the Literature and Culture of the Asia-Pacific Region,* ed. Bruce Bennet and Dennis Haskell, 142–54. Perth: Centre for Studies in Australian Literature, University of Western Australia.

———. 1992b. "The Dark Side of the Dreaming: Aboriginality and Australian Culture." *Australian Literary Studies* 15 (4): 328–33.

———, ed. 1993. *John Romeril.* Amsterdam: Rodopi.

Griffiths, Trevor. 1983. "'This Island's Mine': Caliban and Colonialism." *Yearbook of English Studies* 13:159–80.

Grosz, Elizabeth. 1990. "Inscriptions and Body-Maps: Representations and the Corporeal." In *Feminine/Masculine and Representation,* ed. Terry Threadgold and Anne Cranny-Francis, 62–74. Sydney: Allen and Unwin.

Gunew, Sneja, and Fazal Rizvi, eds. 1994. *Culture Difference and the Arts.* Sydney: Allen and Unwin.

Gurr, Michael. 1993. *Sex Diary of an Infidel.* 2d ed. Sydney: Currency.

Hainsworth, J. D. 1987. *Hibberd.* North Ryde: Methuen.

Hanna, Judith Lynne. 1987. "Patterns of Dominance: Men, Women, and Homosexuality in Dance." *Drama Review* 31 (1): 22–47.

Harley, J. B. 1988. "Maps, Knowledge, and Power." In *The Iconography of Landscape: Essays on the Symbolic Representation, Design, and Use of Past Environments,* ed. Denis Cosgrove and Stephen Daniels, 227–312. Cambridge: Cambridge University Press.

Harris, Wilson. 1988. *The Infinite Rehearsal.* London: Faber.

———. 1992. "The Fabric of the Imagination." In *From Commonwealth to Post-Colonial,* ed. Anna Rutherford, 18–29. Sydney: Dangaroo.

Heath, Jane. 1987. "Malouf: Relatively Speaking." *Weekend Australian,* 18–19 July, 11–12.

Hennessy, Rachel. 1995. "The Sight/Site of the Aboriginal Woman: Representations of Race and Gender by Australian Female Playwrights." Honors thesis, University of Newcastle.

Herbert, Bob. 1980. *No Names . . . No Pack Drill.* Sydney: Currency.

Herbert, Xavier. 1971. *Capricornia: A Novel.* Sydney: Angus and Robertson.

Hewett, Dorothy. 1976. *Bon-Bons and Roses for Dolly* and *The Tatty Hollow Story.* Sydney: Currency.

———. 1979. *The Man from Mukinupin.* Sydney: Currency.

Hodge, Bob, and Vijay Mishra. 1991. *Dark Side of the Dream: Literature and the Post-colonial Mind.* Sydney: Allen and Unwin.

Holloway, Peter, ed. 1987. *Contemporary Australian Drama.* Rev. ed. Sydney: Currency.

Hopkins, Lekkie. 1987. "Language, Culture, and Landscape in *The Man from Mukinupin.*" *Australasian Drama Studies* 10:91–106.

Huggan, Graham. 1989a. "Resisting the Map as Metaphor: A Comparison of Margaret Atwood's *Surfacing* and Janet Frame's *Scented Gardens for the Blind.*" *Kunapipi* 11 (3): 5–15.

———. 1989b. "Decolonizing the Map: Post-Colonialism, Post-Structuralism, and the Cartographic Connection." *ARIEL* 20 (4): 115–31.

———. 1991. "Maps, Dreams, and the Presentation of Ethnographic Narrative: Hugh Brody's *Maps and Dreams* and Bruce Chatwin's *The Songlines.*" *ARIEL* 22 (1): 57–69.

———. 1993. "Transformations of the Tourist Gaze: India in Recent Australian Fiction." *Westerly* 38 (4): 83–89.

Hutcheon, Linda. 1989. *The Politics of Postmodernism.* London: Verso.

———. 1990. "Circling the Downspout of Empire." In *Past the Last Post: Theorizing Post-Colonialism and Post-Modernism,* ed. Ian Adam and Helen Tiffin, 167–89. Calgary: Calgary University Press.

Hwang, David Henry. 1989. *M. Butterfly.* London: Penguin.

Inverso, MaryBeth. 1990. *The Gothic Impulse in Contemporary Drama.* Ann Arbor, Mich.: UMI.

Issacharoff, Michael. 1981. "Space and Reference in Drama." *Poetics Today* 2 (3): 211–24.

Jackson, Earl, Jr. 1989. "Kabuki Narratives of Male Homoerotic Desire in Saikaku and Mishima." *Theatre Journal* 41 (4): 459–77.

Jackson, Rosemary. 1981. *Fantasy: The Literature of Subversion.* New York: Methuen.

Jacobson, Lisa. 1990. "The Ocker in Australian Drama." *Meanjin* 49 (1): 137–47.

Jameson, Fredric. 1984. "Postmodernism; or, The Cultural Logic of Late Capitalism." *New Left Review* 146:53–92.

Jeffords, Susan. 1989. *The Remasculinization of America: Gender and the Vietnam War.* Bloomington: Indiana University Press.

Johnson, Eva. 1989. *Murras.* In *Plays from Black Australia,* ed. Katharine Brisbane, 79–107. Sydney, Currency.

———. 1991. *What Do They Call Me?* In *Heroines,* ed. Dale Spender, 237–55. Ringwood: Penguin.

Jolly, Roslyn. 1986. "Transformations of Caliban and Ariel: Imagination and Language in David Malouf, Margaret Atwood, and Seamus Heaney." *World Literature Written in English* 26 (2): 295–330.

Kaplan, Caren. 1987. "Deterritorializations: The Rewriting of Home and Exile in Western Feminist Discourse." *Cultural Critique* 6:187–98.

Kappeler, Susanne. 1984. *The Pornography of Representation.* Cambridge: Polity.

Katrak, Ketu. 1989. "Decolonizing Culture: Toward a Theory for Postcolonial Women's Texts." *Modern Fiction Studies* 35 (1): 157–79.

Kelly, Veronica. 1981. "A Mirror for Australia: Louis Nowra's Emblematic Theatre." *Southerly* 41 (4): 431–58.

———. 1987a. "'Lest We Forget': *Inside the Island.*" In *Louis Nowra,* ed. Veronica Kelly, 99–113. Amsterdam: Rodopi.

———. 1987b. "Explorers and Bushrangers in Nineteenth-Century Australian Theatre." In *The Writer's Sense of the Past: Essays on Southeast Asian and Australasian Literature,* ed. Kirpal Singh, 119–32. Singapore: Singapore University Press.

———. 1987c. "Apocalypse and After: Historical Visions in Some Recent Australian Drama." *Kunapipi* 9 (3): 68–78.

———. 1988. "'Nowt More Outcastin': Utopian Myth in Louis Nowra's *The Golden Age.*" In *A Sense of Exile: Essays in the Literatures of the Asia-Pacific Region,* ed. Bruce Bennett, 101–10. Perth: Centre for Studies in Australian Literature, University of Western Australia.

———. 1990a. "The Melodrama of Defeat: Political Patterns in Some Colonial and Contemporary Australian Plays." *Southerly* 50 (2): 131–43.

———. 1990b. Review of *Shimada,* by Jill Shearer. *Australasian Drama Studies* 17:224–27.

———. 1992a. "Falling between Stools: The Theatre of Janis Balodis." *ARIEL* 23 (1): 115–32.

———. 1992b. "Louis Nowra." In *Post-Colonial English Plays: Commonwealth Drama since 1960,* ed. Bruce King, 50–66. London: Macmillan.

———, ed. 1998. *Our Australian Theatre in the 1990s.* Amsterdam: Rodopi.

Kermode, Frank. 1967. *The Sense of an Ending.* New York: Oxford University Press.

Kiernander, Adrian. 1992. "The Orient, the Feminine: The Use of Interculturalism by the Théâtre du Soleil." In *Gender in Performance: The Presentation of Difference in the Performing Arts,* ed. Laurence Senelick, 183–92. Hanover, N.H.: University Press of New England.

Kirkby, Joan. 1985. "The American Prospero." *Southern Review* 18 (1): 90–108.

Krishnaswamy, Revathi. 1995. "Mythologies of Migrancy: Postcolonialism, Postmodernism, and the Politics of (Dis)Location." *ARIEL* 26 (1): 125–46.

Kroetsch, Robert. 1989. *The Lovely Treachery of Words: Essays Selected and New.* Toronto: Oxford University Press.

Kruger, Debbie. 1989. Review of *Capricornia,* by Louis Nowra. In *Reviews: Australia's Bicentennial Arts Program, 1988,* ed. Sarah Overton, 247. Sydney: Mead and Beckett.

Lamming, George. 1960. *The Pleasures of Exile.* London: Michael Joseph.

Langer, Beryl. 1991. "The Real Thing: Cliff Hardy and Cocacola-nisation." *SPAN* 31:29–44.

Langton, Marcia. 1993. *Well I Heard It on the Radio and I Saw It on the Television.* Sydney: Australian Film Commission.

Lateo, Karen. 1988. Review of *Hate,* by Stephen Sewell. *Australian and New Zealand Theatre Record* 2 (11): 6–7.

Lawford, Josie Ningali, with Robyn Archer and Angela Chaplin. 1994. *Ningali.* Unpublished playscript.

Lawson, Alan. 1992. "Comparative Studies and Post-Colonial 'Settler' Cultures." *Australian-Canadian Studies* 10 (2): 153–59.

———. 1994. "Un/Settling Colonies: The Ambivalent Place of Colonial Discourse." In *Literature and Opposition,* ed. Chris Worth, Pauline Nestor, and Marko Pavlyshyn, 67–82. Clayton: Centre for Comparative Literature and Cultural Studies, Monash University.

Lee, Dennis. 1974. "Cadence, Country, Silence: Writing in Colonial Space." *Boundary* 3:151–68.

Leer, Martin. 1985. "At the Edge: Geography and the Imagination in the Work of David Malouf." *Australian Literary Studies* 12 (1): 3–21.

Lloyd, Tim. 1989. Review of *Capricornia,* by Louis Nowra. In *Reviews: Australia's Bicentennial Arts Program, 1988,* ed. Sarah Overton, 248. Sydney: Mead and Beckett.

Lo, Jaqueline. 1997. "Tropes of Ambivalence in *Bran Nue Dae.*" Typescript.

———. 1998. "Dis/Orientations: Contemporary Asian-Australian Theatre." In *Our Australian Theatre in the 1990s,* ed. Veronica Kelly, 53–70. Amsterdam: Rodopi.

Loomba, Ania. 1989. *Gender, Race, Renaissance Drama.* Manchester: Manchester University Press.

Low, Gail Ching-Liang. 1989. "White Skins/Black Masks: The Pleasures and Politics of Imperialism." *New Formations* 9:83–103.

———. 1996. *White Skins/Black Masks: Representation and Colonialism.* London: Routledge.

Lowe, Barry. 1989. *Tokyo Rose.* Unpublished playscript.

Lowe, Lisa. 1986. "The Orient as Woman in Flaubert's *Salammbô* and *Voyage en Orient.*" *Comparative Literature Studies* 23 (1): 44–58.

Maes-Jelinek, Hena. 1989. "The Muse's Progress: 'Infinite Rehearsal' in J. M. Coetzee's *Foe.*" In *A Shaping of Connections: Commonwealth Literature Studies—Then and Now,* ed. Hena Maes-Jelinek, Kirsten Holst Petersen, and Anna Rutherford, 232–42. Sydney: Dangaroo.

Makeham, Paul. 1996a. "Across the Long, Dry Stage: Discourses of Landscape in Australian Drama." Ph.D. diss., University of Newcastle.

———. 1996b. "Singing the Landscape: *Bran Nue Dae.*" *Australasian Drama Studies* 28:117–32.

Malouf, David. 1978. *An Imaginary Life.* London: Chatto and Windus.

———. 1983. *Fly Away Peter.* Ringwood: Penguin.

———. 1985a. "A First Place: The Mapping of a World." *Southerly* 45 (1): 3–10.

———. 1985b. "A Splendid Blend of Complex Worlds." *The Australian,* 17 September, 12.

———. 1988. *Blood Relations.* Sydney: Currency.

Mannoni, O. 1964. *Prospero and Caliban: The Psychology of Colonization.* 2d ed. Trans. Pamela Powesland. New York: Praeger.

Marranca, Bonnie. 1991. "Thinking about Interculturalism." In *Interculturalism and Performance: Writings from PAJ,* ed. Bonnie Marranca and Gautam Dasgupta, 9–23. New York: Performing Arts Journal Publications.

Matthews, Brian. 1985. "Australian Colonial Women and Their Autobiographies." *Kunapipi* 12 (2–3): 36–46.

Maza, Bob. 1989. *The Keepers.* In *Plays from Black Australia,* ed. Katharine Brisbane, 167–229. Sydney: Currency.

McCallum, John. 1984. "The World Outside: Cosmopolitanism in the Plays of Nowra and Sewell." *Meanjin* 43 (2): 286–96.

———. 1987a. "The Development of a Sense of History in Contemporary Australian Drama." In *Contemporary Australian Drama,* rev. ed., ed. Peter Holloway, 148–60. Sydney: Currency.

———. 1987b. *Buzo.* North Ryde: Methuen.

———. 1988. "Studying Australian Drama." *Australasian Drama Studies* 12–13:147–66.

———. 1989–90. Review of *Away* and *1841,* by Michael Gow. *Australasian Drama Studies* 15–16:199–202.

McClintock, Anne. 1995. *Imperial Leather: Race, Gender, and Sexuality in the Colonial Context.* London: Routledge.

McDougall, Russell. 1990a. "Music in the Body of the Book of Carnival." *Journal of West Indian Literature* 4 (2): 1–24.

———. 1990b. "The Snapshot Image and the Body of Tradition: Stage Imagery in *The Lion and the Jewel.*" *New Literatures Review* 19:102–18.

McDougall, Russell, and Gillian Whitlock. 1987. Introduction to *Australian/Canadian Literatures in English: Comparative Perspectives,* ed. Russell McDougall and Gillian Whitlock, 1–32. Sydney: Methuen.

McGillick, Paul. 1987. Review of *Blood Relations,* by David Malouf. *CentreStage Australia* 1 (2): 26–27.

McNarn, Maurie. 1979–80. "From Imperial Appendage to American Satellite: Australian Involvement in Vietnam." *Australian National University Historical Journal* 14:73–86.

McRobbie, Angela. 1984. "Dance and Social Fantasy." In *Gender and Generation,* ed. Angela McRobbie and Mica Nava, 130–61. London: Macmillan.

Mead, Philip, and Marion Campbell, eds. 1993. *Shakespeare's Books: Contemporary Cultural Politics and the Persistence of Empire.* Melbourne: University of Melbourne English Department.

Merritt, Robert. 1978. *The Cake Man.* Sydney: Currency.

Mills, Sara. 1991. *Discourses of Difference: An Analysis of Women's Travel Writing and Colonialism.* London: Routledge.

Misto, John. 1996. *The Shoe-Horn Sonata.* Sydney: Currency.

Mitchell, Tony. 1989. "Great White Hope or Great White Hype? The Critical Construction (and Demolition) of Michael Gow." *Spectator Burns* 3:17–27.

———. 1993. "Colonial Discourse and the National Imaginary." *Canadian Theatre Review* 74:18–21.

Moore, John Hammond. 1981. *Over-Sexed, Over-Paid, and Over Here: Americans in Australia, 1941–1945.* St. Lucia: University of Queensland Press.

Morgan, Sally. 1992. *Sistergirl.* Unpublished playscript.

Morley, Michael. 1988. Review of *1841,* by Michael Gow. *Australian and New Zealand Theatre Record* 2 (3): 8.

Morley, Sheridan. 1980. "Drama into History." *Sydney Morning Herald,* 11 October, 19.

Mudrooroo [Colin Johnson]. 1985. "White Forms, Aboriginal Content." In *Aboriginal Writing Today,* ed. Jack Davis and Bob Hodge, 21–30. Canberra: Australian Institute of Aboriginal Studies.

——— [Mudrooroo Narogin]. 1989a. "Black Reality." In *Barungin,* by Jack Davis, vii–ix. Sydney: Currency.

——— [Mudrooroo Narogin]. 1989b. "Towards a New Black Theatre." *New Theatre: Australia* 9:16–17.

——— [Mudrooroo Narogin]. 1990. *Writing from the Fringe: A Study of Modern Aboriginal Literature.* Melbourne: Hyland House.

———. 1993. "World Bilong Tok-Tok." In *The Mudrooroo/Müller Project: A Theatrical Casebook,* ed. Gerhard Fischer, 135–44. Sydney: New South Wales University Press.

Muecke, Stephen. 1983a. "Discourse, History, Fiction: Language and Aboriginal History." *Australian Journal of Cultural Studies* 1 (1): 71–80.

———. 1983b. "Ideology Re-iterated: The Uses of Aboriginal Oral Narrative." *Southern Review* 16 (1): 86–101.

———. 1988. "Body, Inscription, Epistemology: Knowing Aboriginal Texts." In *Connections: Essays on Black Literatures,* ed. Emmanuel Nelson, 41–52. Canberra: Aboriginal Studies.

Mukherjee, Arun. 1990. "Whose Post-Colonialism and Whose Postmodernism?" *World Literature Written in English* 30 (2): 1–9.

Mulvey, Laura. 1975. "Visual Pleasure and Narrative Cinema." *Screen* 16 (3): 6–18.

Murphy, John. 1987. "'Like Outlaws': Australian Narratives from the Vietnam War." *Meanjin* 46 (2): 153–62.

Murray, Peta. 1993. *One Woman's Song.* Unpublished playscript.

Nettelbeck, Amanda. 1992. "Myths of a Nation: History as Narrative Invention in David Malouf's *The Great World.*" In *Myths, Heroes, and Anti-Heroes: Essays on the Literature and Culture of the Asia-Pacific Region,* ed. Bruce Bennett and Dennis Haskell, 132–41. Perth: Centre for Studies in Australian Literature, University of Western Australia.

Novak, Cynthia. 1988. "Looking at Movement as Culture: Contact Improvisation to Disco." *Drama Review* 32 (4): 102–19.

Nowra, Louis. 1977. *Inner Voices.* Sydney: Currency.

———. 1979. *Visions.* Sydney: Currency.

———. 1981. *Inside the Island* and *The Precious Woman.* Sydney: Currency.

———. 1983. *Sunrise.* Sydney: Currency.

———. 1987a. Interview by Veronica Kelly. In *Louis Nowra,* ed. Veronica Kelly, 139–43. Amsterdam: Rodopi.

———. 1987b. "Perfecting the Monologue of Silence." Interview by Gerry Turcotte. *Kunapipi* 9 (3): 51–67.

———. 1988. *Capricornia.* Sydney: Currency.

———. 1989. *The Golden Age.* 2d ed. Sydney: Currency.

———. 1992a. *Summer of the Aliens.* Sydney: Currency.

———. 1992b. *Cosi.* Sydney: Currency.

———. 1993. *Radiance.* Sydney: Currency.

———. 1994. *Crow.* Sydney: Currency.

———. 1995. *The Incorruptible.* Sydney: Currency.

Nugent, Ann. 1987. "A Tragedy on the Grubby Side." Review of *Blood Relations,* by David Malouf. *Canberra Times,* 10 July, 12.

———. 1988. Review of *1841,* by Michael Gow. *Australian and New Zealand Theatre Record* 2 (3): 5–6.

O'Brien, Collin. 1983. Review of *Kullark* and *The Dreamers,* by Jack Davis. *Australasian Drama Studies* 2:125–26.

Olaniyan, Tejumola. 1993. "On 'Post-Colonial Discourse': An Introduction." *Callaloo* 16 (4): 743–49.

Olb, Suzanne. 1988. "The White Problem: Jack Davis' Confronting Realism." *New Theatre: Australia* 6:4–7.

Ong, Walter. 1982. *Orality and Literacy: The Technologising of the Word.* London: Methuen.

Orgel, Stephen. 1987. Introduction to *The Tempest,* by William Shakespeare, 1–87. Oxford: Oxford University Press.

Panozzo, Dina. 1991. *Varda Che Bruta . . . Poretta.* Unpublished playscript.

Parsons, Nicholas. 1994. *Dead Heart.* Sydney: Currency.

Pathak, Zakia, Saswati Sengupta, and Sharmila Purkayastha. 1991. "The Prisonhouse of Orientalism." *Textual Practice* 5 (2): 195–218.

Pavis, Patrice. 1982. *Languages of the Stage: Essays in the Semiology of Theatre.* New York: Performing Arts Journal Publications.

———. 1992. *Theatre at the Crossroads of Culture.* Trans. Loren Kruger. London: Routledge.

———, ed. 1996. *The Intercultural Performance Reader.* London: Routledge.

Perkins, Elizabeth. 1987a. "The Mind on Stage—Deconstructing Conventional Form." *New Theatre: Australia* 2:39.

———. 1987b. "Form and Transformation in the Plays of Alma De Groen." *Australasian Drama Studies* 11:5–21.

———. 1994. *Alma De Groen.* Amsterdam: Rodopi.

Petersen, Kirsten Holst, and Anna Rutherford. 1985. Foreword to *A Double Colonization,* ed. Kirsten Holst Petersen and Anna Rutherford, 9–10. Sydney: Dangaroo.

Phillips, Dennis. 1988. *Ambivalent Allies: Myth and Reality in the Australian-American Relationship.* Ringwood: Penguin.

Pickett, Carolyn. 1991. "If Looks Could Kill: Feminist Themes in Contemporary Playwrights' Work." M.A. thesis, La Trobe University.

Pierce, Peter. 1985. "Perceptions of the Enemy in Australian War Literature." *Australian Literary Studies* 12 (2): 166–81.

———. 1991. "Australian and American Literature of the Vietnam War." In *Vietnam Days: Australia and the Impact of Vietnam,* ed. Peter Pierce, Jeffrey Grey, and Jeff Doyle, 237–74. Ringwood: Penguin.

Porter, Dennis. 1983. "*Orientalism* and Its Problems." In *The Politics of Theory. Proceedings of the Essex Conference on the Sociology of Literature, July 1982,* ed. Francis Barker et al., 179–93. Colchester: University of Essex Press.

Prentice, Chris. 1991. "The Interplay of Place and Placelessness in the Subject of Post-Colonial Fiction." *SPAN* 31:63–80.

Prichard, Katharine Susannah. 1983. *Brumby Innes* and *Bid Me to Love.* Ed. Katharine Brisbane. Sydney: Currency.

Radic, Leonard. 1991. *The State of Play: The Revolution in the Australian Theatre since the 1960s.* Ringwood: Penguin.

———. 1992. Review of *Wahngin Country,* by Jack Davis. *Australian and New Zealand Theatre Review* 6 (2): 53.

Rasul, Kamal Mamand. 1987. "The Archeology of History: An Analytical Study Examining the Strategy of the Historical Construction of the Images and Concepts of the Other in the Context of Colonialist/Orientalist Discourse." *Dissertation Abstracts International* 49:05A. University of Essex, Essex.

Ridgman, Jeremy. 1983. "Interview: Louis Nowra, Stephen Sewell, and Neil Armfield Talk to Jeremy Ridgman." *Australasian Drama Studies* 1:105–23.

Robertson, W. 1928. *Coo-ee Talks.* Sydney: Angus and Robertson.

Romeril, John. 1975. *The Floating World.* Sydney: Currency.

———. 1979–80. "Political Drama in Australia: Why and Wherefore?" Interview by Sophie Elias. *Commonwealth: Essays and Studies* 4:147–54.

———. 1988. *Top End.* Unpublished playscript.

Rowlands, Shane. 1989. "Matrixing: A Post-Colonial and Feminist Writing Strategy." Honors thesis, University of Queensland.

Rubin, Gayle. 1975. "The Traffic in Women: Notes on the 'Political Economy' of Sex." In *Toward an Anthropology of Women,* ed. Rayna Reiter, 157–210. New York: Monthly Review.

Rushdie, Salman. 1983. *Shame.* London: Cape.

Russo, Mary. 1986. "Female Grotesques: Carnival and Theory." *Feminist Studies/Critical Studies,* ed. Teresa de Lauretis, 213–29. Bloomington: Indiana University Press.

Ryan, Simon. 1994. "Voyeurs in Space: The Gendered Scopic Regimes of Exploration." *Southerly* 54 (1): 36–49.

Said, Edward. 1979. *Orientalism.* New York: Vintage.

———. 1990. "Reflections on Exile." In *Out There: Marginalization and Contemporary Culture,* ed. Russell Ferguson et al., 357–66. Cambridge, Mass.: MIT Press.

Salter, Denis. 1996. "Introduction: The End(s) of Shakespeare?" *Essays in Theatre* 15 (1): 3–14.

Sawada, Keiji. 1996. "The Japanese Version of *The Floating World:* A Cross-Cultural Event between Japan and Australia." *Australasian Drama Studies* 28:4–19.

Schaffer, Kay. 1988. *Women and the Bush: Forces of Desire in the Australian Cultural Tradition.* Cambridge: Cambridge University Press.

Schechner, Richard. 1993. *The Future of Ritual: Writings on Culture and Performance.* London: Routledge.

Schechner, Richard, and Willa Appel, eds. 1990. *By Means of Performance: Intercultural Studies of Theatre and Ritual.* Cambridge: Cambridge University Press.

Scolnicov, Hanna. 1987. "Theatre Space, Theatrical Space, and the Theatrical Space Without." In *The Theatrical Space,* ed. James Redmond, 11–26. Cambridge: Cambridge University Press.

Scott, Maurie. 1990. "Karbarra: The New Aboriginal Drama and Its Audience." *SPAN* 30:127–40.

Seaton, Dorothy. 1991. "The Post-Colonial as Deconstruction: Land and Language in Kroetsch's *Badlands.*" *Canadian Literature* 128:77–89.

Sedgwick, Eve Kosofsky. 1991. *Epistemology of the Closet.* New York: Harvester Wheatsheaf.

Sewell, Stephen. 1985. *The Blind Giant Is Dancing.* Rev. ed. Sydney: Currency.

———. 1988. *Hate.* Sydney: Currency.

Sharpe, Jenny. 1989. "Figures of Colonial Resistance." *Modern Fiction Studies* 35 (1): 137–55.

———. 1993. *Allegories of Empire: The Figure of Woman in the Colonial Text.* Minneapolis: University of Minnesota Press.

Shearer, Jill. 1977. *Catherine.* Melbourne: Arnold.

———. 1989. *Shimada.* Sydney: Currency.

Shoemaker, Adam. 1989. *Black Words, White Page: Aboriginal Literature, 1929–1988.* St. Lucia: University of Queensland Press.

Showalter, Elaine. 1981. "Feminist Criticism in the Wilderness." *Critical Inquiry* 8 (2): 179–205.

Siebers, Tobin. 1983. *The Mirror of Medusa.* Berkeley and Los Angeles: University of California Press.

Siegel, Marcia. 1988. "The Truth about Apples and Oranges." *Drama Review* 32 (4): 24–31.

Slemon, Stephen. 1987. "Monuments of Empire: Allegory/Counter-Discourse/Post-Colonial Writing." *Kunapipi* 9 (3): 1–16.

———. 1988a. "Post-Colonial Allegory and the Transformation of History." *Journal of Commonwealth Literature* 23 (1): 157–68.

———. 1988b. "'Carnival' and the Canon." *ARIEL* 19 (3): 59–75.

———. 1989. "Reading for Resistance in Post-Colonial Literatures." In *A Shaping of Connections: Commonwealth Literature Studies—Then and Now,* ed. Hena Maes-Jelinek, Kirsten Holst Petersen, and Anna Rutherford, 100–115. Sydney: Dangaroo.

———. 1990a. "Unsettling the Empire: Resistance Theory for the Second World." *World Literature Written in English* 30 (2): 30–41.

———. 1990b. "Modernism's Last Post." In *Past the Last Post: Post-Colonialism and Post-Modernism,* ed. Ian Adam and Helen Tiffin, 1–11. Calgary: Calgary University Press.

Sontag, Susan. 1973. *On Photography.* New York: Farrar, Straus and Giroux.

Souter, Gavin. 1976. *Lion and Kangaroo: The Initiation of Australia, 1901–1919.* Sydney: Collins.

Spivak, Gayatri Chakravorty. 1985. "Three Women's Texts and a Critique of Imperialism." *Critical Inquiry* 12 (1): 243–61.

———. 1986. "Imperialism and Sexual Difference." *Oxford Literary Review* 8 (1–2): 225–40.

———. 1988. *In Other Worlds: Essays in Cultural Politics.* New York: Methuen.

Stallybrass, Peter, and Allon White. 1986. *The Politics and Poetics of Transgression.* Ithaca, N.Y.: Cornell University Press.

Stam, Robert. 1989. *Subversive Pleasures: Bakhtin, Cultural Criticism, and Film.* Baltimore: Johns Hopkins University Press.

Stephensen, P. R. 1936. *The Foundations of Culture in Australia: An Essay Towards National Self-Respect.* Sydney: Miles.

Stewart, Susan. 1984. *On Longing: Narratives of the Miniature, the Gigantic, the Souvenir, the Collection.* Baltimore: Johns Hopkins University Press.

Stow, Randolph. 1981. *Visitants.* London: Pan.

Strachan, Tony. 1983. *Eyes of the Whites.* Sydney: Alternative.

———. 1986. *State of Shock.* Sydney: Currency.

Strahan, Lynne. 1981. "Aussie Still in Search of Self." *Helix* 9–10:28–35.

Suleri, Sara. 1992. "Woman Skin Deep: Feminism and the Postcolonial Condition." *Critical Inquiry* 18 (4): 756–69.

Suvin, Darko. 1987. "Approach to Topoanalysis and to the Paradigmatics of Dramaturgic Space." *Poetics Today* 8 (2): 311–34.

Swift, Graham. 1984. *Waterlands.* London: Picador.

Tait, Peta. 1994. *Converging Realities: Feminism in Australian Theatre.* Sydney: Currency; Melbourne: Artmoves.

Tapping, Craig. 1989. "Oral Cultures and the Empire of Literature." *Kunapipi* 11 (1): 86–96.

Tate, Nahum. 1969. *The History of King Lear.* London: Cornmarket.

Terdiman, Richard. 1985. "Ideological Voyages: Concerning a Flaubertian Dis-orientation." In *Europe and Its Others: Proceedings of the Essex Conference on the Sociology of Literature, July 1984.* Vol. 1, ed. Francis Barker et al., 28–40. Colchester: University of Essex Press.

Thomson, Helen. 1992. Review of *Sex Diary of an Infidel,* by Michael Gurr. *Australian and New Zealand Theatre Record* 6 (6): 24.

Tiffin, Helen. 1984a. "Commonwealth Literature and Comparative Methodology." *World Literature Written in English* 23 (1): 26–30.

———. 1984b. "Asia and the Contemporary Novel." *Australian Literary Studies* 11 (4): 468–79.

———. 1987a. "Post-Colonial Literatures and Counter-Discourse." *Kunapipi* 9 (3): 17–34.

———. 1987b. "Recuperative Strategies in the Post-Colonial Novel." In *Inventing Countries: Essays in Post-Colonial Literatures,* ed. William McGaw, 27–45. Wollongong: SPACLALS.

———. 1988. "Post-Colonialism, Post-Modernism, and the Rehabilitation of Post-Colonial History." *Journal of Commonwealth Literature* 23 (1): 169–81.

———. 1993a. "Metaphor and Mortality: The 'Life Cycle(s)' of Malaria." *Meridian* 12 (1): 46–58.

———. 1993b. "'Cold Hearts and (Foreign) Tongues': Recitation and the Reclamation of the Female Body in the Works of Erna Brodber and Jamaica Kincaid." *Callaloo* 16 (4): 909–21.

Tompkins, Joanne. 1993. "History/History/Histories: Resisting the Binary in Aboriginal Drama." *Kunapipi* 15 (1): 6–14.

———. 1996. "Re-citing Shakespeare in Post-Colonial Drama." *Essays in Theatre* 15 (1): 15–22.

Trinh T. Minh-ha. 1989. *Woman, Native, Other: Writing Postcoloniality and Feminism.* Bloomington: Indiana University Press.

Turcotte, Gerry. 1987. "'The Circle Is Burst': Eschatological Discourse in Louis Nowra's *Sunrise* and *The Golden Age.*" *SPAN* 24:63–80.

———. 1989–90. Review of *Capricornia,* by Louis Nowra. *Australasian Drama Studies* 15–16:189–91.

———. 1991. "'Speaking the Formula of Abjection': Hybrids and Gothic Discourses in Louis Nowra's Novels." *Westerly* 36 (3): 61–72.

Turner, Graeme. 1986. *National Fictions: Literature, Film, and the Construction of Australian Narrative.* Sydney: Allen and Unwin.

———. 1994. *Making It National.* Sydney: Allen and Unwin.

Twain, Mark. 1969. *Pudd'nhead Wilson.* Harmondsworth: Penguin.

Urry, John. 1990. *The Tourist Gaze: Leisure and Travel in Contemporary Societies.* London: Sage.

Van Toorn, Penny. 1990. "Discourse/Patron Discourse: How Minority Texts Command the Attention of Majority Audiences." *SPAN* 30:102–15.

Varney, Denise. 1989. "The Australian Performing Group: Text and Performance." M.A. thesis, University of Melbourne.

Visel, Robin. 1988. "A Half-Colonization: The Problem of the White Colonial Woman Writer." *Kunapipi* 10 (3): 39–45.

Viswanathan, Gauri. 1990. *Masks of Conquest: Literary Study and British Rule in India.* London: Faber.

Waites, Jim. 1988. Review of *Hate,* by Stephen Sewell. *Australian and New Zealand Theatre Record* 2 (11): 8.

Walker, David. 1976. *Dream and Disillusion: A Search for Australian Cultural Identity.* Canberra: Australian National University Press.

Wallace, Jo-Ann. 1995. "Technologies of 'The Child': Towards a Theory of the Child-Subject." *Textual Practice* 9 (2): 285–302.

Walley, Richard. 1989. *Coordah.* In *Plays from Black Australia,* ed. Katharine Brisbane, 109–66. Sydney: Currency.

Ward, Peter. 1988. Review of *1841,* by Michael Gow. *Australian and New Zealand Theatre Record* 2 (3): 7.

Watego, Cliff. 1989. "Aboriginal Drama." Lecture presented to students in Black Australian Literature course, 16 October, at University of Queensland, Brisbane.

Webby, Elizabeth. 1993. *Modern Australian Plays.* Rev. ed. Sydney: Sydney University Press.

White, Hayden. 1973. *Metahistory: The Historical Imagination in Nineteenth-Century Europe.* Baltimore: Johns Hopkins University Press.

———. 1978. *Tropics of Discourse: Essays in Cultural Criticism.* Baltimore: Johns Hopkins University Press.

White, Richard. 1981. *Inventing Australia: Images and Identity, 1688–1980.* Sydney: Allen and Unwin.

White, Susan. 1988. "Male Bonding, Hollywood Orientalism, and the Repression of the Feminine in Kubrick's *Full Metal Jacket.*" *Arizona Quarterly* 44 (3): 120–44.

Willeman, Paul. 1986. "Voyeurism, the Look, and Dwoskin." In *Narrative, Apparatus, Ideology: A Film Theory Reader,* ed. Philip Rosen, 210–18. New York: Columbia University Press.

Willett, John, ed. and trans. 1964. *Brecht on Theatre.* New York: Hill and Wang.

Williams, Margaret. 1992. *Dorothy Hewett: The Feminine as Subversion.* Sydney: Currency.

Winterson, Jeanette. 1989. *Sexing the Cherry.* London: Vintage.

Wollen, Peter. 1987. "Fashion/Orientalism/the Body." *New Formations* 1:5–33.

Wood, Denis. 1992. *The Power of Maps.* New York: Guilford.

Young, Linda. 1988. "The Experience of Convictism: Five Pieces of Convict Clothing from Western Australia." *Costume* 22:70–84.

Young, Robert. 1995. *Colonial Desire: Hybridity in Theory, Culture, and Race.* London: Routledge.

Zabus, Chantal. 1985. "A Calibanic Tempest in Anglophone and Francophone New World Writing." *Canadian Literature* 104:35–50.

Index

Abject, 130, 153, 156
Aboriginalism/post-Aboriginalism, 8
Aboriginality, 41–42, 51–52, 55, 80, 81, 93, 147
Aboriginal mythology, 55, 74–75, 90, 181. *See also* Dreamtime; Rainbow Serpent
Aboriginal theatre, 3, 4, 10, 14, 51–95, 100, 125, 147–48. *See also* Bennett, Roger; Chi, Jimmy, and Kuckles; Davis, Jack; Enoch, Wesley, and Deborah Mailman; Gilbert, Kevin; Johnson, Eva; Kooemba Jdarra; Lawford, Josie Ningali; Maza, Bob; Merritt, Robert; Morgan, Sally; Mudrooroo; Noonuccal, Oodgeroo; Walley, Richard
Aborigines, non-Aboriginal representations of, 8–9, 34, 41, 107–9, 112–14, 118, 125, 127, 128, 129, 140, 144, 171–73, 175, 182, 210
Agitprop theatre, 195
Allegory, 98, 102, 104–5; of empire, 107; of nationhood, 105; allegorical frameworks, 110; allegorical reading, 105–6
Alterity, 85, 132, 139–40, 174. *See also* Race, racial difference
Ambivalence: in colonial discourse, 29–30, 33, 34, 45, 191; as postcolonial strategy, 8, 97–98, 160, 203, 210
American imperialism/neoimperialism, 124, 186–204, 207, 218, 226
Androgyny, 179
Ang, Ien, 18
Anti-Americanism, 192, 201, 203. *See also* American imperialism/neoimperialism
Anzac legend, 190–91, 192, 199, 209, 215
Apocalypse, 122–23; apocalyptic imagery, 40, 44, 116, 118
Archer, Robyn, 148
Aronson, Linda, *Dinkum Assorted*, 187–89
Arthur, Kateryna, 56, 83
Ashcroft, Bill, 85, 148, 179
Ashcroft, Griffiths, and Tiffin, 6, 11, 23
Asian performance styles, 14, 206. *See also* Chinese theatre traditions; Kabuki; No theatre; Vietnamese water puppetry
Asians, dramatic representations of, 205–39. *See also* Vietnam plays
Attwood, Bain, 8–9
Audiences, 85, 112, 232; bourgeois, 2; dominant/majority, 74, 93–94, 112; and metatheatre, 103, 175, 180; and storytelling, 93
Auslander, Philip, 17
Australian imperialism: in Asia, 200, 218, 229; in the Philippines, 218–29; in the South Pacific, 185, 229; in Vietnam, 194, 197. *See also* Vietnam plays
Australian Performance Group (APG), 207, 208
Authenticity, 7, 11, 40–41, 42, 77, 83, 87, 93, 97, 170, 172, 183

Bakhtin, Mikhail, 42, 73, 87, 131, 133, 137, 139, 141, 143–44
Balme, Christopher, 10, 90
Balodis, Janis, 37, 99, 116; *No Going Back*, 126; *Too Young for Ghosts*, 115, 123–29, 187, 189–90, 209
Banting, Pamela, 17
Barba, Eugenio, 9
Barnes, Mick, 110
Barthes, Roland, 20, 83
Baudrillard, Jean, 226
Bell, Hilary, *Fortune*, 149, 152–59, 168, 222
Bennell, Eddie, *Silent Years*, 75
Bennett, Roger, *Funerals and Circuses*, 91–92
Bennett, Susan, 36

Benveniste, Émile, 86–87
Berndt, Ronald, 54
Bhaba, Homi, 7, 11, 29, 85, 87, 97, 105, 112–13, 173, 204, 210–11, 216, 220, 231
Bharucha, Rustom, 10
Bicentenary, 5, 99–100, 101, 102, 103, 104, 106, 110, 111, 112, 114
Bicentennial plays, 58, 99–114
Binaries/binary systems, 8, 19, 30, 41, 82, 86, 98, 130, 166, 207, 230; gender, 163, 178; race and gender, 23, 212
Body politics, 66–81
Body, 6, 17–18, 44, 66–67, 129–44, 148, 182, 183; Aboriginal, 67–69, 77, 93, 114; bourgeois, 133; discourses of, 74; female, 144, 148, 154–55, 170, 200, 212; grotesque, 130, 132–34, 137–41, 144, 156–57; sexualized, 77; theatricalized, 17–19, 70, 81, 157, 172, 197, 233; theories of, 77. *See also* Body politics
Boire, Gary, 143
Borges, Jorge Luis, 123–24
Bourdieu, Pierre, 125–26, 140
Brand, Mona, *Here Under Heaven,* 148
Brechtian techniques, 23, 56, 63, 75, 89, 166, 172, 183
Bredow, Susan, 111
British Empire, 21, 27, 31
Broinowski, Alison, 192
Brook, Peter, 9
Brown, Paul, 29, 40, 45
Brydon, Diana, 31
Buckridge, Patrick, 99–100
Burvill, Tom, 208
Buzo, Alexander, *Marginal Farm,* 229

Canon: Australian, 46; British, 160, 163–64; imperial, 28, 29, 46, 47, 49, 132. *See also* Counterdiscourse; Shakespeare, William
Carnivalesque, 18, 79, 94, 130–44, 155, 156–57; carnivalesque performance, 86
Carr, Helen, 146
Carter, Paul, 1–2, 5, 13, 15, 53, 60–61, 71, 104, 118–19, 168
Cartesian models, 128
Cartography, 16–17, 62, 115–29, 133; feminist, 165; performative, 157–58; cartographic discourse, 125; cartographic gaze, 62. *See also* Map, mapping
Cathcart, Sarah, and Andrea Lemon, *Serpent's Fall,* 180–84
Chaplin, Angela, 148
Chi, Jimmy, and Kuckles, *Bran Nue Dae,* 77–81, 84, 91
Child-subject, 156
Childs, Peter, and Patrick Williams, 6
Chin, Daryl, 9–10
Chinese theatre traditions, 157
Christianity: Christian imperialism, 65, 79, 87; Christian mythology, 109–10, 181, 183
Cixous, Hélène, 141, 182
Class: and gender, 150, 155; class conflicts, 149
Collins, David, 118
Colonialism/colonization, 2, 6, 11, 17, 30, 110, 139, 140, 186; and Aborigines, 52–53, 61, 62, 66, 69, 78, 100, 121; models of, 36, 129, 145–46; resistance to, 11, 143, 144. *See also* Imperialism
Colonialist discourse, 29–30, 40, 135, 154, 155
Commonwealth Native Title Act, 53
Community theatre, 3–4
Convictism, 5, 36–37, 69, 124, 153; theatrical representations of, 101–4, 132, 144; convict history, 100, 191; convict society, 117, 140; convict system, 103; convict uniform, 21; convict women, 149–55, 159
Copeman, Peter, *Hearts and Minds,* 201
Corroboree, 70–71, 73–74, 75, 77, 80
Costume, 12, 18, 20–23, 67–70, 113–14, 133–34, 135, 136–37, 171–72, 191, 196, 203; costuming codes, 79–80, 120, 212, 213. *See also* Cross-dressing
Counterdiscourse, 7, 13–14, 17, 82, 105, 151, 200, 232; canonical, 13, 27–49; and performance, 13–25, 27–28, 30, 47; counterdiscursivity, 22, 186, 195, 218

Cross-dressing, 18, 114, 172–73, 213, 214. *See also* Transvestite/transvestism
Cross-gender casting, 47

Dalby, Michael, 215
Daly, Ann, 20, 70, 76–77
Da Matta, Roberto, 90
Dance, 19, 44, 57, 70–77, 81, 84, 91, 134–36, 183; and gender, 74, 75–76; as homosexual display, 44; dancer as mythical figure, 57, 58–59, 74–75
Dash, Michael, 129
Davidson, Jim, 130
Davis, Jack, 43, 59, 61, 63–64, 71, 84–85, 93; *Barungin,* 57–59, 64, 90, 100–101; *Dreamers,* 57, 59, 69, 74, 92; *Featherfoot,* 74; *First Born Trilogy,* 59; *Honey Spot,* 75; *In Our Town,* 62–63, 65; *Kullark,* 54–56, 58, 61–63, 65, 68–69, 90; *No Sugar,* 59, 62–63, 65, 69, 73–74; *Wahngin Country,* 59
Davis, Lloyd, 179
De Groen, Alma, 37; *Rivers of China,* 149, 159–68, 175–82, 209, 218
Decolonization/decolonizing strategy, 10, 16, 25, 30, 35, 36, 40, 52, 67, 73, 82, 88, 131
Deleuze and Guattari, 125, 128
Derrida, Jacques, 31, 83, 101
Diamond, Elin, 169
Disease, 144; metaphors of, 212
Dolan, Jill, 182–83
Dollimore, Jonathan, 22–23, 159
Doyle, Jeff, 204
Drake-Brockman, Henrietta, *Men Without Wives,* 148
Dreamtime, 53–55, 57–58, 74, 90
Dunstone, Bill, 171, 175
During, Simon, 99
Dystopia, 41; feminist, 163; dystopian culture, 100, 131, 149; dystopian forces, 132

Edwards, Brian, 7
Einstein, Albert, 15
Enoch, Wesley, and Deborah Mailman, *7 Stages of Grieving,* 92
Enright, Nick, *St James Infirmary,* 193
Evans, Bob, 111
Exile, 12, 16, 31, 160–64

Femininity, 146, 154, 156; feminization, 212–13, 217. *See also* Gender
Feminism/feminist theory, 3, 12, 24; and postcolonialism drama, 14, 145–84, 209, 233
Ferrier, Elizabeth, 66, 125
Filewod, Alan, 12
Finnegan, Ruth, 82–83, 91, 93
Fischer, Gerhard, 10
Fitzpatrick, Peter, 2, 3, 105, 108, 109, 110–11, 205
Foucault, Michel, 15, 120, 143, 151–52, 179–80
Freadman, Anne, 86
Freedman, Barbara, 170, 175–77, 223
Frow, John, 28, 46, 226

Gaines, Jane, 20
Gardiner, Allan, 36
Garner, Stanton, 67
Gay, Penny, 27
Gay theatre, 47; gay and lesbian performance, 3
Gaze: male, 25, 72, 75–76, 176–78, 200, 218, 224; imperial, 24, 66, 104, 120–21, 129, 179, 214; intentional, 41, 126, 166, 169
Gender, 14, 22, 67, 72, 75, 145–47, 149–59, 160, 169; and nationalism, 145, 184, 190, 187–91; and race, 14, 18, 145–46, 229; and war, 188–90, 197, 200, 209–17; gender binary, 228; gender difference, 12, 184; gender inscriptions, 172; gender performativity, 170, 213
Geoghegan, Edward, *Currency Lass,* 170
George, David, 60
George, Rob, *Sandy Lee Live at Nui Dat,* 194–203
Gerster, Robin, 192, 195
Gilbert, Kevin, *Cherry Pickers,* 84
Goldie, Terry, 114

Gothic, 105; Gothic identities, 131; Gothic tropes, 109, 118, 130
Gow, Michael, 2, 5, 28, 37, 99, 109, 194; *Away,* 27, 46–47, 192; *1841,* 100–104, 107–10, 118, 149; *Furious,* 47
Greenblatt, Stephen, 43, 61, 65
Griffiths, Gareth, 7, 11, 23, 112, 118, 186, 205, 207
Griffiths, Trevor, 21, 30
Grosz, Elizabeth, 18
Gurr, Michael, *Sex Diary of an Infidel,* 207, 218–30

Harley, 61–62, 125
Harris, Wilson, 25
Hennessy, Rachel, 147
Herbert, Bob, *No Names . . . No Pack Drill,* 187–89
Herbert, Xavier, 112. *See also* Nowra, Louis, *Capricornia*
Heteroglossia, 42; performative, 87–88
Heterosexuality, discourses of, 35, 213–14. *See also* Sexuality
Heterotopia, 15, 151–52; heterotopic site, 40, 157, 218; heterotopian landscapes, 168; heterotopian vision, 179–80
Hewett, Dorothy, 3, 28, 170, 218; *Man from Mukinupin,* 170–75
Historiography, 2, 102, 104, 106, 159, 231
History/historicity, 1–2, 4–5, 14, 15, 16, 19, 42–43, 45, 46, 145, 149, 190, 207; and Aborigines, 52, 67; and feminist postcolonial drama, 149–52, 157, 163, 167, 168, 172; imperialist, 15, 25, 70–71, 81, 92, 97–99, 231; literary, 112, 114, 159–60, 178; and settler/invader plays, 100–117, 123, 128–29. *See also* Spatial histories
Hodge, Bob, and Vijay Mishra, 7, 8, 99
Homoeroticism, 210, 214, 215, 228
Homosexuality, 210, 215, 228
Huggan, Graham, 127, 224–25
Hutcheon, Linda, 231
Hybridity, 11, 18, 32, 33, 35, 37, 78, 112–14, 117; hybridization, 51, 81, 87, 183, 206

Imperialism, 2, 5, 11, 15, 16, 20, 21, 22, 36, 113, 119, 124–25, 134, 137, 139, 171, 185, 205, 207, 218, 230; and Aboriginal theatre, 52–95; and the family, 157–59; and interculturalism, 10; and manners, 140; and patriarchy, 160, 162–63, 181, 184, 164–65, 189; resistance to, 11, 29, 98, 128, 142, 159, 232; and women, 145–49, 151, 153, 155. *See also* Colonialism; Neo-imperialism
Imperialist discourse, 43, 98, 110, 113, 126–27. *See also* Colonialist discourse
Improvisation, 84, 92–93, 132
Incarceration, 64
Indigenization, 51, 97, 205
Interculturalism, 9–10; intercultural experiment, 217; intercultural theatre, 201
Interpellation, 30, 43, 142
Intersubjectivity, 52
Intertextuality, 29, 46; of oral and written forms, 83; intertextual dialogue, 162; intertextual field, 47; intertextual identity, 183
Issacharoff, Michael, 16, 116

Jackson, Rosemary, 130
Jeffords, Susan, 191
Johnson, Eva: *Murras,* 69, 74, 147; *What Do They Call Me?,* 147
Jolly, Roslyn, 35

Kabuki, 210, 214, 217–18
Kaplan, Caren, 146, 161
Kappeler, Susanne, 178
Katrak, Ketu, 151
Kelly, Veronica, 4, 5, 37, 59, 102, 116–17, 124, 126, 130–32, 138, 144, 218
Kermode, Frank, 122
Kiernander, Adrian, 210
Kirkby, Joan, 45
Kooemba Jdarra, 69. *See also* Davis, Jack, *Dreamers*
Krishnaswamy, Revathi, 161
Kroetsch, Robert, 54, 94

Lamming, George, 115, 162
Landrights, 5, 43, 73–74
Landscape, 15–16, 31, 36, 39, 40, 41, 61, 62, 64, 115–29
Langer, Beryl, 195
Langton, Marcia, 52
Language, 2, 3, 6, 73, 82, 220–21; Aboriginal languages, 85; as counterdiscursive tool, 18, 23–24, 84–85, 141–42; as site of ideological struggle, 42–44. *See also* Orality
Lawford, Josie Ningali, *Ningali,* 147–48
Lawson, Alan, 7, 9, 97
Leer, Martin, 39
Lesbian desire, 72
Linguistic bricolage, 220; linguistic capture, 21, 44–45, 72, 94; linguistic disjunction, 89; linguistic interpellation, 24, 199; linguistic rebellion, 43; linguistic shout, 61; linguistic subject, 43. *See also* Language; Orality
Lloyd, Tim, 111
Lo, Jacqueline, 79
Low, Gail Ching-Liang, 119
Lowe, Barry, *Tokyo Rose,* 201–4
Lowe, Lisa, 205, 207

Malouf, David: *Blood Relations,* 28–29, 31–46, 97–98, 107, 115, 117, 123, 135, 174; *Imaginary Life,* 35
Manichaean discourse, 34, 109. *See also* Binaries/binary systems
Map, 55, 61–62, 167; as motif, 61; mapmaking, 62, 125; mapping, 2, 16–17, 66, 77, 126, 128, 165. *See also* Cartography
Mardi Gras, 3
Masculinity, 74, 154, 188, 191, 208, 209, 211–15, 217; and nationalism, 157, 200, 210. *See also* Mateship
Masking, 216
Masquerade, 18, 23, 216
Maternity, 147, 150–51
Mateship, 189, 191, 199, 209, 215. *See also* Masculinity
Matthews, Brian, 150
Maza, Bob, 85; *Keepers,* 71–73, 93
McCallum, John, 4, 98, 103
McClintock, Anne, 145, 147, 154, 158–59, 184
McDougall, Russell, 131
McNarn, Maurie, 191–92
McRobbie, Angela, 72
Medusa myth, 175–76, 177–78, 180–81, 182
Melbourne Theatre Company, 126
Melodrama, 102
Merritt, Robert, 93; *Cake Man,* 68, 87–88
Metahistory, 112. *See also* Historiography
Metatheatre, 45, 102, 132–33, 202, 203; feminist metatheatre, 169, 170–77, 182, 184; metatheatrical frameworks, 14, 25, 102–4, 152, 222–23; metatheatricality, 79, 114, 196. *See also* Theatricality
Migrancy, migration, 12, 18, 128, 161. *See also* Exile
Migrant theatre, 3. *See also* Multiculturalism, multicultural theatre
Miller, Jonathan, 30
Mills, Sara, 151
Mime, 84
Mimicry, 18, 28, 69, 85, 87, 97, 105, 133, 140, 172, 203, 216
Miscegenation, 32, 81, 112–13, 148, 154, 172
Mise en scène, 20, 28, 62, 137, 171, 180
Missions, missionaries. *See* Christianity, Christian imperialism
Mitchell, Tony, 46, 78, 100
Monodrama, 147, 182
Morgan, Sally, *Sistergirl,* 69, 74, 147
Morley, Michael, 100
Movement, 19–20, 67, 70, 72, 91
Mudrooroo, 51, 84, 91; Mudrooroo/Müller project, 10
Muecke, Stephen, 74, 83, 90
Mukherjee, Arun, 9
Multiculturalism, 99; multicultural discourses, 218; multicultural society, 155; multicultural theatre, 4, 12
Mulvey, Laura, 176, 178

Music/musical forms, 90–91; musical comedy, 170; musical theatre (*see* Bennett, Roger; Chi, Jimmy, and Kuckles; Hewett, Dorothy)
Mythmaking, 104

Narrativity, 169, 173
Nation/nationhood, 22, 23, 99, 144, 157, 160, 184, 186, 191, 229; black, 59; myths of, 100, 153, 156, 232
Nationalism, 3, 24, 99, 145, 148
Nationality, discourses of, 98, 104, 191, 231
Naturalism, 25, 54, 102, 233; naturalistic codes, 75; naturalistic narrative, 57. *See also* Nonnaturalistic theatre
Nature, 16, 31, 37–42, 44, 115; nature-culture dichotomy, 39, 124
Neoimperialism, 5, 12, 186–87. *See also* American neoimperialism
New World, 37–38, 40, 44, 137
New-wave theatre, 2, 3, 4, 148, 187
No theatre, 210, 216
Nonnaturalistic theatre, 14, 16, 23, 25, 195
Noonuccal, Oodgeroo, *Why the Corroborees,* 75
Novak, Cynthia, 70
Nowra, Louis, 2, 5, 18, 28, 37, 99, 114, 116, 128–30, 174, 194; *Capricornia,* 86–87, 100, 111–14, 131–32, 142; *Cosi,* 193; *Golden Age,* 111, 130–36, 143–44; *Inner Voices,* 131; *Inside the Island,* 111, 114, 116–23, 125, 129–30, 144, 192, 199; *Radiance,* 123; *Summer of the Aliens,* 123; *Sunrise,* 192; *Visions,* 131, 134–42, 144
Nugent, Ann, 29

Ocker/Ockerism, 3, 148, 209
Olaniyan, Tejumola, 6
Ong, Walter, 82, 89, 93
Orality, 24, 81–95; oral cultures, 81–82, 85; oral narrative, 182; oral tradition, 60
Orgel, Stephen, 33, 40
Orientalism, 200, 206–7, 211–13, 227–30; Orientalist discourses, 203, 210; Orientalist fantasy, 200

Pantomime, 132–33
Parody, 22, 31, 77, 80, 132–33, 134, 195; parodic modes, 106, 131, 140, 226
Pavis, Patrice, 10, 28
Performative presence, 76–77, 169–70
Perkins, Elizabeth, 162–63, 166
Phillips, Dennis, 192
Photography, 157, 221–24; and imperialism, 41, 143, 222; photographic surveillance, 144
Pickett, Carolyn, 176
Pidgin, 44
Pierce, Peter, 197, 204
Pirandello, Luigi, 169
Play-within-the-play, 104, 152. *See also* Metatheatre
Playbox Theatre, 208
Porter, Dennis, 206
Postcolonialism/postcolonial theory, 5–9, 77, 97–98, 105, 113, 158, 231–33; and feminism, 145–49, 166, 167, 169, 209, 233; and performance, 13–25, postcolonial perspective, 123, 162. *See also* Subjectivity
Postmodernism, 9
Prentice, Chris, 146
Prichard, Katharine Susannah, *Brumby Innes,* 148
Prison imagery, 36, 63, 64, 69, 117. *See also* Convictism; Incarceration
Promenade theatre, 59–60, 92
Prospero-Caliban relationship, 30, 36

Quantum theory, 60–61, 63, 77, 92, 123

Race, 9, 67, 72, 155, 156; and gender, 18, 145–46, 159, 210, 229; race relations, 80, 148; racial difference, 3, 76, 174, 196, 203, 210, 216; racial identities, 100, 205–6; racial purity, 34; racial signification, 77; racial specificity, 183; racism, 69, 92, 95, 114, 155, 156, 199, 202, 205, 206. *See also* Aboriginal theatre; Asians, dramatic representations of

Radic, Leonard, 60
Rainbow Serpent, 55, 180–81
Rape, 30, 32, 125, 150, 155, 176, 177, 178, 187, 189–90; cultural, 134; fantasy of, 225; homosexual, 215; as metaphor, 107, 187
Realism, 19, 112, 201; bush realism, 148. *See also* Naturalism
Recitation, 132, 142. *See also* Ventriloquism
Reconciliation, 45, 46, 52, 66, 175, 182
Republicanism, 5, 99, 232
Rhizomatic model, 16, 24
Ridgman, Jeremy, 194
Robertson, W., 70–71
Role: role doubling, 25, 33, 172; role-playing, 25, 88, 170; role sharing, 164
Romeril, John: *Floating World,* 4, 186, 187, 205, 207–9, 212, 218, 220; *Top End,* 229
Rubin, Gayle, 150, 214–15

Said, Edward, 8, 160–61, 164, 206, 208, 212–13, 229–30
Salter, Denis, 47
Schechner, Richard, 9
Scolnicov, Hanna, 117
Sedgwick, Eve, 215
Settler colonies, 7–8, 11–12, 15
Settler/invader drama. *See* Balodis, Janis; Gow, Michael; Malouf, David; Nowra, Louis; Sewell, Stephen
Sewell, Stephen, 2, 5, 37, 99, 194; *Blind Giant is Dancing,* 192–95; *Hate,* 100, 104–11, 149
Sexuality, 22, 140, 142, 150, 210, 211, 215; female, 34, 141–42, 147, 150–51, 154–55, 211; male, 151; sexual ambiguity, 228; sexual difference, 12, 140, 203; sexual economy of imperialism, 190, 199, 200, 218, 225–27; sexual labor, 150; sexism, 202
Shakespeare, William, 27–28, 173, 175; *King Lear,* 46, 132; *Midsummer Night's Dream,* 46–47; *Romeo and Juliet,* 112; *Tempest,* 21, 29–46, 137, 174; *Twelfth Night,* 46
Sharpe, Jenny, 145
Shearer, Jill: *Catherine,* 149–52, 159–60, 166, 168, 227; *Shimada,* 207, 209–18, 220, 230
Shoemaker, Adam, 54
Silence as performative strategy, 88–89, 131
Slemon, Stephen, 94, 97–98, 105, 106
Sontag, Susan, 41, 143, 221–22
Souter, Gavin, *Lion and Kangaroo,* 116
Space as motif in postcolonial studies, 6, 15–16; alien, 16, 119–20, 121, 125, 129; colonial, 39, 116, 151, 168; contested, 64; discontinuous, 125; imperial, 128; interactive, 116; mythological, 55; phenomenological, 125–26, 127; sexualized, 152–53, superimposed, 123. *See also* Spatial histories
Spacelessness, 40
Spatial histories, 1, 15, 53–66, 123. *See also* Theatrical space
Spectatorship: modes of, 24–25, 120, 179, 182, 222; theories of, 170, 176–78. *See also* Audiences; Gaze, male
Spivak, Gayatri, 7, 18, 67, 146
Stagescape, 115, 116, 120, 124
Stallybrass, Peter, and Allon White, 18, 132–34
Stam, Robert, 141–42, 144
Stephenson, P. R., 187
Stereotype: Asian, 12, 205, 207, 215, 216, 219; gender, 34, 151, 153; colonial, 29, 68, 220; national, 155, 205; racial, 113, 114
Stewart, Susan, 227
Storytelling, 60, 83, 84, 87, 91–93, 147; storytellers, 82, 88, 91, 182
Stow, Randolph, *Visitants,* 31
Strachan, Tony, *Eyes of the Whites,* 229
Strategic essentialism, 18, 67
Subjectivity, 162, 167, 231; Aboriginal, 66–67, 72, 73; and citizenship, 156, 232; diffused, 37; multiple, 232; postcolonial, 5, 17, 70, 144, 157; split, 45
Suvin, Darko, 15, 115–16

Tait, Peta, 3
Tapping, Craig, 82–83
Tate, Nahum, 132
Teacher-student motif, 43, 135
Temporality, 53–56, 92
Terdiman, Richard, 230
Theatrical space, 16, 20, 56, 58, 59–60, 85, 116, 117; diegetic, 116, 119, 120, 128; mimetic, 116, 120, 123, 128; stage space, 40, 56, 57
Theatrical syncretism, 10–11
Theatricality, 44, 79, 102, 124, 170, 171, 175, 195. *See also* Metatheatre
Thomson, Helen, 2
Tiffin, Helen, 9, 11, 13, 17, 22, 25, 28, 142–43, 205, 212
Time: cyclical, 56; journey through, 167–68; linear, 2, 54; nonlinear, 54, 55–56; mythic, 53, 57; spatiality of, 123–24; theatrical, 15, 20, 56
Timelessness, 57
Tompkins, Joanne, 47
Tourism, discourses of, 80, 93, 104, 207, 218, 226–27; sex tourism, 200, 218–27; tourist gaze, 41, 71, 224–25
Translation, 28, 86–87, 114, 142
Transsexual, 228
Transvestite/transvestism, 22–23, 211, 212, 214, 228. *See also* Cross-dressing
Travel as feminist motif, 164–68
Trickster figure, 62, 73, 88
Turcotte, Gerry, 122, 130
Turner, Graeme, 115, 232

Urry, John, 224
Utopia, 40, 44, 149; utopian forces, 132; utopian myths, 41

Van Toorn, Penny, 74, 94
Ventriloquism, 142
Vietnam plays, 47, 116, 189–90, 211, 191–93, 194–201, 218. *See also* American imperialism/neoimperialism
Vietnam War, 47, 190, 191, 192
Vietnamese water puppetry, 201
Voyeurism/voyeuristic gaze, 41, 130, 157, 214, 222–23

Waites, Jim, 110
Wallace, Jo-Ann, 156
Walley, Richard: *Coordah,* 73; *Munjong,* 73
War, dramatic representations of, 186, 207; World War I, 116; World War II, 187–89, 201–4, 208–18. *See also* Vietnam plays
Ward, Peter, 100
Watego, Cliff, 57
Webb, Hugh, 91
White, Hayden, 4–5, 54
White, Richard, 191
White, Susan, 214
Willeman, Paul, 178
Williamson, David, 2, 98, 106
Wollen, Peter, 227
Wood, Denis, 62

Young, Robert, 11

Paperback cover photos (clockwise from top): Michael Leslie (front) and Djunawong Stanley Mirindo, *Bran Nue Dae,* Black Swan/Melbourne Theatre Company, 1993 (photo: Jeff Busby); Stephen Page as the Mimi Spirit, *Murras,* Adelaide Fringe Festival Production, 1988 (photo: Di Barrett); Lynch and Lopez in *Visions,* Paris Theatre, 1978 (photo: Branco Gaica); Stef and Betsheb in *The Golden Age,* Playbox Production, 1985 (photo: David Simmonds).